Melodrama and the Myth of America

DRAMA AND PERFORMANCE STUDIES

Timothy Wiles, *general editor*

Melodrama and the Myth of America

Jeffrey D. Mason

Indiana University Press

Bloomington and Indianapolis

The paper used in this publication meets the minimum requirements of American National Standard for Information Sciences—Permanence of Paper for Printed Library Materials, ANSI Z39.48-1984.

⊗™

Manufactured in the United States of America.

Library of Congress Cataloging-in-Publication Data

Mason, Jeffrey D. (Jeffrey Daniel), date.
    Melodrama and the myth of America / Jeffrey D. Mason.
      p. cm. — (Drama and performance studies)
    Includes bibliographical references and index.
    ISBN 0-253-33686-4 (alk. paper)
    1. Melodrama, American—History and criticism. 2. American drama—19th century—History and criticism. 3. Literature and society—United States—History—19th century. 4. Popular literature—United States—History and criticism. 5. National characteristics, American, in literature. 6. Social problems in literature. 7. America in literature. 8. Myth in literature.
    I. Title. II. Series.
    PS336.M44M36 1993
    810.9—dc20   92-46375

1 2 3 4 5 97 96 95 94 93

Contents

Illustrations

Preface

IN THIS BOOK, I study nineteenth-century American theatre and drama through a glass different from the ones my predecessors chose. The scholars who opened the territory—Hornblow, Moses, Quinn, Hughes, Moody, Hewitt, Wilson—offered panoramic views. Two more recent studies—David Grimsted's analysis of American theatre as cultural history, and Walter J. Meserve's ongoing multivolume history of American drama—also cover wide regions, but with more intensity and depth than the earlier surveys.[1] Yet while I intend this book to serve, in one respect, as a thorough examination of a certain kind of nineteenth-century American theatre, I have chosen to treat not many plays but only five, and I have selected them because they enable me to focus on certain concerns. (I am hoping that intensive study of five drops of seawater will reveal something different about the ocean than cruising the entire vasty deep.) Each of the five was written and produced in America, and each offers an explicit and essentially serious (i.e., not primarily intended to elicit laughter) response to an aspect of the American experience; that is, it presents a considered enactment of "America." (Any play written in America and produced for an American audience does, in some way, confront the American experience—*Spartacus*, for example, addresses the American slavery issue—but I have chosen to treat only those plays that do so overtly.) Moreover, each was exceptionally popular in its time, which I take as evidence that its audiences found its apparent representation of culture consonant with their own conceptions. In every case, the fundamental question is how the audience (probably) "read" the performance of the play, or, to put it another way, how and what the play meant in its time, which leads into considerations of various constructions of America as an idea, and of the very nature and operation of theatre.

In the last decade or two, more and more scholars in the humanities have adopted the practice of beginning any text by pronouncing (or confessing) their specific political and methodological positions, in some cases as clearly and vociferously as a medieval warrior declaiming his titles and antecedents to his enemies before sallying forth into battle. For the record, then, I am a white, male, middle-class, heterosexual member of the professoriate, but I doubt that this information will be significantly useful to my readers. I make no claim, as did my counterparts in generations past, to write from a positivist and implicitly universal point of view, or to represent a centrist or "mainstream" position in discourse which, ipso facto, commands more prestige than "marginal" positions. I do borrow from several current methodologies—deconstruction, semiotics, Marxism, feminism—but I do not feel qualified to identify myself as a disciple of any of them. To embrace a certain methodology, poststructuralist or otherwise, is not always to express a political preference, however the means might help to determine the results. Such a choice can also indicate a preference for certain critical instruments because of what they might reveal when applied to certain material. Some methodologies may also provide the protection of a formalist cloak; that is, the more abstract forms of poststructuralist theory can offer their adherents the same excuse from social concerns that made New Criticism so popular during the McCarthy era. I recognize that poststructuralism has, at least in the United States, become largely identified with leftist politics, but I agree with Steven Watts's contention that even the leftists tend to use a "politics of words" in a way that avoids material issues and so undermines a radical program. On the other hand, as I hope some passages in this book will demonstrate, one may use deconstruction in service of a social critique. Yet even Marxist criticism has become somewhat abstract and apolitical (perhaps desperately so, with the disintegration of the Soviet Union) and so more widely serviceable as an acceptable academic identity. When I employ Marxist theory, I do not mean to promote a Marxist agenda, partly because I do not subscribe to any available version of Marxist doctrine and partly because I believe that the complexity of American society confounds classic Marxism's strict construction of class struggle along bourgeois and proletarian lines. However, I borrow—appropriate, if you prefer—Marxist critical techniques because I believe they can elucidate the operations of any social system, especially one in which capitalism is the dominant mode, and help to reveal the use of text in service of power.

Perhaps the foundation of my position—one evident in the nature of the present study, in the issues I pursue, and in the vectors with which I choose to approach them—is that I believe that there is such a thing as an American culture, that it has a discernible history, and that it is susceptible to analysis as such. That statement is far more complex than it may appear, and in the first chapter I shall begin to address the issues that it implies.

I am a member of the theatre faculty at California State University, Bakersfield, where I direct productions and teach courses in performance and theatre studies, and I could not have wedged this very considerable project into my crowded life without help from many people. The CSUB University Research Council released me from two courses and paid for some clerical assistance during 1988–89, and the Faculty Honors and Awards Committee recommended me for a sabbatical leave during Winter Quarter, 1991. Jerome S. Kleinsasser, Shelley C. Stone III, Manuel Esteban, Edwin H. Sasaki, Ray Geigle, Fred Dorer, and Tomás Arciniega all, in their various administrative capacities at CSUB, supported my work. Jackie Collins helped with the correspondence to prospective publishers. Lorna Frost, who *is* the interlibrary loan department at CSUB, found hundreds of books for me, and

Barbara Tisler produced bibliographies. I received cordial assistance from Christy Gavin and others in the CSUB Library, the staff at the Stowe-Day Foundation Library in Hartford, Rosemary Cullen of the Harris Collection at Brown University, and the staff (especially Susan Naulty) of the Huntington Library in San Marino, which is a wonderfully cozy academic burrow set in a paradisiacal garden. I am very grateful to the following colleagues who read early versions of various chapters: Rosemarie K. Bank, Michael Booth, J. Ellen Gainor, Bruce A. McConachie, Margaret Rose, Richard J. Wattenberg, and Forrest G. Wood. In addition to offering comments and suggestions, which I variously followed or, at my peril, ignored, they have taught me that I cannot please everyone. My greatest professional debt is to Janelle Reinelt, who has been my friend, teacher, and mentor since I enrolled as one of her students in 1978.

Yet the two people who have done the most to make my work possible are my wife, Susan, and our daughter, Ashley. I wish to make clear that I do not thank them as a matter of convention, for I do not take for granted, as might have been typical in my grandfather's time, that their proper place is to maintain the domestic front while I pursue allegedly more important affairs. Susan put her own teaching and acting on indefinite suspension so that we might have a child, and because I had the poor timing finally to find the approach to this study while she was pregnant, she has, to a large extent, been doing the work of two parents for over three years. I do most of my research and writing at home, which has meant that Susan has tried (and usually succeeded) to keep the house relatively quiet (even when she had spent part of the night awake that I might sleep), and that Ashley, at the age of two-and-a-half, learned to respect my seclusion in the study. My family's benefit from this book is largely vicarious, but they are the ones who have made the emotional and personal sacrifices that made the project possible; the "free" time that I have spent on this venture was usually time that I might have spent with them. I have noticed that an unusually large proportion of my colleagues are single, a fact that surprises me less and less as I realize that academic endeavor is largely incompatible with family life, and that the people who will tolerate a scholar (especially one who is also involved in the theatre) as a (frequently absent) husband and father are very, very special indeed.

Earlier versions of portions of this material appeared as follows:

"The Face of Fear." *Melodrama. Themes in Drama* 14. Ed. James Redmond. Cambridge: Cambridge UP, 1992. 213–21.

"The Politics of *Metamora*." *The Performance of Power: Theatrical Discourse and Politics*. Ed. Sue-Ellen Case and Janelle Reinelt. Iowa City: U of Iowa P, 1991. 92–110.

"Poison It with Rum; or, Validation and Delusion: Antebellum Temperance Drama as Cultural Method." *Pacific Coast Philology* 25 (1990): 96–105.

Melodrama and the Myth of America

1

Constructing American Ideology

THIS IS A book about theatre as strategy, or about the strategic uses of theatrical representation in the context of relevant rhetoric, image, and experience. More fully, it is about how America performed "America" during a portion of the nineteenth century—how its people enacted their collective self-concept, or their sense of cultural identity.[1] The study focuses on a series of five plays ranging from *Metamora* (1829) to *Shenandoah* (1889). Each play purports to represent certain historical events or circumstances, and so constitutes a construction of the American experience, designed to reinforce the perspectives that were cherished by its creators and their potential audiences. My investigation lies at the intersection of two rich fields: the study of nineteenth-century American culture, including its literature, politics, and social interactions; and the study of how theatrical events are written, produced, and received. In one sense, it is a demonstration of a certain cultural and especially intertextual approach to theatre studies as applied to only a few examples of one kind of play produced during a brief stretch of decades in one nation—a study of selected nineteenth-century American plays by attempting to locate them in the discourses from which they sprang and to which they contributed, by finding and describing their places in the national imagination.

Theatre is a public art form. That is, while one may produce or contemplate a novel or a painting in absolute privacy, theatre requires interaction between at least two people—the performer and the spectator, to use the conventional terms—and customarily involves many more. No one can participate without reckoning the presence of someone else, and the nature of anyone's participation may change in response to that presence. The solitary reader may react (or not react) with complete lack of inhibition and absolute disregard for what others might think, while the member of a theatre audience will more likely shape her reactions in terms of the effect she believes they will have on the others present and their attitude toward her. She does not act with complete freedom, of course, and there will always be circumstances—matters of society, politics, economics, class, belief—that influence both her intentions and her ability to act on them. Therefore, when I study the production and reception of a theatrical event, I am trying to describe the operative fields of influence and elicit the attitudes of the participants

1

as they wished them known to the others. Insofar as the participants were able to control their behavior, their contributions or responses were constructed, some well in advance, and others on the spur of the moment. If, as in this book, I study the performances of American plays, written on American subjects and produced in America by American artists and for American audiences, and enjoying long and successful runs because of the enthusiastic support of those audiences, I am studying what certain Americans wanted other Americans, and the world at large, to believe that they believed about America as such. Theatre becomes an intricate and reflexive exercise in cultural self-definition.

I have used the term "participant," which may seem general and indeed is so, for whether we refer to a play, a production, or a theatrical event, we refer to a phenomenon whose perception—and therefore whose meaning—is subject to a myriad of influences from the various people involved. Everyone contributes—the playwright writes the script, the manager or director organizes and supervises the production, the designers provide the mise-en-scène, the actors perform the piece, the audience receives it, and the community at large provides the context in which all of these people do their work and perceive the others' contributions. In other words, while some plays may bear the mark of this or that influential artist more than others, all are products of many people's participation. If we draw too clear a distinction between the artists as the producers—as those who compose the piece and lead the event—and the audience members as the consumers—as those who respond to what the artists produce—we are locating the process in a somewhat artificially limited temporal and causal framework, for those artists create what they believe, based on past experience, will elicit a certain kind of response from the audience. The interaction is continuous and infinite.

Above all, what I would really like to elucidate is not only what each artist intended to convey through the production, but what each spectator experienced, felt, and thought as he saw and heard each play—an academic fantasy that leads me into a methodological black hole. Susan Bennett has studied the various factors that can influence response to a theatrical event, ranging from the economics of writing, production, and attendance, to the semiotics and ideological coding of the architecture and milieu of the theatre, to the degree to which the audience can apply familiar codes and conventions to the event. Yet Bennett acknowledges that her goal is elusive; although she offers many approaches, none truly illuminates her central question, instead defining it by its obscurity while marking out the surrounding territory. The black hole analogy is apt because the astronomer cannot see one; she can only argue its presence by the behavior of space in a given region.

One frustration in the study of theatre is that there is so little information on audience composition and especially audience reaction. Bennett cites a variety of reports, some employing audience surveys to identify age, occupation, income, and educational level (93–96), yet such reports and surveys presuppose that to know the audience (even statistically) is to know what they are thinking, or that response correlates accurately with such sociological categories. The most thorough survey I can imagine would involve interviewing each member of the audience at various stages before and after the event—learning of the event, deciding to attend, making arrangements to attend, activities immediately preceding attendance, intermission, the exit from the theatre, the discussion during the following day or week—but even such a survey would elicit only what the spectator is able or willing to articulate; there is no way to get inside his mind and listen to what is going on. I doubt that we can do more than speculate on what motivates people to attend the theatre at all. Bennett cites the example of the New York Metropolitan Opera in order to argue that financial pressure leads to choosing a highly conservative repertory, and she applies this principle to resident theatres without taking into account the example of South Coast Repertory, which defeats probability by offering seasons composed predominantly of new works, but still attracting a large and loyal subscription audience from the notoriously conservative and conventional Orange County population. I speculate that most of SCR's patrons attend not because they cultivate a sincere commitment to theatre as an art form, nor because they share a specific interest in new material, but for a variety of reasons unrelated to the repertory: attendance has become socially acceptable, they hope to signify some sort of social or cultural enlightenment, they wish to support their local flagship theatre rather than drive up to Los Angeles, and so forth.

In summary, I am conceding that an empirical study of theatrical interaction is virtually impossible. We must proceed theoretically, by establishing the probable grounds for the process of communication and understanding, and that is part of my project. Because every artist at least hazards a guess at the nature of the likely public, any theatrical event is carefully constructed in its cultural context. I do not suggest that the playwright, director, or actor wields absolute control over the production or its reception, or that any participant can always freely choose the values that influence her, or even that she is in complete command of the process of constructing her behavior or response, but that the event is largely a function of the fields of influence that are in force at the time. These fields can include the following:

- The economic realities of production and attendance, which can encompass not only those situations specific to the business of theatre but also those related to the economies, both local and otherwise, of the community where the event is offered, and the personal economies of the participants.
- The politics that enfold the event; that is, the power relations of playwright, manager, actor, spectator, civic authority, community organizations, and influential individuals. Such factors can influence what kind of theatrical events are produced, how they are done, who has access

to them in any capacity, and who has a forum for responding to them.
Power can be apparent or actual, and whether an individual perceives it
as one or the other can be a function of that person's relationship to it.
In other words, the community may perceive someone as having power
over others, but that person may not actually be able to influence
others' behavior.

- The social structures within which the event takes place, including considerations of gender, ethnicity, family, religion, class, occupation.
- The prevailing æsthetic, which is, most likely, a function of the other
influences, but which the participants may perceive as working independently.[2]

In other words, we cannot understand the event unless we also identify and consider
the operative contexts and backgrounds that helped to shape the inception, process,
and perception of the event. We must locate the event against what the *Rezep-
tionsästhetik* theorists would call the "horizon of expectations."

Therefore, one of the most daunting questions confronting a theatre scholar
is how broadly to draw that horizon, for theatre can conceivably encompass every
aspect of the human experience and so seems to have no natural boundaries. That
so many theatre historians have devoted their attention to such matters as a company's inventory of costumes or the evolution of a given actor's repertory, and
that so many literary scholars have focused almost exclusively on the formal or
philological qualities of playscripts, may express not so much well-considered disciplinary decisions as desperate but understandable attempts to impose limitations
on topics of colossal dimension. Theatre is like the cosmos; there is always something beyond and behind the object of the present gaze, and the more one reaches,
the more one realizes the depth of infinitude. I, too, have made desperate decisions,
but while I have selected my concerns and delimited my territory, I have cut across
traditional disciplinary lines in hopes of locating theatre in cultural contexts.

There is a fifth prominent field of influence, which is largely a function of
the other four: the discourse in which the event is embedded. Theatrical representation does not, of course, take place in a vacuum or in the isolation of an æsthetic
preserve, but as part of the culture—itself an interactive process—to which it
contributes. Any single element in that process, such as a play, moves—and, indeed,
exists—only in relation to all of the others: the ideas, images, events, impressions,
rationales, values, materialities, and interactions that might have affected its creation
and perception. Taken in the broadest sense, transcending text, this collection of
cultural elements is what I mean by discourse as the context of the play. This
discourse is not limited to other plays, but includes additional experiences to which
the participants had access. In other words, the woman of 1852 who attended a
performance of *Uncle Tom's Cabin* was less likely to "read" it in relation to other
plays about slavery (there were but few, and none quite like that one) than in light
of her nontheatrical experiences with race relations, gender roles, the slavery issue,

sectional politics (in which she could not participate directly), and domesticity, all skewed by her attitudes toward theatre attendance and toward anyone who accompanied her.

Moreover, whatever portion of this discourse adheres to collective memory becomes the cultural residue, which is all that remains accessible. If the life of a play is largely a matter of how its participants perceive its interactive motion through the cultural process, then my study of that life has to do with how I perceive the participants' perception; in other words, what I judge to be relevant in the residue. For example, in the case of *Metamora*, I have examined, among other texts, passages from certain newspapers that enjoyed substantial circulation in New York, where the play was performed many times over a period of years, newspapers whose articles and editorials produced a certain view of "native" for the consumption of their readership and the community at large, a view that informed the public's production of the meaning of *Metamora* (that is, their version/vision/perception of that meaning) as they interacted with and completed Forrest's performance. Ultimately, the newspapers and the play worked to reinforce each other in validating the politics (of white treatment of native populations) and the myths (of the "Indian") of their time. For *The Drunkard*, I have focused on temperance tracts and stories as being most relevant; for *Uncle Tom's Cabin*, the discourse over slavery in a variety of popular venues; and so on.

In a broad sense, my topic involves strategies of (re)presenting experience, a project that is clearly not limited to the theatre. Consequently, one of my preoccupations is the extent to which there are distinctions between texts and between kinds of texts. I interpret Derrida's famous decree—"*Il n'y a pas de hors-texte*"—as not only referring to demarcations between one text and another, or to the boundaries between textual and nontextual experience, but also contending that *all* experience, excepting only the immediate moment, is, in effect, text, since I can know it only through text. (I am using "text" to indicate a composition not only of language but of all kinds of sign systems.) In other words, history, in the sense of past experience, is available and accessible only as text, so I may say that history, in the sense of what I can know of past experience, is composed of text, or that history *is* text. Each text constructs experience and refers both to experience and to all prior texts, so while these texts are, from one perspective, discrete and isolated, they are also connected. They are elements in the cultural process, which I here conceive as the substructure of experience—they are islands in an archipelago, apparently separate only because the ocean obscures their common base—so from another perspective, they are not autonomous and they exist only in interactive and differential relation to each other, which is another way to say that they are contributions to discourse. The principle of intertextuality asserts that meaning is dependent upon the prior body of discourse that influences both creation and reception. *Il n'y a pas de hors-discours.*

To consider a play as text is to confront a certain conceptual and semantic exclusionism on the part of critical discourse, for the most prosaic usage of "text," to indicate a composition of words, usually words as written, seems applicable more to virtually any kind of verse or prose, and less to a play. More functionally, however, the text is the medium of the poem, the means through which the writer realizes the conception or idea known as "poem" by giving it presence, even if unstable or delusory. The comparable medium of a play, as performed, includes not only language—written dialogue and stage directions, and spoken, inflected language—but also image, gesture, movement, presence, spectacle, and audience response. In other words, a play employs multiple sign systems that refer to and interact with each other in what Julia Kristeva calls transposition (59–60). Even in a production of a prewritten playscript, the theatrical event is composed largely of elements which are, according to the prosaic, conservative definition of text, *hors-texte* or, at best, extrapolations from the text. Moreover, because the text is created not only in the writing but also in the performance and reception, it is created anew each time it is performed and perceived.[3] Therefore, any perform- ance—any staged interpretation—may affect the system of signification that the play employs and so may become part of the relevant discourse that forms the intertextual ecology of the play.[4] So if, for purposes of convenience, I use "text" to refer to the embodiment or conveyance of a play, I must expand the meaning of "text" beyond a mere arrangement of language. Because a performance employs several interactive sign systems, the most comprehensive playscript is either a com- plex text (a composition of several voices) or a multitext (several texts working in concert). The metatextual nature of a play demands a consideration of its per- formance and of the influences interacting with that performance—a poetics of audience response and perception and of performer/audience interaction.[5]

To refer to a text as a "play" is to convey only that I may use it in a certain way, according to certain conventions, to help produce a theatrical representation, which is itself a matter of convention. Insofar as a play shapes, represents, and refers to experience, which is necessarily *past* experience, I may also refer to it as "history." If, on the other hand, I describe it as "myth" as opposed to "history," I am claiming universal or fictional qualifies (or effects) in contrast to specificity or factuality. Yet if I propose that myth is a fictional composition and history a factual one, I am counterposing relative, not absolute, terms, for both myth and history are textual representations—both are compositions of signs. Depending on my reading of a text, I may decide whether to regard a given composition as myth or history, and I may change my attitude according to my circumstances, while the text, as such, changes not at all. In the case of a play, that decision is the privilege not only of the reader but of all the participants in the theatrical event. The terms in question—play, history, and myth—are not precisely com- mensurate; they refer variously to the potential uses and potential effects of a text and to the way in which the text uses its material and mediates between the un- knowable event and the reader or spectator.

As audience members experience and process a performance in relation to their own movement through the cultural process, they distill meaning. The perceived residence of this meaning changes from instance to instance, subject to subject, and analyst to analyst—it might lie in the text, the character, the actor, the stage image, the extratheatrical context, or in any interaction between them. In any case, the process that produces meaning in the theatre involves a complex interaction between text and participants amidst the codes and conventions of a given social context, and the social role of theatre twists the question of its meaning into a consideration of how any given play legitimates or promotes a given ideology.

IDEOLOGY AND MYTH

As a concept and as a theoretical basis for humanistic studies, ideology has acquired a pejorative reputation as both the symptom and the means of a sort of conspiracy; to borrow Myra Jehlen's paraphrase, "a system of interested deceit" (5). Marxist usage has rooted the concept of ideology in a perception of a hierarchical socioeconomic system, one in which society evolves through class struggle, each class is defined in relation to every other and to its degree of control over the means of production, class distinctions govern both human relations and societal operations, and the ruling class seeks to ensure its domination through a variety of strategies. Within this paradigm, ideology is the theoretical or philosophical basis according to which a given class competes with other classes in an attempt to structure experience and assert power. Some Marxist writers define the term more narrowly as the scheme of deceit—a fictional plot, if you will—by which the dominant class maintains its power; in other words, in a capitalist society, only the bourgeoisie "have" an ideology, and the proletarian critic takes on the project of revealing its falsities. Such usage relies on class difference, with the members of one class hurling the term as an accusation against those of another—ideology is the pernicious program that some *other* class, never one's own, pursues—so "ideology" takes on inherently negative connotations.[6]

From a position completely outside of Marxist discourse, E. D. Hirsch, Jr., mounts a different assault on ideology as a concept and critical method, decrying its corrosive effect on the elucidation of meaning, and conflating Marxist with deconstructionist critics into an adversarial group against which he defines his own perspective. In his attempt to bolster the concept of truth as absolute—especially truth-in-text as, Hirsch believes, the author controls it—he challenges the Derridean belief that meaning is unstable—that, as he puts it, "all textual commentary is . . . really fiction or poetry"—and accuses Marxists of equating "fiction" with "ideology." He creates an illusory ground for debate when he attributes to the postmodernists the claim that "humanistic inquiry is enclosed within a windowless framework which provides access to no other framework" (147). I would say, rather, that Derrida envisions no framework at all, but an exhilaratingly and distressingly limitless space in which humanistic discourse hurtles. Hirsch damns ideology as that which limits the scholar's vision and so determines the results of inquiry, yet he makes the naïve assumption that a mind can contemplate experience with no assumptions whatsoever. He fails to recognize and acknowledge the ideology that controls his own text, one that derives from his own relationship to power in the academy and in the critical tradition.

The lesson of Hirsch's frustration is that ideology is inevitable in class interaction, and in the operation of the individual within such interaction. We might describe ideology loosely as the sum and intersection of the individual self-interests of those in a given class, a perspective that supports the case that ideology is virtually organic to experience. I do not mean to suggest that ideology is the "center" that Derrida has revealed as delusory, any more than the Derridean space could act as such a center; I mean, rather, that social interaction will, eventually, spur each class to operate according to an evolved or chosen agenda that its constituents or those of another class might identify and describe as an ideology. (One need not be able to articulate an ideology, or even be fully aware of its program, in order to act according to it; an ideology may remain obscure until an observer deduces its influence from the behavior of a class or its members, and then elucidates it.) We might configure social conflict as a battle of ideologies, and the ideology that will most profoundly affect cultural production is, necessarily, that of the dominant class.

Antonio Gramsci elucidated hegemony as the process by which the dominant classes maintain their power not merely through force but also through shaping the subordinate classes' social perception so that they support the status quo, sometimes through a misapprehension of its guiding operations, values, and intentions. The role of theatre in the discourse of power is seldom, if ever, a matter of force, but more a function of the kind of covert coercion that Gramsci described, whether regarded from a Marxist perspective or not. He explained how the intellectuals—which I take broadly to include artists—serve as the "deputies" of the dominant class by helping to foster "spontaneous" consent "given by the great masses of the population to the general direction imposed on social life by the dominant fundamental group" (12).[7]

As I use the term, an "ideology" is a composition of ideas—most importantly, constructions of experience—that serves the interests and sustains the power of a given class, whether "class" is defined in Marxist terms or along more complex paradigms involving ethnicity, gender, sexuality, occupation and so on. I derive this characterization from Louis Althusser's interpretation of Marx's early usage of the term—"the system of ideas and representations which dominate the mind of man or a social group" (158)—and I would like to embrace one of Althusser's own theses, that "ideology represents the imaginary relationship of individuals to their real conditions of existence" (162). He goes on to say that it is not their real conditions of existence, their real world, that "men" "represent to themselves" in ideology, but above all it is their relation to those conditions of existence which is represented to them there. It is this relation which is at the centre of every ideological, i.e. imaginary, representation of the real world . . . It is the *imaginary nature of this relation* which underlies all the imaginary distortion that we can observe (if we do not live in its truth) in all ideology. (164)

I find Althusser's equation of ideology with imagination especially seductive because it resonates with my conception of experience as a matter of construction rather than of positivist essentiality. Moreover, Althusser has suggested that representation deals with neither humanity nor its conditions of existence, but with the *relation* between the two; that is, with an insubstantial bridge over a gap.

Common usage tends to imply that ideology can exist apart from its manifestation, that ideology is prior to and transcendent above the text that conveys it, and that such a text is itself controlled by ideology. Terry Eagleton argues that ideology produces text (*Criticism* 64), thus suggesting that ideology is pre- or sub-*langue*, inhabiting a space beneath the level of text. If I say that any given class structures experience according to its ideology, "to structure experience" may refer not only to the production of text but also to the use of text to convey a perceived shape or pattern in experience. This text is not merely a medium for "expressing" values; the ideology of a class is equivalent to the essential value structure of the class as such, and that structure—that ideology—produces text. Yet ideology is apparent only through text, which raises the question of how one can convey ideology and how the mode of conveyance affects ideology.

To regard text, simply, as a means of expression is to overlook motive and interaction in communication. The term "express" and its cognates and synonyms are seductive and delusive, for they suggest that discourse can flow neutrally, without any intention beyond the compulsion to convey experience. Yet even a bird sings for a reason, and I believe that people structure all texts, with varying degrees of awareness that they do so, to attain certain ends. When individuals band together and act to promote their mutual purposes, they form a class, and the sum and intersection of their motives form the ideology of that class. In other words, any text—any "expression"—is conceived to serve as an instrument in the network of power relations, which pervade and govern human interaction, or discourse. All report of experience is constructed; it does not spring forth unmediated.[8] An ideology is therefore composed of the interests, values, and strategies of a group as they are perceived, by that group and by others, in the context of discourse. Ideology resides in text and discourse; we cannot know it or be aware of it except as it is so revealed. This perceptual relativity of ideology is fundamental. The many discourses that produce the many ideologies occupy a Derridean space of endless reference in which there is no point of theoretical or intellectual rest. I perceive a signifier and then "read" it as an indication or symptom of a correlate signified;

in other words, I recognize a text and assume the presence of an idea. Yet the text is all that I can know, and my understanding of the idea is entirely a matter of my comprehension and interpretation of the text. There is no stability.[9]

Moreover, any text inhabits a referential space which, as in Einstein's physics, is recurved. The text refers back to itself, because even as it speaks, it becomes part of the world that it addresses; it is both subject and object. Because of this simultaneous dimensionality—this positional flickering—we cannot argue, simply, that context determines performance. There is no neutral space, no space outside of space, that the text may occupy either to comment on the human experience or to respond to experiential influence. The text observes experience and is also a part of it; ideology remains amalgamated with text and with culture.

Ideology therefore interacts with the space it inhabits, changing the shape of that space but only as the space itself permits. It is like the energy that creates a wave but is itself invisible without its medium. I claim to see the wave, but in fact I see the water or tall grass respond to the energy that passes through it and changes its appearance. Yet even if I recognize that I perceive an operation not of substance but of energy, how I perceive that energy remains a question of the substance through which it manifests itself. Ideology may influence the shape of discourse, but I perceive it only as the nature of that discourse permits. My present concern is with the discourse that is known as melodrama, which as a form of theatre operates much like myth, and myth is a mode that bears a complex and often paradoxical relationship to ideology, for both treat collective belief.

Myth is a form of symbolic narrative that links the present audience with both past and future; it shapes the raw material of experience, creating a cultural history, and it provides a paradigm for future action and self-contemplation.[10] Myth is inherently allegorical, for the mythic hero is an Everyman—the audience identifies with him and therefore accepts his concerns as compelling—and the mythic world is Everyworld, one the audience embraces as consonant with and resonant of not its own experience—for that has no objective reality—but rather with its perception of and belief in that experience. Because myth can influence and shape perception and belief, the relationships between myth, belief, experience, and humanity are complex and interwoven. There is no clear point of origin, a situation analogous to the bottomlessness of discourse in general.

Myth is the voice not of individuals but of entire peoples; society creates myth, and myth speaks to society. The operation of myth is largely a matter of its collective nature, and a mythology can even help bind disparate peoples together or create the illusion that they are one. To contact many minds at once, myth must employ a semiotic repertoire that time and usage have hallowed and rendered widely accessible, so a mythology is a composition of cultural metaphors. The evocative power of myth is largely a function of the degree to which its signifiers are familiar to the audience; as a myth endures, its figures, images, tropes, and narratives become part of the semiotic repertoire, to the point that they—and the myth as a whole—seem organic or cosmic. For this reason, myth is inherently conservative, relying not on new or revolutionary ideas and significations but on those that have survived the changes of the years. Myth therefore tends to reinforce the dominant ideology, which itself tends to rest on tradition.

While any fictional process, through selection and interpretation, both obscures and reveals its subject, myth is exceptionally powerful because it creates and wields fictions in an attempt to transcend the personal and particular and to convey the experience of an entire culture. Richard Slotkin describes myth as "a complex of narratives that dramatizes the world vision and historical sense of a people," and he goes on to say that "the narrative action of the myth-tale . . . reduces both experience and vision to a paradigm" (6). In so doing, myth can eclipse not only the relevant history but also our perception of the interaction between that myth and that history; we seek to see the object but the myth acts as a veil, hiding the object from view and even usurping its place in our gaze, luring us into misprision.

The semantics of critical discourse tend to blur the distinctions between myth and ideology. Although Slotkin and James K. Folsom see both as "conceptual systems that define a culture's world view and sanction particular social and political structures and behaviors," they draw qualitative and structural distinctions, contending that ideology is composed of concepts—analytic, rhetorical, philosophical, and "open to argument and refutation"—while myth is composed of "evocative symbols, ordered as narratives"—less rational and more given to personification, symbol, and formulaic patterns (5–6). Sacvan Bercovitch depicts them almost as two sides of the same phenomenon when he points out that many scholars assume that ideology "pretends to truth" and therefore seeks "to uncover, rationally, the sinister effects of its fictions," and that while myth is "inherently suspect" because it serves as a vehicle for prescription, the critics seek to reveal its deeper truths (421). In other words, we seek the fiction in ideology-as-"truth," and the truth in myth-as-"fiction."[11] Yet myth and ideology cannot be truly complementary, for the two are incommensurate. The antithesis of myth is not ideology but rather polemic or any other mode that eschews symbol, narrative, allegory, and overt fiction.

Although we may posit myth as being just one of a variety of forms, or sets of signifiers, that may serve as a vehicle for an ideology, a complex of signifieds—that is, if we accept Eagleton's contention that ideology produces text, and so construe myth, as text, as an artifact consequent to ideology—the analysis is too simplistic because it ignores the quality and effect of myth as a vehicle, no matter what "message" it is meant to convey. Because myth employs a highly traditional semiotic repertoire, it conveys a general ideology insofar as it reinforces the dominance of tradition and therefore serves the interests of those groups that identify with the past and the status quo. Ideology reflects distinctions between peoples, but myth tries to bring everyone together, so myth offers an uncomfortable and even dilutive vehicle for ideology. Even to say that myth is the voice of a society is to create a monolith of that society and so both subsume and submerge those individuals who find the face of that monolith at all alien.

THE SENTIMENTAL VISION

The ideological substructure of melodrama is the sentimental vision of humanity, one based on a high regard for emotions, especially sympathy with others, and fraught with profound contradictions that became increasingly debilitating as the nineteenth century unfolded. When Shaftesbury, in 1711, published his proposition that sympathy was one of the "natural affections," he conferred upon humanity a community of feelings and interests.[12] That is, if there is a uniformity of emotions among people, if one person's feelings will inspire like feelings in another, and if one person may feel compassion for another, then people are bound together by more than a social contract. In fact, since what affects one affects others, then self-interest is equivalent to community interest and the distinction between the two does not truly exist. In other words, if I experience sympathy with everyone else—if I believe that everyone else feels as I do, and if I intuit and understand everyone else's feelings—then only if I perversely seek my own distress will I act to the detriment of humanity. If I choose wisely, to act for my own benefit is also to act for the benefit of all, which is, according to common parlance, to act benevolently or virtuously; the consequences of sympathy trick me into virtue in spite of myself. If I am wiser still, I will realize that acting for the good of the community is the best way to ensure my own happiness or satisfaction. Such behavior demonstrates Shaftesbury's "moral sense," which he calls a God-given "natural affection."[13]

One consequence of this syllogism is that feeling is elevated above cold reason. If human feeling is natural (and therefore unavoidable), then emotions are the ultimate arbiters of any situation. The most social of all emotions is sympathy between people—not merely an expression of concern but a sense of mutuality. Yet, paradoxically, although the model establishes an essential subjectivity—experience is defined in terms of individual sensations and attitudes—it argues an emotional community that denies the isolation of the individual.

The sentimental syllogism translates into an abiding faith in the essential goodness of human nature. If each individual, compelled by the circumstances that govern the pursuit of his own interests, acts for the good of all, then each is, for all intents and purposes, virtuous and well-intentioned, and one who strays is not inherently vicious but rather momentarily wayward, and his innate goodness will inevitably re-assert itself.[14] Social change, therefore, is bound to take a positive direction, a promise that reinforced Lockean liberalism and the ensuing American social and political traditions.[15] In fact, because the middle class was (and is) preoccupied with the acquisition of property and needed a justifying rationale, the sentimental reconciliation of self-interest with the public good fit neatly with Adam

Smith's contention that that self-interest and private property are basic to the health of society and that economic liberty permits the utmost production of wealth and therefore the public good, and also with Locke's vision of political power as a means of preserving the individual's freedom to use and dispose of his property with perfect freedom.[16] In other words, Locke, Shaftesbury, and Smith had provided a theoretical means to render bourgeois aspirations not only palatable but downright virtuous.

I described the sentimental vision as ideological in nature because it tends to bolster the interests of the middle and upper classes; one can sympathize with others only if one has leisure to do so and attention to spare. Moreover, the sentimental program assumes—even insists upon—a significant degree of homogeneity in society, and it provides a convenient ground for arguing in favor of the greater good, for those whose interests diverge are clearly marginal and have somehow strayed from the gentility of the "natural affections." The desperate classes—the homeless poor or the workers caught in the maelstrom of industrial society—are either erased from the sentimental paradigm or reduced to objects of philanthropy, as in the case of the humanitarian and reform movements that appeared in America during the antebellum period. In other words, the sentimental sensibility affirms itself by seeking to bring the divergent back to the fold.

The middle class embraced the sentimental vision (and, as of the middle eighteenth century, the novels that conveyed it), and by the nineteenth century had translated it into the philosophy of domesticity, using it to theorize, rationalize, and defend the family. Virtue is defined in domestic terms—the family is sacred, women are canonized as mothers, and children are so innocent and pure as to be virtually saintly. The responsible man works hard (and enjoys his labor) in order to provide for his wife and children, who depend upon him for their livelihood and protection. The virtuous woman remains loyal to her husband in spite of any temptation or assault, so her chastity—sexual exclusivity, really—becomes not only an assurance that her children are her husband's rightful heirs but also a badge of her commitment. Her marriage is, precisely, a sacrament, and she becomes both the defender of sentiment and its paragon. In his 1882 treatise on acting, Gustave Garcia took the sentimental sympathy to its zenith in his conception of a mother's affection for her children.

> Maternal love is the most tender sentiment in living nature. It is the sweetest and most generous movement which the natural instinct can possibly prompt. It is the first inclination in animal economy. . . . The sentiments of a mother are all spontaneous, never reflective or calculating. (136)

The children, who were unfailingly respectful and dutiful toward their parents, served as reminders that all adults began life completely innocent of experience and therefore perfectly virtuous, and they were the objects of their parents' unreserved devotion and dedication. Shaftesbury's "natural affections" were revised into affection—in a more ordinary sense—between family members, the feeling that binds them all together, the commitment that defines their intimacy and relegates all others to the roles of outsiders. The family is the unassailable repository of value, the unanswerable referent.

This ideal model is so clearly and firmly drawn that it virtually mandates an opposite, a dark, alternative model known as "evil" and defined as whatever diverges from virtue. Just as the medieval mind defined Satan as Antichrist, the sentimental mind imagined a perverted world and peopled it with inversions of virtuous characters: the man who fails to provide for his family or who abuses them, the woman who sullies her purity, or the child who somehow wanders from the teachings of his elders. The most heinous criminals are those men who not only neglect their duties but actually threaten or abuse women or children—those most vulnerable creatures in the sentimental imagination—and so displace the precious concepts of chastity and innocence with corruption. This dark alternative creates the Manichæan space so essential to melodrama, and fosters a delicately balanced moral universe that is defined almost entirely of rebounding binary oppositions and whose symmetry suggests a finely conceived mechanism.

Although sentimental culture twisted what Shaftesbury had bequeathed, the potential for a mechanistic interpretation was always there. To valorize feeling and insist on subjectivity, however communal, may seem organic, but the position also suggests a mechanical model insofar as it is deterministic; because the moral sense is a natural affection, all natural men will behave in a certain way. Furthermore, the logical extension of sentimental optimism, especially the proposition that man must constantly progress toward a higher state of grace and goodness, was the belief that man, like a machine, might be perfectible, a proposition that fell neatly into the rationalist, mathematical paradigms of the Enlightenment. While the Newtonian mechanism suggested that effect reliably followed cause, the sentimental version insisted that there was, finally, only one kind of effect, or result, available; after all, according to the conventional wisdom of nineteenth-century America, a benign providence governed human destiny.[17]

The sentimental model bore the potential for devastating effects on the middle class, and it implied a circular model of history. If society is the sum of its individuals, then (1) men undertake moral obligation not only for themselves and their families but also for the community at large, and (2) social ills are the result of individual error, so social progress is a matter of individual reform. If society is no longer stratified and fixed, then social mobility is possible, but it becomes entirely the responsibility of the husband and father. No one seeks to move down in the social milieu, and the opportunity to rise makes stasis unacceptable, so only improvement is acceptable. If the world fails to progress, or if the family fails to move up on the social ladder, it is the individual man's fault. Paradoxically, however, because the supposedly organic movement of the virtuous individual is toward the virtuous state, "change" means a return to what should have been true in the first place. In other words, even though the sentimental interpretation of the world as mechanism offered the promise of perfectibility, it implied not evolution but the restoration of a condition that had, unexpectedly, inexplicably, and unfortunately, been altered. This paradigm encourages a profoundly conservative vision of history, for if "change" is merely a gentle reversion to an approved ideal, culture is constantly in the process of attempting to come full circle and return to its point of origin. Revolution, or even a new idea, becomes anathema, and the "natural" state of society is stasis.

The sentimental vision, therefore, was fundamentally self-contradictory:

- The community of mankind implied harmony of intentions and denied the reality of conflict of interest.
- The value placed on feeling suggested an organic model of the human experience, but the Manichæan polarity and the deterministic implications of "natural affections" both indicated a mechanism.
- Humanity must improve, but improvement might be only a return to the point of origin.
- The individual is responsible for the consequences of his actions, but because the eventual condition of the world seems preordained, he is not truly free to act.
- All are born innocent under the guidance of providence, but the world has somehow fallen into imperfection and must now find its way back.

The middle class found its ideology in the sentimental vision, and its theatre in the plays that flowered on the English-speaking stage during the eighteenth century. The fundamental currency of interaction between audience and performer was sympathy—the seed of the sentimental vision—and it was sympathy that drove the melodrama of the nineteenth century.

MELODRAMA

Melodrama was the predominant dramatic form and theatrical style of nineteenth-century America, and in one sense, this is a book about melodrama. However, it is not a genre study, for I am only slightly interested in the formal characteristics of melodrama as such and in relation to other commensurate genres, such as farce, comedy, and tragedy. To place genre at the center of a methodology is to adopt a formalist position that privileges æsthetics and insists that a text bears an absolute and restrictive literary reality, thus denying the differential freeplay and interaction of the text (and the related event) with its culture, which are, to my mind, its essential processes. I do not mean to argue that form does not exist or that I should ignore it; form *does* exist, and its study can be useful, but I am concerned less with its own qualities and more with those its existence implies. The visible signs of melodrama—the patterns that preoccupy the formalists—interest me principally in that from them I may deduce a point of view, an agenda, or a program. Those visible signs are the result or product of that point of view, not the other way around; the melodrama is set up to convey certain constructions, and its formal characteristics are simply the most appropriate ways to do so. Therefore, when I refer to melodrama, I am discussing not a fixed literary generality but rather an attitude and, more often, the product of that attitude, both of them functions of culture and society, and both flexible in time and space. When I label a certain text a melodrama, I am attempting to describe, briefly and generally, either the response it elicits or the attitude it promotes; or I am indicating that I perceive in it certain qualifies of vision, form, or style—all of which is a more precise way of saying that I am signaling that it is a certain kind of play. "American melodrama" is therefore a certain manifestation of a certain conceptualization of America during a certain period of history, and I wish to elicit its operation in relation to ideology, myth, and representation. While aspects of the following discussion of melodrama may apply to other cases, I intend it more as a theoretical introduction to those melodramas found in the nineteenth-century American theatre.

Any play assumes a set of values, whether it affirms or attacks them, shared among its participants, who represent their culture, speak for it, and respond for it. In a sense, *all* of the participants "write" the play, and indeed, in the theatre of the American nineteenth century, many playwrights enjoyed even less authority over the text than we now consider customary.[18] Plays were not considered literature, and playwrights produced derivative confections of largely interchangeable situations, characters, and stories as popular entertainment for a large, sometimes national audience. I shall therefore refer to the participants as the collective author of melodrama in general. Insofar as melodrama articulates their shared values, it becomes part of the myth-making apparatus of its culture, offering metaphorical and even allegorical action that conveys a world view.

The classic pattern begins with the presentation of a situation as both ideal and normal. The action accelerates as some influence, depicted as external, threatens that situation, and ends when evil is vanquished and the virtuous characters return to the condition they cherish and deserve. The play is therefore the enactment of a dark fantasy concerning the ideal society's dissolution and ultimate (and inevitable) salvation; its threatened loss or destruction inspires the fear that engages the audience's rapt attention, and its subjection to assault indicates its vulnerability while its survival proves its strength. In one sense, melodrama is the expression of sentimental culture's fear that the eighteenth-century optimists might have been mistaken.

The essential action of melodrama is to polarize its constituents, whatever they may be—male and female, East and West, civilization and wilderness, and, most typically, good and evil. By forcing its elements apart until they seem irreconcilably disparate, and then sustaining their interdependent relationship within a shared structure, melodrama provides a paradoxical means of resolving fundamental contradictions. In other words, the melodramatic world is composed of binary oppositions. Individuals are either wholly good or wholly evil, and it is this Manichæan vision that most obviously characterizes melodrama and expresses the fundamental faith of the middle class. Melodrama is the arena wherein hero and heroine contend against villain, and the forces of virtue ultimately defeat the forces of evil.

Yet there are significant distinctions between the villain as a character type, evil as a perceived force, and fear as a generative impulse. The villain customarily serves as the agent or manifestation of evil, but some works we call melodramas employ villains who operate simply as antagonists, without an integral context of evil, while others include that evil without a clearly defined villain standing forth as its avatar. Fear is the only essential component of the three, for it is the emotion from which melodrama springs, inspiring first a conception of evil to rationalize the fear, and then a villain to configure that evil, giving it a form and a voice.

Melodrama works on us in layers, each a bit more removed from our immediate experience but supporting the one before it. The most proximate includes those characteristics that form the familiar descriptive list that sometimes, fallaciously, serves as a definition of the genre: thrilling incident and exciting alternation between disaster and recovery, uninhibited show of spectacle according to the potential of the medium, open display of violence and catastrophe, exaggerated expression of emotion, and the foregrounding of entertainment value at the expense of any subtle meaning or complexity of narrative, all of which carry us away, willy-nilly, with the piece. The second layer involves the leading characters, the hero and heroine earning sympathy and identification, and the villain provoking revulsion and hisses from what is usually assumed to be a mass audience. Each character type configures an idea or concept, thus reinforcing the allegorical quality of the play. The third layer is the struggle between virtue and evil as irreconcilable, absolute opposites, and it is this layer that seems to function as the basis for the rest of the structure. Without this starkly polarized and simplistic conflict, there is only feeble justification for the incident, spectacle, violence, and wild emotionalism that constitute the matter and the fascination of melodrama; that is, the nature of melodrama is a product and an expression of that fundamental, necessary conflict. The extravagance of the representation indicates that semiosis eclipses mimetic or phenomenal considerations; that is, the performance has more to do with conveying the *idea* of experience rather than its mundane actuality.

Yet in theorizing melodrama, we must search for the fundamental layer, that which supports and produces the others. Peter Brooks has said that

> melodrama typically not only employs virtue persecuted as a source of its dramaturgy, but also tends to become the dramaturgy of virtue misprized and eventually recognized. It is about virtue made visible and acknowledged, the drama of a recognition. (27)

In other words, melodrama is a means of revealing the nature of virtue. Yet I contend that because melodrama is, ostensibly, the voice of the virtuous world, then virtue itself is a putative transcendental signified, a given, and an ultimate and unexceptionable referent for moral judgments. Virtue becomes the basis for an essentialist view of society and psychology. Each melodrama must satisfy its audience concerning the nature not of virtue, but of evil, of that which places virtue in jeopardy, of that which virtue fears. "Good" is the world as it should be, stable, safe, and at rest, while "evil" sends the planet hurtling uncontrollably toward some ineffable future. "Good" is the state to which melodrama must inevitably return, while "evil" is the canker to cosmic action, the force that shatters complacency and calls any order into question. "Good" is the self, and "evil" is the other—the stranger. I therefore gaze in a different direction than Brooks, away from the contemplation of virtue and toward the regard of evil, but always evil as virtue sees it and fears it. From virtue's point of view, evil is the unsettler, the destroyer, the vandal, the iconoclast, the unpredictable spirit of negation. Virtue knows that evil will attack, but it never knows how, so it spins apprehensive fantasies. The collective author hopes that all of its constituents are deserving, but evil inspires the fear that virtue might not be inherent, but must be earned, which leads to troubling questions as to the means.[19] The point of melodrama is to enact those fantasies for its sentimental audience—to give evil a mask in order to replay its inevitable defeat and reassure the virtuous that though their fears be valid, their optimism is justified.

The absolute imperative of melodrama is the restoration of the moral, social, and domestic order—and, consequently, the reassurance of the audience—by subjecting its characters to a high degree of risk and uncertainty and then lifting them out of danger. Daniel C. Gerould has asserted that "the universe of melodrama is totally devoid of fatality and inevitability. Contingency rules; things can and will be otherwise. The individual can make of himself what he will" (9). However, this analysis is valid only *within* the structure of melodrama, taken from the perspective of the character herself. While Laura, in Augustin Daly's *Under the Gaslight* (1867), may regard her situation as unpredictably insecure, from *outside* the structure, we can see that her restoration to respectability and comfort is inevitable, and that the play seeks to affirm a vision of reality that makes her continuing misery unthinkable. *She* may see herself as helpless, blown this way and that on the winds of circumstance, but *we* know that virtue must triumph and evil must fall in order to affirm the moral order. From the hero's vantage, the action validates his exercise of free will, but the melodramatic imperative, operating under the guiding hand of divine providence and moving the action toward reconciliation, offers a guarantee that reduces the hero's achievement. By its very nature and method, melodrama must satisfy its audience's expectations rather than present a confrontation with belief and value.[20] The strength of the melodramatic imperative betokens a lurking, covert fear that can drive the machinery. If society can change, if it can evolve or transform into something new rather than experiencing restoration to its former condition, then it is possible for such change to leave the subject behind, rendering him marginal, rejected, and out of place. This is the fear of erasure or of displacement, of being cast aside and left alone.

Melodrama, as I have presented it, makes a myth that seems to express only a portion of the American ethos. It is largely domestic, by which I mean that no matter what the setting or the nature of the action, it is, at bottom, concerned with the family, and it seems to affirm the postsentimental belief in the continuing prog- ress and ultimate perfection of mankind and society. However, it offers little en- couragement for the alleged American love of individualism and freedom and for our sense of romantic mission. Within the system, individual action might seem predominant, but from outside, it is clear that the individuals are only tokens in a deterministic game. Yet melodrama throve in the American theatre.

AMERICA / AMERICA

The principal challenge in theorizing "America"—a clear prerequisite to dis- cussing how America performs itself—is the question of whether there is such a thing at all. The concept of "American culture" seems to insist upon a host of assumptions, principally that there is one homogeneous community with certain qualities that mark it as distinctly American; that is, different from any other. The phrase enforces a certain politics by presupposing the reader's acceptance; it enlists conspiracy. We are a people in that we share a region, a government, a body of law, a network of transportation and communication facilities, a general system of trade, and a certain identity in the international community. We embrace the concept of America as *the* land of freedom (we accept the idea of authority with much more reluctance), where anyone can think, write, say, or do virtually anything at all, where power resides in the populace, who then confer it temporarily on the elected officials and the appointed bureaucracy, and where anyone can rise to the apex of the economic pyramid. Yet there are divisions in American culture, and as both they and our consciousness of them deepen, the word "multiculturalism" seems naïvely optimistic insofar as it attempts to preserve a balkanized but allegedly cohesive American culture.

Yet while there are many American experiences whose diversity denies the validity of any subsuming term, they are connected. I began this chapter by referring to "America," its "people," and "the American experience" in a way that seems to posit uniformity, denying differences between people and blithely ignoring the changes of centuries. Although one might challenge such cultural generalities re- peatedly, rejecting layer after layer of association and inclusion until today's "Amer- ica" splits into 250 million lonely people and a multitude of specific moments—one could, after all, denounce concepts like culture and class as pernicious means to appropriate individuality and erase those qualities held by the minority that is inevi- table in any group—I resist this impulse as more the child of the anger of current academic politics than the expression of a genuine passion for intellectual precision.

To assert difference to such a degree is to deny shared experience and completely disable discourse on the relationships between those individuals and those moments. I will therefore use "America" and its cognates in two ways. First, the terms refer not to something monolithic or fixed, but rather to a process, or a phenomenon in a state of constant formation; they indicate not that any component of that culture has primacy over the others, which are then defined by their difference from the ostensible center, but rather that the system is the product of competitive interaction between all of its constituents; and they refer to all of us who contribute to this interaction and share in the consequent system. Second, the terms refer to an ideal I find implied in the plays I have chosen for the present study. These texts *do* embody assumptions regarding America as a monolith, and part of my project is to explain how they were constructed to bolster those assumptions. This monolith takes the shape of a certain conception of America to which the plays refer, with which they privilege a certain exclusionary vision, and which they revise and re-create.

The fundamental cliché of nineteenth-century American studies is that our ancestors and predecessors lived in a simpler culture where men—white, Protestant, propertied, and confident—frankly wielded virtually all social power, while women, people of color, and recent immigrants were defined in terms of their dependence on and deviance from their self-acclaimed masters. This vision assumes an age of forthright, unashamed patriarchy, when social convention locked men and women into tight gender roles that assured male dominance. Yet this model is simplistic and therefore deceptive. When we refer to that culture as resting on comfortable assumptions of homogeneity and continuity, when we describe that society as the expression of white, male, middle-class assertion of power, and when we accept the pat analysis of the "weaker" ones as clearly disempowered and marginalized, we are accepting a vision derived from a discourse that represented, for the most part, only that culture's dominant voices. It is true, for example, that most plays of the nineteenth century (including all five that I examine in this book) were the work of white men, and that in the melodramas, gender was a key factor in determining the degree of interpersonal power—that is, the freedom to influence one's destiny, measured in terms of options and restrictions—allowed to each of the characters. In simple terms, Man was either villain, the agent of the action, or hero, the often wayward champion of the sentimental social order, while Woman was heroine, the embodiment of virtue, and the passive victim of both the villain's schemes and the hero's weaknesses. The effect was to deny Woman her right to act or choose and to confer both the privilege and the burden of initiative on Man. Yet this confection of convention and expectation is so carefully assembled that it betrays its authors' anxieties; they urge their case too strenuously for us, a century or more later, to accept it as truly reflective of the actuality of their world. To accept that discourse at face value is to overlook its more fascinating qualities. One of the most engrossing aspects of any culture or any discourse is the capacity for oblivious self-contradiction; the best evidence of the complexity of nineteenth-century American culture is the effort its spokesmen expended in urging its simplicity and presenting belief as truth, or myth as history.[21] In other words, I perceive their apparently homogeneous construction as a mask conceived in response to a complexity it hides.

From a certain perspective, there does seem to be an American narrative—a myth of our shared experience. It begins with the "discovery" of the "New" World and the construction of that world as both garden and wilderness, and with the travelers' belief that they held their destinies in their own hands, that they could relocate all of history into the future, there to be rewritten, and so erase the burden of Old World error in a process of limitless beginnings that would free them from ancient, inhibiting European customs and institutions. It continues with the egalitarianism that the settlers developed from the rigors of their trials combined with the Lockean tradition they brought from England, and it moves on with the beckoning temptation of the westering frontier. The myth assures its disciples material plenitude and opportunity for self-improvement, but demands fealty to a sense of mission that could be either romantic or crushingly burdensome.[22] The myth valorizes both the family and the loner, positing them as parallel to the conflicting liberal principles of social contract and individual autonomy, but does not reconcile their contradictory demands, just as it does not offer congruence between the idealism of the American dream with the stolid materialism—the gritty denial of European abstraction and determined appropriation of property as erstwhile aristocratic prerogative—that drives its people. In spite of the complexity and contradictions, this is the myth of the new Eden, the fantasy of the middle class come to America: a prelapsarian, sentimental garden where the natural state of humanity is virtuous domesticity, where industry produces happiness, where sensible people conform to established belief, and where property is the emblem and evidence of moral and worldly success—and that which makes it possible for American commoners to scorn the European aristocracy and caste system—as well as the raison d'être of the new society.

There is a certain beauty in this myth, but as a guiding paradigm it no longer satisfies, and it does not express the profound failure of the American experience. Even as early as the nineteenth century, the actual Americans found that the land denied the myth's abundant promise and that the disappointment led to alienation, guilt, and nostalgia over the nation's acquisition, rape, and loss, as well as to an excruciating sense of frustration. The experience challenges the myth's essential optimism and tenacious faith in the inevitability of progress and ongoing success. Moreover, the myth is composed of pioneer tropes and figures, images that seem increasingly anachronistic as new waves of immigrants come to these shores and find circumstances and episodes only symbolically akin to those of earlier arrivals. Finally, the myth addresses, principally, the white, English, and mostly male experience, treating the natives as Other and virtually erasing the radically different career of the abducted African exiles. The point, however, is not that the myth is imperfect, for that should by now be axiomatic, but that understanding the material is a matter of discerning how discourse treats the myth—how each text works with the myth and changes it. Hollow though the myth may appear today, it enjoyed more currency during the nineteenth century, and there was complex interchange between received narrative, new contributions to discourse, and actual experience.

In this context, *Melodrama and the Myth of America* is a search for the idea of America, the concept that both reflects and determines the American space. I anticipate that the plays I have chosen will elucidate an idea of America that is homogeneous and more stable than the multicultural dialectic that I perceive in my own time. Yet America has, undeniably, a certain continuity in terms of political structures, social antecedents, and cultural traditions, so part of my task will be to find a bridge between the sensibilities of the past and the present, to describe to what extent the idea of America has changed, and to what extent the idea has survived from age to age.

2

Metamora (1829) and the "Indian" Question

JOHN AUGUSTUS STONE'S *Metamora* (1829) was more than a highly popular vehicle for the touring star, Edwin Forrest (1806–1872), more than the most famous and influential of the "Indian" plays of the antebellum stage, and more than a travesty of the history of King Philip's War. It was a political instrument, a means of delicately balancing several components of the American sensibility, projecting the passionate nationalism of the new nation by incorporating, incongruously, an emblematic native American into white narrative, presenting him as an idealized hero who embodied sentimental values, but still reinforcing Andrew Jackson's policy of Indian removal. The play and its performance were also cultural phenomena that occupied specific places in the history of the white construction of Indian as image, and of King Philip in particular. Forrest played Metamora for nearly forty years, until 1868, and drew consistently large audiences, clear indication that many theatre-goers found the sachem appealing and even admirable, even though at least one performance was nearly halted by a crowd of Georgians incensed over Indian removal and states' rights. How Forrest's audiences perceived the play as theatrical event was partly a function of the ideology consequent to their perception of the Indian as fiction and the native as reality, and of themselves as Americans.

In his 1877 official biography of Forrest, William Rounseville Alger offered this assessment of the Indian under the white man's gaze:

> The North American Indian seen from afar is a picturesque object. When we contemplate him in the vista of history, retreating, dwindling, soon to vanish before the encroachments of our stronger race, he is not without mystery and pathos. But studied more nearly, inspected critically in the detail of his character and habits, the charm for the most part disappears and is replaced with repulsion. The freedom of savages from the diseased vices of a luxurious society, the proud beauty of their free bearing, the relish of their wild liberty with nature, exempt from the artificial burdens and trammels of our complicated and stifling civilization, appeal to the imagination. (127)

Alger's white sensibility is drawn to the beauty of the Indian, but a beauty completely dependent on a situation of white construction. There is enough spatial/tem-

Drawn on stone by D. C. Johnston   Lith of Pendleton, Bos

"Mr. E. Forrest as Metamora." From Augustus Toedteberg's *Forrestiana*. Drawn on stone by D. C. Johnston. (Courtesy of the Huntington Library, San Marino, California.)

poral distance to afford a certain æsthetic blur, permitting the white eye to overlook the repulsive actuality and deny, without the appearance of pernicious intention, the subject's humanity; an object is more easily manipulated than a person. More important, the white man assumes the role of the conqueror who, to become civilized and powerful, has not only forfeited his innocence, but has also heroically sacrificed the primal freedom he purports to admire in the Indian. The native is thus appropriated as the object of white nostalgia, as though the white man perceives the Indian as a version of himself—younger and more innocent, but weaker and less sophisticated—a false memory of what he wants to think he could have been. It is a vision borne out of traditions that developed long before Columbus set sail.

The discovery of the New World must have seemed, to the European imagination, to vindicate centuries of legends, stories that sang of paradise on earth, of Atlantis, of the Blessed Isles, of Avalon and Arcadia. To travel to the West was to return to Hesiod's Golden Age, or to Eden itself, to rewrite history from the prelapsarian moment, and to rediscover a mythic life of innocence and peace. However, to find the new Arcadia inhabited was to confront a challenge. The legends operated in a certain way, leading their devotees to cast themselves in a drama of regeneration and form an image of what Western society or its members could become. The idea of becoming implied, in this preevolutionary age, a transformation, and one consequent to a journey from one place, the known and familiar world, to another that was clearly different. In other words, the new Arcadia had to demonstrate essential, fundamental distinctions in relation to the Old World; it had to succeed in whatever respects Europe had failed. The participants assumed roles in this cosmic drama, and therefore any people they met in the new Arcadia were expected to play complementary roles; to admit unsanctioned behavior was to jeopardize the legends themselves. Exploration became an exercise in realizing expectations; for example, as Harry Levin has observed, European writers had speculated that the new Golden Age would be free of the institutions that characterized but hampered European society, so they perceived validation when the sixteenth-century explorers reported finding a simple, primitive people who held land in common (60–61, 65).

However, the search for salutary difference led to a reading of the natives that was intended to confirm white preconceptions but also defined a devastating polarization between native and European, the two elements in a new relationship. Robert F. Berkhofer, Jr. writes that "usually without property, injustice, or kings, and often without work or war," the natives possessed certain "virtues . . . sexual innocence, equality of condition and status, peaceful simplicity, healthful and handsome bodies" that the Europeans believed they lacked (*White Man's Indian* 72). That is, the Europeans found in the natives not only support for their legends, but also expressions of their relative otherness. Their perception of essential and comprehensive difference, and the values by which they perceived it, led them to assert a binary opposition; the primary term was "European" or "white," and the secondary term was "Indian," the word itself being richly expressive of certain attitudes of the namers toward themselves and toward the named. It is a misnomer based on the assumption that the westward mariners would discover the fabled passage to India, it conflates the many diverse original peoples of the Western Hemisphere into a monolith, and its very origins, rooted in European tradition rather than in native self-expression, establish Eurocentrism and the European assumption of cultural hegemony. It is an ethnocentric construct, the product of an act of will and imagination designed to preserve hallowed and cherished beliefs. The binarism established "white European" as the only viable point of reference for the construction of value and perception, and "Indian" as marginal, aberrant, and threatening.[1] Furthermore, this binarism, like any other, offered a certain economy of leverage to anyone who used it. To clarify or more richly define one term is to do the same for the other; to attribute a given quality to one is to imply its opposite in the other. In other words, the assumption of polarization or of opposition takes precedence over the elements themselves; each term must complement the other, so adjusting one redetermines the other. To elaborate the Indian, therefore, became an exercise in self-creation for the Europeans.

Although the valorization of the Indian as exemplar of the Western idyll flowed seductively from the pen, it failed to address the actuality of the colonial experience in what is now the eastern United States. The Europeans who settled that region were not inclined to embrace the primitive life, ideal or otherwise; they preferred to establish a revision of the European civilization they had left behind. For example, those who settled New England sought not an idealized fantasy but a certain kind of life that was, for various reasons, denied them in England. They were, of necessity, practical people, engaged in the demanding business of building homes, churches, farms, and towns, and in order to succeed they needed land, free if possible, and readily acquired—to that portion of the Western myth they did subscribe. When they found their new home already occupied, they inevitably came to regard the natives as competitors and native presence as an obstacle that must be ameliorated or removed, and they adduced theological, political, or imaginative positions to justify what they came to perceive as their necessary response to this increasingly crowded coexistence. The English population grew, cultural interests clashed, and war broke out.[2]

KING PHILIP'S WAR

Up to the time of his death (1661?), the Wampanoag sachem Massasoit had succeeded in nurturing a fragile peace with Plymouth Colony, but at the cost of limiting the tribe's freedom of trade and travel. After Massasoit's death, his elder son, Wamsutta, traveled to Plymouth to request English names for himself and his brother, Metacomet, as signs of mutual goodwill, so the colonists dubbed them Alexander and Philip, after the Macedonian kings. Wamsutta apparently intended to carry on the policy of coexistence with the settlers, but in 1662, the General Court summoned him to Duxbury to respond to allegations that he was forming an alliance with the Narragansetts. He refused to go, but Major Josiah Winslow came with a party and took him at pistol-point. It is possible that Wamsutta was already ill; but it is certain that on his way home after the meeting, he died at Winslow's home in Marshfield.

Metacomet assumed the leadership of his people and renewed his father's covenants.[3] Yet there were disputes over land in Wollomonuppoag, Pokanoket (now Bristol), and Swansea, and in 1667, the English summoned Metacomet to court to answer accusations of conspiracy with the French and the Dutch. After another hearing regarding alleged plots with the Narragansett tribe, the English demanded, at Taunton on April 10, 1671, that Metacomet sign a document of submission in which he confessed that he had broken his covenant with King and Colony "through my Indiscretion, and the Naughtiness of my Heart . . . by taking up Arms, with evil intent against them, and that groundlessly" and promised to yield his "English Arms" (Hubbard 54–55). To ask Metacomet to sign such a statement was impolitic at best, and reveals the colonists' failure to understand their adversaries. The English may have perceived the sachem as unsophisticated, but he was the absolute and hereditary ruler of the third largest tribe in the region, and for that reason probably expected a certain degree of respect. He must have regarded the Taunton Agreement as either a grave, irreparable insult or a severe compromise to his power.

On January 29, 1675, a Wampanoag named John Sassamon was found dead and apparently murdered. He was a "praying Indian," or Christian, who had served as an interpreter for the English during the Pequot War and later taught school in Natick. He switched allegiance to become one of Metacomet's advisors, but he may have been acting as a double agent, for he subsequently returned to the English fold and informed Josiah Winslow, now governor of Plymouth, that the sachem was forming a conspiracy. Some believed that Metacomet then exerted his prerogative under tribal law and ordered the renegade's execution, a possibility that introduced the tricky issue of whether native or English authority should prevail and raised the question of why the sachem, if he did approve the killing, would later bother to disclaim responsibility for exercising what he would perceive as his rightful authority. The settlers accused three Wampanoag tribesmen of murder and, after a trial probably staged for political effect, with a jury including four "praying Indians" as nonvoting members, put them to death in June.

Later that month, a delegation of colonists from Rhode Island met to hear Metacomet's grievances. The sachem and his associates pointed out that Massasoit had protected the English, given them land, and shown them how to plant corn. In exchange, the colonists had poisoned Wamsutta, sold liquor to the natives, manipulated land sales to their unfair advantage, allowed their livestock to invade the natives' own cornfields, and in court had consistently preferred the least credible English testimony over the most reliable native statements. The plea was a litany of frustration, a sketch of how disparate were the customs of the two cultures with regard to man's use of land and the law's use of man. The meeting found no solution, and the natives became increasingly unruly. The settlers complained of vandalism on June 20 and retaliated on the twenty-third by killing a looter. On the twenty-fourth at Swansea, the natives killed nine Englishmen, and the war began.

From the summer of 1675 through the summer of 1676, the fighting decimated New England. In proportion to the population, the loss of life made the war the bloodiest conflict in the history of the colonies and the United States. A dozen towns were completely destroyed, and several others were partially burned. Military costs and the disruption of trade threw the colonial economy into chaos, and the progress of white settlement in New England was severely set back.[4] The natives paid a higher price; their defeat made it possible for the colonists to encroach even faster on the tribes' land, power, and freedom. As for Metacomet, he lost his family and then his life. The English had slowly been gaining the advantage when on August 1, 1676, they captured Metacomet's wife, Wootoneskanuske, and their nine-year-old son; no one knows exactly what happened to the two of them, but they were probably sold into slavery in Spain or the West Indies. On August 12, Captain Benjamin Church led a band of English and native troops to Metacomet's base. A brave had turned informer to avenge the death of his brother, whom the sachem had killed for daring to suggest a negotiated peace. Church's troops surprised the encampment, and when an Englishman's gun misfired, a renegade Wampanoag named Alderman shot his own chief dead. Church ordered his men to cut off the head and hands (one of which he awarded to the killer), and then to draw and quarter the body in the manner of an English execution.

SAVAGISM

It was, in one sense, a war over land, a struggle to see who would dominate southern New England in the 1670s—approximately twenty thousand natives living in scattered villages under the decentralized rule of many sachems, or about twice as many English, living under four highly organized colonial governments that were inclined to overlook their differences in order to stamp out a common threat. Yet there was a more abstract dimension to the conflict, one rooted in white conceptions of race and religion. Sixteenth- and seventeenth-century European thinkers had grappled with the phenomenon of the Indian, some suggesting that Indians were not descended from Adam at all, and others arguing that they were drastic degenerations of the human race; the fundamental question was whether or not they had souls, an issue that would affect the way in which the explorers dealt with them—or, rather, with how the explorers justified their dealings. William Bradford himself considered the natives to be little better than beasts, and he implicitly denigrated them by describing North America as "unpeopled" (Drinnon 48–49). Although most of the colonists were Puritans, Separatists, and Quakers, who were accustomed to managing significant differences between themselves and others, they found the natives to be completely alien in virtually every way. If the settlers were God's elect, the Indians were surely a fallen race to whom the Lord had sent His favorite emissaries. Roy Harvey Pearce has explained that

> the Puritans carried to its extreme the logic of seventeenth-century Christian imperialism. God had meant the savage Indians' land for the civilized English and, moreover, had meant the savage state itself as a sign of Satan's power and savage warfare as a sign of earthly struggle and sin. The colonial enterprise was in all ways a religious enterprise. (20)

The 1629 Charter of the Massachusetts Bay Colony specifically charged the settlers to "wynn and incite the Natives of Country to the Knowledge and Obedience of the onlie true God and Sauior of Mankinde, and Christian Fayth, which in our Royall Intencon, and the Adventurers free Profession, is the principall Ende of this Plantacion." The colonists fought the war not only to defend their accomplishments and to control the natives' land, but also to assert a conception of God and man, a conception that informed the histories of the war that began appearing even before the last battle.

When Stone wrote *Metamora*, most of the available accounts of King Philip's War were those written in colonial times, and it was in relation to them that writers in the early nineteenth century offered their interpretations. Perry Miller has explained the Puritan conception of history as insisting that "there was no place for contingency, fortune, or accident either in the past or in the future, and no nation could ever attain to a destiny other than what had been appointed. . . . The future was just as secure and as unalterable as the past." In a sense, the historian had to discover, record, and elucidate, after the fact, a cosmic play in which events were God's expression of Himself through humanity, whose apparent acts of will were simply means to fulfill His intentions (463–64).

This vision carried a crushing burden, for if success was God's will, then so was failure, so the official apologists read the war either as God's test of His people or as a form of warning or punishment. History was therefore the record of God's authority over the human race as each lonely soul sought grace amidst the trials that the Lord had set before him. As Richard Slotkin and James K. Folsom have observed, the principal historians were members of the ruling theocracy, forging myth in service of an ideology that sought to bolster their society's hegemony over nonbelievers, both red and white (6). In essence, the historians faced three tasks: (1) to explain why God had brought this disaster to pass, (2) to exculpate the colonists, and (3) to define the Indians, and especially Metacomet, as the agents of evil.

By 1677, several accounts of the war were published in London and Boston, but I shall concentrate on the contributions of three authors: Nathaniel Saltonstall, a Boston merchant; William Hubbard, a Harvard-trained minister who made a reputation writing sermons and histories; and Increase Mather, educated at Harvard and at Trinity College in Dublin, whose response to the war constituted the beginning of his interest in the native situation and of his activity as an historian, and who later became president of Harvard and one of the most powerful men in New England.

Although there is no evidence to indicate that Metacomet controlled any war parties besides his own Wampanoag bands, the historians singled him out as the focal point of the trouble and cast him as the whipping boy for their fear and hatred (Simpson and Simpson 6, Leach 241). Saltonstall accused him of forming a conspiracy to avenge the Sassamon affair, and Mather vilifies him as "the perfidious and bloody Author of the War and woefull miseryes that have thence ensued" (193). Hubbard refers to him as "a Salvage and wild Beast" who retired to a swamp until "the Messengers of Death came by Divine Permission to execute Vengeance upon him" (265). The historians also cast Sassamon in a principal role, recognizing that the case against Philip depended largely on the interpreter. Mather presented him carefully as one "who had submitted himself unto . . . the protection of the *English* and dutifully informed on the "*profane Indians* [who] were hatching mischief" (47). Hubbard treats him more cynically, describing him as a "very cunning and plausible Indian" who shifted loyalties frequently, but still blames Metacomet for "contriving" Sassamon's death (60–61).

To those colonists most closely involved, the most painful memories of the war involved the natives' treatment of those they captured. Saltonstall relates native atrocities in sensuous detail and claims that

> many have been destroyed with exquisite Torments, and most inhumane barbarities; the Heathen rarely giving quarter to those that they take, but if they were women, they first forced them to satisfie their filthy lusts and then murdered them; either cutting off the head, ripping open the Belly, or skulping the head of skin and hair, and hanging them up as Trophies; wearing men's fingers as bracelets about their necks, and stripes of their skins which they dresse for Belts.
> (*New and Further* 100–101)

This passage defines the "Heathen" as violators, vandals of colonists' bodies and of the women's sexual sanctity, yet the use of "exquisite" and "lusts," as well as the provocative detail, seems to invite the reader to contemplate forbidden horrors—it becomes a form of colonial pornography that mingles sexual with racial politics.

Out of the raw material of the war, the historians created melodrama. The colonial armies crushed the natives because they impeded white expansion and defied the settlers' zealous enterprise, but to justify the struggle according to the Puritans' ethical standards, colonial apologists cast Philip as a villain whose evil transcended temporal concerns. They condemned him (and, by implication, all refractory natives) for rejecting English religion and denying English authority;

in essence, for maintaining a tenacious hold on his own cultural identity. Puritan theology gave them an anomalously theatrical cosmic vision: God was an *über-regisseur* who had entrusted the colonists with a sacred mission and then permitted Satan to lead a series of antagonists against them in an apparently endless divine melodrama. They had little doubt as to where Philip fit into this casting structure, and his villainy assured their heroism.

On an earthly plane, the Puritan historians read the war as a conflict between barbarism and civilization, an interpretation that proved useful as people throughout the colonies confronted the challenge of theorizing their experience. They wished to sustain the image of the New World as Arcadia, but they had no intention of putting primitivism into effect. To validate their course of action and demonstrate that the Golden Age need not be defined in the terms that the legends encouraged, they revised the prevailing white/Indian binarism. They redefined "Indian" as "savage," which by contrast and exclusion—the leverage of the binarism—legitimated "civilization" as their own distinguishing achievement. Pearce has argued that the colonists' conception of culture approved man's progress "from a lesser to a greater good, from the simple to the complex, from savagism to civilization," a paradigm that assured the eventual destruction of the savage "as one who had not and somehow could not progress into the civilized. . . . [T]he Indian was the remnant of a savage past away from which civilized men had struggled to grow. To study him was to study the past. To civilize him was to triumph over the past. To kill him was to kill the past" (48–49). In his 1828 dictionary, Noah Webster defined "savage" as the opposite of "civilized" and cited native Americans as exemplary savages in that they were faithful and grateful, but also cruel, revengeful, and barbaric. The concept of savagism permitted the colonists to argue that Arcadia—the *true* Arcadia—was the product of efforts like theirs spent in a virgin land. The savages were a sort of mistake, a flaw in the legend that might, under divine guidance, inspire colonial heroism but that had to be erased to make room for the future. Real Arcadians rose above savagism, and in order to do so, they had to seek it out, reveal it as the enemy, and destroy it.

The typical strategy for asserting savagism was to relate atrocities, in horrified detail, to elicit the reader's disgust and revulsion for the Indians, and sympathy for their victims. One source of such anecdotes was Henry Trumbull's *History of the Discovery of America*, a book popular enough to require thirteen printings from 1802 to 1831, plus seven printings of its successor, *History of the Indian Wars*, from 1841 to 1854. Trumbull offers lurid descriptions of savages torturing savages; but his more effective stories were actual reports borrowed from white settlers. The following letter was posted in Charleston on August 6, 1792:

> Mrs *Thresher*, to avoid if possible the fate with which she was threatened, fled with an infant of about five or six weeks old in her arms, and leaped into the river; the Indians pursued, shot her through each thigh and right breast, stabbed her in the left breast with a knife, cut her arm nearly off, and then scalped

her. In this horrid situation she remained until the neighbors could assemble in sufficient numbers to cross the river and pursue the Indians. . . . [W]hen informed by her physician that it was impossible for her to survive much longer, she with a fortitude that is rarely to be met with, called her friends around her, and in a calm but pathetic manner, gave her hand to each one, wishing them a better fate than had befallen herself and family. . . . (*Discovery* 149)

Mrs. Thresher becomes a sentimental heroine, suffering the tortures of the saints and maintaining her Christian virtues to the last, and the narrative is all the more compelling due to Trumbull's choice of a mother and an infant as his victims. Such accounts offered theatre of the nightmare, a Grand Guignol gone mad, as helpless people witnessed butchery but were too civilized to be able to return it in kind. Other writers published, during the 1820s and 1830s, descriptions of torture by fire, scalding, scalping, and amputation. Still others promoted the savagist agenda in terms of disapproval; in his preface to *Nick of the Woods* (1837), Robert Montgomery Bird condemned the "North American savage" for waging war on women and children (29). Bird's is a sentimental and apparently naïve perspective, and his attitude clarifies that the culture that contrived and accepted the civilized/savage binarism was itself essentially sentimental defining "civilization" largely in domestic terms—family, romantic love, and filial devotion.

The most famous and still influential vehicles for the savagist agenda were the Leatherstocking tales of James Fenimore Cooper, whose Indian has overshadowed all others as well as the actuality of the natives, and has so pervaded novels, plays, and the films and television shows of our own age that to read his tales today, even for the first time, is to experience a sense of familiarity, of old acquaintance. Even those authors who do not employ Cooper's construction must define their Indians in relation to his. He used the concept of the savage for sensational effect and as a foundation for creating certain characters in his most popular novel, *The Last of the Mohicans* (1826). He balanced his narrative on a casting structure of opposites: the Indians and the whites, the dark woman and the fair woman, and the vicious warrior and the more sympathetic brave. One of the more bloody scenes begins when an Iroquois covets an Englishwoman's shawl and grabs her infant as a bargaining chip. When another warrior takes the shawl, the first smashes the child's head against a rock and then brains the mother before she has a chance to ask God for retribution. The presence of the mother and child as victims to Indian (and male) cruelty serves as an emblem for the entire novel. The Huron's tomahawk saves not only the young woman's soul but also the entire sentimental sensibility, for the mother, as a concept, must survive, stainless, to continue to serve as an emblem of sentimental values and as the pure background against whom the warrior's cruelty becomes clear.

The early historiography of King Philip's War had already established Metacomet as a savage, and some later writers bolstered the image. In the 1827 edition of Thomas Church's *History of Philip's War*—the account published closest to the premiere of *Metamora*—editor Samuel G. Drake's annotations reinforced the image of Philip as treacherous and deceitful, scarcely able to restrain his violence towards Sassamon and the English; and on the subject of the sachem's demise, Drake mused, "Thus fell the celebrated King Philip, the implacable enemy of civilization" (123).[5] Trumbull presented Philip as a conniving, vicious villain:

> [T]he Indians commenced an indiscriminate murder of the defenceless inhabitants of Swanzey, sparing not the tender infant at the breast! . . . [T]he savages, not content with bathing their tomahawks in the blood of the defenceles [*sic*] inhabitants of Swanzey, had, it was discovered, in many instances detached their limbs from their mangled bodies, and affixed them to poles which were extended in the air! Among which were discovered the heads of several infant children . . . (*History of the Discovery* 39–41)

Trumbull manages the scene carefully; as the English discover Philip's plots and then realize the carnage at Swansea, the reader moves with them. By casting the settlers as defenseless infants, Trumbull uses the leverage of the binarism to make the Indians' brutalities all the more horrible.

THE ROMANTIC WARRIOR

Yet white culture developed another model of the Indian, one presented in competition with the savagist paradigm. As events led toward the establishment of the republic in the late eighteenth century, those who had once identified themselves as European colonists now desired a new self-image. In spite of the diverse peculiarities of religion, nationality, or economic circumstance that had driven each group here, all communities shared the experience of dislocation to a certain destination, and they sought a characterization of their consequent sense of homogeneity. They arrogated for themselves the title of "American," but they then required a means to justify this self-construction as denoting more than just a transplanted European; they needed to define the new name in terms of the new land. Their perspective had reversed; as Europeans, they could cherish their identity as exiles from their own history and reject anything native as "other," but as Americans, European values and symbols became the alien antagonists against which they demarked their national identity. Furthermore, anything incontrovertibly American offered attractive raw material for the (re)formation of myth. Although the concept of Indian as Satanic villain had thrived throughout most of the colonial period, the nation's apologists now sought a native heroism and so reconsidered the potential of the Indian. The problem was how to elevate those who were historical enemies not only of westward progress, but of civilization itself as white culture defined it. While the "savage" label had been usefully pejorative enough to excuse the colonists from imitation, it also obliterated the Indian as Arcadian, and Arcadia with him. The solution was the "noble" savage, a return to the idealism of Montaigne and Rousseau.

The phrase is delicately balanced, gently maintaining the inferiority of the savage to the civilized, but using the idea of ennoblement to resonate with the most time-honored forms of legitimation in the stratified society of the Old World. Moreover, this was a Romanticist investiture; the savage derives his nobility from his kinship with natural forces and from a certain tendency to deal in abstractions, gracefully rising above the merely mundane complications of the expanding American nation. The poets located the vision in the distant past, a nostalgic image that Americans accepted with increasing ease as the frontier receded, putting more and more distance between the hostile tribes and the eastern cities. This Romantic revision not only rejected the hostile and restrictive Puritan model but also restored the dream of the uttermost West as a primitive idyll that inspired white longing. Even though the noble savage was a construction of white imagination intended to provide an identity for the natives, the governing binarism—the guide for white relations with the natives—now became covert, simultaneously defining and denying difference between the two elements.

One of the first noble savages in American literature was Logan, a chieftain whose entire family was murdered in a white ambush, and whose famous oration appeared in print in 1775.[6] Thomas Jefferson lent his considerable influence to the nobility of the savage by including Logan's speech in *Notes on the State of Virginia* (1787) as proof of the noble savage's innate ability to match Cicero or Demosthenes. During the peace negotiations for the War of the Earl of Dunmore, Logan sent the following message to Lord Dunmore, then Governor of Virginia:

> I appeal to any white man to say, if ever he entered Logan's cabin hungry, and he gave him not meat; if ever he came cold and naked, and he clothed him not. . . . For my country, I rejoice at the beams of peace. But do not harbour a thought that mine is the joy of fear. Logan never felt fear. He will not turn on his heel to save his life. Who is there to mourn for Logan?—Not one. (188–89) [7]

The speech certainly appealed to white imagination, and in 1823, Joseph Doddridge published a closet drama named *Logan*. The title figure is "the last of a long race of chiefs" who "smells nought but blood" and hears "nought but the war whoop, and death halloo" (21). His integrity, mercy, and wistful reluctance elevate his bloody plans; because he makes war with regret, perceiving no other options, his nobility transcends his savagery.

Philip Freneau promoted the new image in "The Prophecy of King Tammany." The Lenni Lenape chieftain contemplates the proliferating, aggressive Europeans that have invaded his land, and he weeps for his people's loss. He mourns the Indians' inability to resist the white men militarily, but he resigns himself and climbs onto his funeral pyre and smiles to think that his troubles are nearly over; another "last" Indian making way for the inevitable onslaught of white civilization.

Yet this was fiction, no matter how compelling, and some Americans, remembering their personal experiences with the natives, were not persuaded to discard the savagist agenda in favor of Indian nobility. In 1814, Washington Irving entered the debate with a direct attack on the savagist position and the actuality that seemed to support it: "Traits of Indian Character," later reprinted in the popular *Sketch Book*. Irving argued that the "unfortunate aborigines" were not only dispossessed during the colonial period, they were also "traduced by bigoted . . . writers" who applied the terms "savage" and "pagan" in order to justify the mistreatment. He warned against generalizing on the Indian character based on the example of those natives who are "corrupted and enfeebled by the vices of society" because they live in proximity to white settlements, and he described them as "mere wrecks and remnants of once powerful tribes," victims of poverty that "corrodes their spirits, and blights every free and noble quality of their natures." He blamed the whites for teaching cruelty to the natives by burning their villages and taking their lands. Such reasoning became a typical component of noble-savage orthodoxy; if the actual natives were disappointing, the logical object of blame was the civilization that had polluted them. Like Freneau, Irving gazes nostalgically back to a beatific past, and forward to the poetry that will exploit it after the few remaining tribes follow their ancestors into oblivion:

They will vanish like a vapor from the face of the earth; their very history will be lost in forgetfulness. . . . Or if, perchance, some dubious memorial of them should survive, it may be in the romantic dreams of the poet, to people in imagination his glades and groves, like the fauns and satyrs and sylvan deities of antiquity. (286–88, 292, 297)

The factual case for the noble savage grew stronger when, in 1819, John Heckewelder, a Moravian missionary, published an account of his experiences living, during 1762 to 1810, near the tribes of the Six Nations in the region of the Susquehanna, Allegheny, Cuyahoga, Huron, and Muskingum rivers—what is now Pennsylvania and northeastern Ohio. He defended the natives as just, generous, kindly, and naturally eloquent: "Every person who is well acquainted with the true character of the Indians will admit that they are peaceable, sociable, obliging, charitable, and hospitable among themselves, and that those virtues are, as it were, a part of their nature" (102, 132, 330).

In spite of the savagist legacy of writers from Saltonstall to Trumbull, the figure of Metacomet moved easily into the noble tradition. In 1814, Irving published "Philip of Pokanoket," a delicately ironic piece of propaganda contrived to discredit the settlers and establish the natives as a noble, wronged race with whom all patriotic Americans might justifiably feel sympathy.[8] He begins with a wistful gaze back into the days before civilization, then describes the seventeenth-century chieftains as "a band of native untaught heroes, who made the most generous struggle of which human nature is capable; fighting to the last gasp in the cause of their country, without a hope of victory or a thought of renown." He attacks the Puritan position directly and insists on Philip as hero, "a true-born prince, gallantly fighting at the head of his subjects to avenge the wrongs of his family; to retrieve the tottering power of his line; and to deliver his native land from the oppression of usurping strangers." He depicts Philip as waging a daring guerrilla war on the settlements, and miraculously eluding capture again and again to hide in the New England swamps, where the hapless English cannot follow. Finally, Philip retreats to Mount Hope, where he is "defeated, but not dismayed," because "little minds are tamed and subdued by misfortune; but great minds rise above it." Irving construes Philip as

> a patriot attached to his native soil,—a prince true to his subjects, and indignant of their wrongs,—a soldier, daring in battle, firm in adversity, patient of fatigue, of hunger, of every variety of bodily suffering, and ready to perish in the cause he had espoused. Proud of heart, and with an untamable love of natural liberty. . . . With heroic qualities and bold achievements that would have graced a civilized warrior, and have rendered him the theme of the poet and the historian, he lived a wanderer and a fugitive in his native land, and went down, like a lonely bark foundering amid darkness and tempest—without a pitying eye to weep his fall, or a friendly hand to record his struggle.

In Irving's hands, Philip became an anachronistic American patriot who led a band of freedom fighters, seeking against hope to "deliver his native land from the oppression of usurping strangers" (299, 306, 314–16).

This new conception of Metacomet first appeared in imaginative literature with James Wallis Eastburn's Romanticist poem, *Yamoyden* (1820). He sets the action in forests, "wood-crowned hills," rocky ramparts, and shadowy coves, with mists "wildly wreathing" and idealizes Indians in general by presenting Metacom as a fearless, noble hero whose wampum crown is "a studded coronet, / With circling plumage waving high" (7, 24). In "Metacom" (1829), John Greenleaf Whittier offers the sachem as a warrior who can find meaning only in death. He leaves his dying curse against the English and predicts the chaos of the Revolutionary War.

> The bed of yon blue mountain stream
> Shall pour a darker tide than rain—
> The sea shall catch its blood-red stain,
> And broadly on its banks shall gleam
> The steel of those who should be brothers. . . .

The morning star hangs in the sky as dawn arrives and with it, Metacom's stoic death.

Red as the naked hand of Doom,
The English volley hurtled by—
The arm—the voice of Metacom!
One piercing shriek—one vengeful yell,
Sent like an arrow to the sky,
Told when the hunter-monarch fell!

Cooper himself appropriated Metacomet for *The Wept of Wish-Ton-Wish* (1829), depicting him as a great ruler and elder statesman, an avatar of George Washington. He has come to Narragansett territory to advise and mediate, and presides over a postbattle council with calm dignity in spite of a fresh wound that slowly drips blood from beneath the blanket he has thrown over his shoulder. Metacom is a visionary, a prophet who intuits the present and future truth about the inevitable dealings between red and white. He consents to meet with his Narragansett counterpart, Conanchet, and listens courteously to a friendly Englishman who has come to present the colonists' case. When an English band fires on them, the chief brains an inadequate lookout but controls his passions to spare the ambassador. Clearly, Stone had ample precedent for the creation that he offered to Forrest.

EDWIN FORREST, AMERICAN

In 1828, the actor decided to commission an American play as part of a nationalist agenda that supported his personal ambitions as the first major American touring star. He had made his professional debut at the Walnut Street Theatre in 1820, toured from Pittsburgh to New Orleans, and appeared in Albany with Edmund Kean, playing Richmond to his Gloucester. In 1826, Forrest chose Othello for three prominent occasions: his New York debut at the Park Theatre, his first star billing at the Chestnut Street Theatre in Philadelphia, and his first starring appearance at New York's Bowery Theatre on November 6. Not yet twenty-one years of age, he played Marc Antony, Lear, and Shylock, and his salary rose to $200 per performance. The time was opportune for Forrest to present himself as the champion of American play writing; in 1827, a critic writing for the *American Quarterly Review* had complained about the sorry state of the American theatre, both its writing and its production, and called for a "National Drama . . . one appealing directly to the national feelings . . . and, above all, displaying a generous chivalry in the maintenance and vindication of those great and illustrious peculiarities of situation and character, by which we are distinguished from all other nations" ("American Drama" 339). English actors, managers, and playwrights had dominated the American stage since its slow development during the colonial period, and when Forrest began to attempt major roles, he was competing with the likes of Kean, Junius Brutus Booth, and William Charles Macready.

Alger reports that during the early years of Forrest's career, some scorned him simply because he was an American; now the actor hoped to capitalize on his nationality (176–77). At Forrest's request, on November 22, 1828, William Leggett published the following offer in the *Critic*.

> To the author of the best Tragedy, in five acts, of which the hero or principal character shall be an aboriginal of this country, the sum of five hundred dollars, and half of the proceeds of the third representation, with my own gratuitous services on that occasion. (qtd. in Moody, *Forrest* 88)

Forrest appointed a play-reading committee: Fitz-Greene Halleck, a popular writer; James Lawson, an editor and playwright; James G. Brooks, an essayist and poet; Leggett, an editor, poet, and playwright; Prosper M. Wetmore, a poet; and William Cullen Bryant, the editor of the *New-York Evening Post*, author of several "Indian" poems, supporter of Jackson, and friend of Forrest.[9] Out of fourteen plays, they chose *Metamora*, and Wetmore wrote a prologue to exhort the audience, in rhyming couplets, to give a sympathetic hearing to a native "subject, and bard, and actor."[10]

Metamora became only the first of many strategies Forrest devised to promote his American program. One specific concern was the development of American literature, especially the drama, and on January 8, 1834, in a letter to a literary society in Albany, he wrote,

> In a country like ours, where all men are free and equal, no aristocracy should be tolerated, save that aristocracy of superior mind, before which none need be ashamed to bow. . . . The parasitical opinion cannot be too soon exploded which teaches that "nothing can be so good as that which emanates from abroad." Our literature should be independent. . . . (qtd. in Alger 179–80)

He enclosed one hundred dollars for the purchase of "books purely American." On April 2 of that year, a few months before leaving on a trip to Europe, he gave a farewell performance of *King Lear* at the Arch Street Theatre and at the curtain call announced, to repeated cheers, that "I feel grateful for the honorable support I have received in my anxious endeavors to give to my country, by fostering the exertions of our literary friends, something like what might be called an American national drama" (qtd. in Rees 104). On July 16, after a rendition of *The Broker of Bogota*, someone asked why he did not intend to perform in England, and he answered that

> to deserve and enjoy the good opinion of the intelligent American Public bears with it reward enough to satisfy all my aspirings, both after fame and emolument; and I should blush for that servile and degraded spirit, that could deem the English stamp, in our country, necessary to the formation of a complete and current reputation. (*Evening Post* July 17, 1834)

Forrest also expressed his patriotism in extratheatrical contexts. While visiting Paris during January of 1835, he wrote a letter to Leggett and referred to one of Jackson's ultimata to France as "once more *Americanizing* Americans, and [reviving] within them that love of country which the pageantry and frivolity, the dreamy and debasing luxury of this metropolis serve materially to enervate" (qtd. in Moody, *Forrest* 116). In a Fourth of July speech delivered in 1838, he asked

> Where does the sun, in all his compass, shed his beams on a country freer, better, happier than this? . . . Where are the foundations of private right more stable, or the limits of public order more inviolately observed? Where does labor go to his toil with an alerter step, or an erecter brow, effulgent with the heart-reflected light of conscious independence? Where does agriculture drive his team a-field with a more cheery spirit, in the certain assurance that the harvest is his own? Where does commerce launch more boldly her bark upon the deep, aware that she has to strive but with the tyranny of the elements, and not with the more appalling tyranny of man? (13)[11]

He went on to ask, "What bounds can be set to the growth of American greatness?" (24) The *United States Magazine and Democratic Review* offered this comment on the speech:

> No one can read Mr. Forrest's excellent oration, without feeling and believing that he is an American, true to his national vocation, and who fully appreciates the peculiar mission of his country. He has drank deep of the pure and invigorating waters which flow from the fountain of American Democracy. The fervor of his language attests the strength of his patriotism—patriotism deeply imbued with the philanthropy which contemplates his country as designed, by her example, to shed the light of her moral truth, by gradual progression, into the remotest corners of the earth, for man's emancipation. ("Mr. Forrest's Oration" 56)

During the next few months, Forrest was mentioned as a candidate for Congress. The New York nominating committee made a formal invitation, but on October 17, Forrest declined (Moody, *Forrest* 176–77).

He contrived his career to become an icon of American masculinity—forthright, muscular, and upstanding—so it was no mere coincidence that he attracted the enthusiasm of the nativist societies of the mid-1840s and became the excuse for the jingoistic Astor Place Riot of 1849. Forrest and Macready had carried on a transatlantic rivalry for over a decade, including the 1843–44 season, when they toured many of the same cities and played many of the same roles, culminating in one night in New York City when they played the same role in different theatres. Finally, on May 10, 1849, after a performance earlier that week had already been disrupted, Macready walked out on the stage of the Astor Place Opera House to play Macbeth, but Forrest's "supporters" once again stopped the performance and proceeded to destroy the auditorium while a mob outside threw bricks and stones at the theatre. Finally, the militia fired on the mob; by the end of the night, at least 31 people had died and over 150 were wounded.[12]

The riot offers a historiographical challenge; theatrical concerns may have been only incidental, and the rivalry may have merely provided a convenient pretext for those who wished to foment a disturbance to further their own ends. Certainly

E. Z. C. Judson—also known as "Ned Buntline," the dime novelist—and his nativist cronies had little interest in the theatre per se and were more concerned with promoting the aims of their Order of Native Americans, which included opposing foreigners and Catholics in the name of patriotism; because some still associated the American theatre with English plays and artists, it was a vulnerable target. The handbill rhetoric asked whether English or Americans should rule in New York, accusing an English steamer crew of threatening any Americans who dared to "express their opinion" at Astor Place, and calling on free workingmen to stand by their right to "liberty of opinion" in the best tradition of 1776. On the evening after the riot, speakers addressed a gathering at City Hall Park to accuse the militia of being "the right arm of despotism" and the tool of the aristocracy who found Macready amusing, to interpret the riot as a war between public authority and the people of the city, and to deny that Forrest paid them to put his rival down (Moody, *Astor* 130, 179, 187–93).

Some contemporary observers tried to marginalize the event on the grounds that it *was* a strictly theatrical phenomenon; those who scorned the stage may not have been at all surprised to hear that a mob of working-class thugs had rallied around the childish rivalry. The *Boston Traveller* wondered why other newspapers had bothered "to dignify the paltry quarrel between two actors," and the *Herald* of Newburyport accused Forrest of fomenting the riot with his poor manners. On May 9, the day before the riot, the *Tribune* referred to the performers' "miserable vocation" and went on to demand that the "incurably vicious" stage, that "systematic corrupter of Popular Liberty" undertake "to teach nobler lessons and juster principles than those exemplified in the outrage on Macready" (Moody, *Astor* 226–27, 120).

No matter what status we ascribe to the riot, it confirmed that Forrest was a prominent nationalist, one around whose name others would rally. Alger did his best to present Forrest as a superlative, exemplary American.

> No one among all our distinguished countrymen has been more thoroughly American than Edwin Forrest. From the beginning to the end of his career he was intensely American in his sympathies, his prejudices, his training, his enthusiasm for the flag and name of his country, his proud admiration for the democratic genius of its institutions, his faith in its political mission, his interest in its historic men, his fervent love of its national scenery and its national literature. He was also American in his exaggerated dislike and contempt for the aristocratic classes and monarchical usages of the Old World. . . . [A]ll his life long he felt something of the Native American antipathy for foreigners, and cherished an exaggerated sympathy for many of the most pronounced American characteristics. . . . His creed was always purely democratic; and so was the core of his soul. . . . [A]ll members of our nationality . . . should . . . [recognize] the true qualifications for American citizenship only in the virtues of American manhood, the American type of manhood being simply the common type liberalized and furthered by the free light and stimulus of republican institutions. (39, 43)

Bruce A. McConachie has pointed out that the development of the star system during the early nineteenth century—both in the theatre and in politics—revealed a gap between theory and practice, between egalitarian rhetoric and the actual stratification of the population into stars and extras (15). Forrest operated like one of our own politicians today, working to convince his audience that he was a common man like themselves, yet still claiming the heroic stature that earned their applause. For Forrest to identify himself so closely with Metamora, then, was for the actor to appropriate a compelling and complex image as a means to promote himself as a certain kind of actor and public figure during a specific era in American history, and that act of appropriation contributed to the perception of the Indian as a role to which all Americans did have access. Like the bald eagle and the buffalo, the Indian had been enlisted into a service composed of American symbols that satisfied the needs of whites in search of cultural myth.

METAMORA

The play begins with the white colony mired in intrigue. Mordaunt is an unhappy expatriate who helped execute Charles I and then, at the time of the Restoration, fled England. He hopes to reclaim his position by marrying his daughter, Oceana, to Lord Fitzarnold, who in turn covets the dowry that the young woman will bring. Oceana loves Walter, a poor young man whose guardian is Sir Arthur Vaughn, who left the strife of the English court to "woo contentment in this wilderness."[13] Walter resolves to resist Fitzarnold, tries to provoke him when meeting his ship on the quay, and aggressively establishes his democratic credentials by telling one of the men that "thou knowest one who will not take a lordling by the hand, because his fingers shine with hoops of gold—nor shun the beggar's grasp if it be honest" (209).[14] Oceana tells Mordaunt that she detests Fitzarnold, but her father promises that if she will not help him restore his honor, he will take his own life. Just as she is about to swear compliance, Walter stops her, Mordaunt strikes him, and only her intercession prevents a fight.

Meanwhile, Stone has introduced Metamora. Walter meets Oceana in the woods, where she mourns at her mother's grave, and she explains how the sachem saved her from a panther:

> High on a craggy rock an Indian stood, with sinewy arm and eye that pierced the glen. His bowstring drawn to wing a second death, a robe of fur was o'er his shoulder thrown, and o'er his long, dark hair an eagle's plume waved in the breeze, a feathery diadem. Firmly he stood upon the jutting height, as if a sculptor's hand had carved him there. With awe I gazed as on the cliff he turned—the grandest model of a mighty man. (207)

With the audience thus prepared, Metamora enters, having just won a bare-handed fight with a wolf and hurled it over a cliff. He permits Oceana to bind his gash with her scarf, remembering that her mother nursed his own father, Massasoit, back to health and that he "loves the mild-eyed and the kind, for such is Nahmeokee," his wife (207).[15] He gives Oceana an eagle plume to wear in her hair, promising that no Wampanoag will harm anyone bearing the feather.

Through Walter, Stone shapes the audience's perception of Metamora, referring to him as a "great chieftain" and "the noble sachem of a valiant race—the white man's dread, the Wampanoag's hope" (207). He marvels at "that lofty bearing—that majestic mien—the regal impress sits upon his brow, and earth seems conscious of her proudest son" (207) and explicates the sachem in sentimental terms: "Is justice goodly? Metamora's just. Is bravery virtue? Metamora's brave. If love of country, child and wife and home, be to deserve them all—he merits them" (208). With these encomiums and a few scenes demonstrating Metamora's tender regard for his wife and infant son, Stone establishes the sachem as man, husband, and father in the best nineteenth-century, middle-class, sentimental tradition.

Yet Metamora dreams of white scalps while sleeping in his village, and then awakes to ponder his tribe's prospects:

> Yes, when our fires are no longer red, on the high places of our fathers; when the bones of our kindred make fruitful the fields of the stranger, which he has planted amidst the ashes of our wigwams; when we are hunted back like the wounded elk far toward the going down of the sun, our hatchets broken, our bows unstrung and war whoop hushed; then will the stranger spare, for we will be too small for his eye to see. (210)[16]

Escorted by Captain Church and his band of musketeers, Sir Arthur arrives to invite Metamora to attend the English council, where Errington, the Puritan leader, asks the sachem bluntly whether he plots with the Narragansetts against the colony, and then accuses him of harboring a banished Englishman. The chief assures Errington that he would not deny shelter to his "rarest enemy," and he alludes to the Christian Bible, which counsels charity to strangers. He complains of English snares, of "fire water," and of the pollution of the clear streams, but when Errington suggests that he relinquish his lands to the colony and relocate, Metamora vows that he will never "forsake the home of his fathers" and reminds Errington of how kindly Massasoit treated the English when they first arrived (213). He claims his prerogatives as firmly as any Jacksonian:

> Climb upon the rock and look to the sunrise and to the sunset,—all that you see is the land of the Wampanoags, the land of Metamora. I am the white man's friend; but when my friendship is over I will not ask the white man if I have the right to be his foe. Metamora will love and hate, smoke the pipe of peace or draw the hatchet of battle, as seems good to him. He will not wrong his white brother, but he owns no master save Manito, Master of Heaven. (qtd. in Alger 242–43)[17]

He turns to leave, but an officer ushers in Annawandah, one of Metamora's principal advisors, intending that he testify to having murdered Sasamond at Metamora's command. The chief reminds the warrior of their long friendship and then asks the English, "can he speak to you the words of truth, when he is false to his brother, his country and his god?" (214).[18] Annawandah cannot bring himself to speak in Metamora's presence, and finally the sachem stabs him to death and declares war before running out unharmed. Mordaunt is accidentally shot in the English volley, and seeing a chance that he might lose Oceana's dowry, Fitzarnold resolves to marry her that night and sail for England at dawn.

Metamora asks his people for war, proclaiming that the English are encroaching and will soon destroy the red man as they destroy the forests, and relating a dream in which Massasoit called upon him to sharpen his spear, all to the accompaniment of thunder rolls and lightning flashes:

> The pale-faces are around me thicker than the leaves of summer. I chase the hart in the hunting-grounds; he leads me to the white man's village. I drive my canoe into the rivers; they are full of the white man's ships. I visit the graves of my fathers; they are lost in the white man's corn-fields. They come like the waves of the ocean forever rolling upon the shores. Surge after surge, they dash upon the beach, and every foam-drop is a white man. They swarm over the land like the doves of winter, and the red men are dropping like withered leaves. (qtd. in Alger 243)

He sends Nahmeokee to ask the Narragansetts for an alliance, and then leads his warriors to storm Mordaunt's home. The sachem is wild with battle, and when his men capture Mordaunt, he tells the pleading Oceana that she might as well quell the storm or melt the rocks as secure his mercy, and then commands his warriors to "Drag him away to the fire of the sacrifice that my ear may drink the music of his dying groans" (217). When Oceana places her eagle feather on Mordaunt's bosom, the chief spares him in favor of throwing her, now featherless, into the flames of the English dwelling, but finally scorns to vent his fury on so weak a victim. He then hears the English bugle approaching, expediently declares a victory, and leads his men off as Walter embraces Oceana.

The English capture Nahmeokee and her baby, and Errington resolves to hold her until she answers his questions, but Oceana reveals to Fitzarnold that the woman is Metamora's wife and might be traded for the English prisoners. He promises to advocate for Nahmeokee, but when alone, reveals to the audience his plan to secure her release to the furious English populace, who will undoubtedly kill her and inspire the Wampanoags to execute Walter, whom Sir Arthur has commissioned as his emissary on behalf of the English captives, and who arrives in the Indian camp just as Kaweshine, the prophet, is preparing to burn his prisoners. Metamora refuses to parley on the ground that his warriors want more blood, but a messenger brings news of Nahmeokee's capture. The sachem orders his men to hold Walter hostage, telling him that "If one drop fall from Nahmeokee's eye, one hair from her head, the axe shall hew your quivering limbs asunder and the ashes of your bones be carried away on the rushing winds" (221). He finds Nahmeokee in danger from "the fanatic herd" and threatens that if the English imprison and execute him, his warriors will kill their captives. Nahmeokee persuades him to forbear, so he becomes a hostage while she returns to their village to release the prisoners. Metamora then escapes through a secret passage leading to Mordaunt's family crypt, where he finds Fitzarnold about to rape Oceana, who is communing with her dead mother. The Indian kills the Englishman to punish him for plotting against Nahmeokee, then returns to his village with Oceana.

He gathers the warriors and, like Irving's Philip, appears more as a patriot than a savage as he addresses them in the manner of Patrick Henry:[19]

> Prepare for the approaching hour if ye love the high places your fathers trod in majesty and strength. Snatch your keen weapons and follow me! If ye love the silent spots where the bones of your kindred repose, sing the dread song of war and follow me! If you love the bright lakes which the Great Spirit gave you when the sun first blazed with the fires of his touch, shout the war song of the Wampanoag race, and on to battle follow me! Look at the bright glory that is wrapped like a mantle around the slain in battle! Call on the happy spirits of the warriors dead and cry, "Our lands! Our nation's freedom! Or the grave!" (224)

Kaweshine advises peace; Metamora is about to stab him, but Nahmeokee intervenes. He relents, but when he hears the English approach, tells her, "Come not near me or thou wilt make my heart soft, when I would have it hard like the iron" (225). He kneels to pray to Manito:

> [B]reak thou the strength of the oppressor's nation, and hurl them down from the high hill of their pride and power, with the loud thunder of thy voice. Confound them—smite them with the lightning of thine eye. . . . They come! Death! Death, or my nation's freedom! (225)

The Wampanoags lose the battle, but Nahmeokee frees Oceana. Metamora retreats to his rocky stronghold to find Nahmeokee alive but their little son dead, shot by an English musket. Metamora mourns:

> His little arms will never clasp thee more; his little lips will never press the pure bosom which nourished him so long! Well, is he not happy? Better to die by the stranger's hand than live his slave. (225)

He tells his wife that "the palefaces are all around us, and they tread in blood. . . . We are destroyed—not vanquished; we are no more, yet we are forever" (226). They can neither fly nor fight, and if the whites do not kill Nahmeokee, they will enslave her. Metamora shows her the only weapon he has saved from the battle, her brother Coanchett's knife. She realizes what he intends and assures him, "I rejoice at it" (226). He asks her to look up into the air to see their son "borne onward to the land of the happy, where the fair hunting grounds know no storms or snows," and where the spirit of her murdered father beckons. The English approach as they embrace, and he stabs her to death. "She felt no white man's bondage—free as the air she lived—pure as the snow she died! In smiles she died! Let me taste it, ere her lips are cold as the ice" (226). Errington has bribed Kaweshine to lead Church and his men to the hiding place, and Metamora—"the last of his race" defies them, challenging them to meet him, one by one, in combat. When Church gives the order to fire, the sachem (anachronistically) echoes Logan, saying, "I would not turn upon my heel to save my life." As the principals form a tableau, he curses the English and dies.

Stone retained the general shape of the actual events—mutual defiance between the parties, the interpreter's death bringing a crisis, and Church finally trapping the sachem on his own ground—but the playwright's revisions of history elevated Metamora and created the showcase role that Forrest desired. There is no Wamsutta in this story, so Metamora is no one's younger brother. Stone never mentions Puritanism explicitly, and except for a few ambiguous allusions to faith and zeal, and for Mordaunt's implied support of Cromwell, he excises from the story a religious and political issue that might have distracted attention from the sachem's heroism. While the actual Metacomet signed a capitulation, Metamora meets with the English only to scorn them and reinforce his personal and tribal pride. Metacomet was never clearly linked to Sassamon's assassination, but Metamora welcomes personal responsibility. The actual war evolved through a series of subtle, escalating provocations, but Metamora defies the English in open council, declaring and initiating the war on the spot, and then mustering his warriors as the charismatic leader of his people. Metacomet's wife and son were captured and later sold into slavery, but Stone replaces such indignities with the sensational scene where Metamora stabs Nahmeokee himself. Metacomet died ignominiously in a scramble as Church's men surprised his camp, but Metamora anticipates the soldiers' arrival, challenges them to fight him singly, and invites the volley that kills him, a champion to the last.[20]

Stone's creation bears some resemblance to the characters he might have encountered in Irving, Whittier, and Cooper; it certainly supports the noble-savage revision of Metacomet. His Metamora is an impressive man, strong and brave, but unfailingly tender and solicitous toward women and children, especially his own, and he is a dedicated leader of his people—just, loyal, and so devoted to the welfare of his nation that he will die for its freedom in the best tradition of white America. Yet he is subject to dark passions, demonstrating a savage love of war, war for the sake of blood and battle, and we wonder whether he killed Sasamond and Annawandah partly to satisfy some compulsion. He relishes the prospect of torturing Mordaunt and very nearly violates the sentimental code by subjecting Oceana to a fiery death. To suggest that he is a classic hero of melodrama is to overemphasize his more sentimental qualities, however admirable they be. Metamora satisfies the criteria in time of peace, but when the passion of battle dominates him, his carefully delineated regard for women and his sense of righteousness struggle with his more savage tendencies. Pearce has argued that Metamora is an exemplar of neither the savagist nor the primitivist tradition, too complex and "civilized" a character for the first, and insufficiently idealized for the second (177). Yet this analysis is unduly limited; Metamora makes more sense if considered in the context of Jacksonian society. Marilyn J. Anderson points out that he is a patriot in the Jacksonian style, and suggests that the impending Indian removal made the protagonist's plight all the more effective for Forrest's earlier audiences ("The Image of the Indian" 802). Walter J. Meserve asserts that Metamora was a perfect hero for the Jacksonian period—patriotic, devout, sentimental, a champion of love and honor who confronted his adversaries directly, even violently (49–50). If these are typical Jacksonian values—brutality and sympathy, each in its place—then Metamora embodies them accurately. In any case, audiences could excuse his less domestic qualities on the grounds that he, like any American hero, fought against the English.

In locating the play in relation to the discourse and events of the 1830s, the central issue is one of politics, of the extent to which Metamora has the power to influence his own destiny. Power resides in white society—in its law, its army, its narrow vision, and its ideological facility—and though Metamora be a great warrior and chief, feared and respected by all, he remains a political outsider. The very structure of the play demonstrates his exclusion; it is a quite conventional melodrama (involving Fitzarnold, Oceana, and Walter as villain, heroine, and hero) with the Indian story grafted on.[21] The English make token gestures toward including Metamora in the social processes that eventually destroy him, but the very nature of their offers submerges his people's interests. Metamora's strength and energy give him the appearance of mastery, but he is denied access, so he is effectively helpless. Like most "last" Indians in the Romantic vision, Metamora is a victim of forces for which he is not responsible. Only through his inability to acquiesce does he contribute to his own destruction, a doom that the play presents as inevitable, and that conveniently leaves the field clear for the English characters to carry on with their lives.

Stone also exploits the safety inherent in the theatrical event. A play, as a reenactment, transforms its material into history, which in turn removes that material from the arena of present concern; since the material of Metamora was already history that had been shaped and reshaped by many hands, this distancing effect was multiplied.[22] Stone's white audience could admire Metamora and sympathize with him, but as audience, they were not required to act on his behalf. To see his fall enacted heroically before their eyes, was to be assured of a fait accompli whose relegation to the distant past absolved them of responsibility and whose finality made their intervention pointless.

INDIAN REMOVAL

The relationship of Metamora to the issues of action and accountability makes the play more than just another embarrassing white exploitation of native Americans; it was also a provocative ideological phenomenon—perhaps even a useful instrument—during the period of Indian removal.[23] Like King Philip's War, removal was an intense expression of the gulf separating two cultures. Both the war and removal were struggles to dominate the land, the natives perceiving it as a resource that all share, and the whites defining it as private property, the foundation of liberal society, and the raison d'être for their new nation. The American concept of freedom depended on an unlimited supply of unoccupied land that offered any man the chance to repeat the Lockean experience of the first immigrant and found his own society, a scenario that presented a nation of self-created, independent individualists living freely under a minimal government. Native presence therefore came to be seen as an unacceptable obstacle to white aspirations, and American energy—and therefore American law—precluded coexistence of red and white nations within the same territory.

The concept of the Indian blocked the whites from understanding the natives. In continuing to revise and reconstruct the binary opposition—"American" versus "Indian"—the whites had engaged in an ongoing diacritical examination of both signs and the cultures they allegedly represented. By redefining "Indian" according to the demands of the changing times, and by implicitly assigning the natives roles ranging from primitive aborigines to fabulous inhabitants of the legendary Arcadia, the colonists and their heirs had obscured the natives' actuality and whatever self-created identity they had, and reduced them to objects of the white men's gaze, a relationship where, inevitably, the gaze itself determined perception more powerfully than the object in question. So constructed, the natives consequently became an obscure mystery to the interlopers, who, because they seldom sought to understand the natives on their own terms, failed to find a sensible manner of coexistence. The whites displaced them, but prevented themselves from knowing them. Furthermore, having invented "America" as a nation and as a culture, the whites took upon themselves a revision of the colonial mission—to transform their new nation into the conception they had imagined. Like everything and everyone else, the natives had to be Americanized.

Since the beginning of the colonial period, the whites' need to control the natives had required theorizing their relationship to the natives in such a way as to justify intervention and manipulation. The solution was paternalism, a framework in which the whites were cast as fathers and the Indians as children. In the cliché oration, the white emissary assures the red chieftain that the King of England regards the natives as his children, and so will treat them kindly; the government of the new nation tried to substitute the presidential image for the king, and so assumed official responsibility for "Indian affairs." This hegemonic strategy is delicately balanced, for it purports to express concern while veiling the underlying assumptions (1) that white authority has the prerogative to determine native destiny, (2) that the natives need white intervention, and (3) that the natives will, if properly approached, accept and even welcome white supervision. Such paternalism was fundamental to the discourse of removal—the discourse, composed of rhetoric and image, in which *Metamora* was embedded.

The white government justified its subsequent course of action by precluding any options that required compromise or disadvantage on its part. When Thomas Jefferson first proposed removal in 1803, he conceded only two possible choices for the survival of the natives, and the ensuing debate found no others: first, to assimilate, that is, to adopt Christianity and an agricultural society, which the whites accepted as the hallmarks of civilization; and second, to sustain the old way of life beyond the reach of white influence. Andrew Jackson himself saw citizenship or removal as the only two viable alternatives open to the Cherokee, and in a treaty of 1817, he offered land to any Cherokee who would remain in the East and become a citizen. This strategy of treating the natives as individuals rather than nations disempowered the tribes and made white appropriation much easier. The provision was politically astute, for by giving each individual native land, conceding him the right to sell it as he pleased, and encouraging him to become a citizen, Jackson had, to white eyes, demonstrated the best of intentions by offering the natives everything that the whites themselves wanted. Moreover, as Michael P. Rogin has observed, liberal ideology enabled Jackson and others to argue that the natives had a choice and that the transactions were contracts between equal parties acting freely and independently; this paradigm virtually absolved the government of responsibility and therefore of guilt (212). That the offer imposed a drastic change on native life and offered no genuine options within native value systems did not matter to the majority of the white public. From colonial times on down, the whites had treated the natives not as the sovereigns of their land but as its owners; by reducing the natives' claims to matters of deed and purchase, the whites could confer a comfortable legitimacy on their encroachments. This legal manipulation went all the way to the Supreme Court; in *Johnson and Graham's Lessee v. M'Intosh* (1823), Chief Justice John Marshall ruled that the European nations who had colonized the New World had evolved the principle that discovery conferred both title to the land and the right of acquiring it from the natives. He carried the logic a step further to propose "that discovery gave an exclusive right to extinguish the Indian tide of occupancy," and asserted that the United States had assumed these rights from its colonial overlords and was therefore acting according to precedent. Finally, he offered the rationale that the natives, as savages, were ungovernable, and that "to leave them in possession of their country was to leave the country a wilderness" (Williams 5: 688, 692). Marshall's decision reinforced the general policy that neither the American people nor their government were guilty of improper or unjust behavior, rather, the blame lay in the past.

Proremoval rhetoric tended to adopt a paternalistic strategy to urge the alleged best interests of the natives. A politician or bureaucrat, if eager to expedite progress while avoiding a callous appearance that would disaffect sentimental constituents, could adopt the preservationist rationale to appear benevolent while justifying the dispossession and transportation of tens of thousands of people. Certain mission-aries supported removal on the grounds that exposure to white culture tended to corrupt the natives. Under this rationale, removal would create an evangelical island within the continent, isolated from the infection of civilization gone awry while the dedicated faithful brought light to the waiting heathen.

During the last few months of his second term, James Monroe made removal a formal legislative issue. He presented his plan on December 7, 1824, and in January of 1825 asked Congress to pass a law to transport the tribes to beyond the Mississippi, install a government for them, and "civilize" them. The issue moved slowly under John Quincy Adams's administration until July of 1827, when the Cherokee nation raised the political temperature to a critical level by adopting a constitution modeled after America's own and by declaring sovereignty over parts of Georgia, North Carolina, Tennessee, and Alabama. As soon as Jackson was declared victor in the 1828 election, Georgia, Alabama, and Mississippi formally extended their jurisdiction over natives within their boundaries and abolished the tribe as a legal entity; Georgia went so far as to disenfranchise the natives and announce a public lottery of their lands.

All parties now pressed the debate, and influential voices spoke out for removal. In 1828, James Fenimore Cooper offered *Notions of the Americans*, written as a series of letters introducing America to an imaginary European correspondent. Cooper urged the superiority of white over red, averred that due to "the peculiar habits and opinions of these people," white benevolence could achieve little with them, and maintained that neither the United States nor the individual states had ever taken native land without treaty or purchase. He then presented the straight government line regarding the resolution of native presence in Georgia, assuring the reader that "in order to secure the rights of the Indians more effectually," the United States planned to buy the tribes' land and improvements and replace them, "acre for acre," west of the Mississippi, where they would be disturbed no more (277, 282–93, 286). In a rationale that applied simultaneously to removal and to his own novelistic endeavors, Cooper asserted that beyond the Mississippi there were "specimens of loftiness of spirit, of bearing, and of savage heroism, to be found among the chiefs, that might embarrass the fertility of the richest invention to equal" (287).

Jackson designed his own rhetoric carefully; at his first inauguration, he an-nounced that

> it will be my sincere and constant desire to observe toward the Indian tribes
> within our limits a just and liberal policy, and to give that humane and considerate
> attention to their rights and their wants which is consistent with the habits of
> our Government and the feelings of our people. (Richardson 2: 438)

Yet in his first annual message to Congress in December of 1829, he warned against the existence of the native nations as a threat to states' rights (Richardson 2: 457–

59). On December 11, the *New-York Evening Post*, which was then carrying daily advertisements for the opening of *Metamora*, supported Jackson in an editorial that reduced the "Indian problem" to a question of states' rights, hailing as "clear and convincing" Jackson's argument that the principle demanded that (1) the natives could not be allowed to maintain a separate government, and (2) the federal government could not intervene.[24] The writer magnanimously conceded the tribes the rights of "possession and occupancy of their lands," and reinforced the idea that the natives "may or may not remove, as they shall themselves incline" to lands where their permanent residence was guaranteed, the alternative, of course, being submission to state law and authority. The article established that Jackson's government was doing all it could for the natives within its constitutional limits.

One of the most powerful and persuasive spokesmen for removal was Lewis Cass, then governor of the Michigan Territory, whom Jackson later appointed as his Secretary of War and therefore the cabinet-level supervisor of Indian affairs, an office that Cass occupied from 1831 to 1837. In January of 1830, the *North American Review* published his comments on removal and the state of the Indian in general. Cass reinforced the savagist model of the Indian, alleging that the warriors despised labor, ascribed disgrace to any endeavor besides battle and the hunt, cultivated a fatalistic indifference to death or misfortune, and followed their impulses without moral restraint or assessment of consequences (73–74). Representing the Indians as exotic but still alien and barbarian, Cass found cause for concern (and, less explicitly, for condescension) in the Indians' alleged preference for hunting and casual subsistence farming over European-style agriculture, and in their "inordinate attachment . . . to ardent spirits" (65–66). He reduced the Indians to objects when he wrote, "They stand alone among the great family of man, a moral phenomenon, to be surveyed and observed, rather than to be described and explained" (70). He then scorned the Romantic tradition in favor of "the soberness of truth and reality."

> Rousseau and the disciples of his school, with distempered imaginations and unsullied reason, may persuade themselves of the inferiority of civilized to savage life; but he who looks abroad over the forests of our country, and upon the hapless beings who roam through them, will see how much they endure, that we are spared. It is difficult to conceive that any branch of the human family can be less provident in arrangement, less frugal in enjoyment, less industrious in acquiring, more implacable in their resentments, more ungovernable in their passions, with fewer principles to guide them, with fewer obligations to restrain them, and with less knowledge to improve and instruct them. (73)

By late twentieth-century standards, this point of view is almost laughably Eurocentric and suggests that the author was blind to the limitations of a vision that did not—indeed, could not—admit even the possibility of a valid native perspective.

To forestall debate, Cass regretfully reviewed the unsuccessful but sincere efforts to ameliorate the inevitable Indian decline, referring to attempts at education "in the hope that principles of morality and habits of industry would be acquired," and to the missions, "where zealous and pious men devoted themselves with generous ardor to the task of instruction, as well in agriculture and the mechanic arts, as in the principles of morality and religion" (67). He expressed his perplexity that none of the Indians had benefited from white aid or seemed inclined to change "their manners," and insisted that the failure of the relationship was not at all the fault of the whites, but rather due to some "inherent difficulty, arising from the institutions, character, and condition of the Indians themselves."

> As civilization shed her light upon them, why were they blind to its beams? Hungry or naked, why did they disregard, or regarding, why did they neglect, those arts, by which food and clothing could be procured? Existing for two centuries in contact with a civilized people, they have resisted, and successfully too, every effort to meliorate their situation, or to introduce among them the most common arts of life. (72)

Cass artfully enlisted the reader to his own position and included him in his discourse, encouraging his sense of value as a member of civilization, congratulating him on those philanthropic efforts that did not succeed but whose attempt excused him of further responsibility in that regard, and emboldening him to admit his intolerance for "distempered imaginations" and to blame the Indians for their own troubles. By condemning the Indians for their departure from Euro-American values, he sanctioned others who would, possibly with great relief, follow his example.

Cass assured his readers of the ongoing concern of the American government, but referred to the "inevitable" retreat of the "aboriginal population" which was "produced by the access and progress of the new race of men, before whom the hunter and his game were destined to disappear," and argued that "a barbarous people, depending for subsistence upon the scanty and precarious supplies furnished by the chase, cannot live in contact with a civilized community" (64). He concluded that "the only means of preserving the Indians from that utter extinction which threatens them" was removal, compared the prospect of "a tribe of wandering hunters" who "have a very imperfect possession of the country over which they roam" to the productive potential of white civilization, and assured the reader that "we" will not impose removal through force, but will "liberally remunerate" the Indians for all ceded lands and respect the treaties (66, 77, 76, 84). Conceding that "the Indians are entitled to the enjoyment of all the rights which do not interfere with the obvious designs of Providence, and with the just claims of others," he yet insisted that "our right of jurisdiction over them . . . is perfect," and although "unnecessary restraints" should not be imposed on the Indians, only "we" can be the judges (76, 88). Cass made the government's case, clearing the path and stopping up the holes.

Jackson's advocates proposed bills in both houses of Congress in February of 1830, and in spite of National Republican support for native rights, both measures passed with most of the legislators voting along party lines. Jackson signed removal into law on May 28, and on that same day, the *New-York Evening Post* ran another article on the issue, referring to the bill as a "plan of removing the Indians to a tract of country where they shall forever be free from state jurisdiction." The writer concluded that

> the very title of the bill itself,—"a bill to provide for an *exchange* of lands with the Indians," &c. shows that no undue exercise of power is intended. . . . [T]here is nothing arbitrary, nothing tyrannical, nothing calculated to tarnish the honor of the country, and make our want of faith a byword in other lands.

The writer goes on to ask

> whether it would not be for the ultimate advantage of the Indians, as well as conducive to the interests and happiness of the whites, to remove the former from within the limits of the states, to a tract of country west of the Missis-sippi . . . the removal only to take place with the free consent of the Indians themselves.

This argument rests on the assumption that the whites and the natives were equal parties entering into bona fide negotiations, and that the natives, whether as tribes or as individuals, had an opportunity to choose, without coercion, between viable alternatives.

In his second annual message, on December 6, 1830, Jackson presented a rationale that either echoes Cass or demonstrates the consistency of perspective between the two men.

> Humanity has often wept over the fate of the aborigines of this country, and Philanthropy has been long busily employed in devising means to avert it, but its progress has never for a moment been arrested, and one by one have many powerful tribes disappeared from the earth. . . . But true philanthropy reconciles the mind to these vicissitudes as it does to the extinction of one generation to make room for another. . . . What good man would prefer a country covered with forests and ranged by a few thousand savages to our extensive Republic, studded with cities, towns, and prosperous farms, embellished with the improvements which art can devise or industry execute, occupied by more than 12,000,000 happy people, and filled with all the blessings of liberty, civilization, and religion? (Richardson 2: 520–21)

He announced that the government's "benevolent policy" would not only free the Indians "to pursue happiness in their own way," but also encourage them "to cast off their savage habits and become an interesting, civilized, and Christian com-munity" (Richardson 2: 520). He argued that the government was not responsible for the Indian decline and that he was offering terms that many whites would welcome.

> Can it be cruel in this Government when, by events which it can not control, the Indian is made discontented in his ancient home, to purchase his lands, to

give him a new and extensive territory, to pay the expense of his removal, and support him a year in his new abode? How many thousands of our own people would gladly embrace the opportunity of removing to the West on such conditions! (Richardson 2: 521)

On December 28, Jackson asked Congress to set aside an Indian territory west of the Mississippi, and in 1831, the government initiated a series of treaties that would put removal into effect. The treaty of February 28 with the Seneca nation includes the language typical of all such treaties, promising that the United States would "grant them by patent, in fee simple to them and their heirs forever, as long as they shall exist as a nation and remain on the same, a tract of land" (Kappler 2: 328). The phrase "to them and their heirs forever," repeated in treaty after treaty, became an ironic comment on the value of the government's promises and a hallmark of the entire history of Euro-American treatment of the natives. The debate continued, but had more to do with politics than with genuine concern; on December 14, 1831 (possibly in response to the National Republican party's attack, two days earlier, on Jackson's policy), the *New-York Evening Post* tried to bury the issue by referring to the "Indian question" as "settled," an assertion made in spite of the fact that removal was only just beginning.

Some tribes resisted; the Cherokee nation sought help from the Supreme Court, whose majority opinion was that they were not entitled to redress under the Constitution, and in 1835, a minority faction of the tribe signed a removal treaty. The *Post* continued to project complacent benevolence; on December 6, 1837, the paper described removal as "the settled policy of the country" and expressed satisfaction that the Choctaw and Cherokee had abandoned hunting for farming and seemed ready for "a simple form of government." Yet by 1838, fifteen thousand Cherokee still refused to leave their home region, so Martin Van Buren ordered Winfield Scott to remove them by force; some were raped and murdered by soldiers, and thousands died on the consequent "Trail of Tears." Ultimately, about 70,000 people, mostly from the southeast, were transported.

Set against the discourse of removal, *Metamora* became an expedient resource for the implementation of ideology. The primary assumption in the whites' reasoning was that American concerns and values were paramount and unexceptionable; all issues had to be measured accordingly. During the 1830s and 1840s, schoolbooks, leading literary magazines, and political journals took for granted the march of white civilization and justified removal in the name of Providence or Progress (Satz 55). As of the mid-1840s, the doctrine of Manifest Destiny offered blanket justification for any means Americans might adopt to achieve the end that God had ordained for them; for both society at large and individuals who held political power, the concept provided a way to disclaim responsibility for the unpleasant consequences of their actions. To absolve the nation from guilt, the government cited the liberal tradition and assured the people that due process was respected and that the natives had given consent in exchange for appropriate compensation. To those who protested, the demagogues insisted that the natives were beyond all but the most desperate help, assuring the public of their paternalistic concern as well as their regret at the solution, which they presented as the next inevitable stage in a decay that was part of the organic process of the Indian character. Such discourse conferred upon contingent matters the irrevocability of the past, and to a people so accustomed to dealing with the Indian rather than the native—with the construct rather than the actuality—the rhetoric rang true. Removal became a performance of a passage that was already inscribed in history, and the disposition of the natives became a matter of doom or fate, which neither good intentions nor benevolent government policy could alter. Amidst such attractive and convenient rhetoric, the opposition to removal, such as it was, withered. The ideology of America was well served.

THE SACHEM'S AUDIENCE

During the 1830s, when Forrest established *Metamora*, Americans displayed a variety of attitudes toward the natives. The "Indian" wars were by no means over, the Black Hawk War, fought in Illinois, ended in a massacre in the summer of 1832, and the Seminole War broke out in the southeast in 1835. Yet for some, natives were a source of amusement. In 1837, the *Weekly Herald* was given to making fun of them, employing gossip-column witticisms to describe Black Hawk and his party—"objects of terror to females, of wonder to children, and astonishment to negroes"—and relating how they superstitiously refused to have their likenesses painted but found Catlin's portraits and landscapes fascinating, how the umbrella intrigued them, and how their conversation consisted principally of grunts.

Others professed concern. On October 11, 1837, the *Morning Herald* predicted that removal would follow removal, that those natives sent west would have to move again "as the march of our race goes onward reclaiming the forests and the prairies from a state of nature," and possibly driving them into the Pacific Ocean. The writer then attributes to all natives a Plains-style dependence on the buffalo for food, clothing, and shelter, and expresses concern that their "improvident natures" will lead them to kill off the herds to sell the skins to white traders. He then observes that the removal policy was concentrating the native population and increasing the possibility that the tribes would form an alliance against the whites to wreak a "terrible retribution." On November 4, 1837, the *Weekly Herald* described the natives as a "noble and unhappy race" that "is rapidly becoming extinct," and reinforced the concept of the fading noble savage by reporting that "they are rapidly sinking into the stream of oblivion, and soon nothing of them will remain but the memory of their past existence and glory." The writer avoided considering the causative connection between white politics and native ruin.

Some found the natives disappointing in comparison with the noble savage.

In 1833, Washington Irving's twenty-year-old nephew, John Treat Irving, Jr., traveled through Pawnee country on the Platte River, and two years later published *Indian Sketches*. Corroborating his uncle's belief that white civilization had tainted the natives who lived too intimately with it, he confessed a disappointment that derived from not realizing that "the wild savage could no more be compared with his civilized brother, than the wild, untamed steed of his own prairie, could be brought in comparison with the drooping, broken-spirited drudge horse, who toils away a life of bondage, beneath the scourge of a master" (14). He scorned the "civilized Indian" as boring and having little "to enlist the feelings," mourned the greatness that they had lost under white influence, and predicted that before two hundred years had passed, only "a few wretched beings" would remain, "strangers in the land of their fathers" (21–22). On October 24, 1836, Job R. Tyson delivered an address to the Society for Commemorating the Landing of William Penn, proposing that the Indian was no icon but a mere man, bereft of culture and development, and so dominated by his animal tendencies (7). He imagined the Indians' past glory and mourned their decline: "That race once so free, so powerful, so full of heroic fortitude and high-minded honour, are dwindled into a miserable remnant, for the most part of base dependents and degenerate debauchees" (16).

Yet some writers kept hoping. Timothy Flint promoted removal because he imagined "a sort of Arcadian race between our borders and the Rocky mountains, standing memorials of the kindness and good faith of our government" (240). In spite of a generally pessimistic tone, J. T. Irving could not resist a certain romantic hope that in the freedom of the prairie, the Indian would thrive: "His head droops not; his eye quails not; and not a single feature yields in submission to his fellow man. He is unrestrained in body; unfettered in spirit; and as wayward as the breeze, which sweeps over the grass of his own hills" (114). George Catlin's accounts, first published as letters in New York newspapers during 1832 and 1833, may have done much to keep the romance alive, for he proposed that the Indian of legend—and of his own paintings—was the Indian who lived farthest from white civilization.

The image of the Indian had not, therefore, developed in a straight line but had become increasingly diverse with the passage of time, the accretion of experience, and the growing complexity of political rhetoric—variously a figure of fun, a source of disappointment, an object of alleged concern, a symbol of romance, or, for a few settlers on one frontier or another, a palpable and genuine enemy. In presenting *Metamora*, then, Forrest faced the challenge of creating a character that would shape audience response within these options and at the same time reinforce the public image he sought.

The ongoing appeal of *Metamora* was a tribute to Forrest's success in burying the comic and disappointing aspects of the Indian, sublimating white fear and concern, and foregrounding the sachem as American hero. To the extent that Alger served as Forrest's amanuensis—the biography was based largely on the actor's recollections during the last few years of his life, and the general tone is unreservedly adulatory—his comments on the play may offer a guide to the performer's hopes for audience response to the play and the character.[25]

> [T]he English are made to represent power and fraud, the Indians truth and patriotism; and when their fugitive king pauses on a lofty cliff in the light of the setting sun, gazes mournfully on the lost hunting-grounds and desecrated graves of his forefathers, and launches his curse on their destroyers, every heart beats with sorrow for him. (242)

Furthermore, Forrest wanted his audience to regard his performance as authentic. Alger reports that in 1825, Forrest left an engagement in New Orleans and traveled north to visit Push-ma-ta-ha, a young Choctaw chief whom Alger described (or Forrest remembered) as being

> in the bloom of opening manhood, erect as a column, graceful and sinewy as a stag, with eyes of piercing brilliancy, a voice of gutteral music like gurgling waters, the motions of his limbs as easy and darting as those of a squirrel. His muscular tissue in its tremulous quickness seemed made of woven lightnings. His hair was long, fine, and thick, and of the glossiest blackness; his skin, mantled with blood, was of the color of ruddy gold, and his form one of faultless proportions. (126–27)

Forrest lived with the tribe as one of them, dressing, eating, and living as a Choctaw and taking part in their hunts and dances. Alger assures his readers that the experience conferred upon the actor "an accurate knowledge of the American Indian," which he put to good use when playing Metamora (138). Whether or not Forrest actually visited the Choctaws, or even visited them in the circumstances he describes, the anecdote illuminates less his youth and more his wish, as an old man looking back on his career and reminiscing for his official biographer, to construct his past in a certain way to serve certain ambitions. Metamora was one of Forrest's staple roles and one of the few that only he performed for the duration of his career.[26] The intended effect of the Push-ma-ta-ha story is to confirm the actor's meticulous verisimilitude and legitimize his portrayal of the Wampanoag sachem.

In spite of the play's durable popularity, the published reviews were not all what Forrest might have desired. Soon after the play opened at the Park, the *Irish Shield and Monthly Hilenan* condemned the "meagre and miserable dramatic abortion" as "utterly destitute" and "absolutely defective," being a "mere pantomimic exhibition of stage tricks and mannerisms, factitious touches and clap-traps." The critic proposed that Stone, realizing the weakness of his poetry, had "resorted to the last resource of dullness, spectacle and conflagration." The critic did offer ambiguous praise for Forrest himself: "In such a tame, unintellectual representation as this, which requires only *postures* and *grimaces*, we might pronounce Mr. Forrest's 'sayings and doings' faultless, with the exception of his roaring rant in the Council-Chamber" ("New-York Stage" 468). Several years later, in its review of December 28, 1837, the *Morning Herald* slammed the "furious melodrame" and announced, "Nothing indicates more surely the low ebb of the drama in our city than the toleration of such a piece as this, under the professed name of tragedy. . . . [T]hat an audience should have the patience to sit by and listen to the miserable twaddle of the . . . *dramatis personæ*, is almost incredible."[27] The critic treated Metamora more kindly, calling the character "an excellent representative of the Indian of poetry" and comparing him with Sarpedon in that both lived and died for "glory in war, and indolence in peace." He offered Forrest a backhanded compliment and managed to denigrate Indians at the same time.

> He has a large fund of that *sang froid* and self-sufficiency requisite to portray the stoicism of the red man. His hoarse voice, uncontrolled by art—his sullen features, his dogged walk, his athletic frame, and his admirable personations of the transitions of the mind from calmness to passion, are lofty and enviable qualifications for the attainment of excellence in this range of the drama.[28]

In spite of the writer's generally sneering tone, he conceded Forrest's accuracy in portraying an Indian.

> He is truly the impersonation of the Indian of romance. The Indian in his *true* character never *can* find a representative among the whites. Disgust, rather than admiration, would ensue, but if the author made him successful, our prejudices would revolt at the scene.

In 1830, the *American Quarterly Review* found no room for æsthetic distance, decrying Forrest's "ferocious savage" and describing the play as an account of "the reckless cruelties of a bloody barbarian, who stabs his subjects like pigs, and delights the white men of the present day, by burning the villages of their forefathers, and involving women and children in one indiscriminate massacre" ("Dramatic Literature" 145).[29]

The *Post* continued to offer Forrest its warm support while abetting removal by legitimating the concept of the vanishing Indian. On July 29, 1834, the *Evening Post* described a dinner given in Forrest's honor, where in a lengthy toast, William T. McCoun referred to *Metamora* as "wholly American in its character and incidents," and described the title figure as "a strong and natural portrait of one of the most remarkable warriors of a race, the last relics of which are fast melting away before the advancing tide of civilization."[30] Three years later, on October 11, 1837, a review in the same newspaper asserted that Metamora was "a faithful and spirited portraiture of one of the most heroic of that aboriginal race of men who were once the sole denizens of this continent, but of whom now but few and degenerate relics remain."

The distinction between the portrait and the actuality is crucial to understanding the performance and its reception. Forrest claimed to be representing a genuine, if generic, Indian, and cited his time with the Choctaws as supporting evidence. The only tangible artifacts of Forrest's portrayal are several engravings and drawings depicting his costume as Metamora. Most of them show him wearing a tunic that accentuates his shoulders and covers the hips like a kilt or short skirt, fringed leggings, a knife thrust into the left side of his belt, and two to five long feathers thrust into a headband worn over long, straight hair.[31] Variations include an axe thrust into the right side of his belt, a pouch hanging on his right hip, either a long-muzzled flintlock or a longbow in his right hand, decorative belts crisscrossing his chest, and long sleeves cut to leave his lower arms free. The costume bears little resemblance to what we know of Wampanoag dress, and looks more like an idealization of what a nineteenth-century Sioux warrior might have worn on a cold day. The critics for both the *Herald* and the *Post* realized that Forrest offered a representation not of an actuality—neither Metacomet nor an authentic native of the Jacksonian period—but of the conception that his public cherished, a romanticized vision whose validity his audience may, for emotional and political reasons, have wished to urge.[32] In other words, Forrest and his public had covertly recognized yet another binarism, but this time not between red and white, rather between red and "red," between "degenerate relics" and the "Indian of romance."[33] To reserve respect for the romantic, semihistorical fiction was to deny it to the actual native. This strategy left only contempt for the disappointingly real native and disempowered him, virtually making the case that he should embrace his own luxuriously melancholy demise, for as a mere relic, he probably deserved to melt away.

In only one recorded incident did Forrest's audience seem to interpret Metamora as a representative of the actual Indians. James E. Murdoch was playing an engagement in Augusta, Georgia, in 1831, when Forrest arrived to star in *Metamora*. All went well until the sachem denounced the English council and declared war.

> [A]s the chief rushed from the stage he was followed by loud yells and a perfect storm of hisses from the excited audience, who seemed ready in their fury to tear everything to pieces. Order was with difficulty restored, and the performance continued till the curtain fell upon the dying chief amid unqualified evidences of disapprobation. (298–99)

Murdoch relates that Forrest then realized that the Georgians read the play as "a positive protest against the policy which had deprived the Indians of Georgia of their natural rights and driven them from their homes"; they accused the actor of contriving a deliberate insult and "felt indignant at any reference to the stealing of Indian property, and especially so at being menaced with the tomahawk and scalping-knife of the red man's vengeance" (299). (The performance probably fell very close to the March 18 verdict of *Cherokee Nation v. Georgia*.) One angry lawyer announced that

> Any actor who could utter such scathing language, and with such vehemence, must have the whole matter at heart. Why . . . his eyes shot fire and his breath was hot with the hissing of his ferocious declamation. I insist upon it, Forrest believes in that d——d Indian speech, and it is an insult to the whole community. (299–300)

Forrest attempted *Metamora* once more, but "to empty benches," and the rest of his engagement suffered as a result of the controversy.[34]

Metamora served the political exigencies of its time. Because white writers typically defined native culture as "other"—whether through Puritan denunciation or Romantic panegyric—all Indian narratives offered strong melodramatic potential, and the history of Metacomet was particularly rewarding.[35] *Metamora* created a myth, an idealized vision, that permitted its audience to enjoy the beauty of the Indian while abusing the native. At the same time, Forrest's performance and his prominent nationalism helped annex the Indian into the American mythic structure by presenting Metacomet, as Metamora, as an American patriot, an emblem of honesty, integrity, and masculinity in the American version of the sentimental tradition.[36] The key element in this chemistry was Forrest himself, playing the role of "Indian" while signifying Euro-American values, his mimesis at odds with his semiosis. He and Stone appropriated the poetic Indian in order to promote the white man's inaccurate self-concept as the free, lonesome hunter, living in harmony with the land that bore him, a myth that was mostly humbug. Yet they also redefined Metacomet as a paragon in the sentimental tradition, inscribing the Indian with just those male virtues that white Americans admired and that the actor portrayed so effectively. Their version of the mythic Indian set a standard that no actual native—indeed, no person of any background—could hope to match, and so vindicated both nostalgia and removal.

"Fearful Quarrels, and Brutal Violence, Are the Natural Consequences of the Frequent Use of the Bottle." Plate VI of George Cruikshank's *The Bottle* (1847). (Courtesy of the Huntington Library, San Marino, California.)

3

The Drunkard (1844) and the Temperance Movement

THE ANTEBELLUM TEMPERANCE movement, as we view it from our comfortably retrospective vantage, seems virtually to invite melodrama, for its essential concerns were the sanctity of the family and the preservation of the middle class, and its vision of the human condition encompassed only heroes, villains, and victims. Yet even though antebellum temperance drama expressed reform doctrine faithfully, the movement scorned the plays and relegated them, through resolute neglect, to a marginal position.[1] They scarcely appear in the organizations' reports, the reformers' memoirs, and the later histories; even the most prominent and still durable play, W. H. Smith's *The Drunkard; or, The Fallen Saved* (1844), is notable by its absence from mainstream temperance commentary.[2] There was even hostility from those whose cause the plays purported to support; in 1843, the board of selectmen in Worcester, Massachusetts, closed down a well-intentioned and well-attended touring production entitled *Moral Exhibition of the Reformed Drunkard*, and the *Journal of the American Temperance Union* approved, arguing sarcastically that

> This is the right way to prevent our cause from ever enlisting the serious, enlightened and reflecting portion of the community. It is a great cause, the cause of God and humanity, and needs not the aid of buffoonery, mountebanks, and theatrical exhibitions, which are, after all, money-making affairs. ("Theatrical Exhibitions")[3]

The reformers do not seem to have regarded the plays as providing significant assistance in their struggle.

In spite of the potential for florid melodrama that nearly every temperance tale demonstrates, the social and moral abyss that separated theatre from the movement was very nearly insuperable. The audiences for theatre and for the temperance message were nearly mutually exclusive; respectable people did not, by and large, attend the theatre, but only respectable people, or those who aspired to respectability, were likely to heed the temperance polemic. One temperance journal referred to the theatre as "the 'devil's trap' for the youth of our country" ("Theatrical Exhibitions"). Nevertheless, the playwrights fell neatly into step with the "official" temperance literature of the antebellum period—a wide variety of tracts, sermons, songs, poems, stories, and novels—all the writers demonstrating a remarkably homogeneous perspective as they produced a body of discourse that not only expressed their self-conscious attitude to a specific historical situation, but also fostered a myth that promoted the ideology of the rising middle class.

THE POLITICS OF DRINKING IN ANTEBELLUM AMERICA

The temperance activists of the early nineteenth century represented alcohol not only as a threat to the general health but also as the cause of social disorder, which they believed to be increasing. If, as the sentimental position maintained, man was born innocent and essentially virtuous, then the presence of crime and immorality indicated the operation of a corrupting influence. The activists worked to establish the causative link between alcohol and disorder, especially crime; to condone drinking was to encourage criminals, but to make society sober was to make it stable and safe. This was, of course, a highly simplistic analysis, and as Ian R. Tyrrell has observed, it ignored such factors as the operations of a capitalist system that was likely to foster unrest and anxiety by relegating most of its participants to the roles of helpless victims of market fluctuations (129). However, the paradigm facilitated persuasive platform rhetoric.

The movement faced a struggle because its fundamental demand ran counter to American habits of the time. While actual drunkenness was disparaged, drinking itself had been an integral part of American manners from the earliest colonial days down through the federal period; taverns served as community centers, politicians were expected to "treat" during an election, and most laborers drank on the job as a matter of course. As W. J. Rorabaugh has observed, copious social drinking had become linked with basic American values; "all men were equal before the bottle, and no man was allowed to refuse to drink" on the grounds that abstention betrayed a supercilious attitude. Moreover, drinking, especially to the point of intoxication, was an act of choice and self-will and an exercise of liberty that confirmed the individual's autonomy (151). The reformers countered by arguing that the drinker was enslaved to demon rum and only through the use of reason and moderation could he restrain his appetites and find true freedom in adherence to a certain morality. This strategy was an attempt to replace rough-and-tumble individualism with an essentially sentimental conception of man as responsible to society and to God. The reformers also pointed out that the typical American was drinking more and turning increasingly to whiskey, rum, and other "spirituous liquors"; according to Rorabaugh, in 1830, the average adult drank, each week, nearly a fifth of hard liquor and over half a gallon of cider.[4] Yet there was resistance to other beverages: water was unsafe in many communities, milk was not available to those who lived too far from a dairy, tea was perceived as foreign and unpatriotic, and coffee was usually too expensive (Rorabaugh 97–100). To wean Americans away from cider, the activists had to promote a viable alternative.

The first organization dedicated specifically to temperance and claiming wide-spread influence was the Massachusetts Society for the Suppression of Intemperance (MSSI), founded in 1813. The members had observed a decline in public morality—working on Sunday, swearing within the hearing of respectable folk, drinking to excess in public—and saw it as a significant reason why they seemed to be losing both deference and political power; some joined in search of a way to reestablish their authority over the lower classes. Composed largely of clergy, merchants, and professionals, the society censured only immoderate drinking, aspiring to change, by virtue of the members' own admirable example, the manners and morals of the uneducated and allegedly uninhibited common people. The MSSI, therefore, was dedicated not to reforming its own membership, but to instituting a paternalistic program for others; to control drinking among the working class was to control the working class morally, politically, and economically. The society's program was somewhat old-fashioned; the plan was to limit drinking by enforcing colonial-style regulations on the public taverns, which, the members believed, should be owned and operated only by responsible individuals. Although the MSSI rolls counted four thousand in 1818, the group declined during the early 1820s, largely due to its narrowly Federalist/Congregationalist identity, which alienated not only laborers but also Methodists and Baptists, and by 1823 the organization had virtually disappeared (Tyrrell 33–44; Dannenbaum 16–17).

Led by Justin Edwards, a reformer and Congregationalist minister, a group of evangelical Christians founded the American Society for the Promotion of Temperance (ATS) in 1826. Like the MSSI, the ATS drew its membership largely from the patrician class, mostly in New England, but its leaders were more inclined to be involved in other reform and missionary organizations; many also belonged to the American Tract Society, which published material in support of evangelical Protestantism and by 1851 distributed nearly five million temperance pamphlets. Yet the new organization departed from the MSSI precedent to adopt a different reform strategy, foregrounding the eternal, rather than the temporal, consequences of intemperance, and arguing that drink eroded man's moral sense, deafened him to the call of religion, and jeopardized his immortal soul. ATS members were concerned not with the lower-class drunkard but with those people who were relatively temperate and respectable. They scorned the moderate drinker—commonly perceived as a respectable, Christian gentleman—as one whose indifference and ambiguous example impeded reform, and they argued that moderate drinking led to heavy drinking, with all the consequent pauperism and crime, so they called for complete abstinence from spirits. They attacked distillers and liquor traders, especially those who attended church, for legitimating drinking by making it a business. ATS membership was impressively large; by 1834 the group recorded seven thousand chapters with 1.25 million members, or approximately one out of twelve Americans (Tyrrell 54–77; Dannenbaum 17–20; Rorabaugh 202).

The link between the temperance movement and evangelical Protestantism reveals the vast and powerful substructure lying beneath most reform efforts that followed the Second Great Awakening. To attend a revival and "get" religion was to subscribe to an extreme version of the sentimental agenda, one that argued that since man was perfectible, he should set about perfecting both himself and the world around him with all dedication and energy; hence the overwhelming output of the American Tract Society. Furthermore, the revivalists operated on the assumption that every man *could* be "saved," an idea that resonated harmoniously with American egalitarianism and eroded the Calvinist exclusivity of the "elect." According to Joseph R. Gusfield, the religious man demonstrated his spiritual status through the outward signs of industry, responsibility, thrift, and sobriety, all of which increased his personal wealth and contributed to the improvement of his community; he became a bootstrap member of the middle class, and temperance was one of the new habits that announced his superiority over the less enlightened (45–46). Revivalism thus served the greater needs of American free enterprise; Rorabaugh has suggested that the temperance movement, more than some other reforms, succeeded because it managed to satisfy both the devotion to materialism and the hunger for salvation (202).[5]

In 1833, the Apprentices' Temperance Society became the first temperance organization in New York City to embrace total abstinence from all alcoholic drinks, whether spirituous or fermented.[6] The society's leadership was predominantly those mechanics—self-improving, success-oriented entrepreneurs—who employed the journeymen and apprentices in their respective trades; that is, men of responsibility and ambition. Teetotalism spread, and in 1836, the National Temperance Convention at Saratoga adopted the teetotal position and established the American Temperance Union (ATU) as the new national organization (Tyrrell 140–41, 144). Members of the temperance groups took a pledge; an apparently typical one from 1836 reads as follows:

> We, whose names are hereunto annexed, believing that the use of intoxicating liquor, as a beverage, is not only needless, but hurtful to the social, civil, and religious interests of men; that it tends to form intemperate appetites and habits, and that while it is continued, the evils of intemperance can never be done away;— do therefore agree, that we will not use it, or traffic in it; that we will not provide it as an article of entertainment, or for persons in our employment; and that, in all suitable ways, we will discountenance the use of it throughout the community. (*Temperance Manual* 12)

In 1839, the Executive Committee of the ATU triumphantly reported "continual progress . . . in the work of purification" and claimed that drinking survived no longer in polite homes but chiefly in

> tippling-houses, dram-shops, taverns, splendid hotels; in the navy, in steam-boats, at public dinners and evening parties; at treats, at election and political meetings; at gatherings about judicial tribunals; at the seats of State Legislatures and (peculiarly humiliating) of the National Congress. (qtd. in Dorchester 311–12)

As teetotalism rose, so did working-class leadership in the temperance movement. The New England patrician who proscribed hard liquor was acting completely
to his own advantage; he probably drank wine as part of the social rituals of his
class, preferring it to spirits, and if he could control local laborers, both his business
and his political interests were more likely to thrive. Such a man may have already
faced difficulties with the ATS, whose evangelical model insisted that only the
regenerate could proselyte; in other words, he could not drink wine while urging
his employees to abstain from spirits. On the other hand, the mechanic who embraced teetotalism was taking the initiative and the power away from his social
superior and proclaiming, in essence, that if he had to give up his drink for the
improvement of society, then the patrician should sacrifice his as well. Such teetotalers probably derived even greater resolve from the fact that such luminaries
as Jefferson and Burr were known wine drinkers whose example had reinforced
the correlation between class and beverage.[7]

With the founding of the Washingtonian Temperance Society in 1840, the working class offered a serious challenge to patrician control of the movement.[8] The
early members were former drinkers, dedicated to recruiting and reforming other
men like themselves. Because they had personal experience with drinking (unlike
their patrician predecessors), they rejected the principle that the drunkard was beyond hope, affirming instead that he could and must be saved, a revision that
accommodated even penitent liquor sellers. Ultimately, Washingtonian membership
included not only former drinkers but also lifelong teetotalers, and it crossed class
boundaries to include laborers, employers, and professionals. Still, the bulk of the
members were artisans and skilled tradesmen, people who worked in small shops
where owner and employee shared interests to a significant degree, and who also
were inclined to regard temperance as a sign of the middle-class status they desired.
Some were former liquor sellers who might have hesitated to join the ATU but
who discovered that their fellow tradesmen in the Washingtonian societies accepted
them as men who were simply trying to make a living for their families. Moreover,
a seller who renounced his business set an impressive example and invigorated
the organization. The group stressed self-help, but some members offered converts
new jobs and new housing, realizing that the deprivation of basic necessities and
the lack of supportive company could easily return a man to his original and destructive habits. By the end of 1841, the Washingtonians claimed two hundred
thousand members in the North (Dannenbaum 33–38; Tyrrell 159–62, 175–76,
200).

The typical Washingtonian experience meeting demonstrated an unintentional
theatricality, resembling a revival as members and converts signed the pledge, acknowledged their past weakness, and described their aspirations for the future.
Ironically, however, the Washingtonians and the evangelicals were uneasy with each
other. The societies were nonsectarian and, for that era, relatively secular, seeing
sobriety as the path to God (although some members did not attend church), while

the evangelicals saw religious conversion or acceptance of God as the best means to sobriety (Dannenbaum 39). Insofar as it satisfied some of the same emotional and social needs, the experience meeting displaced the revival or evangelical church service, but with speakers instead of preachers; Tyrrell explains that the act of reform offered the drinker regeneration and the "secular equivalent of a religious conversion," because "for faith in God, reformed men substituted faith in self; for belief in ultimate salvation, they substituted belief in immediate reform" (172). The meetings were open to the public, and the societies welcomed even the most destitute and apparently irredeemable drunkards; the more desperate the case, the more dramatic the decision to reform.[9] The "experience speech" was a highly public form of confession, appeal for absolution, and, through the assemblage's enthusiastic approval, a means of immediate transformation from derelict to citizen; it was a mode of performance, with player, script, audience, and mutually agreed-upon conventions governing the interaction. Benjamin H. Estes—a self-confessed rum seller of twenty years' experience—reported an experience speech in which the man confessed fifteen years of drunkenness, degradation, and loafing

> around the markets and wharves without any regular means of subsistence, sleeping in the markets and on the side-walks, almost without clothes, or friends, and that all he sought for was rum; and that his appetite was so craving that he would stoop to the meanest calling to obtain a little rum. (6)

The miscreant was a family man whose wife, after enduring poverty, misery, and wretchedness, finally sought "protection" with friends. After relating his troubles, he presented himself to the assembly as a happy and prosperous citizen, restored to health, family, church, and prosperity, and all due to his decision to sign the temperance pledge.

The Washingtonian florescence did not last long; the organization went into a decline during the years from 1843 to 1845. One possible cause was the probability that the experience meetings had used up all the conceivable variations of confessional narrative and no longer engaged audience interest as they once did. Furthermore, by the mid-1840s, many believed that the battle was won and so lost interest in the temperance struggle as a whole. Indeed, according to Rorabaugh, the average annual adult consumption of spirits fell from 5.2 gallons in 1830 to 2.1 gallons in 1845; this decline combined with the shift from cider to beer and reduced the consumption of absolute alcohol from 7.1 gallons in 1830 to 1.8 gallons in 1845.[10] To join a temperance organization had become less a radical gesture and more a conventional one, and by the 1850s, sobriety had become firmly associated with middle-class respectability (Gusfield 50).

I would like to abstract two significant points from this brief historical review. First, the leadership of the temperance movement passed from the patrician class, to reform-oriented lay and clerical evangelical protestants, and finally to the upwardly mobile artisan classes, each group influencing the perceptions of the next and so blending the rhetoric across class lines, much as the solera method mixes vintages. In her study of the temperance movement in Boston, Jill Siegel Dodd tabulates various records from 1837 to 1859 and concludes that there was a positive correlation between level of wealth and upward mobility (in terms of occupation or accumulation of property) on the one hand, and support for temperance on the other. In other words, those who resisted temperance were less likely to own taxable amounts of property or to rise economically or professionally. Laborers, and especially immigrants and unskilled workers, were more likely to drink on the job, as had long been customary, and to view temperance as an upper-class program for divesting them of a cherished pleasure. However, those who aspired to middle-class status were more inclined to adopt middle-class habits in anticipation of their rise.

Second, by the time *The Drunkard* appeared in 1844, the movement had already effected a significant change in America's drinking habits, and indeed would not achieve further measurable success until after 1919, when the Eighteenth Amendment attempted to impose prohibition from the federal level. During the years when most of the known antebellum temperance dramas were produced, from 1844 to 1858, American drinking remained stable. In other words, the temperance dramas, no matter what the intent of their creators and supporters, rather than helping to change attitudes to a significant degree, were instead affirming a vision that had already come true; they were conservative rather than revolutionary, demonstrating a high degree of consonance between their myth and their ideology. The plays appeared only when the mainstream temperance rhetoric and publications, as well as the nature and policy of the organizations, had evolved to the point at which popular theatre was possible.

THE TEMPERANCE MESSAGE

Through the early 1830s, temperance propaganda tended to prefer relatively rational persuasion that addressed the problem and its consequences in straightforward terms. The points most often repeated were that liquor was harmful rather than useful, that the drinker tended to develop an uncontrollable appetite for it, that it was a waste of money, and that it jeopardized the family. One of the earliest and most influential advocates was Benjamin Rush, the prominent physician, former member of the Continental Congress, and signatory of the Declaration of Independence. His views were still popular in the 1830s, and the American Tract Society circulated 172,000 copies of his pamphlet entitled *The Effect of Ardent Spirits upon the Human Body and Mind* (Marsh, *Half Century* 27). Rush earnestly listed eleven groups of symptoms of intemperance, including both unusual "garrulity" and unusual silence, unusual good humor, a tendency to disclose secrets or to tell others their faults, and "certain extravagant acts which indicate a temporary fit of madness. These are singing, hallooing, roaring, imitating the noises of brute animals, jumping, tearing off clothes, dancing naked, breaking glasses and china, and dashing other articles of household furniture upon the ground or floor" (1–2). Edward Hitchcock, in his *Essay* of 1830, gravely assured his readers that

> the unnatural excitement, which a moderate and occasional use of alcoholic and narcotic substances produces, is unfavorable to clearness and vigor in mental operations. The dizziness of the brain, and exhilaration accompanying their use, especially that of alcohol, what are they, but incipient delirium, and the premonitions of apoplexy. (17)

Justin Edwards adopted a variety of means toward direct suasion. In *The Well-Conducted Farm*, he stressed the benefits of temperance—better health, longer life, and a national saving of $30 million per year that would no longer be spent on spirits—and assured his readers that if the presently temperate would remain so, intemperance would disappear in one generation as the drinkers died out and left no successors. Doubtless responding to the belief that alcoholic beverages fortified both body and mind, he wrote *On the Traffic in Ardent Spirit* to argue that liquor was neither necessary nor useful but rather harmful in that it wasted property, destroyed reason and the soul, increased disease, caused poverty, exposed children to dissipation and crime, and created widows and orphans.

Such essentially intellectual appeals soon paled in comparison with the temperance narratives that rose in popularity during the 1830s. This was the decade when the movement shifted clearly away from patrician control and moderation, and toward artisan control and teetotalism. The new membership was perhaps less inclined by temperament and education to respond to dry persuasion, and the newly adamant position may have required a more vivid, extreme means of exhortation. Whether oral or written, and no matter what its other stylistic or formal qualities, each narrative marked out a carefully chosen position on a perceived continuum between fiction and truth. That is, for the narratives to establish the highest degree of credibility and achieve the utmost in effect on their listeners and readers, they had to insist on their authenticity; an overt fiction was less likely to impress and persuade than even an apparent history.

The authors of the earliest narratives presented their stories as straight reportage; some of these allegedly factual accounts were simple anecdotes offered as evidence to support the writer's case. The 1832 ATS report listed a child who burned to death because the parents were too drunk to help, a couple who drowned while inebriated, a captain who ran his steamship aground on a rock and killed over one hundred passengers, and a mother who supplied the rope for her grown son to hang himself (*Permanent Temperance Documents, Fifth Report* 31–32).[11] *Who Slew All These?* is a four-page tract that tells the story of a couple with five sons who opened a public house and declined from temperate respectability into dissolution and death—the wife goes insane, the husband becomes a "beast," two sons die, and one suffers an injury that deranges him. In his *Temperance Manual*,

Edwards displayed a taste for grotesquerie when he related the stories of a man who got drunk after his wife died and "in high glee dragged her across the room by the hair of her head, and threw her into the coffin," and of "a father [who] took a little child by his legs and dashed his head against the house, and then, with a boot-jack, beat out his brains" (21, 71).

Another strategy that appeared in the early 1830s was the generic speculation based on the presumptively shared experience of speaker and listener, or of writer and reader. In his *Address on the Effects of Ardent Spirits*, published as a widely circulated tract, Jonathan Kittredge asked the reader to remember someone he knew who grew up in a respectable family with all the advantages and began a business and a family, but who "grew fond of ardent spirits" and so neglected his responsibilities and finished his life as a "useless pest," who, drunk, "staggers through mud and through filth, to his hut" where "he meets a weeping wife and starving children" (3). This scenario was, Kittredge affirmed, not a work of imagination, but a representation of a widespread and familiar reality. Another master of speculation was actor John Bartholomew Gough, who gave up drinking and became a temperance lecturer.[12] In 1844, he described

> the wife of the drunkard as she sits in her destitution and misery, in the cold damp cellar, or the rickety garret, working her fingers to the bone, that she may gain a morsel of bread for her band of half-starving, half-naked, shivering children; hearing no sound but their cries for food and fire. The scene of early days and her youthful bloom—the time when she pledged her all to the man who has now deserted her—his broken promise—his progressive steps in vice—his waning love—his brutality—his indifference to her wants—and the deep, utter midnight darkness that has settled upon her hopes and happiness, are all brought before the mind, as though they were daguerrotyped upon the wall. (qtd. in Marsh, *Temperance Recollections* 127)

He went on to describe the drunkard, sitting apathetically in the "groggery . . . carelessly steeping the little left of his sensibility in the damning bowl."

One of the most compelling narrative modes was the testimonial, written in first person and nearly always implying its impeccable verisimilitude, much like the experience speech it frequently resembled so closely. In a tract published in 1840, the anonymous author adopted the narrative voice of a wife and mother who sank from prosperity to the poorhouse. "She" realizes how her troubles began through her own folly, as she, "young and thoughtless," poured out wine for her companions from "elegant decanters, sparkling so brilliantly":

> Oh that wine! that wine! how like the serpent it stole into the Eden of our bliss, and stamped a curse upon me and mind, unutterable and indescribable. . . . I laughingly urged those who were temperate to drink *only one glass*. Like a fool, I was sporting with the very temptation, the most fatal to the peace and happiness of families. (2–3)

She bears five children while her husband develops his business, but after nine years, she realizes that he has become a drunkard.

> I covered my face with my hands, and burying them deep in the pillow, I tried to shut out the frightful idea. Oh, God! what an hour of agony—of deep, un-utterable agony was that! the husband of my bosom—the beloved of my heart—the father of my children, prostituting his intellect and debasing his character, by intemperance. Could it be? (5)

He insists, repeatedly, that one glass will not hurt him, and he continues to buy drinks from a "rum-selling Christian." His creditors foreclose on their home, one son dies of scarlet fever, two more drown in a boating accident, and the remaining two ultimately become "the most profligate and abandoned sailors in the navy" (16). The husband turns to common labor and she takes in sewing, but they starve. "I was miserably wretched. How could it be otherwise? I was the wife of a drunk-ard" (16).

One of the most famous temperance narratives combined the modes of re-portage and testimonial. Timothy Shay Arthur's *Six Nights with the Washingtonians* purported to be a virtual transcript of what he saw and heard at a series of ex-perience meetings in 1840 and 1841; he published the accounts first in his news-paper, the *Baltimore Merchant*, then as pamphlets, and then collected in book form in 1842.[13] The stories themselves reinforced patterns that had become familiar, and dealt with the principal characters that troubled the temperate imagination. In "The Broken Merchant," a man drinks away his inheritance and destroys his heroically faithful daughter's marriage prospects, but then signs the Washingtonian pledge and instantly reforms. One of the tales in "The Experience Meeting" involves a young mechanic who drinks more and more until his wife dies, but a stranger—a reformed drunkard—rescues him. "The Moderate Drinker" finally loses his busi-ness at the age of fifty, his wife opens a boardinghouse to maintain the family, he spends more and more time ill and in jail for debt, but finally signs the pledge. The titles of the other stories reveal their focal points, all personalized to configure the problem and inspire the reader to self-examination: "The Tavern-Keeper," "The Drunkard's Wife," and "The Widow's Son."

Even the overt fictions in the temperance canon demonstrated their authors' concern for compelling realism in service of doctrine. In two early collections of short stories—*The Club Room* (1845) and *Illustrated Temperance Tales* (1850)—Arthur reinforced the presence of the narrative voice by occasionally addressing the reader directly and by writing each story almost as a transcript of a series of events, sometimes beginning a tale with allegedly unmediated dialogue. In Arthur's most famous novel, *Ten Nights in a Bar-Room, and What I Saw There* (1854), the narrator is a business traveler who passes through a small town several times over a period of years, and so witnesses the various stages of the fall of a miller-turned-innkeeper and his family; the traveler becomes a spectator of an ongoing and ostensibly historical drama.

THE TEMPERANCE NARRATIVE

As a group, these stories employ a somewhat consistent narrative and address the same concerns over and over again; the use of generic speculation suggests that at least some orators and writers were aware that they were improvising variations on a theme. Temptation is virtually irresistible, for man is inherently weak and somewhat naïve regarding the potential consequences of his actions. Drink itself precludes and displaces all other interests, endeavors, and concerns. The inevitable consequence of drinking is decline into disaster; the mere fact of tippling compromises respectability, and the reprobate falls into one or more of a list of dire consequences—a very public loss of wealth, property, and prospects, sometimes through the thunderclap of foreclosure; an equally public loss of position and consequent shame and disgrace; madness; or death, sometimes visited upon innocent victims rather than the drunkard himself, and occurring through fire, drowning, violent accident, or a vague spiritual dissolution or exhaustion. The drunkard is almost always a man, and a man with a family; as in the harangues by Kittredge and Gough, the wife and children (soon to be widow and orphans) are helpless, weeping, starving, half-naked victims of the drunkard's betrayal.

The strategy essential to this discourse was the equation of sobriety with prosperity and middle-class respectability, and of drink with poverty and disgrace. As the movement gathered strength and turned toward teetotalism, the narrative insisted more and more vehemently that to take one drink was to take another, that social drinking led to an uncontrollable craving that would certainly lead to destruction.[14] This linkage was not entirely abstract; the time, effort, and especially money that the drinker spent on alcohol would, in the best of all possible bourgeois worlds, have been better invested in business. Drinking became a matter of misdirecting potential capital; if a man had excess funds to spend on drink, he could, instead, put them in a savings account and not only enable his own social rise but also help finance the larger operations of the capitalist system (Rorabaugh 204, Dannenbaum 80). Furthermore, the man who drank was less likely to perform efficiently on the job. All of this theorizing led to the assumption that if sobriety led to success, then one could recognize the successful man by his sobriety; the manner of his outward behavior was accepted as an indicator of his inner nature.[15]

The temperance narrative evolved from one approach to another; I shall call them the "censorious" and the "regenerative" narratives. The earlier examples design a chain of events moving from temptation to dissolution and concluding with disaster, leaving the drunkard to his just deserts and using the relentless parable to threaten the reader. These censorious narratives served the general program of warning away the temperate and wasting no effort on the drunkard himself, whom

the writers assumed to be unsalvageable. Only as of the mid-1840s, in response
to the Washingtonian position that the drinker could and should be saved, did authors
like Arthur round out the threatening pattern with reform and redemption. These
regenerative narratives assume the shape of an inverted arc as the young family
man (usually "in business" as a clerk or merchant, sometimes a mechanic) takes
to drink and slides into complete moral and financial degradation before renouncing
alcohol and fulfilling his destiny as he rises on the ladder of economic success
and social prestige.

The family was the temple of antebellum middle-class sentimentality, so the
temperance narrative's readers saw their favorite fears realized in the husband's
fall and the consequent disgrace and debasement of his loved ones. His lapse demonstrates the possibility of downward mobility and so places everyone in jeopardy,
especially the children, those representatives of the next generation, who could
become corrupted. Because he deserts her or fails to support her, his wife becomes
the reluctant head of the family on a merely temporary basis, and because she
can do no more than piecework on a very modest scale—sewing or making artificial
flowers—she can provide only the barest subsistence for herself and her children,
thus demonstrating the necessity and propriety of male hegemony. She scarcely,
if ever, reproves him, but suffers silently and so confirms her heroic moral stature
and worldly helplessness; she is the completely irreproachable victim.

The presence of a victim leads to the question of responsibility. There are
essentially only two alternatives—either it is the drinker's fault, or it is not. From
one perspective, the regenerative narrative holds the drunkard responsible, for to
save himself and his family, he must exert his will, sign the pledge, and reform.
To require or expect this act of will implies that he made a free choice to drink
in the first place, and if he is free to choose, he must be responsible for that
choice, especially since he made it *before* the rum rendered him incompetent. This
perception of responsibility derived in part from the middle-class burden of mobility; while a fixed socioeconomic hierarchy excuses the individual from ambition
by rendering it pointless, the fluid model that admits the possibility of improvement
also imposes expectations that some must have found difficult to satisfy. To fail
to rise is to confront the consequent sense of guilt; all choices come into question
and blame hovers ominously over the individual's head.

However, to blame the drunkard would be drastic. Because his error has
wreaked havoc on the family, poetic justice would certainly demand his death, but
such a denouement would deny the hope that the regenerative narrative sought to
offer. The drunkard could not be held responsible because he had to have a chance
to reform and set the example that encouraged moral behavior. Furthermore, the
narrative emphasizes the point that the drunkard does not enjoy one moment of
his debauchery, and his sense of guilt helped to win the sympathy of the reader.
Michael Booth has observed, with reference to the plays, that the typical drunkard

never lost hold of his conscience, perceiving himself as a "moral criminal" and drinking partly in an attempt to forget his remorse (210). In other words, he drinks to forget that he is drinking, a paradox that would be comic were it not so truthful.

Since the drunkard seemed beyond blame, the temperance apologists looked for other scapegoats, and the most convenient one was an abstraction—temptation. To succumb to temptation was to demonstrate weakness and poor guidance rather than malice, and also to provide a model to whom the average reader or listener could easily relate. The concept of temptation implied a certain reluctance on the part of the drunkard; as one fictional sufferer complained, "temptation allured me from the flowery route, till in the gloomy labyrinth of guilt my honor, peace, reputation, comfort, all are lost!" (C. W. Taylor 25). Also, because temptation was located outside of the drunkard, the narrative could present him as a victim, and because temptation had neither face nor name, it became an inescapable given that obviated any impulse to remedial action.

Another candidate for blame was the source of the liquor. Some of the stories imply a hierarchical concept of transgression, attributing more fault to the rum seller, and sometimes the private host, than to the drunkard. *Who Slew All These?* suggests that the unfortunate family's demise was all the more horrible because they not only drank but operated a public house. In "The Experience Meeting," a remorseful tavern-keeper not only transforms his establishment into a "temperance grocery," but also destroys $200 worth of stock because its consumption would entail a far greater moral cost. Such stories contended that the cause of intemperance is the rum seller himself; if the taverns were closed, the problem would disappear. Yet they did not challenge the system that encouraged such men to go into the tavern business in the first place. In other words, the narrative naïvely expected, on moral grounds, behavior that the institutions of production and trade simply did not foster.

Not a single example of temperance literature suggested fundamental social change as a solution to the problem; every temperance narrative assumed that some form of individual action was necessary. In his study of the temperance movement in Victorian England, Brian Harrison accuses the reformers of claiming to rescue "isolated individuals from among the countless victims of an unjust social system which they did little to rectify" (356). He argues that signing a pledge was merely a momentary expression of will but did not change the conditions—poverty, alienation, and insecurity in an industrialized, capitalist society—that inspired and encouraged the drinking in the first place. This is an essentially Marxist point of view; the *Communist Manifesto* lumps "temperance fanatics" together with philanthropists, humanitarians, and other reformers who composed that part of the bourgeoisie that wished to redress social grievances in order to promote the continuance of bourgeois society. Marx insisted that only "a change in the material conditions of existence, in economic relations" could truly improve the lot of the workers.[16]

To define the problem as a private one absolved society of any blame for the individual's downfall, for if the individual bears the burden of changing his life, there is no need to change the social status quo, which is therefore reinforced and affirmed.[17]

This delicate juggling of responsibility—now you have it, now you don't—relies on the evangelical model of behavior. The equation of reform with conversion appropriates the concept of divine intervention; the reprobate affirms his freedom by choosing to accept God's mediation, but the mediation itself demonstrates that the individual is not truly in control. Like a sinner, the drunkard is not evil but merely weak, so temptation leads rapidly to corruption, and like a regenerate Christian, the reformed drunkard returns to his original state of innocence and also, in many cases, rises above his former level of prosperity.

To first excuse the individual from accountability for his errors, and then to expect him to choose a new course of action, is simultaneously to validate and to vitiate the exercise of free will. Furthermore, this paradigm sets reason above passion (here, appetite) but without explaining how one may bring rationality to bear at the crucial moment. Both ambiguities reinforce the evangelical model, suggesting that the solution to any problem lies in inspiration and intuition (probably the product of divine intervention), a position that further renders pointless any attempt to rectify the situation by operating on its causative factors. In other words, the narrative purports to embrace a liberal point of view but cannot explain the allegedly inevitable success of the autonomous individual without allowing for an ineffable factor.

The covert contradictions in the temperance narrative reveal the high degree of tension that it embodies. To the late twentieth-century sensibility, the narrative, as narrative, is itself intemperate, given to extravagance and implausibility. Yet the narrative's mode of expression is part of its message, and not simply a matter of the rhetorical style of a certain place and time. The pressure of inherent paradox created stress, which burst forth in the tendency of some speakers or characters to express themselves in an overwrought manner, creating a highly exaggerated delineation of the issues and participants in the temperance scenario. Following is a passage from one of Gough's tirades.

> Ye mouldering victims! wipe the grave dust crumbling from your brow; stalk forth in your tattered shrouds and bony whiteness to testify against the drink! Come, come from the gallows, you spirit-maddened man-slayer, give up your bloody knife, and stalk forth to testify against it! Crawl from the slimy ooze, ye drowned drunkards, and with suffocation's blue and livid lips speak out against the drink! . . . [L]et the past be unfolded, and the shrieks of victims wailing be borne down upon the night blast! Snap your burning chains, ye denizens of the pit, and come up sheeted in the fire, dripping with the flames of hell, and with your trumpet tongues testify against the damnation of drink. (qtd. in Marsh, *Temperance Recollections* 128)[18]

Gough, perhaps drawing on his experience playing romantic melodrama during the Jacksonian period, virtually presented himself as an ancient Biblical prophet, calling down the fury of heaven upon demon rum. During a lecture in Savannah, William A. Caruthers asked his audience to imagine the drunkard:

> But hark to that shrill and piercing scream and see the wild and frantic creature, as with one bound he clears the bed and lights in the midst of them. His nostrils dilated, his eye red with agony, and his whole countenance ghastly with the extremity of mortal terror. (19)

The word nearly incarnates the image, a man become a driven, bestial hellion. A clergyman in Pittsfield peopled the local tavern with ghosts and supernatural phenomena when speaking on the occasion of the death of a drunken mechanic.

> For what would you be the man who sold that bottle of spirits? For what would you own that money? Oh! if the man be here who owns it, and has got it, let him look at it! Don't you see the blood on it? In your bar-room, by the cask, don't you see that mangled body? Don't you hear the steps of the naked feet of the orphans? Don't you see the wild eye and the pale face of the broken-hearted widow? (qtd. in Marsh, *Temperance Recollections* 134)

This is not gratuitous effusion but a heightened and scarcely restrained level of expression that was symptomatic of the emotional and social turmoil felt by the temperance speakers and their audiences; they were desperately afraid, so they cried out. From here, there was only a short distance to melodrama.

MELODRAMA AND THE NARRATIVE

The temperance narrative resembled the melodrama of its time in two major respects. Classic melodramatic practice involves setting up an ideal whose threatened loss or destruction inspires the fear that engages the audience's rapt attention, and that withstands the attack of some pernicious force, thus proving both its vulnerability and its strength. To incarnate that ideal, much nineteenth-century American melodrama, like the antebellum temperance narrative, located all social value in its most unassailable repository, the family—the universal object of sympathy and the most convenient means of perpetuating the culture and its economy.

As an ideological method, melodrama rests on a generalized and simplistic conception of virtue, which functions as a transcendental signified and ultimate referent for moral judgments. Both the temperance narrative and the melodrama, true to the antebellum culture in which they were embedded, translated this conception into the all-encompassing, ultimate code word, "respectability."[19] Respectability was more than a matter of certain forms of everyday behavior; the narrative and the melodrama defined it as a matter of business. The respectable man takes advantage of his society's offer of personal freedom in order to further his material progress, which not only supports his family but sustains the wealth of the community. Drinking *is not* respectable—not only because it releases inhibitions and confuses one's sense of propriety, but also because it hinders economic achievement. In spite of their constant, sensationalistic appeal to the emotions, the narratives and the plays express the shattering impact of compulsive drinking in economic terms; the visits to the dramshops waste the capital that the drunkard should be conserving, and when he ceases to provide, his family loses the home that is their bastion and symbol. In other words, the drunkard's moral collapse inevitably produces a corresponding economic catastrophe; the loss of property and financial security becomes the outward sign of the inner waywardness. Once fallen, the drunkard despairs.

The quintessential temperance admonition is that success requires respectability, but its basic assumption is delusory. The equation of sobriety with prosperity assures the audience that the capitalist system is composed entirely of winners, that every man can begin humbly, accumulate capital, and increase both the public and his private prosperity. In the *Manifesto*, Marx accused all bourgeois reformers, which he called "conservative socialists," of wishing for a bourgeoisie without a proletariat, a condition they hoped to achieve by elevating the workers to the middle class; he interpreted this strategy as the futile positing of the possibility of a modern society without its "revolutionary and disintegrating elements." Whether myth or naïve strategy, the scenario served to sustain business, for the clerks were more likely to work hard if they believed that they could rise in the class structure. Yet the actual system required the individual to profit from others' labor and to defeat competitors in the open market; surely his own rise would deny those other aspirants the success and respectability that they, too, seek. The temperance myth offers a utopia—one especially seductive to those in business—where markets and prosperity increase without limit.

Temperance drama became popular in America only after the rise of the regenerative narrative, which offered a more pleasant alternative to the more rigorous censorious version and provided a more congenial model for popular plays. British plays like Douglas Jerrold's *Fifteen Years of a Drunkard's Life* (1828) and T. P. Taylor's *The Bottle* (1847) did follow the censorious pattern and ground the drunkard down as far as imaginatively conceivable, but although these plays were produced in the United States, those actually written in this country emphasize reclamation. Perhaps more important, the regenerative narrative developed in response to the growing numbers of urban artisans and tradesmen who were joining the movement; these people were more likely to support a sensationalistic temperance melodrama than were the New England evangelical Protestants.[20] Gusfield has observed that after the temperance leadership passed down from the patrician class, "parades became a standard form of persuasion, and banners, flags, and outdoor meetings were typical parts of the program" (49). The tone of the movement became more popular and more inclined to ceremony, drama, and emotionalism.

There were eighteen temperance dramas known or believed to have been produced during the antebellum period, and although many more appeared after the Civil War (especially during the period from 1873 to 1879, doubtless reflecting the enthusiasm associated with the founding of the Women's Christian Temperance Union in 1874), some were intended as parlor dramas or didactic dialogues, and none achieved the notoriety of such antebellum standouts as *The Drunkard* or William W. Pratt's 1858 adaptation of *Ten Nights in a Bar-Room*.[21] Moreover, *The Drunkard*, first produced at the Boston Museum on February 12, 1844, may be the earliest American temperance drama still extant.[22] There is little doubt that the play was popular; Harry Watkins, an actor, claimed that the Boston production racked up 130 performances during 1844–45, and P. T. Barnum recalled that his 1850 production drew not only the usual theatre audience but also significant numbers of "the most respectable people" in New York, and that thousands— many of them men whose wives brought them to the Museum for this purpose— signed the pledge that he kept at the box office (Skinner and Skinner 70; Barnum 264–65). [23]

THE DRUNKARD

In trying to employ the techniques of those who had produced the narratives, the temperance playwrights faced an obstacle. Even if they presented the play as reportage, generic speculation, or testimonial, the presence of actors on a stage, working within the conventions of antebellum theatre and the expectations of the audience, added a fictional layer that was difficult to ignore and that diluted the "truth" of the piece in spite of the actuality of performance.[24] For *The Drunkard*, playwright W. H. Smith ameliorated the problem by playing the role of the drunkard himself and apparently letting it be known that he was a reformed drinker who had signed the pledge and "was playing his own life" (Skinner and Skinner 70). The play thus became a sort of clumsy autobiographical documentary.

Like many melodramas of the period, *The Drunkard* employs a mode that I shall call "exegetical representation."[25] The technique combines elements of pageant and lecture as the characters do not enact their roles as much as demonstrate them for the audience, and the asides and soliloquies are only the most obvious means for constructing the action even as it unfolds. This mode is not a matter of theatrical naïveté or ineptitude, even though it may seem so to those who judge all representation according to the practices of psychological realism. Neither is it an inspired prefiguration of Bertolt Brecht's alienation effect, although both Brecht and the temperance dramatists communicated for didactic purposes. Exegetical representation is more the consequence of expectations borne out of the American traditions of stump speeches, revivalist sermons, and schoolroom lessons. The primary purpose is to galvanize the audience into accepting the message and acting upon it; the æsthetic of performance is only a by-product.

In the opening moments of the play, Smith introduces both the heroine as an embodiment of virtue, and the villain as virtue's bane. Old Middleton has died and bequeathed to his son, Edward, a cottage that he had been renting to the widowed Mrs. Wilson, who now worries that her home will be sold and that Mary, her grown daughter, "will be left exposed to the thousand temptations of life, a penniless orphan." With these opening lines, Smith presents the women as the appropriate and deserving objects of the audience's regard and sympathy, the help-less and innocent victims of events outside their control. He then introduces the evil, conniving Lawyer Cribbs, who (we later learn), seeks to avenge himself on Middleton's father, who "detected me in an act of vile atrocity" but pardoned, pitied, and (so he thinks) despised him.[26] This is the only rationale Smith offers for Cribbs's irredeemable wickedness, and throughout the play, he presents the lawyer as a consummate artist of deceit and trickery, a formidable villain who could corrupt all but the strongest.

The lawyer ascribes Old Middleton's recent financial trials to "bad speculations, unlucky investments, false friends," but also happens to mention that he himself was one of the dead man's trusted advisors (281). Smith therefore seems to absolve the unfortunate by defining disaster as the product of unseen, ineffable forces, but also presents Cribbs, as villain, as the agent of depreciation. Cribbs somewhat judgmentally describes Edward as "a gay young man . . . fond of the world, given somewhat to excess . . . giddy, wild, and reckless," and protests his reluctance as he advises the women to move as soon as is convenient, suggesting Boston as a likely prospect for relocation. This interaction establishes the women's sweet gull-ibility while conveying Cribbs's hypocrisy and duplicity to the audience, and it sets the precedent of utterances that certain characters may interpret one way while the audience, assumed to be more critical, may interpret another.

Mrs. Wilson has saved thirty dollars to buy winter fuel, but she owes rent and so advises Mary to see Edward and "give him the money, and tell him your sad story. . . . [H]owever wild a youth may be, when abroad among his associates, no gentleman ever insulted a friendless and unprotected woman" (282). The decision and its rationale serve to reinforce the women as not only virtuous but also assuming virtue in others.

Once alone, Cribbs keeps no secrets from the audience, referring to "that in-terview of mock sympathy and charity" and resolving to see the women evicted in revenge for some unspecified "wrongs" done him by the late Mr. Wilson. Hiding and watching as Mary sets off to see Edward, Cribbs refers to him as "this dissipated collegian" and expresses fear that "such a man can have no pity for the children of poverty, misfortune's suppliants for shelter beneath the roof of his cottage" (283). Mary sees the young man approaching and hides in the bushes while Edward assures Cribbs that he would not think of evicting the women.

I cannot think of depriving them of a home, dear to them as the apple of their eyes—to send them forth from the flowers which they have reared, the vines which they have trained in their course—a place endeared to them by tender domestic recollections, and past remembrances of purity and religion. (283)

He brushes off Cribbs's attempts to discredit the women's value as tenants, and then utterly scorns the lawyer's roguish implication that Edward wants to keep Mary in the cottage to ensure her accessibility. He demands to know whether Cribbs realizes that the "poor girl" has neither father nor brother; he protests his respect for the lawyer's "gray hairs" but assures him that had his father, that paragon of old age,

> heard you utter such foul sentences to his son; had he heard you tell me to enter, like a wolf, this fold of innocence, and tear from her mother's arms the hope of her old age, he would have forgotten the winters that had dried the pith within his aged limbs, seized you by the throat, and dashed you prostrate to the earth, as too foul a carcass to walk erect and mock the name of man. . . . [B]egone; your hot, lascivious breath cannot mingle with the sweet odor of these essenced wild flowers. Your raven voice will not harmonize with the warblings of these heavenly songsters, pouring forth their praises to the Almighty power, who looks with horror on your brutal crime. (283–84)

At that, Mary rushes from the woods to ask for mercy for Cribbs, who cannot stand to see her tears and exits, telling the audience that "I'll be terribly revenged for this." She offers Edward the rent, but he advises her to keep it as a portion of her dowry and, first apologizing for speaking so plainly, describes the special qualities that he has already noticed in her.

> The charm of mental excellence, noble sentiment, filial piety. These are the beauties that render you conspicuous above all the maidens I have seen. These are the charms which bind captive the hearts of men. I speak plainly, for I speak honestly, and when I ask you to keep that money as a portion of your dowry, need I say into whose hands I would like to have it fall at last. (284)

She is overwhelmed, but invites him to visit the cottage, which he describes as "a casket, invaluable for the jewel it contained."

This first presentation of Edward works against Cribbs's unflattering construction of him and presents him as an upstanding young man in the best sentimental tradition. He cultivates unlimited respect for the domestic ideal and champions the purity of womanhood even while urging his respect for age and proclaiming his filial piety. When Mary rushes on, his actions suit his words as he not only refuses to take any advantage of her but declares the most honorable possible intentions.

They marry and declaim their bliss in extravagant terms.

> EDWARD: Dearest Mary, ah, now indeed, my own; words are too poor, too weak, to express the joy, the happiness that agitates my heart. Ah, dear, dear wife, may each propitious day that dawns upon thy future life, but add another flower to the rosy garland that now encircles thee.

> MARY: Thanks, Edward, my own loved husband, thy benison is echoed from my inmost heart. (288–89)

Years pass, and Edward and Mary have a little daughter, which not only fulfills their marriage according to the domestic conventions, but also provides an object for audience sympathy even more poignant than Mary herself. One day, however, a local farmer remarks to a friend that Edward had missed church that Sunday and had been noticed that afternoon in a tavern. We next see him, "dress rather shabby," asking for brandy in a country barroom; Cribbs has inveigled himself into Edward's confidence and started him drinking, so the pattern of temptation and dissolution has already begun. In spite of Edward's halfhearted protests, the landlord and Cribbs press him with whiskey (his reluctance and their insistence serve to shift culpability off of his shoulders) until he is drinking Cribbs's health and calling for drinks for all present. He picks a fight, the other man knocks him down, and William, Edward's foster-brother, runs in to take him, now ashamed, home to Mary.[27]

Cribbs is pleased that his scheme is working so well, and hides to hear Edward articulate his self-loathing, but also his continuing weakness, in a soliloquy.

> Is this to be the issue of my life? Oh, must I ever yield to the fell tempter, and bending like a weak bulrush to the blast, still bow my manhood lower than the brute? Why, surely I have eyes to see, hands to work with, feet to walk, and brain to think, yet the best gifts of Heaven I abuse, lay aside her bounties, and with my own hand, willingly put out the light of reason. . . . Oh, how my poor brain burns! my hand trembles! my knees shake beneath me! I cannot, will not appear before them thus; a little, a very little will revive and strengthen me. . . . Now, for my hiding place. Oh! the arch cunning of the drunkard!

He goes to his hiding place, brings out a bottle, looks around, and drinks while Cribbs "exults."[28]

> So, so, it relieves! it strengthens! oh, glorious liquor! Why did I rail against thee? Ha, ha! [*Drinks and draws bottle*] All gone! all! Of what use the casket when the jewel's gone? (293)

Because in his first scene Edward described Mary as a jewel in a casket, the echo suggests that the bottle has displaced her in his regard. Cribbs advises Edward to sell the cottage to raise the money he needs, but he clings to the facts that his father built it and his family now lives there, and consequently indicates that his fall is not yet complete.

> [T]o take the warm nest from that mourning bird and her young, to strip them of all that remains of hope or comfort, to make them wanderers in the wide world, and for what? To put a little pelf into my leprous hands, and then squander it for rum. (294)

Cribbs persuades him to visit his house for a little brandy, telling the audience, "He's lost."

Mary and Julia, her little girl, are clean and neat, but dressed very poorly. This was virtually a formula treatment of the drunkard's family, based on the theory that outward show was an accurate expression of inner character; no matter how impoverished, they maintained appearances and their self-respect to the best of their abilities. Julia wants to know why Mary is crying and why Edward was too sick that morning to eat his breakfast. Mary cannot bear to answer her and retreats into her sick mother's room saying, "Oh, *Religion!* sweet solace of the wretched heart! Support me! aid me, in this dreadful trial!" Edward returns, drunk and singing. He has slipped and fallen against the elm tree that his father had planted on the day that he was born, and in a fit of pique, he chopped it down, protesting hysterically, "Why should it flourish when I am lost forever? Why should it lift its head to smiling Heaven while I am prostrate?" (295) There is a groan offstage, and Mary discovers that her mother has died. Aghast and blaming himself, Edward decides to leave, tearing himself away from Mary's frantic pleas, insisting that "madness is my strength; my brain is liquid flame." He still knows right from wrong, but still cannot help himself, and sinks further yet.

The scene shifts to New York, where Cribbs gives Edward a dollar and satisfies the conventional temperance dogma by advising the audience, "Before sundown he's a few yards nearer his grave" (296).[29] The lawyer assures him that Mary and Julia are thriving back at the village, thinking of him only to pity him and wish that he could become respectable. Edward wonders "how can one become respectable, without a cent in his pocket, or a whole garment on his wretched carcass?" Since this was one question that no temperance narrative ever addressed in pragmatic terms, Cribbs invites him to forge Arden Rencelaw's name to a check for five thousand dollars. Edward is shocked; he has not and will not sink low enough to contrive deliberate injury against another.

> What! forgery? and on whom? The princely merchant! the noble philanthropist! the poor man's friend! the orphan's benefactor! Out and out on you for a villain, and coward! . . . Wretch as I am, by the world despised, shunned and neglected by those who should save and succor me, I would sooner perish on the first dunghill—than that my dear child should blush for her father's crimes. Take back your base bribe, miscalled charity; the maddening drink that I should purchase with it, would be redolent of sin, and rendered still more poisonous by your foul hypocrisy. (296)

Cribbs is furious, but predicts that Edward will change his mind when he is starving. Edward, awash in self-pity, rushes off to trade his handkerchief for the brandy that he craves.

Mary is neither flourishing nor living in the village; she has demonstrated her loyalty by coming to New York to find Edward, and is living in "a wretched garret" that, according to the stage directions, "indicates want and poverty." She is cold, tired, and hungry, sewing on "slop-work" in order to feed Julia. She prays that if Edward were restored to her, she could bear anything, but she worries over her daughter.

> [S]he was fortunate to-day, sweet lamb, while walking in the street in search of a few shavings, she became benumbed with cold. She sat down upon some steps, when a boy moved with compassion, took from his neck a handkerchief, and placed it upon hers; *the mother of that boy is blessed.* (298)

The boy gave Julia a few cents to buy a loaf of bread, half of which lies on the table to tempt Mary's hunger. She refuses to eat it, for to do so would be to rob her child. Cribbs visits to suggest that she change her lodgings and to try to persuade her to forget Edward, assuring her that other women, not so respectable, are willing to accept his presents and do not mind the liberties a man might take. Mary is horrified.

> Man, man, why dost thou degrade the form and sense the *Great One* has bestowed upon thee by falsehood? Gaze on the sharp features of that child, where famine has already set her seal, look on the hollow eyes, and the care-worn form of the hapless being that brought her into life, then if you have the heart, further insult the helpless mother, and the wretched wife. (299)

She rejects all of Cribbs's slurs on Edward's character and behavior, insisting that he is merely weak. Then Cribbs urges his own affection for her and tries to take her hand. In the following dialogue, Cribbs reveals himself as the ultimate sentimental horror, the man who would use his strength not to protect but to force himself—the word "rape" could hardly be mentioned—on a woman, while Mary both overtly interprets his actions and declaims the conventional domestic vision of female honor.

> MARY: Wretch! [*Throws him off*] Have you not now proved yourself a slanderer, and to effect your own vile purposes? But know, despicable wretch, that my poor husband, clothed in rags, covered with mire, and lying drunk at my feet, is a being whose shoes you are not worthy to unloose.
> CRIBBS: Nay, then, proud beauty, you shall know my power—'tis late, you are unfriended, helpless, and thus—[*he seizes her, child screams*]
> MARY: Help! mercy! [*She struggles*] (299)

William runs in to protect Mary and insult Cribbs on behalf of the audience.

> You're a bad case of villainy versus modesty and chastity, printed in black letters, and bound in calf. . . . Nature made a blunder. She had a piece of refuse garbage, she intended to form into a *hog*, made a mistake, gave it your *shape*, and sent it into the world to be miscalled man. (299)

He evicts the lawyer and takes Mary and Julia to a comfortable boardinghouse where he is staying.

Bereft of coat and hat, Edward has been sleeping on the ground near a tavern.

The landlord comes looking for his horse, and the two argue over their relative claim to respectability. The landlord tells Edward that though he may have been respectable once, like Lucifer, he has fallen beyond reclamation, and Edward serves the standard ideology by casting the blame back in his face; rum sellers may have been invited to Washingtonian meetings, but only in order to change occupations.

> You speak as if you were not the common poisoner of the whole village. . . . Eternal curses on you! Had it not been for your infernal poison shop in our village, I had been still a man—the foul den, where you plunder the pockets of your fellow, where you deal forth death in tumblers, and from whence goes forth the blast of ruin over the land, to mildew the bright hope of youth, to fill the widow's heart with agony, to curse the orphan, to steal the glorious mind of man, to cast them from their high estate of honest pride, and make them—such as I. (300–01)

He begs the landlord for brandy and begins to throttle him as William runs in to break them up. Edward writhes on the ground in delirium.

> Here, here, friend, take it off, will you—these snakes, how they coil round me. Oh! how strong they are—there, don't kill it, no, no, don't kill it, give it brandy, poison it with rum, that will be a judicious punishment, that would be justice, ha, ha! justice! ha, ha! . . . [I]f the globe turns round once more, we shall slide from its surface into eternity. Ha, ha! great idea. A boiling sea of wine, fired by the torch of fiends! ha! ha! (301)

This delirium tremens scene became one of the play's principal attractions and may have carried the morbid fascination of novelty. According to Rorabaugh, delirium tremens did not even appear in America until the 1820s, and the typical victim was subject to hallucinations that expressed an uncontrollable fear of persecution—that someone was trying to kill him, that snakes or rats were chasing him, or that the devil was coming to claim his soul (169–72).[30] Edward's fit not only reflected an actuality that some spectators may have witnessed and others were eager to see, it provided an opportunity for a bit of bravura acting in the most sensational style.

William goes for help, and just as Edward is about to drink a lethal dose of poison, Rencelaw enters to prevent him. At this point, the drama—like most temperance theatricals—becomes a modern morality play, with Rencelaw contending against Cribbs's influence for mastery over Edward's soul.[31] Rencelaw introduces himself as "one of those whose life and labors are passed in rescuing their fellow-men from the abyss into which you have fallen." He tells Edward that he, too, was once a drunkard, but took the pledge that he now administers to "those who would once more become an ornament to society and a blessing to themselves and those around them" (302). The eleventh-hour entrance of Edward's savior discourages the audience from considering genuine solutions to the problem and instead fosters the belief that change in fortune, for good or ill, is outside anyone's control. At the same time, his demand that Edward free himself through an act of will locates the responsibility in the individual. Rencelaw is an agent of the dominant ideology, come as deus ex machina to restore Edward and his world to their proper, if ambiguous, state.[32]

We next see Edward in Rencelaw's house, dressed decently, looking well, reunited with his family, and full of gratitude.

> Oh! what joy can equal the bright sensations of a thinking being, when redeemed from that degrading vice; his prisoned heart beats with rapture; his swelling veins bound with vigor; and with tremulous gratitude, he calls on the Supreme Being for blessings on his benefactor.

Edward's conversion is actually somewhat mild in comparison with those of later stage drunkards, but he sets the pattern.[33] There is little in the way of transition; we have little sense of time passing, and the transformation seems to be an instantaneous result of accepting Rencelaw's help, remembering his duty to God, and renouncing the bottle altogether.

Meanwhile, Cribbs attempts to swindle Rencelaw with his forgery scheme, but William sees him pay fifty cents to a street boy to deliver the check, and later informs Rencelaw. The lawyer returns to the village, but William helps the police apprehend him. Among other crimes, Cribbs had forged a false will for Edward's grandfather and thus inherited much of his property, but now the true will is discovered, so the family fortune falls to Edward. Although the cliché Victorian ethic holds that success requires both virtue and industry as demonstrations of worth, Edward has had success thrust upon him without earning it, a resolution that clarifies the melodramatic pattern of return to an order that is offered as normal, no matter what events have intervened. Cribbs, on the other hand, refuses to repent: "I have lived a villain—a villain let me die." His refusal to change conveys the same message as Edward's embrace of the pledge; that is, the individual can be what he wishes to be. The restoration of the hero and the punishment of the villain make the case for determinism, but the emphasis on will creates the illusion of choice.

The play closes in a way that clarifies the antebellum use of the tableau to express a theory of personal and social change. The action finishes in the cottage, "everything denoting peace and tranquil happiness" and now elegantly furnished, where Mary is sewing and Julia sings "Home, Sweet Home" to Edward's flute. In the final image, Edward sits at the table praying, one hand on the Bible and the other pointing to heaven, with Mary standing by his shoulder and Julia kneeling at his feet. It is not a change of circumstances as much as a restoration, and its stasis recalls George Cruikshank's illustrations on the subject of temperance, each image capturing a level in the drunkard's decline. In both the engravings and the play, people move from moment to moment—from image to image—and each moment seems both fixed, in that the artist or playwright catches and holds it, and kinetic, in that the representation is composed of signs and icons that refer to the allegedly inevitable consequences of the present action. From either perspective, the vision is deterministic, which made it eminently suitable for antebellum melodrama in general and for the antebellum temperance message in particular. Moreover, the virtual synonymy between illustration and stage representation reinforces the idea of a theatrical æsthetic that seeks not to "live" the action (as we might in a typical contemporary "realistic" play) but rather to illustrate or demonstrate both the action and its significance, especially its moral point.

THE OPERATIONS OF DISCOURSE

The heyday of *The Drunkard* continued well past the 1840s; Moody estimates that there were at least 450 productions across the nation from 1844 to 1878 (*Dramas* 279).[34] The temperance movement, however, turned its attention away from the concepts of suasion and individual moral choice, and toward political action aimed at the rum seller; that is, legal prohibition. In 1851, the state of Maine passed a law outlawing the sale of liquor and revoking all existing licenses; while earlier antilicensing legislation had required that officers prove a sale in order to obtain a conviction, this measure empowered them to secure warrants for search and seizure of contraband (Tyrrell 254–55). From 1852 to 1855, twelve northern states and territories passed laws modeled after Maine's, inspired partly by the intransigence of immigrant workers, mostly Irish and German, who persisted in drinking and contributed to the fear of disorder that had inspired the temperance movement a generation earlier (Tyrrell 297–98).[35] To focus on the rum sellers was to relinquish the struggle over the individual and assign guilt, once and for all, to the trade and to the (faceless) society that made it respectable and offered it legal protection. The reformers had realized that addiction was a compelling force and that willpower alone was sometimes inadequate; to be saved, the truly lost would have to be cut off from the supply at the source (Dannenbaum 81, 83). Furthermore, passing legislation against the trade was easier than trying to wean thousands of drinkers away from temptation; enforcing the law was a different matter, but at least one had the satisfaction of seeing it written into the books. However, the Maine Law may have been too radical, and so caused a backlash of opposition by drinkers (both immigrant and native) and sellers. Enforcement also proved difficult, and most of the states modified or repealed their legislation during the 1850s and 1860s as enthusiasm for political temperance declined (Tyrrell 282, 304).

T. S. Arthur published *Ten Nights in a Bar-Room* in 1854, just in time to promote the Maine Law and ride on its popularity. An honest miller named Slade sells his business to buy a local inn, which becomes the center of all idleness and vice in the village. Joe Morgan grumbles against Slade, the landlord, for taking his last dime, conveying the conflicting message that his drinking and his profligacy disgust him, but that he is compelled, beyond his understanding and control, by the opportunity that Slade offers. Joe reforms, buys the old mill, and dedicates himself to running it more profitably than ever, but Slade, his family, and his cronies slide downhill, and the novel ends as the good people of Cedarville resolve to outlaw taverns. Although Pratt's close adaptation retained Arthur's pro–Maine Law message, by the time the play appeared in 1858, faith in political action had already began to fade. Other plays of the latter 1850s were even farther out of step; both *The Drunkard's Warning* (1856) and *The Fruits of the Wine-Cup* (1858) embraced a straight Washingtonian line. Both were commercial productions—the first at Barnum's Museum and the second at the Bowery—and it is likely that the managers waited until radical ideology had become conventional before risking their investment. The leaders of the movement may have regarded the plays as alien to their sensibilities, but the managers apparently made use of a ready opportunity to tap into their audience's fears.

Antebellum temperance melodrama validates middle-class ideology even while it fosters social delusion. It affirms the sentimental agenda, the propositions that each individual is essentially good and well-intentioned, that personal industry and righteousness will perfect the individual, and that the health of the state depends on individual reform. By defining respectability as virtue and therefore absolute and unimpeachable, the narrative bolsters the hegemony of the system and of those who control it. Specifically, it asserts that drink causes most, if not all, social evils, a reductionist position that precludes investigation.

As opposing metaphors for a vision of society, the temperance plays offer sobriety and drunkenness, which become the principal constituents that the melodrama, as it must, forces apart until they seem irreconcilably polarized, but then sustains in coexistence within its structure. While earlier temperance dogma accepted moderate drinking, by the time the plays appeared, teetotalism was the only sanctioned doctrine, so with the reforming drunkard's rise from the gutter up to the affluence that the middle class craved, the narrative implies that disgraceful poverty and wealthy respectability are the only two options. This is, obviously, a binary opposition, one that privileges sobriety and defines drunkenness as a departure from the norm. Yet because the narrative expends such extraordinary effort to reclaim the man who fell so easily, it seems to indicate that man will naturally gravitate to indulgent sensualism, and that only constant attention will keep him balanced on the edge of respectability. The narrative validates its fear better than its hope.

I have been presenting a deconstruction of temperance melodrama that may seem to define it as a theatrical conspiracy to keep the many happy so the few could profit; this would be what Eagleton has called a "vulgar Marxist" analysis (*Marxism* 14). Yet I agree with him that there can be many factors that mediate between the system and the text, and also with Chantal Mouffe, who has pointed out that a society divides on more than economic class lines, suggesting a paradigm that includes criteria related to gender, faith, and ethnicity (89–90). In antebellum society, economic motivations competed with matters of religion, social status, nationalism, and gender for the influencing of people's behavior. I suggest that the ideological uses of popular literature or entertainment are seldom self-conscious and never clear—in spite of the implied claim of exegetical representation, that the play makes a precise argument—and, more important, that there is an emotional component to social loyalty and consequent action that pure Marxism, insofar as it is a scientific method, may not be able to take into account. The temperance narrative succeeded not necessarily because it was able to address its audience's actual status, but because it was able to resonate with the audience's aspirations and dreams; the solera metaphor of temperance rhetoric implies a conflation of classes, if not in fact, in the imaginations of those for whom it was produced. In other words, we process experience according to our self-image (including our perception of our future potential), not according to a supposedly objective assessment of our condition by some outside party.

In the famous delirium tremens scene of *The Drunkard*, when Edward Middleton writhes on the ground and screams at his hallucination, he defines himself as subject and the chimerical snake as object, but it is only an apparition, part of his own imagination. The antebellum temperance reformers looked for an object of blame and sought to define rum as outside of their society, external, and therefore a viable villain. Yet they could not poison the snake with rum, because his mouth was full; he was swallowing his own tail.

From John P. Jewett's illustrated edition of Stowe's *Uncle Tom's Cabin; or, Life Among the Lowly* (1863). Original design by Billings, engraved by Baker and Smith. (Courtesy of the Huntington Library, San Marino, California.)

4

Uncle Tom's Cabin (1852) and the Politics of Race

The object of these sketches is to awaken sympathy and feeling for the African race, as they exist among us; to show their wrongs and sorrows, under a system so necessarily cruel and unjust as to defeat and do away the good effects of all that can be attempted for them, by their best friends, under it.

—Stowe, *Uncle Tom's Cabin* 9

These negroes are, as a race, inferior in mental and moral force to the white race with whom they live. . . . As the white race is the permanently strong, and the negro race the permanently weak, it follows that so long as the two races live together, the negro must be the servant of the white. . . . [T]he white race are the natural rulers. . . .

—Review of *Uncle Tom's Cabin, North American Review*

I's knows I's wicked!

—Topsy, in Aiken's *Uncle Tom's Cabin*

IN THE STUDY of any of the theatrical versions of Harriet Beecher Stowe's *Uncle Tom's Cabin*, one of the central issues is the performance of race. America is a racist society, a fact that reveals the ideology of America as a hypocrisy, yet an incontrovertible truth in a nation that has not yet moved beyond the phenomenon of two-and-a-half centuries of slavery—of whites legally and systematically subjugating blacks. The politics of race pervades every aspect of our culture, and of all the juxtapositions, the division between black and white is most devastatingly and perhaps irreconcilably profound; the very semantics of the terms reveals an underlying conception of absolute opposition. The dominant white majority appropriated the native American by inventing the Indian and incorporating it into American myth, but the alienation of black from white, the fundamental differential relation between the two, makes even such a hegemonic rapprochement virtually impossible. To stage *Uncle Tom's Cabin* is to perform America's conception of race in the context of relative access to social power and cultural expression; it is to represent black and white in relation to each other. The story depicts racial

difference; or, more accurately, it conveys a white vision of blackness, and a somewhat less self-conscious vision of whiteness. The white/black binarism seems to
invite classic melodramatic treatment, but while neither the novel nor any of the
plays translates it into a simple equation with good and evil, it remains a starkly
drawn index of the division of America.

Antebellum white writers, both pro- and antislavery, agreed that the whites
were responsible for the care of the blacks. Proslavery advocates tended to link
this belief with paternalism and argue that the slaves were not competent enough
to be freed, while antislavery activists insisted that the only appropriate exercise
of the whites' responsibility was to free the slaves and restore their humanity in
the liberal tradition. Either way, the sense of responsibility enforced the necessity
of choosing a course of action. To a large extent, *Uncle Tom's Cabin*, as novel or
as play, represents the experience of white sensibility confronting that burden of
choice.

The best-known dramatization was written in two parts by George L. Aiken,
a young actor, for the company run by his cousin's husband, George C. Howard.[1]
The first part, which ended with Little Eva's death, opened at the Troy Museum
on September 27, 1852 and closed October 25. The second, entitled *The Death
of Uncle Tom; or, The Religion of the Lowly*, opened on October 26. The company
then combined the two parts into the complete play, running it without the customary afterpiece from November 15 through December 1. A. H. Purdy brought
the play and some of the Troy company to his National Theatre in New York City
on July 18, 1853, and the production ran for 325 performances through May 13,
1854.[2] Like all the Uncle Tom plays, Aiken's was an attempt to capitalize on the
audience that Stowe had created, and with the other productions, it repaid the original
author by generating increased interest in the novel.[3] The order of the experience
became untraceable; one could not see the play without reference, direct or by
reputation, to the novel, and vice versa, so of the discourse in which Aiken's play
was embedded, the dominant text was the play's immensely popular source.

In any form, the story enjoyed an astounding popularity—the novel sold over
three hundred thousand copies during its first year of publication, and attendance
at theatrical productions during the 1850s alone may have surpassed that figure—
but as we gaze back to the antebellum era, the foreshortening of our vision and
our perception of the Uncle Tom myth may tempt us to find in the story's celebrity
an indication of a high degree of sympathy between its audience and the emancipation we may now regard as eventually inevitable.[4] Yet there are certain pitfalls
in such an assumption. First of all, the novel and the plays were not necessarily
identical, or even similar, in their presentations of slavery and in their depictions
of the nature and relationships of black and white Americans. Second, we cannot
assume that the antebellum audience responded to the same features of the myth
that we now find significant or even salient. Third, we must acknowledge certain
disparities between the groups participating in the various relevant aspects of ante-

bellum culture. Whatever else it was, or is, the novel was part of the tradition of sentimental fiction, written by a woman for what the author herself may have presupposed to be a predominantly female audience, while the evidence that we typically examine to take the pulse of the era—the lees of politics, society, and business—represents, almost entirely, the work of men in a community where men retained all direct political power and most of the social control. As for the plays, their presenters faced a dissonance between audience and message; that is, those Northerners most likely to support an antislavery program were probably disinclined, because of their religious and moral conventions, to attend the theatre, while the typical antebellum play-goer probably exemplified the northern majority view and resisted slavery only insofar as it threatened to spread and upset the economic equilibrium.[5] As both story and polemic, the novel itself was, more than most, embedded in the social discourse of its time, a dialectic of North and South, of antislavery and proslavery, of abolitionism and gradualism, of liberalism and racism, of extension and compromise, of sentiment and pragmatism, and of idealism and expediency. My task, over a century later, is to offer a reconstruction of how the cultural environment might have shaped both creation and perception, to assess the rhetorical currents, and to suggest how antebellum audiences might have perceived the operation of Aiken's play.[6]

THE SLAVE SYSTEM

Stowe expanded the politics of race to encompass the entire process of American society, identifying slavery as its salient sin and hurling a challenge at her readers with her principal polemic thrust: that slavery is neither the sum of individual moral aberrations nor a regional peculiarity, but a social system that carries and controls everyone who promotes or condones it. Her character St. Clare reduces the situation to the strong taking advantage of the weak simply because they are able to do so:

> [B]ecause my brother Quashy is ignorant and weak, and I am intelligent and strong,—because I know how, and *can* do it,—therefore, I may steal all he has, keep it, and give him only such and so much as suits my fancy. . . . Because I don't like work, Quashy shall work. . . . Quashy shall do my will, and not his, all the days of his mortal life, and have such chance of getting to heaven, at last, as I find convenient. . . . Talk of the *abuses* of slavery! Humbug! The *thing itself* is the essence of all abuse! . . . And he who goes the furthest, and does the worst, only uses within limits the power that the law gives him. (261–62)

St. Clare agrees with Alfred, his twin brother, that both the southern planter and the English capitalist appropriate the lower classes "body and bone, soul and spirit, to their use and convenience," and that the "slave-owner can whip his refractory slave to death,—the capitalist can starve him to death" (269). The comparison reinforces Stowe's contention that slavery is more than a legal eccentricity.

Yet the horror of the slave system is that it not only dehumanizes the black man, it also corrodes the white man's soul. First of all, ownership inevitably corrupts any master; the slave system makes "every individual owner an irresponsible despot," and even if "men of honor" survive its influence, "the ruffian, the brutal, the debased," who form the majority, can "own just as many slaves as the best and purest" (513–14).[7] Stowe's "men of honor" are St. Clare and Shelby, but while the former is too fastidious to drive slaves on a plantation, he cannot quite bring himself to free his servants, and the latter incurs debts and so must sell both Tom and Harry in spite of his wife's dismay and Eliza's anguish. Shelby's situation is a melodramatic cliché; Stowe reveals nothing about the nature or cause of his embarrassment and so makes him seem like a helpless victim of Business as an impersonal and mysterious force.[8] Not only are these "men of honor" unable to palliate the abuse of their own slaves, they cannot interfere in the treatment of others at the hands of the "ruffians." St. Clare assures Ophelia that "a man of honorable and humane feelings" can only "shut his eyes" and "harden his heart" before the inevitable reality that "a whole class,—debased, uneducated, indolent, provoking" will be bound over, unconditionally, to "people who have neither consideration nor self-control" (258–59). One of Legree's fellow travelers on the Red River, disgusted by the planter's brutality, tells another passenger that

> it is you considerate, humane men, that are responsible for all the brutality and outrage wrought by these wretches; because, if it were not for your sanction and influence, the whole system could not keep foot-hold for an hour. If there were no planters except such as that one . . . the whole thing would go down like a mill-stone. It is your respectability and humanity that licenses and protects his brutality. (395–96)

If ownership corrupts, then so does the trade itself. Stowe presents Haley, a slave trader, as the inevitable product of his profession and insists that to play such a role in such a system would degrade anyone, caustically suggesting that anyone, "with proper effort and cultivation," could grow callous to human suffering and reach "that stage of Christian and political perfection which has been recommended by some preachers and politicians of the north," and that "it is the great object of recent efforts to make our whole northern community used to them, for the glory of the Union" (157). Yet Stowe blames not the trader but the "enlightened, cultivated, intelligent man" who upholds public sentiment and supports the system that creates the trader's profession (161).[9] This is, perhaps, the most disquieting message of the Uncle Tom story; that the slave system will inexorably poison the whites involved in it, eroding or denying those cherished qualities that they associate with their whiteness. St. Clare points out that his brother embraces the concept of a toiling lower class as requisite to an upper class that "acquires leisure and wealth for a more expanded intelligence," but St. Clare argues that the system degrades the blacks, whose "vicious, improvident, degraded" presence in turn degrades the whites:

> They are in our houses; they are the associates of our children, and they form
> their minds faster than we can; for they are a race that children always will
> cling to and assimilate with. . . . We might as well allow the smallpox to run
> among them, and think our children would not take it, as to let them be
> uninstructed and vicious, and think our children will not be affected by that.
> (269, 272)

St. Clare has anticipated James Baldwin's observation that "the oppressed and the
oppressor are bound together within the same society; they accept the same criteria,
they share the same beliefs, they both alike depend on the same reality" (583).
Mrs. Shelby struggles to reconcile the slave system with her sense of morality
but, when faced with the sale of Tom and Harry, condemns the attempt as futile
and acknowledges slavery as "a curse to the master and a curse to the slave"
that even "kindness, care, and instruction" cannot mitigate (48).

Having established the devastating effect of the slave system on southern whites,
Stowe then insists on the responsibility of the entire American nation, not just the
traders and plantation owners; in the words of William Ingersoll Bowditch, a Garrisonian attorney, "we are a nation of slaveholders!" (126). A sense of guilt inspired
many antislavery advocates; Arnold Buffum, who had helped found the American
Anti-Slavery society, denied any wish to interfere in the affairs of the slaveholding
South, but also insisted that the South not impose the demands of the slave system
on the nation as a whole:

> We complain, that by the action of the national Government, and also of the
> governments of many of the non-Slaveholding States in *support* of Slavery, we
> are made participants in the crime of robbing men of their natural rights—we
> wish to absolve ourselves from such crime. (qtd. in Pease 424)

Stephen Symonds Foster, a radical abolitionist minister, in 1843 offered a similar
interpretation of the national involvement in the slave trade:

> It is a common but mistaken opinion, that to constitute one a slaveholder he
> must be the claimant of slaves. That title belongs alike to the slaveclaimant and
> all those who, by their countenance or otherwise, lend their influence to support
> the slave system. . . . [A]ll who, through their political or ecclesiastical con-
> nexions, aid or countenance the master in his work of death, are slaveholders,
> and as such, are stained with all the moral turpitude which attaches to the man,
> who, by their sanction, wields the bloody lash over the heads of his trembling
> victims, and buries it deep in their quivering flesh. (13)

Stowe contrived part of her New Orleans auction scene to convey the outrage
of the slave trade and to illustrate its national scope. Susan and Emmeline are
sold to pay their bankrupt owner's creditors, the largest being a respectable New
York firm whose senior partner has misgivings but condones the sale anyway
because thirty thousand dollars was "rather too much money to be lost for a principle" (383). Stowe asks her northern readers to consider whether slavery deserves
their protection, and maintains that "the people of the free states have defended,

encouraged, and participated; and are more guilty for it, before God, than the South, in that they have *not* the apology of education or custom" (515). St. Clare points out northern hypocrisy, assuring Ophelia that northern whites dislike blacks more than their southern counterparts and that they "loathe them as you would a snake or a toad" (211). He insists that the pious Northerners would rather send the slaves to Africa and then send missionaries after them rather than bring "the heathen" to their own villages and devote the necessary time, attention, and money to bring about their "education and elevation" (366). He knows that no tradesman would accept his butler as an apprentice, and that no school would board his maidservants.[10]

The whites cannot escape. Whiteness becomes equivalent to depravity, cruelty, and impotence, so to be white is to be damned. "White" is defined as that which oppresses "black," and therefore renounces its own right to humanity. Stowe drives the point home with her depiction of Legree, the worst possible master, a man who would rather use up his slaves—expecting seven years' work (and only that much life) out the hardiest—than care for them. She arranges his outward appearance to express his essence, introducing him as

> a broad, muscular man, in a checked shirt considerably open at the bosom, and pantaloons much the worse for dirt and wear. . . . From the moment that Tom saw him approaching, he felt an immediate and revolting horror at him, that increased as he came near. He was evidently, though short, of gigantic strength. His round, bullet head, large, light-gray eyes, with their shaggy, sandy eye-brows, and stiff, wiry, sun-burned hair, were rather unprepossessing items, it is to be confessed; his large, coarse mouth was distended with tobacco, the juice of which, from time to time, he ejected from him with great decision and explosive force; his hands were immensely large, hairy, sunburned, freckled, and very dirty, and garnished with long nails, in a very foul condition. (387–88)

This portrait terrifies because it is the apotheosis of white America and the harbinger of the future generations, both North and South. Stowe presents Legree as the icon of the white race and so suggests to thousands of readers that they are damned.

The issue of northern involvement reached a political crisis with the passage of the Fugitive Slave Act as part of the Compromise of 1850. Intended to amend and reinforce a similar law passed in 1793 but thereafter largely ignored, the new legislation gave a master the right to "pursue and reclaim" a fugitive slave by "seizing and arresting" the person in question, haling him or her before a court that would hear the case "in a summary manner"—that is, offering no trial by jury—and presenting proof that "the person so arrested does in fact owe service or labor to the person or persons claiming him or her."[11] The fugitive's testimony was specifically disallowed as evidence; only the alleged master's word carried weight, and since he could present it as a deposition, the fugitive could not confront his accuser or cross-examine him. As for other involved parties, the law commanded "all good citizens . . . to aid and assist in the prompt and efficient execution of this law, whenever their services may be required," and specified a fine of up to one thousand dollars and a prison term of up to six months as punishment for anyone hindering the efforts of masters or their agents, harboring or concealing fugitives, helping fugitives to escape, or rescuing fugitives from the custody of their masters. Any "claimant" who anticipated a rescue attempt could file an affidavit to that effect and expect the arresting officer to maintain custody and deliver the fugitive "to the State whence he fled."

The new law provoked outcry. Ralph Waldo Emerson objected to being required to hunt slaves and observed that "slavery was no longer mendicant, but was become aggressive and dangerous" ("Fugitive" 216). He contended that the Constitution, the Supreme Court, the Missouri Compromise, and the sovereignty of free states had all proven inadequate against the onslaught of slavery, and that Daniel Webster's efforts to preserve the Union had, ultimately, failed.

> I fear there is no reliance to be put on any kind or form of covenant, no, not on sacred forms, none on churches, none on bibles. . . . If slavery is good, then is lying, theft, arson, homicide, each and all good, and to be maintained by Union societies. ("Fugitive" 220)

Henry David Thoreau condemned the courts for asking not what was right, but rather what was constitutional, which he described as "a very low and incompetent standard" (103). However, in spite of abolitionists' efforts to aid fugitives and protect free blacks, in spite of citizens being arrested for refusing to help the bounty hunters, and of mobs trying to prevent the return of fugitives, the northern public eventually acquiesced and some even endorsed the new compromise.[12]

This new legislation forced Stowe to reconsider the relationship of faith to law, of God's will to temporal regulation. She related her surprise when she heard of "Christian and humane people" actually cooperating in returning fugitives into slavery (513). Because the legality of slavery made it unassailable in some people's minds, Stowe had to establish that the law itself had subverted higher principles. Unable to conceive of a true Christian who would deny succor to a fugitive, she created the character of Mrs. Bird, who argues that if men like her husband are willing to pass a law admonishing her against helping runaways, then they make a mockery of law itself. She points out that the Bible tells her to feed the hungry and clothe the naked, she refuses to accept the possibility that she could impair the public good by obeying God, and so she concludes, with no hesitation, that she will break the new law as soon as she gets a chance. In other words, to live as a Christian woman, according to the dictates of the Bible and her own conscience, she must violate the law; she becomes, as critic Elizabeth Ammons has observed, a mother who uses the cult of motherhood to challenge the patriarchy rather than reinforce it (163).

The Fugitive Slave Act implicated the North in the slavery issue as never before. Because ordinary people were now legally obligated to help return runaways, they were clearly and specifically involved in supporting the slave system, no matter how much their local legislators might ban slavery, and no matter how much they and their neighbors might speak, write, or pray against it. On a deeper level, the law forced northern whites to acknowledge their relationship with all black Americans. The whites could no longer ignore the blacks as a distant abstraction, nor could they dismiss the racial politics that characterized American culture and inexorably drew in each individual. When Stowe's novel appeared, with the Uncle Tom plays close behind it, the northern populace was too engaged in the problem to view the story lightly.

ABOLITIONISM AND RACISM

The general public, from 1852 to our own time, seems to have regarded Stowe's novel as an abolitionist work, one that so galvanized Northerners that they were willing to go to war. To designate the book in that way reflected both a certain semantic laxity—in that "abolitionist" has been used as an umbrella term for various antislavery views—and a misapprehension of the author's position. Nowhere in the book does Stowe promote an abolitionist program; she recommends colonization while hoping that individual Southerners might emancipate their own slaves and individual Northerners might aid the fugitives. This conservative position may have consoled readers who might otherwise have found her antislavery passion disquieting, but writers in both the North and the South interpreted her antislavery sentiment as directly supportive of abolitionism. Predictably, southern critics attacked the story while southern authors produced a series of "anti-Tom" novels to refute Stowe's depiction of the slave system.[13] In the North, periodicals ranging from the *North American Review* to *The Liberator* read the story as an abolitionist tract.[14]

Likewise, reviews of the Uncle Tom plays emphasized their alleged abolitionist sentiment. The newspapers seem to have overreacted, responding more to the idea of a stage version than the actuality, and sometimes expressing a sense of indignation that thousands of play-goers apparently did not share.[15] To those newspapers who supported the Union above all, even the prospect of an Uncle Tom play was an outrage. Referring to a production (probably of H. C. Conway's version) planned for Boston, the *New Orleans Weekly Picayune* warned its readers that

The stage is to be employed in depicting to the people of the North the whole body of the people of the South as living in a state of profligacy, cruelty and crime—tyrants who fear not God, and cruelly oppress their fellow creatures; and the drama is thus enlisted among the promoters of sectional discord, whose end inevitably would be the disruption of the Union. . . . The tendency of all these anti-slavery demonstrations in the North—abolition novels, abolition lectures, pictorial abolitionism, and now the abuse of the stage to the purposes of

calumny and insult in aid of abolitionism—is to create a more intense international enmity than could ever rage between nations of different languages and
institutions. . . . The success of the attempt must be a dreadful calamity, the source
of innumerable horrors to both sections and both races; and even if it should
not prove to be successful, the attempt itself is a great crime, meriting universal
abhorrence. (" 'Uncle Tom' ")

We might dismiss this as a typical and specifically southern response, but the
New York Herald presented a similar position in a review of Charles Western Taylor's
version, referring to "the pernicious abolition sympathies" of the novel and scolding
Purdy for committing "a serious and mischievous blunder" by producing the piece.
The writer maintained "that any such representation must be an insult to the South"
and assured his readers that Taylor's was "a crude and aggravated affair" that offered

> the most extravagant exhibitions of the imaginary horrors of Southern slavery.
> The negro traders, with their long whips, cut and slash their poor slaves about
> the stage for mere pastime, and a gang of poor wretches, handcuffed to a chain
> which holds them all in marching order, two by two, are thrashed like cattle
> to quicken their pace. Uncle Tom is scourged by the trader, who has bought
> him, for "whining" at his bad luck.

The writer expressed concern that "the audience appears to be pleased with the
novelty, without being troubled about the moral of the story, which is mischievous
in the extreme," and went on to promote the political compromises—including
the Fugitive Slave Law—that had been forged to protect the Union.

> And yet, here in this city—which owes its wealth, population, power, and pros-
> perity, to the Union and the constitution, and this same institution of slavery,
> to a greater degree than any other city in the Union—here we have nightly
> represented, at a popular theatre, the most exaggerated enormities of Southern
> slavery, playing directly into the hands of the abolitionists and abolition kidnappers
> of slaves, and doing their work for them. . . . It is a sad blunder; for when our
> stage shall become the deliberate agent in the cause of abolitionism, with the
> sanction of the public, and their approbation, the peace and harmony of this
> Union will soon be ended.

Yet when Purdy produced Aiken's version, one even more likely to arouse southern
ire, his business prospered. William Lloyd Garrison wrote to his wife that he preferred the Boston production (undoubtedly of Conway's play), but *The Liberator*
gave the National's production of Aiken's play an unqualified rave:

> It is better by one hundred per cent. than the version of the Boston Museum.
> If the shrewdest abolitionist among us had prepared the drama with a view to
> make the strongest anti-slavery impression, he could scarcely have done the work
> better. O, it was a sight worth seeing, those ragged, coatless men and boys in
> the pit (the very *material* of which mobs are made) cheering the strongest and
> the sublimest anti-slavery sentiment! The whole audience was at times melted
> to tears, and I own that I was no exception. . . . I wish every abolitionist in

the land could see this play as I saw it, and exult as I did that, when haughty pharisees will not testify against slavery, the very *stones* are crying out! (" 'Uncle Tom' on the Stage")[16]

A Southerner visited New York, found several thriving productions of *Uncle Tom's Cabin*, and in a piece for the *New Orleans Daily Delta*, drew troubled conclusions regarding northern sentiment:

I see in Southern papers, the suggestion that Uncle Tomism is dead in the North. Such is not the case. The rising generation will be infected by it to an extent no one can foresee, and "the Softs" in politics—which means, literally translated, Uncle Tomites—are of either Whig or Democratic party in political power. A volume could be written upon the Abolition tendencies of the North. The editors of Southern papers should examine behind the scenes of public opinion here, and they would find, in spite of the pro-slavery appearances in Congress, that the real current moves the other way. ("Letter from New York")

While Aiken hardly promoted orthodox abolitionist doctrine, there is a certain resemblance between the rigor of the Garrisonian vision and the clean, well-defined morality that melodrama affirms. Insofar as melodrama cannot help but define evil clearly and in the blackest terms, Aiken's audiences and critics may have discerned, to their pleasure or their distress, the abolitionist mood.

Yet apparently one could cultivate abolitionist sentiment without supporting abolitionist activism. The Quakers founded the first antislavery society even before the Revolution, but it was not until the years following the War of 1812 that the proliferating reform organizations adopted various antislavery positions and fostered the formalization of the movement.[17] The early societies promoted gradual emancipation, a judicious program of reform and legislation that was designed not only to permit time to make a transition from one supply of labor to another, but also to solve the problem of what to do with the freed blacks, a formidable hurdle that stymied some antislavery conservatives and provided a convenient rationale for proslavery advocates. In its review of Stowe's *Uncle Tom's Cabin*, the *North American Review* declared, "To send them away is impossible; to emancipate them, equally so. It would destroy great interests, it would endanger the peace of society, it would be disastrous to themselves" (477). However, there was increasing support for immediate emancipation on the grounds that slavery and its tolerance were sinful, a position that led to the flowering of abolitionism and, in 1831, the founding both of a newspaper, *The Liberator*, edited by Garrison, and of an organization, the New England Anti-Slavery Society, whose Annual Report of 1833 called for immediate cessation of "all title of property in the slaves," for the slave trade to be regarded as a felony, and for the education and employment of the freed blacks ("Extracts" 21).

The abolitionists were the radicals of their time, so perceived by most white Northerners and even by many gradualist antislavery activists, a fact that calls into question the tendency of collective American memory to valorize them as the visionary leaders whose struggle led to the now-hallowed phenomenon of emancipation.[18] *The Liberator*, no matter how compelling or eloquent recent retrospection construes its jeremiad, was actually a relatively obscure journal whose circulation probably never rose above three thousand (a majority of the subscribers being freed blacks), while the more moderate *National Era* boasted a circulation of twenty-five thousand as of 1853 (Dillon 213).[19] Mainstream politicians regarded abolitionists as fanatics. Through the 1840s, the major national political parties did their utmost to avoid the slavery issue, either omitting it from their platforms altogether, offering support for the Missouri Compromise, or referring piously to states' rights, a code phrase that represented their attempt to absolve the federal government of having to act on the slavery question at all. The congressional gag rule against slavery petitions survived from 1836 to 1844. Men like Daniel Webster and Henry Clay, even though they disliked slavery, saw the issue itself as less important than its potential effect as the wedge that could split the Union; in *The Liberator*, Garrison insisted that the maintenance of union with slaveholding states was completely unacceptable, and the slogan "No Union With Slaveholders" appeared on the masthead of every issue. Both the Whigs and the Democrats accepted slavery in the South and supported the Compromise of 1850 in order to avoid dividing their constituencies (Foner 187, 189).[20] Men like Garrison turned Webster's priorities upside down by defining the Union as that which protected and assured certain basic rights with which slavery was unacceptably dissonant. Only the Liberty Party attacked slavery openly, and consequently never won more than 3 percent of the popular vote in a presidential election; when the party split from the Free Democrats in 1852 to demand both abolition and equal rights for free blacks, its support fell to an insignificant level (Foner 139, 187; Blue 246–47).[21]

Antislavery sentiment was not necessarily altruistic and was even, in some cases, an overt expression of racism. Many whites objected to the idea of assimilating millions of freed blacks into white, "mainstream" American society; some feared that if the freed slaves were allowed to remain, either race war or amalgamation—a possibility many dreaded—would inevitably follow (Richards 30–31, 44–45).[22] Merton L. Dillon has pointed out that the abolitionists, no matter how much their mission was aligned with cherished religious and democratic principles, were clearly agitators whose denunciations of the slave system cast guilt on all Americans, whose wish to incorporate black people into society—and even concede them equal participation—threatened certain laborers' job security, and whose insistence that white Americans discard their racial prejudice ran counter to fundamental fears and biases (66–68, 77). Even some of the less racist anti-abolitionists were inclined to express concern over the economic upheaval that would result from divesting the southern plantations of their laborers and then trying to find jobs for the freedmen (Ratner 136). Some publicly denounced abolitionists as fanatics who attacked not only southern slaveholders but Northerners as well, and in 1836, Connecticut banned abolitionist speakers from the pulpits of the Congregationalist churches (Sorin 126). As Lorman Ratner has put it, many in the North found the abolitionist agenda to be "unreasonable, radical, dangerous, and unlawful" (138). During the 1830s, antiabolitionist sentiment reached the point of violence as a mob ran riot through the black neighborhoods of New York City, Garrison barely escaped lynching in Boston, and in Cincinnati (then Stowe's home), the office of the *Philanthropist*, James G. Birney's abolitionist newspaper, was sacked.

For the vast majority of the American public, the genuine antebellum slavery issue was not abolition but extension; this was the question that informed the Missouri Compromise, the Wilmot Proviso, the Compromise of 1850, and the Kansas-Nebraska Act. None of these measures sought to abolish slavery in the South; all attempted to settle the ongoing dispute regarding the spread of slavery into new territories. Yet even opposition to extension was frequently an attempt to serve the interests of the whites rather than the blacks. Antiextension Democrats during the latter 1840s opposed slavery because they saw it as a threat to free labor; they reasoned that employers might prefer to buy slaves than hire wage-earning workers. They believed that very presence of slavery eroded the dignity of honest labor, a position they supported by pointing to the class prejudices of southern society, and those that Stowe herself adopted in *The Key to Uncle Tom's Cabin* (365–66). Some people supported the Wilmot Proviso in hopes of restricting the West to whites only. The Free Soil Party had displaced the Liberty Party with a more moderate antiextension, free-labor platform, but Frederick J. Blue has argued that the Free Soilers attracted some support because the covertly racist aspect of their platform appealed to Northerners who were also inclined to favor discriminatory legislation against blacks (81–82). Dillon reports that even though sympathy for fugitives and hostility toward the slave system seemed to increase during the 1850s, legal proscriptions against free blacks continued (192). Anti-Negro sentiment pervaded the North; even in those New England states that allowed the black man to vote, there was discrimination as well as legislation restricting his employment to menial occupations; Illinois, Indiana, Iowa, and Oregon barred blacks from entering their territory at all (Foner 261). Ironically, therefore, many whites adopted an antislavery position to express their hatred of black people, and they might have found comfort in the fact that not a single one of the slaves in Stowe's novel ends up settling in the North—they remain on their southern plantations, they emigrate to Liberia, or they die.

Given so ambiguous a social and political context, the popularity of the novel and the plays seems inexplicable. If the majority of the potential readers and spectators perceived abolition as unacceptably radical, opposed extension largely from racist motives, and actively discouraged the migration of free blacks to the North, then we might feel compelled to suppose that those who did buy the books and theatre tickets comprised a collection of marginalized minority groups—freed blacks, abolitionists and other reformers of radical leanings, and especially women who disagreed with the male direction of society but could do little to change it. Yet both the novel and the plays offered the opportunity to cherish abolitionist sentiment without actually subscribing to a strict, abolitionist agenda, and so tapped into a much larger audience.

THE COLONIZATION MOVEMENT

Stowe did offer explicit support for one organized antislavery program. The great conundrum of the antislavery movement was the disposition of the freed blacks, and through the example of the Harris clan, Stowe promotes colonization—the transportation of freed slaves to Africa, there to form a new nation. This was hardly a new idea; similar proposals had appeared as early as the 1770s and attracted the support of Thomas Jefferson, and in 1816, Robert Finley, a Presbyterian minister and schoolmaster, offered the rationale that colonization would free the slaves to realize their potential and form a civilized, Christian society (Staudenraus 15–22). The fulfillment of human potential, combined with the promise of a new Christian state, was a prospect that held great appeal for Stowe, who believed that Africans had long been repressed by their white conquerors, that slaveholders had failed to give their charges credit even for appreciating the value of religion, and that the emancipated slave would, like the self-improving George Harris, demonstrate "self-denial, energy, patience, and honesty," embrace any opportunity to educate himself, find respectable employment, and raise a conventional, middle-class, devout family. Emerson had adopted a similar position when praising the advances made by blacks emancipated in the British West Indies.

However, support for colonization was not necessarily synonymous with friendly intentions toward black Americans. The most naïve position was that colonization offered an opportunity for blacks to return to their former homes, a rationale that free blacks themselves attacked on the grounds that they had been Americans for several generations and that to send them to Africa made no more sense than to ship the Pilgrims' descendants to England. Another position, also well-meaning, held that if emancipation were achieved, white America would never accept the assimilation of millions of blacks, who could find true freedom only by relocating. Robert Goodloe Harper, a Baltimore lawyer, articulated a third position, which also anticipated irreconcilable differences between black and white populations in a fully emancipated America, but directed concern away from the "degraded" black race and toward the effect they—"idle and useless, and too often vicious and mischievous"—might have on white America:

> These persons are condemned to a state of hopeless inferiority and degradation by their color. . . . Whatever justice, humanity, and kindness, we may feel towards them, we cannot help considering them, and treating them, as our inferiors; nor can they help viewing themselves in the same light, however hard and unjust

they may be inclined to consider such a state of things. . . . Be their industry
ever so great, and their conduct ever so correct, whatever property they may
acquire, or whatever respect we may feel for their characters, we never could
consent, and they never could hope, to see the two races placed on a footing
of perfect equality with each other; to see the free blacks, or their descendants,
visit in our houses, form part of our circle of acquaintance, marry into our families, or participate in public honors and employments. (qtd. in Pease 19)

Even though the antislavery advocates argued that black "depravity" was a natural
consequence of the conditions of enslavement, proslavery forces argued that society
would be better off if the blacks were kept under control, and as late as 1832,
Henry Clay defended colonization as a means of avoiding the problems inherently
consequent to a free black population (Staudenraus 184–87). The final rationale
for colonization appealed principally to Southerners. While some opposed colonization because its possibility disrupted plantation discipline and its actuality would
deprive them of their labor force, others, especially after Nat Turner's uprising
in 1831, supported it as a means of getting rid of the troublesome free blacks;
they had no intention of emancipating and transporting those slaves that remained
useful. Under Garrison's outraged leadership, the abolitionists used this program
as a means of discrediting the colonizationist movement altogether.

The debate flowered in the 1840s and early 1850s, leading into the period
of *Uncle Tom's Cabin*. Black abolitionist minister Henry Highland Garnet pointed
out that blacks had been colonized once and could not be recolonized (25), while
Martin Robison Delany, a black physician and journalist, damned the American
Colonization Society—the northern group that had raised money to transport the
willing free blacks who eventually founded the Republic of Liberia—"as one of
the most arrant enemies of the colored man, ever seeking to discomfit him, and
envying him of every privilege that he may enjoy."[23] He went on to say, "We
believe it to be anti-Christian in its character, and misanthropic in its pretended
sympathies" and referred to Liberia as "a deep laid scheme of the slaveholders of
the country, to *exterminate* the free colored of the American continent" (31–32,
169). William Goodell, a white abolitionist editor whose *Slavery and Antislavery*
appeared in the same year as *Uncle Tom's Cabin*, contended that colonization had
done little to encourage emancipation and had rather validated slavery while ob-
structing abolition, discouraging education for blacks, and denying blacks the right
of freedom in their native land (344–49). Maria Weston Chapman mocked the
colonizationist position:

Yes; to make slavery stronger by exalting prejudice as an ordination of divine
Providence; to make slavery safer by eliminating that dangerous element, the
free black; to make its term longer by stultifying national conscience. See that
society making the laws of slave States more cruel, the men of the free States
more obdurate, the situation of the free men of color more difficult and insup-
portable, as a part of its plan. (1–2)

While the antislavery forces continued in this vein, the general populace reconsidered colonization as public opinion swung toward emancipation and people once again confronted the problem of absorbing millions of freed blacks into hitherto white society; Abraham Lincoln himself—who opposed black suffrage—endorsed colonization on the condition that the emigrants remove voluntarily. According to Eric Foner, procolonization sentiment revived in the 1850s due to an increase in anti-Negro legislation in the North, exclusionary legislation in the West, and the belief that some southern states were moving toward expelling or enslaving their free blacks (294, 274). One of the few antislavery spokesmen to offer his support to the program was James G. Birney, discouraged by the setbacks to the cause and convinced that there was no object in free blacks' remaining in America to suffer the abuse of the racist white majority. In his *Examination* of 1852, he acknowledged that Liberia was no paradise, but he offered it as the least objectionable alternative.

Stowe's support of colonization therefore represented a retreat to a conservative program of questionable alignment. She envisioned a classic antebellum reform scenario, where northern white Christians make reparations to black fugitives by opening the doors of the churches and schoolhouses and "receive them to the educating advantages of Christian republican society and schools, until they have attained to somewhat of a moral and intellectual maturity, and then assist them in their passage to those shores, where they may put in practice the lessons they have learned in America" (516). In a letter to a friend, Stowe's character George Harris rejects America in favor of African nationality because he imagines Liberia as "a republic formed of picked men" and a haven that will, due to God's design, rise above the oppressive schemes of those who encouraged the colony for the wrong reasons (502). He argues that while as an individual he can do little for America's slaves, as a member of the Liberian nation, he can join with others and speak out. Birney had warned black America that to migrate to Liberia was to undertake the hard work of carving a civilized nation out of a hostile wilderness; George assures his friend that he expects "to work *hard*; to work against all sorts of difficulties and discouragements; and to work till I die" (504). He will build Stowe's African utopia, "an enlightened and Christianized community" (10).

THE GOOD SAMARITAN

Ultimately, however, Stowe's novel throws the responsibility for reform onto the individual. After marshaling effective arguments and evidence to damn the slave system, she wrings her hands and asks her readers to consult their consciences. She flatters the men and women of the South and coaxes them to admit that they have, secretly, acknowledged the great evils of the slave system.[24] She beseeches her readers to ensure that they feel "right," that their feelings are "in harmony with the sympathies of Christ" (515). She asks them to pray. Stowe's recommendations subvert her own analysis of slavery as a system by reducing its reform to a personal level, to transactions between individuals in spite of the fact that the suffering at issue was a matter of racial oppression, not of individual qualities. The Quakers help the Harris family escape to Canada, the conveniently wealthy Madame de Thoux finances George's university education in Paris, and then George leads the family to Liberia. Ophelia takes Topsy to New England, where she is eventually baptized and sent to Africa as a missionary teacher, and George Shelby frees his own slaves, but apparently has no plans to persuade his neighbors to follow his example. Stowe's sensibility demands emancipation, but she sees it more as a matter of individual conscience and moral suasion than as a problem demanding social and political action.

Her attitude was fairly typical of the various antebellum reform movements, and it placed her in the mainstream of antislavery sentiment. The American Anti-Slavery Society encouraged free blacks in their efforts at self-improvement:

> By means of education, industry, and piety, with a due sense of your individual and collective responsibility, you will attain at an early day, every desirable object for yourselves and your posterity. You will exert a most happy influence upon the emancipation of your and our enslaved brethren—cause the hearts of your friends to rejoice, and be amply rewarded in your own peace and prosperity. God will smile upon all the work of your hands and make you and your children blessed. (qtd. in Pease 195–96)

In a program similar to Stowe's, Angelina Emily Grimké asked not for the reform of southern society, but for southern women to emancipate, educate, proselyte, pray, and, if necessary, disobey the law. Stowe's sister, Catharine Beecher, opposed the abolitionist societies, and especially women's participation in them, and argued, "Woman is to win everything by peace and love; by making herself so much respected, esteemed and loved, that to yield her opinions and to gratify her wishes, will be the free-will offering of the heart. But this is to be all accomplished in the domestic and social circle" (100).

The preoccupation with individual action derived in part from the evangelical model of behavior, one which David Brion Davis explains as being based on a confidence in the efficacy and validity of instantaneous conversion: "The evangelical movement, traditional in overall theology and world view, emphasized man's burden of personal responsibility, dramatized the dangers of moral complacency, and magnified the rewards for an authentic change of heart" (*Age of Revolution* 46). In other words, revolution begins with revelation, and history moves ahead one soul at a time; the evangelicals could not legislate conversion and so came slowly to the idea that they could legislate social reform. The entire antislavery movement was closely identified with evangelical revivalism, and as Ronald G. Walters has pointed out, evangelical rhetoric pervaded antislavery discourse as the speakers played on the relationships between slavery, slaveholding, and the bondage of the soul, and the immediatists drew a parallel between repentance and emancipation—both required an act of Christian will, and both were best done at once (38). Much of the passion of Stowe's novel springs from her conviction that the slave system violated her conception of Christianity. Davis has observed that Protestant tradition had forged complex links between sin and slavery; sin was a form of spiritual enslavement that could justify a temporal power's imposing actual bondage, but "John Wyclif had agreed with Augustine that bondage to sin was the only servitude that mattered, and that physical slavery, being a consequence of sin, was of no concern to the elect" (*Western Culture* 292, 296). Therefore, to attack the slave system, the reformers had to challenge the logic that over three million people must be sinners because God had placed them in slavery, suggesting instead that they were innocent and that their slavery was a consequence of the sin of the society that had wrongfully enslaved them. By attributing to the slave innocence rather than iniquity, the reformers were adopting an essentially sentimental construction of the black man, while simultaneously appointing themselves the indictors of the white man's collective sin. Yet the evangelical reliance on individual conscience—its assumption of good intentions—let racism thrive by failing to control the "ruffians," that is, those lacking in sympathy and scruple.

Stowe's predilection toward individual Christian acts of domestic kindness was even clearer in her own dramatic adaptation of the novel, *The Christian Slave* (1855). [25] She wrote little that was new—most of the dialogue consists of verbatim transcriptions from the novel—so its interest lies in the choices she made in terms of inclusion and exclusion.

The first act follows the story up to the moment that Haley drives Tom away from the Shelby plantation, but except for Eliza's farewell to Tom and Chloe, Stowe's selections differ from Aiken's. [26] The action begins in Uncle Tom's cabin itself with a nearly complete transcription of the dialogue from chapter 4, starting with the handwriting lesson and finishing with the preparations for the prayer meeting. We then learn of Shelby's deal with Haley, but whereas Aiken had chosen the negotiating scene, in which little Harry's future is still contingent, Stowe selected the conversation between the Shelbys. We lose the tension of the transaction, which is now a fait accompli, but instead we hear Mrs. Shelby express her anxious views on slavery and establish a feminine perspective in contrast with her husband's fatalistic business sense. Over one-third of the act is devoted to Eliza's escape, but rather than depict her frantic quest for freedom and her daring flight across the frozen Ohio, Stowe tells the story through the byplay of Sam and Andy, the hostlers who plan and then enjoy their sabotage of Haley's pursuit, and then report to the amazed Shelbys. The act closes with Tom's farewell to Chloe and the rest, including the entire dialogue wherein Tom gives George his parting advice.

Except for the one private scene between the Shelbys, the first act presents events through the eyes of the slaves, who depend largely on hearsay and limited observation for information regarding the whites, and who learn of the whites' transactions only when the arrangements are complete and concern them directly. Even the operations of the slave trade are kept obscure; Loker and Marks are omitted entirely, and Haley appears as a minor character, entering only to become the butt of the stable boys' mischief and to take Tom away in chains.

Act Two concerns events in the St. Clare household and shifts to an almost exclusively white point of view. Stowe includes virtually the complete text of the ongoing discussion of slavery between St. Clare, Marie, and Ophelia from chapter 16; Eva is present, but comes and goes principally to reinforce sentiment rather than to provide a central focus. Although the act seems to have more to do with St. Clare's personal confusion than with Eva as the exemplar of faith, the plantation home thrives as long as she lives, and withers after her death. St. Clare contemplates the last judgment and feels his mother's presence near him, and we see his death scene from the servants' point of view as they run "distractedly to and fro" in the courtyard below; Tom enters to announce, simply, "He's gone," the others mourn him, and the play moves from this grief to the godless torment of Legree's plantation. The key is the scene in which Eva reads Revelation with Tom, not only 15: 2–3 but also 4: 2–4. Completely innocent, she recites the beautiful imagery as a harbinger of the new Jerusalem, but seems unaware of the prerequisite apocalypse. The final act of the play therefore appears as a depiction of the world that God, having explored both black and white versions of domesticity, has blasted in preparation for the final glory.

The central figure in Act Three is Cassy, the quadroon who loved her white master, virtually imagined herself his wife, bore two children by him, begged incredulously for mercy when he sold the entire family to pay his gambling debts, and confronted further sorrow when Legree purchased her, abused her, and made her his mistress. The act opens with an entirely new scene that depicts Cassy, alone, mourning her lost children and singing a Spanish song that she learned from their duplicitous father:[27]

> Hay une seno todo el es propio mio,
> Do mi cabesa enferma reclino,
> Und bosa que nie si yo nio,
> Ojos que lloron cuando lloro no.
>
> This was a bosom all my own,
> That oft sustained my aching head;
> A mouth which smiled on me alone,
> An eye whose tears with mine were shed. (49)[28]

Upon meeting Emmeline, Cassy tells her, "You have come to the gates of Hell! Come with me. I'll show you the way" (50). Tom helps the other slaves, reads them the Bible, and receives a flogging for refusing to punish another slave.[29] Cassy then tells him the story of her life, transferred almost verbatim and complete from chapter 34, forming a monologue almost twenty minutes long. She then invites him to kill Legree, who is lying in a drunken coma with an axe nearby, but Tom refuses and encourages her to run away. The next five scenes focus on Cassy's conspiracy with Emmeline. We last see the two women hiding in the garret, watching Legree's posse prepare to hunt them down; Legree has a short soliloquy that develops a fragment from the original:

> It's all that Tom, I know! Did n't I see the old wretch lifting up his black hands, praying? I *hate* him! I HATE him! And is n't he *mine*? Is he not MINE? Can't I do what I like with him? Who is to hinder, I wonder? I'll try once more to-morrow. If I don't catch them—I'll see what I'll do! (64)

The play finishes as George Shelby enters to hold Tom's hand one last time. In this last scene, the only variation from the novel is a repetition of the dying man's last phrase: "Who — who — who — shall — separate — us from — the — the — *love of Christ?* LOVE! LOVE! LOVE of CHRIST!" (67) With that, Stowe's play draws to a close; she does not finish the story of Cassy and so does not offer the Liberian denouement of the novel.

To those who see *Uncle Tom's Cabin* only as an antislavery tract, the most puzzling change from novel to play may be the complete omission of the slave auctions, for nowhere are the abuses of slavery—the treatment of people as property, and the callous disregard for family ties—more evident. The inherent theatricality of such scenes gave them great potential to engage the audience's emotions, a point that professionals like Aiken and, several years later in *The Octoroon* (1859), Dion Boucicault doubtless recognized. Yet throughout *The Christian Slave*, Stowe retreats from intense action, and even in Act Three treats concubinage and flogging much more delicately than in the novel. Stowe had minimal experience even as an audience member, so it is possible that she made her choices out of naïve perplexity as to what was stageable, but it is more likely that she was expressing a certain set of values regarding what a respectable sensibility could tolerate on stage.

The most notable omission is George Harris, that angry revolutionary whose dreams Stowe could not criticize but whose violent methods she could not, apparently, condone outside the safety of the silent, printed page. Without George, the blacks have no model for active struggle, and we are left with a cast of sweet, docile slaves whose greatest defiance involves hiding a beech nut under Haley's saddle. By remaining passive, the black characters leave all the initiative to the whites, a scenario that may grate against late twentieth-century sensibilities, but one that sets up the theme of the faithful's resignation to the will of God.

By emphasizing the themes of Christianity and domesticity, *The Christian Slave* leaves ambiguous the questions of what to do about the slave system and how to cure America's racial cancer. Each act presents a different kind of family setting and measures its failure in Christian terms. On the Shelby plantation, the blacks try to live as Christians but cannot because the slave trade disrupts their families. The St. Clares struggle, each in his or her own way, to resolve the slave system with their faith (or, in Augustine's case, his wistful lack of faith), but they cannot find peace because such resolution is impossible. On Legree's plantation, the slave system has destroyed the family altogether, and although the word of God makes inroads into the pervading misery, evil is so strong that Tom can only pray to Jesus to give him "the victory." Stowe structures the interaction not as a matter of social relations, but as one of God and the individual.

THE SENTIMENTAL ARGUMENT

Sentiment was the foundation of Stowe's sensibility—sentiment based on her compulsive sympathy with slavery's victims—and both the novel and the plays succeeded largely through the emotional experience they offered. Stowe's fundamental assumption is that all men and women, both black and white, are essentially well-meaning and bound by a common humanity. The depth of her feeling was such that she could find philanthropy lacking if not pursued with a full heart: "O, ye who visit the distressed, do ye know that everything your money can buy, given with a cold, averted face, is not worth one honest tear shed in real sympathy?" (120) St. Clare confesses that his great failing as a planter was that he could too easily imagine himself in the slave's place, filling his cotton-picking bag with surreptitious rocks to make his weight and appease the overseer. Baldwin scorned the novel because "the wet eyes of the sentimentalist betray his aversion to experience, his fear of life, his arid heart" (579), but for Stowe's audience, the tears were the meat of the story.

The heart of the sentimental world is the family, and Stowe stated simply, "The worst abuse of the system of slavery is its outrage upon the family" (Key 257).[30] The white antebellum home was built on the sanctity of marriage, and the typical northern sentimental sensibility was dismayed at reports that southern slaveholders made little effort to keep married slave couples together; hence George and Eliza Harris and their marriage that is not legally binding in the eyes of the white law. William Goodell, who had no patience with those who criticized the abuses of slavery without attacking the system that made them inevitable, pointed out that the disruption of family was fundamental to the master's maintenance of power, arguing that "the idea of the unlimited control of the master, and the absolute defenselessness of the slave" made "the absence of legal marriage, and of the protected family relation . . . manifestly essential to the idea of human chattelhood" (379). Since slaves could not truly marry, and since those who considered themselves married could be so easily separated, sexual relations were, almost by definition, promiscuous and sinful. The final outrage was that the slave women, living without the protection of a husband in the white manner, were subject to casual rape by their white masters. Where individuals cannot commit to one another, there can be no family and no home; John William Ward proposes that "the tragedy of the Negro is that he has, quite literally, no home. . . . The Negro's world is defined by separation and loneliness, a terrible solitude" (485). The apotheosis of this homelessness is the row of squalid shacks on Legree's plantation, a prison that prevents its residents from becoming anything more than alienated inmates, afraid to reach out to each other.[31] However, as compelling as this line of protest may be, it seems to submerge the essential problem of racism by asking that black people be conceded family lives modeled after the white experience; if the conditions are changed, then the cause need not be addressed.

The slaves' homelessness is all the more painful and complete because the system also separates children from their parents. In the auction scenes, mothers beg to be sold with their children, but invariably mother and child go to different owners; the separations undercut the smug southern gentry who assure each other that slave families are usually left intact. Hearing that Haley has purchased Harry, Eliza is transformed: "Pale, shivering, with rigid features and compressed lips, she looked an entirely altered being from the soft and timid creature she had been hitherto" (50). She risks her own comfort and security to save her son from being sold down the river and to keep her with him. When Haley tells Lucy that he has sold her son, the news virtually kills her; she collapses to a sitting position, her hands slack at her sides, seeing nothing, and too shocked to weep. Even Tom's prayers and sympathy cannot console her, and in the dark of night, she steps over the side of the steamboat into the river. One of Cassy's greatest sorrows is the loss of her children, and she is not truly restored until she finds her daughter, Eliza, and Eliza's children, Harry and little freeborn Eliza. Cassy, the most ravaged victim of the slave system, committed the ultimate act of desperation when she killed her own child with laudanum to save him from his own life. Stowe condemns not her, but the institution that shaped her decision, urging the "anguish and despair" that shatter thousands of families at each moment and drive "a helpless and sensitive race to frenzy and despair" (514). Tom himself cannot—indeed, does not wish to—restrain his grief when the time comes to leave his children in Ohio:

> Sobs, heavy, hoarse and loud, shook the chair, and great tears fell through his fingers on the floor: just such tears, sir, as you dropped into the coffin where lay your first-born son; such tears, woman, as you shed when you heard the cries of your dying babe. For, sir, he was a man,—and you are but another man. (55)

As always, Stowe is not satisfied with representation alone, so she asks her reader to imagine herself in such a predicament, referring to Eliza's strength as she turned her furtive steps away from Shelby's plantation.

> If it were *your* Harry, mother, or your Willie, that were going to be torn from you by a brutal trader, to-morrow morning,—if you had seen the man, and heard

that the papers were signed and delivered, and you had only from twelve o'clock
till morning to make good your escape,—how could *you* walk? (67–68)

Stowe feminizes the reader, implicitly suggesting that the entire sentimental argument, if not the entire novel, is actually addressed to women, and implying that
only women can understand the issues that she finds most compelling.

Yet Stowe apparently realized that the gulf between black and white experience
was too dark and deep, that the white readers could not empathize with the agony
of the blacks, so she offered little Eva, a figure of incalculable impact on a sentimental public that was, at least at the domestic level, passionately devoted to
children.[32] Black parents feared losing their children; to translate that anxiety into
white terms, Stowe linked loss or separation with death—a calamity that Stowe's
white, northern readership could more easily understand and that was more likely
to inspire them to antislavery sentiment. Eliza wins Mrs. Bird's full sympathy and
cooperation when she asks whether she, too, had ever lost a child. Such loss is
the ultimate disaster and most vivid emotional experience in the sentimental world;
Mrs. Bird, her sons, and her servant dissolve into tears. Many of Stowe's white,
northern readers had watched little ones die, so the author was opening a vein of
feeling that had great potential to evolve into antislavery sentiment. Jane Tompkins,
as part of her effort to reconsider the nineteenth-century American sensibility and
to challenge subsequent antisentimental values, rejects the explanation of the popularity of lachrymose childhood deathbed scenes as a symptom of weakness in the
literature of the period and of triviality of emotion in its readership; she sees instead
a "relationship of these scenes to a pervasive cultural myth which invests the suffering and death of an innocent victim with just the kind of power that critics
deny to Stowe's novel: the power to work in, and change, the world" (130). With
the death of little Eva—the incarnation of Christian perfection who passes "from
death into life," a child so idealized that even southern critics found her unexceptionable—Stowe forged an adamantine chain from death to separation to slavery
itself; to weep for Eva is to weep for all little children, black or white, who are
taken from their parents. No matter how alienated from the blacks they might
have felt, few white readers could deny sympathy to Eva, so to associate her parents'
grief with the sorrow of slave parents was to present a powerful argument. Stowe
calls to the "mothers of America," to remember their dead children:

By the sick hour of your child; by those dying eyes, which you can never forget;
by those last cries, that wrung your heart when you could neither help nor save;
by the desolation of that empty cradle, that silent nursery,—I beseech you, pity
those mothers that are constantly made childless by the American slave-trade!
(514–15)

The burden of Stowe's appeal is that the black mother loves her child as deeply
as the white mother, that the enslaved black harbors the same values and affections

as the free white, that, in essence, the black and white sensibilities are virtually the same—a position that flew in the face of antebellum conventional wisdom.

RACIALISM AND MISSIS HARRIET

The sentimental vision provided a troubling challenge for white America. The concept of sympathy seemed to require whites to take blacks to their bosoms, but the vast majority of antebellum whites, both Northerners and Southerners, took for granted their racial superiority over blacks. As James A. Rawley puts it, "It was a rare American who doubted the anthropological assumption of African inequality, an occasional one who favored legal equality, a nearly non-existent one who favored social equality" (259–60). In 1828, at the height of his popularity, James Fenimore Cooper suggested that Virginia and the Carolinas might as well enfranchise their twelve-year-old boys as their blacks, and proposed that "there is no doubt that the free blacks, like the aborigines, gradually disappear before the superior moral and physical influence of the white" (2: 265, 1: 286). In 1853, the *North American Review* defined blacks as inferior beings who might improve under white influence but, once separated, would relapse "speedily into barbarism." The anonymous author reasoned that the black man, weaker than the white, should be the servant: "It is his happiest position. His docility, his good temper, his bodily vigor, his intellectual weakness, all fit him for it. As a servant, under just treatment, he thrives and rejoices, and is tormented by no ambition for a higher sphere" (477). That author's opposition to emancipation was founded in his skeptical appraisal of black capabilities:

> Ignorant, improvident, without self-sustaining energy of character, and of limited intellectual faculties, they are incapable of providing for their own support or caring for their own interests. Freedom to them would be like freedom to children, or to the domestic animals. It would be helplessness, abandonment, the absence of guidance and protection. Thus deserted, indolence, vice, and poverty would speedily degrade them below even their present condition, and they would gradually dwindle away and disappear. . . . (477)

He ignored the entire history of the slave trade to argue that slavery had to continue simply because there was no other way to handle the black minority:

> It is not slavery that is the curse of the South; it is Africa. It is the presence of an alien, inferior race, with whom amalgamation is degradation and corruption of blood, who can never be citizens; whose natural tendency is not to improvement, but to barbarism; who make industry ignorant, unskilful, and abject; who form no part of the people, though a large proportion of the population; and who are thus a source of weakness, and not of strength. (489)

George Fitzhugh, in *Sociology for the South* (1854), contended that slavery was the best way to care for an inherently improvident portion of the population (83).

Such rhetoric seems to brand Stowe's contemporaries as the most flagrant kind of racists, a designation apparently justified by the combination of the systematized oppression of southern slavery with the more subtle repression of northern legislation. Yet a more historically accurate term would be "racialism," a doctrine that explained certain behavior patterns by attributing to the various races, for good or ill, certain special qualities. In the winter of 1837–38, Alexander Kinmont expounded the racialist point of view in a series of lectures given in Cincinnati, where Stowe then lived. He asserted that African civilization had not developed as far as European, and that to hurl Africans into a European culture was to put them at an inevitable disadvantage. He believed it appropriate that the white race should "bear the torch of science and moral improvement in advance of the other races" but that in later epochs, gentler leadership might be more appropriate (193–94). He suggested that the blacks would eventually develop a "far nobler civilization," one based on "all the milder and gentler virtues" where their "singular light-heartedness" would no longer be a vice, and where they could cultivate "that natural talent for music with which they are pre-eminently endowed, to say nothing of their willingness *to serve*, the most beautiful trait of humanity" (191). He went on with an analysis that might have appealed to Stowe, suggesting that "the sweeter graces of the Christian religion" grow better in the "Ethiopian" than the Caucasian mind (218). George M. Frederickson has explained the use of "romantic" racialism—that is, racialism where the white gaze found exotic and even admirable qualities in other races—in the context of some whites' dismay at antebellum politics, materialism, and expansionism, all apparently concomitant to the collapse of traditional values. If the Anglo-Saxons were "aggressive, warlike, and domineering," then they had better look to the Negroes for a more Christian model (*Black Image* 108–109). Like the native American, the black became reconstructed by the white gaze. The romantic racialists hoped to ameliorate the problems of white society by blending in the softer tendencies they saw in black people (not through interracial marriage, but through cultural mingling and sharing), but no matter how well-meaning, their approach was inevitably hegemonic because it appropriated the black for white use and reserved for the white those qualities that led to social and racial power. They sought to free the slave from the plantation, but only to engage her services in a subtler fashion.

The most pernicious use of racialism appeared in the work of certain southern writers who wished to reassure their concerned compatriots that they were not actually enslaving their fellow men, that black and white were in fact two different species, not mutually descended from Adam or Noah at all.[33] The utility of this position is clear: if black and white are different species, then there is no more objection to one enslaving the other than to either owning a draft horse. It was against such politically dangerous use of racialism that Stowe aimed her sentimental defense of the black person. Yet her good intentions led to the promotion of what have become the stereotypes with which white America has demeaned and disempowered black America.

Under Stowe's white gaze, the typical black man is an amusing child, "naturally patient, timid and unenterprising," and almost invariably good-natured, well-meaning, and doggedly loyal to the point where the well-treated slave, limitlessly grateful, will not run away even if given the chance. He is somewhat educable; Tom—an experienced and capable plantation manager in his forties—struggles "with a respectful, admiring air" through his handwriting lesson with the thirteen-year-old George Shelby, and marvels, with Chloe (who exclaims that "words is so curis"), at "how easy white folks al'us does things" (34). Stowe cites various acquaintances of her husband's to prove how well the black man can succeed with education and opportunity, but none is a professional, and all are tradesmen or artisans. If a black man is honest, it may be partly because he is too innocent to conceive of knavery; Stowe assures us that Tom will not steal because of "an impregnable simplicity of nature, strengthened by Christian faith" (240). Black people have certain natural abilities; Harry and Topsy sing and dance on request, and Dinah reigns supreme in the kitchen because cooking is "an indigenous talent of the African race." They also demonstrate amusing quirks; Adolph so admires St. Clare that he steals his clothes, handkerchiefs, and cologne to become as much like his master as he can, and Dinah is steadfastly committed to running her kitchen in an intuitive and feudal manner that seems completely irrational to Ophelia's white mind. Moreover, the black man is fascinatingly foreign, an "exotic" who harbors "a passion for all that is splendid, rich, and fanciful" (195).[34] Tom sees St. Clare's mansion as an Aladdin's palace, inspiring Stowe to speculate that Africa's ascendancy will offer the world a new opulence:

> In that far-off mystic land of gold, and gems, and spices, and waving palms, and wondrous flowers, and miraculous fertility, will awake new forms of art, new styles of splendor; and the negro race, no longer despised and trodden down, will, perhaps, show forth some of the latest and most magnificent revelations of human life. (212–13)

It will, of course, be a Christian kingdom, for the black man is gentle, docile, childlike, forgiving, and willing "to repose on a superior mind and rest on a higher power."

All of this may seem disquietingly familiar, an exhausted, embarrassing cliché, but the important point is that Stowe's creation is an essentially comic one that expresses her fundamental cosmology. In relation to God, man is but a child, bearing only as much responsibility for his actions as God will impose. Since man cannot be held accountable at the ultimate level, God will offer forgiveness, so the error that would shatter the tragic figure will only earn forbearance for this fallible creature. Furthermore, and with specific regard to the black slave, if he is fundamentally innocent—if his bondage is not, as John Wyclif might have argued, punishment for his essential corruption—then he is as a little child. He is akin to Eva. For Stowe to attribute sophistication to one of her black characters would be to allow the possibility that they are responsible enough to deserve to be slaves, which is the risk she takes with George Harris. That is, if Topsy commits her misdeeds with a sense of sin, then her bondage is an appropriate return. Stowe *must* draw her blacks as amusing, endearing children, for to depict them as adults in the liberal tradition would be to justify their damnation.

Stowe sets up black and white as polar opposites; in spite of her faith in shared sensibility, these are mutually exclusive terms. Each is what the other is not, and each defines the other in terms of contrast and absence. Her blacks are "essentially unlike the hard and dominant Anglo-Saxon race" (9). George Harris remarks that although the blacks are "not a dominant and commanding race, they are, at least, an affectionate, magnanimous, and forgiving one," and takes for granted that God has entrusted the destiny of the world to the "hot and hasty Saxon" (503). Stowe, like a mother trying to excuse her children's weaknesses, says that "they are not naturally daring and enterprising"—like the Anglo-Saxon—but home-loving and affectionate (118).[35] Stowe is, clearly, one of Frederickson's romantic racialists, drawing the comparison with the utmost in sympathy for the black man, probably unaware that she reserves for the white man those qualifies that ensure power.

From this theoretical basis, Stowe creates her characters according to their relative blackness, blending "blood" and color as though she were mixing paint. Those she designates as fully black are most likely to demonstrate the qualities that she attributes to their race, no matter how contradictory and diverse the examples of Tom, Topsy, and Sambo might be. Those she designates as part white demonstrate the intelligence, initiative, restlessness, and love of liberty that she associates with the white or, more specifically, the Anglo-Saxon race. St. Clare predicts an uprising based on mixed racial heritage:

> If ever the St. Domingo hour comes, Anglo Saxon blood will lead on the day. Sons of white fathers, with all our haughty feelings burning in their veins, will not always be bought and sold and traded. They will rise, and raise with them their mother's race. (315)

The mulatto man, like George Harris, is dissatisfied and dangerous, while his female counterparts—Cassy the quadroon, Eliza the octoroon—are virtually helpless objects of white male sexual desire, their blackness (however invisible) connoting their availability and titillating promise. Their enslavement is all the more pathetic because they are more white than black (if that phrase can mean anything), their appearance and "white" manners making them irreproachably desirable, but their black ancestry darkens both their skin and their potential for respectability. It is somehow impossible to imagine one of Stowe's fully white women submitting, however unwillingly, to such a nightmare of sexual exploitation; she would, literally, die first. Cassy is not only demeaned as property in a white world, she is demeaned as a sexual toy in a male world, condemned by the "tropical warmth" of her "blood" to surrender and enter regions that Stowe herself can scarcely imagine.[36]

Of all the blacks in the novel, Tom engages Stowe's deepest concern. He is the ultimate Christian, abused beyond ordinary endurance, even declining the temptation to kill Legree when he has the chance, and submitting not merely because he is black but because his faith tells him he must. Yet his blackness shines, magnifying with his trials until it dominates the story as powerfully as the whiteness of Melville's whale. Baldwin has argued that in Stowe's mind, "black equates with evil and white with grace," and that because Tom is "jet black" and "born without the light, it is only through humility, the incessant mortification of the flesh, that he can enter into communion with God or man" (581). In Baldwin's interpretation, the black slave pleads with God to wash him until he is white, "for black is the color of evil; only the robes of the saved are white" (584). The paradigm suggests that whiteness leads to salvation—which may have seemed true, and unconscionably so, from Baldwin's bitterly ironic black perspective in 1949—but of all the whites in the novel, only Eva is transfigured, Eva, the perfect child who was perhaps not of the earth at all. Tom, however, dies a mature man who has lived to know both joy and grief, and who has chosen, knowing the consequences, according to God's word, which is the only word that means anything to Stowe. Yet before God he is still a child, like Eva, and his death, no matter how deep the agony, is not a tragedy but a regeneration and a return to love. His blackness brings him to "the victory"; it is the depth of the novel.

Nowhere is Stowe's vision of the black/white contrast clearer than in the juxtaposition of Topsy and Eva as "representatives of their races" and of "the two extremes of society":

> The fair, high-bred child, with her golden head, her deep eyes, her spiritual, noble brow, and prince-like movements; and her black, keen, subtle, cringing, yet acute neighbor. . . . The Saxon, born of ages of cultivation, command, education, physical and moral eminence; the Afric, born of ages of oppression, submission, ignorance, toil, and vice! (287)

If Eva is the exemplary Christian child, the living saint, Topsy is her polar opposite, a child who has *not* had a Christian upbringing and who is deficient in nearly every way, a goblin, a "sooty gnome from the land of Diablerie." She acknowledges no parents, does not know how old she is, and can scarcely distinguish a lie from the truth, knowing only that when she is whipped she must confess something, even if she has not done it. In place of a sense of right and wrong, she has only an amoral cunning that has enabled her to survive. Ophelia, the exemplar of northern self-righteous naïveté, finds Topsy to be an inexplicable, uncontrollable phenomenon, more a creature than a child, who knows nothing of kindness, who scorns whippings, and who finds New England values incomprehensible. However comic, Topsy is the ultimate calamity of slavery—a child who has been wasted.

BREAKDOWN

As Topsy moves from Stowe's hands into Aiken's, she signals the play's marked debt to the popular theatrical tradition of Negro minstrelsy. Minstrelsy was based more on belief than on fact; that is, it was a rendering of an idea rather than of actuality. While it is undoubtedly true that southern whites came to regard their black slaves' songs and dances as forms of entertainment, minstrelsy did not originate on the plantation; it was essentially a stylized version of northern whites' imaginative conception of black folk performance, and most of the minstrel performers were northern whites with little or no firsthand experience of black people, much less southern slaves. Robert Toll has suggested that minstrelsy catered to northern white audiences who were curious about blacks but wanted to be reassured that the two races were quite different, and he believes that the characters' plausibility led some gullible members of the public into accepting the minstrels' caricatures as realistic portrayals (34, 38).

The effect of minstrelsy on the white conception of the black man is probably incalculable. Certainly the technique of portrayal rendered the Negro more a clown than a man. Carl Wittke has described the typical makeup, which included big lips, distended mouth, shining white teeth, and fright wigs (141). Toll interprets the style of performance as a denigration of black people:

> They dressed in ill-fitting, patchwork clothes, and spoke in heavy "nigger" dialects. Once on stage, they could not stay still for an instant. Even while sitting, they contorted their bodies, cocked their heads, rolled their eyes, and twisted their outstretched legs. When the music began, they exploded in a frenzy of grotesque and eccentric movements. Whether singing, dancing, or joking, whether in a featured role, accompanying a comrade, or just listening, their wild hollering and their bobbing, seemingly compulsive movements charged their entire performance with excitement. (36)

Robert Lumer has argued that the minstrel troupes, who stayed clear of the controversy over slavery, sought commercial success, which was most available if they presented the black slave "in the most laughable, most grotesque way possible" (58). This re-creation of the plantation slave was, as Wittke described him, "lazy, shiftless . . . careless," and fond of watermelon and crap games:

> He always was distinguished by an unusually large mouth and a peculiar kind of broad grin; he dressed in gaudy colors and in a flashy style; he usually consumed more gin than he could properly hold; and he loved chickens so well that he could not pass a chicken-coop without falling into temptation. . . . [T]he Negro's alleged love for the grand manner led him to use words so long that he not only did not understand their meaning, but twisted the syllables in the most ludicrous fashion in his futile efforts to pronounce them. (8)

The caricatures evolved into a set of recurring types: the sentimental, kindly, loyal Old Uncle with his white hair; his female counterpart, the Mammy; and the "yaller gal," as fair and beautiful as a white woman but as exotic and available as the African slave (Toll 76–79).

Minstrel shows depicted not only the slave but slavery itself. In his discussion of minstrelsy as a peculiarly urban form of entertainment, Alexander Saxton has argued that minstrelsy promoted slavery by affirming the owners' point of view and presenting the institution as benign and desirable (18). Toll has analyzed the minstrels' construction of the plantation as an "idealized, interracial family," characterized by the slave party, which suggested that black slaves were playful—but loyally deferential—children who passed their days singing, dancing, frolicking, and eating their fill under the benevolent toleration of their kindly "parents," the master and the mistress. This romanticized plantation was a mythic sanctuary for both black and white, where "Negroes wanted only a chance to play and to love and serve their beloved white superiors," and the whites enjoyed their superiority and sense of patriarchal wisdom (72–80). If a minstrel show depicted an exslave in the North, it was to reinforce further the rosy image of the plantation he had left behind. If a slave did run away, it was usually not to escape from the brutality of the plantation, but to join his family. Toll argues that through the early 1850s, the minstrel shows made it possible for northern audiences to weep over the pathos of separated families and at the same time sigh over the beauty of the plantation, and to applaud the runaway's search for freedom while accepting his love of his master. Slavery was simply part of the minstrel show, and therefore required no action (86–87). The performances took contradictory aspects and issues from real life and resolved them on stage; the slave system became pleasant and compassionate. Moreover, the minstrel caricature displaced the black actuality; the white performers had found an image that their white audiences embraced eagerly as reassuringly different without providing any threat or call to action.

Stowe probably had even less experience of minstrelsy than of plantation life, but her creation of Topsy seems to spring from the minstrel model and prefigure the Little Rascals, probably an indication of the high degree to which minstrelsy drew upon the cultural currents of the antebellum era. When St. Clare asks for a song and a dance, Topsy becomes the harbinger of countless variety turns:

> The black, glassy eyes glittered with a kind of wicked drollery, and the thing struck up, in a clear shrill voice, an odd negro melody, to which she kept time with her hands and feet, spinning round, clapping her hands, knocking her knees together, in a wild, fantastic sort of time, and producing in her throat all those odd guttural sounds which distinguish the native music of her race; and finally, turning a summerset or two, and giving a prolonged closing note, as odd and unearthly as that of a steam-whistle, she came suddenly down on the carpet, and stood with her hands folded, and most sanctimonious expression of meekness and solemnity over her face, only broken by the cunning glances which she shot askance from the corners of her eyes. (278–79)

Along with little Harry's skit for Shelby and the slave men's song on the Red River, Topsy's dance reinforces the cliché of the happy Negro with a natural rhythm, an ear for simple tunes, and a complete lack of inhibition in performance. Stowe even depicts Topsy as a little black pickaninny clown, with her hair "braided in sundry little tails, which stuck out in every direction" (278).[37]

THE SAFETY OF THE STAGE

By 1852, minstrelsy had so defined the stage Negro that when George C. Howard asked Greenbury C. Germon to play Uncle Tom in the Aiken première, he had to convince him that the role would *not* require a standard, black-faced, song-and-dance performance. Germon's reservations were probably indicative of the preconceptions harbored by many people in Howard's prospective audience, for the popularity of minstrelsy had inured spectators to a depiction of blacks and the black world that was flagrantly stylized and was, as a theatrical form, fast becoming routinized. Anyone planning to stage *Uncle Tom's Cabin* had to confront the question of whether the audience would take the black characters and their problems at all seriously.

Aiken presents Topsy as virtually the same breakdown-dancing puppet as in the novel, but he subtracts the context of Stowe's analysis and, to a large extent, Ophelia's point of view. He includes the scene where Eva's love apparently converts Topsy, but the stage action moves mechanically from Eva's declaration to Topsy bursting into tears to the two children exiting as Topsy exclaims, through her tears, her comic catchphrase, "I's so wicked!" Without Stowe's elaboration of the moment—Eva as angel emanafing a ray of heavenly love that penetrates Topsy's dark, heathen soul—there is little substance, and the exit line is a hook for laughs. Topsy mourns Eva's passing as in the novel, cherishing the lock of hair, but undercuts the sincerity of her emotion by shifting, in an instant, from vehement sobbing to the saucy exit line, "I ain't half so wicked as I used to was." Aiken encourages the audience to laugh at her conversion.

> Dar's somethin' de matter wid me—I isn't a bit like myself. I haven't done anything wrong since poor Miss Eva went up in de skies and left us. When I's gwine to do anything wicked, I tinks of her, and somehow I can't do it. I's getting to be good, dat's a fact. I 'spects when I's dead I shall be turned into a little brack angel. (57)

She is, as Aiken's St. Clare says, an "incorrigible imp," and the playwright makes the most of her in the Vermont scenes as she offers malaprop mischievous comment on the folly of Ophelia and Deacon Perry, and provides a comic foil for Cute. If Saxton's analysis is valid, then Aiken's appropriation of minstrelsy's figuration contributed to the tendency of his play to bolster the slave system that it purports to attack.

Slavery was not only an institution, it virtually defined the relationship between black and white in antebellum America, so Aiken's performance of race depended largely on his treatment of slavery. While Stowe's retreat from activism weakened her own presentation of slavery as a system, Aiken attenuated the issue even farther by making it trivial and often comic. The script permits and encourages responses that were quite congenial to the majority of Aiken's potential audience—to applaud and approve one individual's fight for liberty and another's hold on his faith, to regard cruelty toward slaves as reprehensible but aberrant and unusual, and to enjoy the plight of helpless, beset heroines and the mischief of comic darkies. This melodrama defines and locates slavery, its central generative evil, in such a way as to absolve society as a whole, and therefore its potential audience, from guilt. Slavery becomes not a system that forms part of the integral workings of the entire American culture, but a somewhat localized instrument for separating certain people from those they love. It is not an institution, but a collection of cases and anecdotes, so the play presents not a dialectic of class and economics, but specific interactions between villains and victims. Even though Aiken transfers whole sections of dialogue intact from the novel, he lifts them out from the discursive narrative that contextualized their meaning for the reader and clarified Stowe's ideology as the framework for the whole.[38] When he does turn narrative into dialogue, it is to reinforce sentiment, as when Legree recites most of the story about his dead mother.[39] He cuts most of the ongoing debate between St. Clare and Ophelia, and even omits any reference to colonization—the Harrises will escape to Canada, taking with them the problem of what to do with freed blacks, and therefore protecting the American status quo—and so avoids offending anyone with strong feelings on that subject. In general, Aiken authorized his audience to disapprove of the specific abuses that he represented on stage, but he excused them from doing anything about the reality beyond the stage door.

In Aiken's hands, the trials of George and Eliza are concerned primarily with the integrity of the family; slavery becomes, at times, little more than a pretext for those who would wrest the couple apart. With very few changes, the sequence of scenes in Act One could be revised into a fairly conventional series of melodramatic episodes involving a young mother and her child running away from any villain's evil clutches. In the opening scene, George has "lost his place in the factory" and, embittered, cannot live up to his own standards as a husband and father. Given that these are mulatto characters, the actors in the 1850s, who were white, probably did not play them in classic blackface with nappy wigs. If so, the scene may have resembled any other encounter between a troubled white couple who faced the classic melodramatic situation of having to deal with misfortune visited upon them by some unseen, external agency.[40] Aiken employed this and other melodramatic conventions—debts of inscrutable origin that jeopardize the security of innocent parties, and the patterns of captivity and escape—that appeared over and over again in plays that had nothing to do with slavery or black Americans.[41] Aiken presents slavery as mere background to the Harrises' domestic situation: George complains that his abusive master can employ him at his own caprice, bitterly reminds Eliza that the law does not recognize their marriage, challenges the right of any man to set up as his master, and denies that the United States is his true country, promising that "I'll fight for my liberty, to the last breath I breathe! You say your fathers did it, if it was right for them, it is right for me!" (30). Yet his resolution to live free or die is more a faint echo of Revolutionary rhetoric, calculated to produce reflexive applause from the audience, than a critique of slavery, and he further attenuates his alleged argument by assuring Eliza that she has little to complain about because she has been educated and kindly treated, which is exactly the point that proslavery pragmatists would have raised to support the slave system as such. As George fights for his freedom, the underlying motivation is, more than in the novel, his wish to reunite with Eliza and Harry and become a true family; the final tableau of Act Two displays George and Eliza kneeling "in an attitude of thanksgiving" with little Harry between them. While Stowe emphasized the family and domestic values as among slavery's chief victims, Aiken virtually presents the effect without the cause.

As Eliza prepares to climb out of the tavern window to make her famous escape across the frozen Ohio River, Aiken turns the audience's attention not to the system she flees, but to the flight itself and the beleaguered heroine, the classic focal point of sympathy and concern.

> Powers of mercy, protect me! How shall I escape these human blood-hounds?
> Ah! the window—the river of ice! That dark stream lies between me and liberty!
> Surely the ice will bear my trifling weight. It is my only chance of escape—better
> sink beneath the cold waters, with my child locked in my arms, than have him
> torn from me and sold into bondage. He sleeps upon my breast—Heaven, I
> put my trust in thee! (16)

David A. Grimsted has objected to this speech as cheap and trite, an illustration of midcentury dramaturgy's preference for explanation at the cost of "complexity . . . verisimilitude and honest emotion" (237). Yet the æsthetic and operation of such melodrama differ radically from what Grimsted seems to expect. Harry Birdoff has described the play's tableaux: fully sixty seconds spent to burn in the images of Legree raising his whip to strike Tom, Eva sitting on Tom's knee to hang a wreath around his neck, and a "convoy of angels" lifting Eva up to "a better world" (50–51). Aiken is employing exegetical representation, albeit somewhat different in style than in the temperance dramas, choosing allegorical images to accentuate the message that action and dialogue have conveyed. The very purpose of a speech like Eliza's is to communicate directly to the audience, to involve them, and to teach them, explicitly, the meaning of the staged incident. This does not mean that the play lacked subtlety or that the audience was unduly dense; it means, rather, that the form placed ideas and their delineation in the foreground, rather than attempting to imply them in a more delicate fashion according to the values that naturalistic or realistic representation assumes.

Aiken seems to treat the religious aspect of the myth with more reverence than he does the political and social issues, but primarily to exploit the sensational possibilities of Eva's death, and he, perhaps unintentionally, further deflects attention away from the problem of racism. Eva is the same saintly child as in the novel, an idealized incarnation taken far beyond actuality, reading the Bible and singing hymns with Tom, and trying to reform Topsy with the light of her love. When she tells Tom, "I'm going before long," he responds with a revision of a brief dialogue that, in the novel, he shared privately with Mammy: "It's no use tryin' to keep Miss Eva here; I've allays said so. She's got the Lord's mark in her forehead. She wasn't never like a child that's to live—there was always something deep in her eyes" (46). Because the two are alone on stage, this could only be addressed to the audience, so both actors cease to represent their characters even within the conventions of midcentury performance. Tom has stepped out of the story to address the audience, but not in the manner of the standard aside, and Eva sits next to him, an icon, the Bible in her lap, her finger pointing up to heaven; because he speaks as though she is not there at all, Tom reminds us of Eva's symbolic value. Aiken has, in essence, staged a religious tract, and the moment offers a hint of the tableau that will close the play.

After Eva warns her father that she will be "leaving" soon, he asks the audience a question that Stowe, in the novel, had asked her readers:

> Has there ever been a child like Eva? Yes, there has been; but their names are always on grave-stones, and their sweet smiles, their heavenly eyes, their singular words and ways, are among the buried treasures of yearning hearts. It is as if heaven had an especial band of angels, whose office it is to sojourn for a season here, and endear to them the wayward human heart, that they might bear it upward with them in their homeward flight. When you see that deep, spiritual light in the eye when the little soul reveals itself in words sweeter and wiser than the ordinary words of children, hope not to retain that child; for the seal of heaven is on it, and the light of immortality looks out from its eyes! $(47-48)$[42]

Lewis Saum's study of private correspondence from the antebellum era indicates that some parents repressed their love for their children for fear that if they cared too much, the little ones would be taken from them (88). By including St. Clare's ruminations, Aiken is clearly playing upon such anxieties. Both St. Clare's soliloquy and Tom's comment on Eva pull the audience into the action by suggesting the link between Eva and children the spectators might have known and lost.

The more lingering Eva's dying, the greater its impact and capacity to move a sentimental audience. The review in the *New York Atlas* emphasized the compulsive sentimental appeal of "the enacting of Eva, by Little Cordelia Howard" as "one of the most delectable and affecting specimens of the *art dramatique* we ever beheld" (176).[43] Because the conclusion is foregone—few in the audience could have but known that Eva would die—the excitement resides in the staging of the journey, which Aiken effects carefully: the child reaches a crisis and the family assembles with Ophelia standing at the head of the bed, St. Clare leaning over his daughter, and Tom and Marie kneeling at her feet. Eva is as a monarch or a saint, dying beautifully with her closest retainers in fond attendance, and her death struggle ceases as she gazes joyfully into eternity before passing on. Yet this treatment of Eva permits the white, northern antebellum audience to accept her as a child, not as a specifically white child. Her saintliness implies a universality that erases her color and excludes the question of the racial and economic privileges that make possible the beauty of her passing.

Tom is a virtual minister, sent to officiate at Eva's passing, comfort the bereaved father, and attend him at his death. As Tom himself says, "the Lord's given me a work among these yer poor souls, and I'll stay with 'em and bear my cross with 'em till the end" (11). He is the conscience of the play, a sort of uncle-confessor who expresses concern over St. Clare's dissipations and then sits on the grassy bank to read Revelation with Eva. His paraclerical status illuminates the similarities between the readings of the novel's character that Baldwin and Ammons, in spite of their differing perspectives, offer; Baldwin condemns Stowe because in her quest to purify all blacks of the state of sin that (she covertly believes) their color betrays, Tom "has been robbed of his humanity and divested of his sex" (581), while Ammons describes Tom as a black male version of the sentimental nineteenth-century heroine. Each writer sees Tom as somehow emasculated.[44] Tom as a black man— especially as a strong, mature black man, as depicted in the novel and in the earliest productions of Aiken's play—carries a great potential for sexual threat, especially, perhaps, to the antebellum white woman's sensibility, but also to the sentimental audience in general.[45] For the character to succeed, the author must remove that threat, but to Baldwin's dismay, the threat takes the sexuality with it. Ammons sees Tom

> as a stereotypical Victorian heroine: pious, domestic, self-sacrificing, emotionally uninhibited in response to people and ethical questions. . . . [T]he characterization insinuates Tom into the nineteenth-century idolatry of feminine virtue, sentimentalized in young girls and sacrosanct in Mother. (172)

Ammons's argument virtually deconstructs itself; if Tom is a heroine, then the requisite qualities are only arbitrarily feminine and the very concept of heroine assumes an infinitely circular trajectory. Yet Tom-as-minister suggests Tom-as-priest, and the priest is the man who wears a skirt, the man who does not function—sexually or socially—as a man. Tom's religious value catapults him beyond considerations of sexuality and gender, and resolves some of the complications that his blackness presents.

As in the novel, the staged Tom is also a nearly passive victim, but Aiken retains only a small portion of the Christian dedication that Stowe used to elevate

Tom from wretch to martyr. In his first appearance on Legree's plantation, Tom soliloquizes as "Old Folks at Home"—a minstrel song—plays in the background:[46]

> I have come to de dark places; I's going through de vale of shadows. My heart sinks at times and feels just like a big lump of lead. Den it gits up in my throat and chokes me till de tears roll out of my eyes; den I take out dis curl of little Miss Eva's hair, and the sight of it brings calm to my mind and I feels strong again. . . . Dere's de bright silver dollar dat Mas'r George Shelby gave me the day I was sold away from old Kentuck, and I've kept it ever since. Mas'r George must have grown to be a man by this time. I wonder if I shall ever see him again. (67)

Aiken retains all of Tom's obligatory remarks—that he will work "while there's life and breath in me" but will die before he will flog another person, that Legree cannot buy his soul, and that he forgives his own murderer—but the playwright omits most of the struggle that leads, in the novel, to Tom's exclamation, "What a thing 't is to be a Christian!" (486). Without the depth of his faith, Tom is more an object of abuse than a man who claims his own spirituality by making a choice to submit.[47] Stowe's Tom is a black Christ who dies that others might live; Aiken's is still a pastor, but not one of divine magnitude.

To the extent that Aiken depleted the story by disarming its treatment of slavery and religion, he replenished it with laughter. Comic characters and interactions dominate approximately half of the play, and while their presence reflects the conventions of midcentury dramaturgy, it also serves to deflate any attack on slavery that other parts of the play might attempt. Ophelia (who is on stage more than any other character in the play) is far more risible than in the novel; she never confronts her own prejudice and hypocrisy, and after she leaves Louisiana, she becomes a stock comic spinster whose scenes with Deacon Perry deny the sentiment that is the substance and point of the Harris subplot. Phineas Fletcher is a travesty of his more principled predecessor; while we can hardly help but like him and applaud the emancipation of his slaves and his stalwart support of George and Eliza, his transparent Quaker role and idiosyncratic speech make him seem such a clown that we must wonder if he truly believes in anything he does. Gumption Cute undercuts the entire issue of the cruelty of slavery when he tells Marks that he shrinks from "setting myself up as a target for darkies to fire at" and that "though it was dreadful trying to my feelings to flog the darkies . . . I got used to it after a while, and then I used to lather 'em like Jehu" (53, 51). The point of Cute is that he has no feelings, and if he can flog the "darkies" without remorse, then perhaps Haley's and Legree's abuses are equally meaningless. As always, farce renders violence harmless, and racism becomes a matter of individual quirks, of the crotchets of a soulless clown.

Stowe leaves Legree disquietingly alive, but Aiken stages his death, offering grotesque entertainment even while resolving the action. When George Shelby travels up the Red River in search of Tom, he brings with him Marks, the lawyer, who tries to arrest Legree for the murder of St. Clare. In the scuffle, Marks shoots Legree, who exclaims, "I am hit!—the game's up!" and falls abruptly dead. The planter's two assistants, Sambo and Quimbo, enter, laughing, to carry him off stage. Suffering from his master's beatings, Tom expires, and the play closes with a tableau:

> *Gorgeous clouds, tinted with sunlight.* EVA, *robed in white, is discovered on the back of a milk-white dove, with expanded wings, as if just soaring upward. Her hands are extended in benediction over* ST. CLARE *and* UNCLE TOM *who are kneeling and gazing up to her. Expressive music.—Slow curtain.* (88)

No matter how comic Legree's death, and no matter how extravagant the final tableau, the two events are commensurate with the terms in which the play has presented its material. On Aiken's stage, neither racism nor slavery is a genuine problem, so neither merits an earnest solution. Ludicrous though it may be, Legree's demise conforms to a standard theatrical convention which, like most, is an expression of a deeper reality: it enforces closure by enacting the ritualized demise of evil itself. To kill Legree is to abolish slavery, but without any real-world complications, and when this death is combined with the tableau of transfiguration, Aiken has created more than a cliché happy ending; he has solved the problems that the play ostensibly reveals. The melodrama has presented slavery as only superficially threatening within the limits of the stage, and it has afforded its audience a typically overblown, vicarious emotional experience that has little to do with the complex problems of the actual world. The theatricality, extravagant though it may be, serves the underlying operation of the play and provides an appropriate resolution less to the action itself and more to the spectatorial process. The denouement is reassuring within the limits of that process: slavery drops dead with Legree, and the more deserving characters receive their heavenly reward, so the audience may enjoy the sensation, however illusory, of having achieved what the play implies is morally right, but without having to make any effort or take any initiative. Legree's murder and Eva's transfiguration are not rehearsals for actions the audience might undertake upon leaving the theatre; these are artificial solutions which, like the problems that the play mocks and simplifies, prevail only within the stage representation. The play legitimates the essential conservatism of the middle-class by solving a distasteful problem without subjecting society to fundamental reform—by transfiguring it, if you will, into shallow artifice.

Stowe's novel rested on her conception of slavery as a system; when Aiken removed that footing, he replaced it with the more comfortable melodramatic world view. Melodrama satisfies because it resolves the complexities and brings its action to complete closure. Aiken's dramaturgical dialectic leaves the audience with no specific ground of meaning; the elements of the play cancel each other out— wherever Aiken elicits concern, he deflates it with laughter, sentiment, or melodramatic formula—so when the audience leaves the theatre, all is settled. *Uncle Tom's Cabin* becomes a self-contained world, resolving its own momentary inconsistencies and offering no correlation to the genuine issues it purports to address. Stowe traced the quest for human value within the destructive oppression of slavery, while Aiken followed the stylized mumming of simplified characters within the neat limits of melodrama.

The final moments of the play clarify the fundamental tension between Stowe's Christian vision and the ideology of midcentury melodrama. Stowe explored the complexities of life, dying, and death, but melodrama insists on the simplicity of the essential life/death binarism and scorns the final journey except as an excuse for suspense. In melodrama, death operates in two spheres. Within the fiction—that is, as far as the characters themselves are concerned—it is the ultimate calamity, the vandal that destroys the stability of the family, especially when it takes the husband and father, and so leaves widows and orphans (like St. Clare's slaves) helpless before the onslaught of an apparently random world. Outside of the fiction—from the point of view of the playwright, performers, and audience—death is the necessary convention for dramatizing the defeat of evil. Melodrama itself is a means to incarnate and expiate its audience's fears; "evil" is the name of those fears, and the villain is its agent. The villain must die to lay fear to rest, and virtue must triumph to affirm the world view that melodrama's audience cherishes and to restore the moral order.

That very restoration—the absolute imperative of melodrama—leads the play to confirm the fundamental racism of American society. The discourse of race and racism defines a space, and while neither the novel nor the play can conceivably escape from that space, each takes up a different position within it. Stowe attempts to challenge the validity of race as the primal factor in defining the discourse of human relations, but Aiken accepts the discourse without question, and instead of disputing its terms, he employs them—therefore embracing and reinforcing them—to give his audience a reassuring experience. In both treatments, race remains the currency of interaction. No matter what the characters' allotted destinies—George's freedom in exile, Tom's jubilee, Eva's beatitude, or Legree's certain damnation—their racial identities are their salient features as individuals and as interactive members of a community.

The characterizing feature of the discourse and space of racism, at least in its American formulation, is that slavery in America involved blacks as slaves and whites as masters. Race therefore mandates class, and class is strictly associated with race; as Frederickson has demonstrated, American racism evolved—and took on many of the characteristics that endure today—during the first half of the nineteenth century to become an ideology intended to rationalize slavery (*Black Image* 47–50). It is truly an ideology, for it protected, and possibly still protects, the interests of that certain class known as white Americans. The novel disapproves of racism, but its sentimental foundation makes its position vulnerable; if feeling is the ground for one's belief, then to satisfy the demands of feeling is to mollify the individual and, potentially, remove the need for action, and although sympathy assumes essential equality, philanthropy is inherently paternalistic.[48] Stowe is therefore susceptible to palliatives instead of solutions, and her philanthropic strategies ensure the endurance of racial hierarchy. The play muffles its ostensible appeal even more than the novel; to the extent that it personalizes slavery and racism, and so leaves American society tacitly uncensured and intact, the audience has no motivation to pursue a program of reform or revolution. Aiken even succeeds in preserving whiteness as a viable alternative; by killing Legree, he eliminates the idea of the white man as the source of evil, while at the same time expiating the guilt of the white audience.

5

My Partner (1879) and the West

ON SEPTEMBER 16, 1879, Bartley Campbell's *My Partner* opened at the Union Square Theatre in New York City.[1] It was not the first play to treat the adventures of the California gold county; the Wallacks had produced *Fast Folks* in San Francisco in 1858, while New York theatres had offered, within the space of one year, Bret Harte's *Two Men of Sandy Bar* (1876), Joaquin Miller's *The Danites in the Sierras* (1877), and *Ah Sin* (1877), by Harte and Mark Twain.[2] Yet *My Partner* was the most popular of these plays, and Campbell located it not only in relation to the actual California experience, but also—and much more importantly—in relation to what his predominantly eastern audience believed about that experience, in both specific and general terms. The fundamental question of the play involves how melodrama (re)constructs myth, or, more precisely, how this certain play, as a mimetic and semiotic composition employing the form, style, and conventions of melodrama, the culture's predominant theatrical medium, shapes and revises not so much experience as another such composition, the culture's most powerful historical narrative and richest expression of ambition, the myth of the West.

THE WEST

Once upon a time, our entire hemisphere was "the West." Since the beginning of collective European memory, the known world and the maps that measured it had found the ultimate western boundary in the swells of the Atlantic, an impenetrable vastness that had encouraged generations of fantasies concerning what might lie beyond the sunset. When Europeans realized that their ships could cross the water and reach not Asia but completely unfamiliar lands, they wondered whether their dreams were materializing, whether God were expanding the limits of human experience to include ancient mysteries. As Seneca had written, in anticipation of Columbus's voyage, "Today the sea has capitulated and submits to human terms . . . any skiff may wander at will over the deep. All boundaries have been abolished . . . the whole world may be freely traversed. . . . Thule shall no longer be land's end" (*Medea*, Act Two).

Most of what is now the United States has been defined as the West at one

"Washing for Gold." From *Our New West* by Samuel Bowles (1869). (Courtesy of the Huntington Library, San Marino, California.)

time or another since the early 1600s, when the first English-speaking colonists completed the Atlantic crossing and stood on the beach to gaze westward into the inscrutable forests. Once the eastern seaboard was settled, the West became the territory beyond the Appalachians, but Daniel Boone led his party through the Cumberland Gap in 1775, the Erie Canal opened in 1825, and by the 1830s, Independence, Missouri, was the western outpost and point of debarkation for what Americans today still tend to regard as the West, as both region and mythic construct: the trans-Mississippi West, the vast land of prairies, mountains, and deserts that lies beyond the big river. The legends of this West grew out of what drew people to it and how they lived when they arrived: French and English trappers had been collecting pelts in the Old Northwest since the mid-1600s and by 1825 were holding rendezvous in the Rockies; loggers harvested Northwest timber as early as the 1820s; and, always, the farmers hitched up their wagons and moved west even before the government opened the territories, searching for new fields to subdue with the plow, domesticating the country with their families, and reaching the Pacific Coast by the early 1840s.[3]

Yet it was the discovery of gold that most dramatically galvanized the nation and focused the general gaze westward toward the fabulous fortunes that seemed so accessible. James Marshall picked up his famous nugget only nine days before Mexico ceded California to the United States—a confluence of events that abruptly relocated the American dream to the riffles in a sluice box and brought it to full fruition in those lovely mountains where, so the tale ran, a man need not work but merely bend down to find a fortune waiting at his feet.[4] Even before its discovery by Spanish sailors, the mythic pressure on California was stronger and the experience more intense than on the West at large; this Pacific haven was the apotheosis of the western promise, named after the imaginary island in Garcí Ordóñez de Montalvo's romance, and generating a mystique that still survives.[5] As David Wyatt has said,

> The American settlement of California marked the end of western man's Hesperian movement. So great was the beauty of the land that it conferred on the completion of the quest the illusion of a return to a privileged source. As the sense of an ending merged with the wonder of beginnings, California as last chance merged with California as Eden. It proves a garden but briefly held. The city that rises like an exhalation, San Francisco, burns and rises again and again. (xvi)

The beauty of the landscape may have ravished the newcomers, but it was the possibility of quick wealth that drew them in; it was the gold rush that changed the Easterners' perception of California, mandated a rapprochement between Eden and Mammon, rendered delightfully convenient the rhetoric and the rationale of Manifest Destiny, and inspired the plays by Campbell, Harte, Miller, and Twain.[6]

The discovery of the "New" World had encouraged—even required—the European wanderers to vindicate the Arcadian or Edenic legends by enacting the old narratives, by taking roles in a drama of regeneration. To posit that the New World or the American West offered limitless opportunity is not quite accurate, for Old World storytellers had already anticipated the nature of that opportunity and the manner of its realization; that is, cultural myth, accumulating over centuries, had already imagined the future and inscribed it on collective aspiration. The migrating Europeans and their restless descendants were charged with a mission, with the responsibility to live up to mythic expectations, so they found not precisely freedom, but rather a prescription for freedom. To move west and there reconstruct the East was to fail; the West was the future, and if the great migration led to repeating the past, there was no point in leaving home. The myth defined the westward movement as part of the constant becoming of western culture, as the final journey toward the perfection of mankind. The migrants therefore carried an emotional burden, and it is this burden that, to a large extent, shaped the narrative and performative responses to the westward experience.[7]

The deepest foundation of the myth of the West was a classic binary opposition that used the settled East as a point of reference and defined the West as alien, divergent, exotic—different. This opposition provided the foundation for Frederick Jackson Turner's vision of the westward movement as colonization; he posited "wilderness," "primitive," and "savage" on the one side, and "institutions," "civilization," and "democracy" on the other. When he defined the frontier as "the outer edge of the wave—the meeting point between savagery and civilization," Turner did not clarify whether "savagery" was a matter of land or people—whether the pioneers had to meet the challenge of a wilderness or of the "primitive" people who already lived there. He seemed to conflate the two alternatives, suggesting that the colonist adopts native ways partly out of imitation and partly because the land demands them (3–4). As with any binary opposition, depending as it must on a rigid conception of difference, the supposedly polar elements twist back on each other and refuse to remain stable—in this case, the very process of migration merges East with West and reveals as virtually arbitrary the distinction between "Easterner" and "Westerner" (even today, especially in California, it seems that most Westerners were once Easterners). The distortion reveals that we *think* that we speak in geographic terms—the West is a region, and the frontier is the interface between East and West—not realizing that our usage of "West" refers, more richly and more often, to what happened when Europeans and Easterners moved into the North American continent; the "West" is less a region or the people in it, and more an experience as contemplated from a Eurocentric perspective. The essential East/West opposition is only superficially geographical, and even in that sense became more and more blurry as the so-called frontier moved westward, yet myth and discourse have persisted in accepting both its validity and its apparent meaning.

This persistence may derive partly from the fact that California remains the most vivid inspiration and vessel of the myth of America—the vision of an Eden, a dream of limitless possibilities, and a sense of eternal beginnings. It is a land within a land, the home of expectations, separated from the rest of the nation by distance, topography, and mutual suspicion. To concede that California is, ultimately, no different from the other states and territories is to include California in the general failure of the American dream and to preclude any new attempts to realize it. Any expression of California as such, including *My Partner*, must move within the space of mythic expectations.

THE DISCOURSE OF CALIFORNIA

Nineteenth-century residents of the settled East learned of California principally through what were in essence travelogues—chronological reports, sometimes day-to-day, of authors' journeys, the very form of which served to cast subject, writer, and reader in specific roles and to construct California in a certain way. In any such account, the writer defines himself as a traveler, moving freely through space and time and sending reports back to the reader, who, unlike the writer, is bound to a specific place and probably also to commitments such as family and conventional employment.[8] Any reader/writer relationship is political, assuming for the writer a voice and an opportunity to speak, while relegating the reader to passivity; in the case of the travelogue, especially the accounts in question, the reader is especially denigrated as one who chose to remain home, safe in the East, one for whom the admired experience is only vicarious. Moreover, to validate the journey, and therefore the traveler himself, the writer must present the subject— California or the West—as a source of wonder and an object of admiration; otherwise there would be no reason to undertake the journey or write the account, and even less reason to read that account. The writer urges California's magnificence to valorize himself and at the same time legitimate the fantasies of the reader, who is taking time from more conventionally constructive pursuits to learn about a place he cannot apprehend on his own. To describe is to appropriate; the writer makes California his own and therefore assigns carefully differentiated positions of relative proximity (and therefore status) to himself and the reader. Yet because California has no volition in this process, because California is only as the writer presents it, although the writer purports to mediate between California and the reader, in actuality, the writer locates California in a position to seem to mediate between himself and the reader, to become the veil through which reader and writer perceive each other. Writing becomes (as always) an exercise in self-construction, and the material is less the point of the exercise and more its field or medium.

Within this paradigm, the writer promotes California to elevate himself. Richard Henry Dana, Jr., wrote of the wealth of California's forests, rivers, and plains, "with a soil in which corn yields from seventy to eighty fold," and exclaimed, "In the hands of an enterprising people, what a country this might be!" (172). He not only describes the region but also constructs himself as the discoverer and his point of view as worthy of respect and attention; in other words, he is the man with the energy and determination to leave the security of Harvard and sail to the other side of the continent in 1835, well before most others, and the man with the perception to foresee the future.[9] T. J. Farnham presented his journey of 1840 as a seamless adventure, characterized by encounters with the exotic Spanish and natives, and dominated by the landscape. He claimed that only from an incoming ship could one appreciate the "surpassing beauty and magnificence" of the San Francisco Bay:

> One must approach it from the sea; have a full view of the lofty shores north and south, rising at intervals into lofty peaks girded at their bases with primeval forests of evergreen cedars and pines mottled with the boughs of the oak, the ash, and the plane.[10] . . . [T]he Bay is . . . a broad sheet of water stretching off, north and south, the largest and best harbor of the earth, surrounded by a country, partly wooded, and partly disposed in open glades and prairies of the richest kind, covered with the flocks and herds of the Missions, and deer, and elk, and bears. (139)

Farnham cannot help interpreting the Bay in terms of its potential wealth—its promise as a harbor, the richness of the surrounding fields, and the plenitude of animal life. In his report on the expedition he led through California during 1844, John C. Frémont depicts the beauty of the flowers and trees, and relates his pleasant ride through the San Joaquin Valley—a relief after his struggles through the winter snows of the high mountains—toward a pass in the southern Sierra, where he pauses to contemplate the scenery one last time before heading into the desert toward Utah:

> [W]e continued up the right-hand branch, which was enriched by a profusion of flowers, and handsomely wooded with sycamore, oaks, cottonwood, and willow, with other trees, and some shrubby plants. . . . Gooseberries, nearly ripe, were very abundant on the mountain . . . the air was filled with perfume, as if we were entering a highly cultivated garden; and, instead of green, our pathway and the mountain sides were covered with fields of yellow flowers, which here was the prevailing color. . . . [W]e rode along between green trees and on flowers, with humming-birds and other feathered friends of the traveller enlivening the serene spring air. (254–55)[11]

Edwin Bryant, in a report of his travels during 1846–47, one much more stiffly factual than Farnham's and more comprehensive than Frémont's, considered the fertility of the land, the perfection of the native raspberries, and the probable future of the San Francisco Bay region which, he predicted, "under American authority . . . will rise with astonishing rapidity" (324). Yet even he allowed himself a temporary preoccupation with the sheer beauty of the landscape near Donner Lake:

The sublime altitude of the mountains, their granite and barren heads piercing the sky; the umbrageous foliage of the tall pines and cedars, deepening in verdure and density as the forest approaches the more gentle and grassy slopes along the banks of the lake, the limpid and tranquil surface of which *daguerreotypes* distinctly every object, from the moss-covered rocks laved by its waves to the bald and inaccessible summits of the Sierra—these scenic objects, with the fresh incense of the forest, and the fragrant odor of the wild rose, constituted a landscape that, from associations, melted the sensibilities, blunted as they were by long exposure and privation, and brought back to our memories the endearments of home and the pleasures of civilization. (230)

Like so many other eastern writers, Bryant, even though he acknowledges the presence of the native and Spanish populations, emphasizes the concept of California as a vessel ready to be filled, a richly sexual image of a virgin land, untried, unclaimed, but irresistibly inviting to the male adventurer who is willing to conquer, penetrate, and possess this pliant, welcoming new world. Bryant even appropriates the region on behalf of his eastern readers when he assures them that "it seems to be a settled opinion, that California is henceforth to compose a part of the United States, and every American who is now here considers himself as treading upon his own soil, as much as if he were in one of the old thirteen revolutionary states" (327). California is the ultimate land of opportunity and a space in which aspiration thrives; to make the journey is to find the dream.

After the discovery of gold, the travelogues took on a new urgency. The promise of beauty and rich farmland was enticing enough, but the prospect of wealth, of easy fortunes expressed in terms that even the urban cynics could embrace, was overwhelmingly seductive. Now the writer/traveler could dangle before his readers' eyes descriptions and reports that could engage rapt interest almost as well as the actual nuggets. The classic goldfield story was the anecdote about an easy "find," like Walter Colton's tale of the little girl who brought her mother an interesting rock that turned out to be a lump of gold weighing six or seven pounds. Colton was a minister who served as alcalde of Monterey from 1846 to 1849; he was not given to effusion, but even he could not resist the excitement of prospecting when he arrived in the gold country on September 30, 1848:

[W]e wound over a rough, rocky elevation, and turned suddenly into a ravine, up which we discovered a line of tents glittering in the sun's rays. We were in the gold mines! I jumped from my horse, took a pick, and in five minutes found a piece of gold large enough to make a signet ring. (273)

He tried panning, but disliked standing in river mud, so instead turned to chipping particles of gold out of the layers of slate on the wall of a ravine. This process was easy and rewarding, but he observed that a team of four or five men operating a nine-foot cradle could earn at least one hundred dollars a day.

A much more enthusiastic champion of the golden dream was E. Gould Buffum, who lived in California for three years from 1847 to 1849 and spent six months in the goldfields.

> I shall never forget the delight with which I first struck and worked out a crevice. . . . I had slung pick, shovel, and bar upon my shoulder, and trudged merrily away to a ravine about a mile from our house. . . . [T]here at the bottom strewn along the whole length of the rock, was bright, yellow gold, in little pieces about the size and shape of a grain of barley. Eureka! Oh how my heart beat! I sat still and looked at it some minutes before I touched it, greedily drinking in the pleasure of gazing upon gold that was in my very grasp, and feeling a sort of independent bravado in allowing it to remain there. When my eyes were sufficiently feasted, I scooped it out with the point of my knife and an iron spoon, and placing it in my pan, ran home with it very much delighted. I weighed it, and found that my first day's labour in the mines had made me thirty-one dollars richer than I was in the morning. (46)

He concedes that digging for gold involves strenuous labor under severe conditions, but he insists that, for a man willing and able to work, "there was never a better opportunity in the world to make a fortune, than there is at present in California" (109).

There was little difference in response between men like Colton and Buffum, who had come to California before Marshall's discovery, and the eastern journalists who invaded the Sierra along with the argonauts. Bayard Taylor reported his reactions when first visiting the Mokelumne diggings during 1849–50:

> The gold was of the purest quality and most beautiful color. When I first saw the men carrying heavy stones in the sun, standing nearly waist-deep in water, and grubbing with their hands in the gravel and clay, there seemed to me little virtue in resisting the temptation to gold-digging; but when the shining particles were poured out lavishly from a tin basin, I confess there was a sudden itching in my fingers to seize the heaviest crowbar and the biggest shovel. (65–66)

He scorns those who fail and who "cry out with such bitterness against the golden stories which first attracted them to the country," insisting that the gold is there for those who can understand the clues Nature leaves to her "buried treasures." His own "golden story" is calculated to locate the reader—the Easterner, naïve to the ways of the mining camps—in an imaginary Sierra stream, glittering in the sun as the prospectors—the brave ones, the vanguard—release its treasures. Taylor assures his readers that "there is more gold in California than ever was said or imagined: ages will not exhaust the supply" (69). In an almost gluttonous assessment of the region's potential ten years later, Horace Greeley concurred, assuring his readers that California would continue "to produce gold abundantly" (244). As editor of the New York *Tribune*, he wielded considerable authority, and his firsthand experience, combined with his use of statistics and display of business acumen, doubtless increased the influence of such passages. Others depicted the gold rush as a romantic quest, but Greeley legitimated the effort as eminently practical and therefore responsible and even respectable. Yet the mystique survived; long after gold mining had become more an industry than a matter of individual initiative, Mark Twain, in *Roughing It* (1872), cultivated the myth of the goldfields with a reminiscent look back at the way life was in the "early" days:

> [Y]ou will find it hard to believe that there stood at one time a fiercely-flourishing little city, of two thousand or three thousand souls, with its newspaper, fire company, brass band, volunteer militia, bank, hotels, noisy Fourth of July processions and speeches, gambling hells crammed with tobacco smoke, profanity, and rough-bearded men of all nations and colors, with tables heaped with gold dust sufficient for the revenues of a German principality—streets crowded and rife with business—town lots worth four hundred dollars a front foot—labor, laughter, music, dancing, swearing, fighting, shooting, stabbing—a bloody inquest and a man for breakfast every morning—*everything* that delights and adorns existence—all the appointments and appurtenances of a thriving and prosperous and promising young city. . . . They fairly reveled in gold, whisky, fights and fandangoes, and were unspeakably happy. The honest miner raked from a hundred to a thousand dollars out of his claim a day. . . . (369–70)

The acquisition of the gold becomes both the source and the metaphor for the effulgence of frontier life during the gold rush.

Yet the landscape prevailed. In her letters from the gold country, written during 1851–52, Dame Shirley wrote that one late winter day broke

> with all the primeval splendor of the birth-morn of creation. The lovely river—having resumed its crimson border . . . glides by, laughing gaily, leaping and clapping its glad waves joyfully in the golden sunlight. The feathery fringe of the fir-trees glitters, like emerald, in the luster bathing air.[12] A hundred tiny rivulets flash down from the brow of the mountains, as if some mighty Titan, standing on the other side, had flung athwart their greenness, a chaplet of radiant pearls. Of the large quantities of snow which have fallen within the past fortnight, a few patches of shining whiteness, high up among the hills, alone remain; while, to finish the picture, the lustrous heaven of California, looking "further off" than ever, through the wonderfully transparent atmosphere, and for that very reason, infinitely more beautiful, bends over all the matchless blue of its resplendent arch. (107)

Even the pagan reference scarcely compromises the presentation of California as Eden, where the natural world retains its divine beauty and mankind can have another chance to begin history.

Such a response was even more characteristic of those who, in the 1850s and 1860s, visited Yosemite Valley, whose landscape even the practical Greeley found irresistible:

> That first full, deliberate gaze up the opposite height! Can I ever forget it? The valley is here scarcely half a mile wide, while its northern wall of mainly naked, perpendicular granite is at least four thousand feet high—probably more. But the modicum of moonlight that fell into this awful gorge gave to

that precipice a vagueness of outline, an indefinite vastness, a ghostly and weird spirituality. Had the mountain spoken to me in an audible voice, or began to lean over with the purpose of burying me in its crushing mass, I should hardly have been surprised. (258)

Each eastern writer who visited Yosemite presented himself as its discoverer and conveyed not only a description of its wonders but also subliminal instructions to the reader regarding how to position himself in relation to both the spectacle and the intrepid man who reported it. Charles L. Brace stood on Inspiration Point and decided that neither the Alps nor "even Niagara itself, was so full of the inspiration of awe" as Yosemite Valley, demoting those other "sights" by arguing that "all other scenes of grandeur and beauty must fade away in my memory when this vision is forgotten," and aligning himself with divine vision when he asserted that "before the mighty powers which had shaped this tremendous gorge, and in presence of this scene of unspeakable and indescribable beauty and majesty, man and his works seemed to sink away to nothingness" (100).

Yet even the commonplace landscape ravished traveler and reader. Clarence King, the mountaineer and geologist, stood at the summit of Pacheco Pass (forty miles southeast of San José) and gazed east across the San Joaquin Valley, toward the Sierra Nevada.

> Brown foot-hills, purple over their lower slopes with "fil-a-ree" blossoms, descended steeply to the plain of California, a great, inland, prairie sea. . . . Miles of orange-colored flowers, cloudings of green and white, reaches of violet which looked like the shadow of a passing cloud, wandering in natural patterns over and through each other, sunny and intense along near our range, fading in the distance into pale bluish-pearl tones, and divided by long, dimly seen rivers, whose margins were edged by belts of bright emerald green. Beyond rose three hundred miles of Sierra half lost in light and cloud and mist, the summit in places sharply seen against a pale, beryl sky, and again buried in warm, rolling clouds. . . . Dusky foot-hills rose over the plain with a coppery gold tone, suggesting the line of mining towns planted in its rusty ravines—a suggestion I was glad to repel, and look higher into that cool, solemn realm where the pines stand, green-roofed, in infinite colonnade. . . .
>
> While I looked the sun descended; shadows climbed the Sierras, casting a gloom over foot-hill and pine, until at last only the snow summits, reflecting the evening light, glowed like red lamps along the mountain wall for hundreds of miles. The rest of the Sierra became invisible. The snow burned for a moment in the violet sky, and at last went out. (23–24)[13]

King presents California as, to paraphrase Henry Nash Smith's vision of the Mississippi Valley, the Garden of the West, while others saw this Californian garden as a prolifically fertile working farm and eagerly tallied produce of the fields under the steady sunshine. Greeley described the potential of California's "thirty millions of acres" (a phrase he repeated, with variations) for vineyards, fruit orchards, and fields of grain. Albert D. Richardson visited California in 1865 and reported that one wheat farm near San José yielded a hundred bushels to the acre after one planting, and sixty bushels in a subsequent "volunteer" crop. He described the astonishing circumference and weight achieved by onions, turnips, tomatoes, beets, squash, and watermelons exhibited at agricultural fairs, and claimed that "a peach twig a foot long, stuck in the ground in 1858, bore fruit the next year." He savored the local custom of serving fresh fruit—grapes, figs, peaches, strawberries, and pears, all in season—for breakfast, and listed the achievements of a one-acre "garden" belonging to a friend in Placerville:

> The oleander bloomed upon the porch, and the garden air was fragrant with rose and fuchsia, honeysuckle and heliotrope, nasturtium and sweet verbena. It was only the first week of July; but strawberries, (the second crop—the same vines produce four or five times a year,) raspberries, blackberries, cherries, plums, apricots, figs, early peaches, pears, apples and grapes were abundant. (452, 453, 388)

Like every other aspect of the West, this garden is the best of its kind, an Eden, but an orderly one, producing according to these eastern writers' delighted values. To write of California in this vein becomes a virtual exercise in gluttony, a gastronomical celebration of the glorious West. California was a Greeleyan fantasy, a land of unutterable beauty that was eminently productive.[14]

As the population of California grew, the literature on California peopled the mythic space as well. The East's discourse on the West had taken on a new intensity after the Civil War as the public gaze turned toward the Pacific and the railroad spanned the continent, and in 1868, San Francisco's *Overland Monthly* published "The Luck of Roaring Camp" and brought fame to Bret Harte.[15] His stories came to dominate the literary construction of California during the 1870s; travel writer Mary E. Blake once referred to "the traditional Westerner, the man whom Bret Harte created and the world has taken as a type, fearless, dashing, yet gentle" (81). Harte distilled the population of the mining camps, the trails, and the sudden cities into a handful of vivid types—the lonely miner who has left his wife and family in the East while he hunts for the strike that will make them all rich, the devoted partners working a claim together, the impeccable gambler, the madcap teamster, the picturesque but dim-witted working-class Mexican, the even more picturesque but debonair aristocratic Mexican, and Colonel Starbottle, the renegade Kentucky gentleman come to the West as orator, attorney, duellist, drinker, and dandy. Harte's Californians are fortune hunters, seekers after dreams drawn from all parts of the globe and thrown together, helter-skelter, to form a haphazard society in which men's destinies are governed more by a Dickensian operation of coincidence and the ironic past than by their own considerable wills and energies.

This California differs from the theatrical model in one essential respect: evil has little presence. Harte peopled his stories with those whom the respectable, conventional East regarded as beyond the fringe of polite society, yet few, if any, act from malice; all mean well. Harte can scarcely imagine a man, no matter how rough in appearance or action, who does not shed a tear in response to the slightest evocation of the sanctity of home and family. The presence of tiny Tom Luck does not convert the miners, for they need no conversion; it rather reveals their allegedly innate kindness, altruism, and talent for nurture. Men revere women, and all the more so if they resemble the migrants' memories of the wives, mothers, and sisters they left behind. Harte's California is a land of wild beauty and limitless potential, but also a rough country where the basic goodness of human nature survives and proves the indomitability of the individual.[16] In 1877, E. S. Nadal wrote in the *North American Review* that Harte's books express "the scenery and society of the country [and] describe the life of a remote region and of a rude frontier people. But that life was an extravaganza of the traits of our whole democratic society" (81). If, in "The Story of a Mine" (1867), Wiles attempts to dupe Concho out of his quicksilver mine, he is an exception that demonstrates the pattern. Far more typical is Dick Bullen, who, in "How Santa Claus Came to Simpson's Bar" (1872), rides a worthless mare fifty miles, fords the torrent of Rattlesnake Creek, and takes a bullet from a highwayman in order to bring a sick boy a few broken toys for Christmas. Harte excludes evil to affirm an essentialist and sentimental vision of human nature; Patrick D. Morrow argues that "Harte saw California in mythic and archetypal terms and wrote parables which showed the Eastern reading public that picturesque Western scenes really were a part of universal experience and truth" (128–29). More importantly, Harte had created the characters that would, in the minds of millions of Americans (mostly Easterners) inhabit the paradise that the earlier writers had described and defined; he had invented the cast of Californians and set the pattern for their interactions. He prevailed over the national imagination so successfully that writers like Campbell had to work with Harte's material and on his terms.

MY PARTNER

My Partner follows in the traditions of the travelogues and Harte's stories. The play begins with a love triangle between Mary Brandon and two mining partners named Joe Saunders and Ned Singleton. Mary loves both men, but Ned promises to marry her, and she has sexual relations with him. Joe, not suspecting that he and his partner are interested in the same woman, is about to declare his love and propose marriage when he learns the nature of Mary's involvement with Ned; he demands that his recreant partner marry the girl within three days (a nicely arbitrary deadline that invites mishap!), and proceeds to dissolve their partnership. Before Ned can keep his promise, he receives a visit from Josiah Scraggs, an old acquaintance and secret enemy of Mathew Brandon, Mary's father. Scraggs suggests that Mary has been Joe's mistress, and in the ensuing scuffle he picks up a knife and kills Ned. The miners arrest Joe for Ned's murder, months pass, Mary returns from a mysterious prolonged absence to attest to Joe's character, and Joe suddenly proclaims that they were secretly married in order to ensure the restoration of her father's affections and protect her from Scraggs's slanders. Before the jury can hang Joe, Wing Lee produces a torn shirt that incriminates Scraggs, and the lovers look forward to a happy future.[17]

Campbell locates his action in the California landscape; the mountain country is a virtual paradise that confers an Edenic innocence on its inhabitants. Poetic justice flows not from religion or moral abstraction, as in most midcentury melodrama, but from the land itself. Joe refers to "California, where the trees are larger, and men's hearts bigger than anywhere else in all creation," and when young Grace Brandon asks whether there is any place like California, Sam Bowler, her suitor, answers, "Except heaven, and California up here in the mountains is so close to it that none of us want to leave it" (58, 56). Even the blustering, hard-drinking Major Britt's inflated politician's rhetoric conveys an essential faith in the land when he calls his constituents' attention to

> the top of Siskiyou, where the stars drink dew from the daisies and the singing of the Klamath comes mingled with the rustle of the pines . . . the moon like a beacon in motion, afloat upon a sea of azure; the dark pines whispering to each other, the river flashing like liquid silver, and singing as it flows, while the great dome of Shasta, clad in its mantle of eternal snow, shames by its purity and proportion the fabled fabrics of pagan Rome. (56–57)[18]

The community is upset when circumstances subject Joe, an upright man, to a charge of murder, but the last-minute discovery that saves the victim also restores and vindicates the people's faith.[19] Nothing can remain wrong in this Eden; error and transgression settle effortlessly into resolution as the innocent and well-intentioned find ultimate reward. California is the land of kept promises, a garden where dreams grow and hopes flourish.

Yet California also carries the burden of the myth of the West, especially the West as wilderness, and Campbell, like most who have written on the subject, in order to mediate between his audience and the West that he constructed for them, evidently felt compelled to confront the central problem of how to define the West, as wilderness, as distinct from the East, as civilization. This issue was of central, if underlying, concern with regard to plays like *My Partner*, because the subject was western and the audience, like the playmakers, was eastern, so the phenomenon of difference suffused and controlled the entire experience and the production of meaning. Moreover, to apply melodrama to the myth of the West is to confound both. The melodramatic vision wraps its disciples in a Manichæan straitjacket that compels them to make choices and define their terms of existence according to the polar model, to see elements only in pairs, identify with one as the embodiment of virtue, and shun the other as the avatar of evil. East and West seemed so clearly opposed that this tradition insisted on a similarly irrevocable choice—to identify with one as the embodiment of virtue, and shun the other as the avatar of evil. Yet because American mythology had valorized both wilderness and civilization, rendering untenable the rejection of either, both audience and playmakers were forced into a dilemma that Rosemarie Bank explains:

> On the one hand . . . the virgin frontier is distorted and can be corrupted by civilization because civilization exploits and exploitation is not inherently tied to understanding the need to reward good and punish evil—the major ethical check upon the doctrine of manifest destiny. On the other hand, utopia is the product of civilization because the frontier environment does not exist without regulation once people are gathered together within that environment, and those who possess the gifts of civilization—education, culture, know-how—are the best equipped to lead that society toward an affirmation of good and away from evil. (158)

The audience's own values force them to acknowledge an essential ambiguity in what they would rather perceive as an opposition.

Campbell subscribes to the fundamental distinction (East/West, civilization/wilderness) but at the same time denies that it has substance, arguing instead that the West is becoming what the East can no longer be, and that the ideals upon which the East was supposedly founded are more fully realized in the clear air of the Siskiyous. He reduces evil to one aberrant individual; once the malefactor is cast out, the land is clean again. In spite of the arrival of women, politicians, and organized religion, Campbell's characters remain eternally located on the frontier; they have their wilderness and their civilization, too.

The issue of whether East/West is equivalent to civilization/wilderness suggests the question of whether female/male is equivalent to either dichotomy.[20] Traditional cliché and convention hold that the East is polished, educated, civilized, and female, while the West is rough, crude, violent, and male. Men pioneered Campbell's mining community in the Siskiyous; should we then conclude that they are men of the wilderness or vanguards of civilization? When Joe says that "there ain't no happiness where there ain't no women" (60), does he express a desire for a complement to his wildness, or does he recognize that men and women need each other in order to establish domestic civilization? The women seem more refined and sensitive than most of their male counterparts, but this comparison probably obtains in virtually every play written during the period, whether set in the West or not. That the men revere Mary and Grace as toddlers demonstrates Campbell's debt to Harte more than it clarifies his stance on the gender question.[21] Furthermore, the precise history of the characters scarcely supports careful distinctions because none is native to the West: Scraggs, Wellington Widgery, and the Brandons are from England, and the rest are from the eastern United States. Because Mary and Grace grew up in California, they seem to have the best claim to the title of Westerner, yet if we accept the conventional qualities of the West, melodrama's vision of gender roles militates against there being a genuinely western woman at all; to adopt "western" behavior she would unsex herself.[22] The clearest expression of the East/West opposition appears not in any male/female pairing, but in the juxtaposition of Scraggs with Joe.[23] Indeed, the characters' style and behavior are less a matter of their relative western quality and more a function of their various roles as hero, heroine, villain, father, and comic.

Through most of the play, gender relations are governed by an impeccably conventional conception of honor. Men must treat women honorably or take the consequences; when Scraggs "forgot himself" with Mary's mother, Brandon had to whip him to remind him of his manners, and when Joe discovers that Ned Singleton had slept with Mary, he not only insists that they marry as soon as possible, but also cuts himself off from his old partner.

> Look at that poor, trembling child standing there, who tells you she hasn't slept for days and nights; whose faith has slipped from her, whose head is bowed, whose heart is crushed. I mean that you shall do her right, that here in the moonlight, on the threshold of that home you have robbed of its purity and peace, you shall solemnly swear to do this poor, motherless child justice. (62)

Joe defines the values, identifying the man as criminal and the woman as victim, and supporting the Victorian convention that absolved the woman of full culpability while denying her the right to take responsibility or credit for her own actions. Joe would protect Mary, but he disempowers her in his effort to live up to the ethic that Britt explicitly defines as medieval: "it delights me to see such unaffected chivalry encased in flannel shirts. That's the stuff out of which great states are made. The pioneers of California stand before you; every one of them a knight in courtesy and a king in honor" (67). Even a miner bears art invisible escutcheon; when Ned proposes to swear by his honor, Joe, distraught at his partner's lapse, insists that he find "something purer than that—by the eternal stars that are looking down upon us now, by the memory of your mother." Later, when Joe faces execution for a murder he did not commit, he tells Brandon, "It's not death I fear—I hope no one here thinks that—but the shame of such an end, the bitter, burning shame" (62, 87).

The most controversial question in *My Partner* concerns Mary's status as simultaneous heroine and fallen woman. She has slept with Ned of her own free will, giving a consent that nearly destroys her. Her sense of shame drives her to contemplate suicide in the river, she explains to Ned how she suffers, and when she returns from her brief exile, she calls herself "a sinful wretch" and assures Grace, "I know that I am unworthy of your love any longer" (85, 86). When she sees her father—the man whose honor, according to convention, she has stained, and the man who demands to know whether she has "a right to rest on my breast"— he waves her from him, but she sinks to her knees and cries, "Mercy! Mercy!" while music plays in the background. In spite of her exaggerated efforts to expiate her sin, Campbell has driven his heroine into an untenable position—she slept with a man out of wedlock, delayed marrying him until it was too late, ran away to bear his child, who died, and then returned in disgrace to marry another man so that he might protect her and save her father's feelings.[24] Joe is the agent of Mary's salvation, and he uses the classic excuse to enlist the audience's forgiveness:

> I've forgotten everything but that you was a poor child raised out here in the wilderness, without the same chance as most wimmen, and little as I know about Scripter I feel sartain Heaven will not be too hard on *a poor gal as had no mother to guide her*." (94; emphasis added)[25]

Mary looks to Joe for guidance, and Campbell gives her so artificially conventional a position that he robs her of any vestige of good sense. She tells Grace that although she once loved Ned, "Since then I have seen with a purer, truer vision; the love of that man in his grave was a shallow stream, lovely to look upon in the sunlight of prosperity, but not deep enough to launch one's barque of life upon." Yet she also sustains the prevailing conception of honor by returning to clear Joe not with proof, but with her belief in him, in his "great good heart, . . . noble soul, [and] tender, patient, self-sacrificing nature" (93, 86). While she realizes that her statement may not free him, she believes that it would have been "cruel and cowardly" to stay away. She risks calumny by acting on her faith in virtue, her belief that sincerity deserves credit and that the outward signs of righteousness (in Joe's case) offer a reliable indication of inner nature and past deeds.

Joe is a hero for the Siskiyous—honest, industrious, and rough. One character concedes that Joe may lack education (even Ned attended college), but "if ye measure gentlemen by their manhood, there's enough of Joe to make a dozen of yer coronet fellows" (50).[26] The *New-York Times* reviewer described him as

> the ideal being whose heart and soul never swerve from their guiding conscience. He is not necessarily improbable, because he is so much better and nobler than men in general. With his prototype we are familiar, for the genius of Bret Harte has described him under many aspects.

Joe is a man of sensibility, however unsophisticated, compelled by his love for Mary and his loyalty to Ned to leave the settlement, but torn at the idea of cutting old ties. He's also a man of strict principle, not only insisting that Ned swear to marry Mary, but even protesting that he is simply unable to shake Ned's hand until the two are married. Yet his feelings govern him in the end, for he returns to the cabin to make amends, only to find his partner dead with a knife in his back. He is as much a part of the California landscape as any of these newcomers can be, and he equates Mary with Eldorado:

> I've seen your eyes in the glitter of the bright gold in the wash, in the stars that looked through the branches on the lonely mountain side, and the thought that you might some day be my own sang its song of hope in my heart as ye hear that river now singing to the willows that bend over it. (60)

Mary, distracted with shame, replies, "If I were only worthy of such devotion, I would give all the gold in the Sierras."

Scraggs is Joe's opposite, polished, well-spoken, class-conscious, and meticulously sensitive to insult. He was a clerk in Brandon's father's countinghouse in London, he courted the woman that Brandon later married, and now he seeks to ruin his old rival: "when I've broken his heart, and can lie down on his pauper grave and beat upon it with my bag of shining gold, then I'll feel my triumph is complete." Where Joe speaks from the heart, Scraggs says whatever he must; the rascal manipulates conventional morality to his own purpose when he tells the returned Mary that "you owe obedience to your father. 'Tis your duty to tell the truth." He proves himself the ultimate Victorian villain by preying principally on women—he turns his best energies toward destroying Mary's reputation—and at the very last, rejects Brandon's sympathy with a threat: "I don't want your sorrow! I despise your pity! Besides you have none to waste! Go to Lady Mary and hear her story, or will I tell it to you here, before all your friends?" (52, 88, 98) Yet Scraggs, like the typical villain, like the misguided drunkard, falls victim to his sense of guilt and self-loathing, stymied by Joe's heroic marriage to Mary, and unable to bring himself to go near the pile of gold he stole from Ned in order to divert suspicion.

Campbell carefully constructs Scraggs's murder of Ned to project certain attitudes on the participants. When Scraggs declares that Mary is Joe's mistress, Ned refers to the statement as a "vile slander" and starts to choke him. Scraggs grabs a knife—one lying on the table, not one that he brought with him—and stabs Ned, who releases him and falls into a chair. The dastard stabs the miner again, fatally, only when Ned rises and starts for him. Scraggs's first comment is "I had to do it! It was self-defense." In this romanticized mining-camp culture, the community approves and admires the man who will forthrightly kill someone who needs killing, and scorns a man who kills haphazardly and will not stand behind his deed. Scraggs does not plan Ned's murder, has little cause to kill him, and does so almost by accident when, Campbell implies, a more masterful man would have avoided striking the final blow. Once the deed is done, Scraggs further proves how craven he is by doing everything he can to disclaim responsibility and throw suspicion on others, in contrast to Joe, who openly declares his willingness to kill the scoundrel if he tries to disgrace Mary. Joe—who refers to the early days when three men were killed as the "good times"—is the paragon of the mining community, while Scraggs is alien in every way.

THE PASTORAL MINES

Campbell's presentation of the murder and subsequent trial followed the growing tradition of gold-country fiction and anecdote. Mining-camp customs in the early 1850s established the now-legendary model: when a crime was discovered, the men would immediately convene a miners' meeting—an impromptu jury composed of whoever happened to be available—and mete out justice with more efficiency and expediency than careful consideration, but always in the best liberal tradition of relying on the judgment of the honest, forthright common man, possessed of an infallible sense of fairness. Evidence was less important than the community's perception of the man and the crime; if the accused were believed to be upright and to have had just provocation, he was likely to go free. This romantically primitive form of justice, developed intuitively by unlettered men far from established authority, supports Turner's concept of "perennial rebirth," of the reinvention of social institutions as each group of pioneers develops civilization amidst the wilderness and further promotes the myth of the westward movement. However, the accounts of contemporary observers (Easterners all) create an equivocal assessment of the system's success. Dame Shirley describes how a miners' meeting condemned a man to death for having stolen gold dust from his partners. They hanged the miscreant three hours after delivering a verdict, and the execution was carried out by the "more reckless part of the community" with so little finesse as to be undeniably cruel, but in spite of her regret, Dame Shirley avers that "there is no doubt, however, that they seriously *thought* they were doing right, for many of them are kind and sensible men. They firmly believed that such an example was absolutely necessary for the protection of this community" (87).[27] Bayard Taylor concedes that punishments were severe, but believes harshness was necessary to maintaining order in the absence of effective government, and assures his readers that camp law was exercised by an elected alcalde and empaneled juries (71).

In his 1884 study of mining-camp government, Charles Howard Shinn argued that camp law derived from the egalitarian concept that all the miners worked government land, and therefore all had equal opportunity to use and benefit from its resources, which were so "inexhaustible" that no one could become wealthy enough to exert power over the others. In this "unconscious socialism . . . clothes, money, manners, family connections, letters of introduction, never before counted for so little," and social and financial equality was available to anyone willing to work with a pan and a pick. Shinn reported that in the "Arcadian era" of 1848, when only about eight thousand miners worked the hills, each man left his cabin open for the use of passing travelers and no one bothered to guard his store of gold, for crime, particularly gold stealing, was virtually unknown, and "a man capable of stealing from his comrades in these busy, friendly camps, was hopelessly hardened, was capable of all the crimes of the Decalogue" (110, 119). Those few exceptions were, by consent of the mining community, whipped, banished, or hanged.

The process of justice in *My Partner* confirms the myth of the West in that individual honor, loyalty, love, and inspiration prevail in the end, and even though the law is rough and raw, right will out and evil will fall. Joe Saunders's trial moves from the reality of the 1870s, when law in California had become more formal, to an imaginative ideality. Rather than try him immediately, his peers wait six months—a convenient and unexplained contrivance that permits Mary to disappear, have her baby, and return. Rather than hold a relatively informal inquest in the nearest saloon, the judge and jury convene in the courtroom. Conviction is looming when Wing Lee brings Major Britt the crucial torn shirt, all the townspeople rush into the sitting room of the Golden Gate Hotel to serve as an impromptu jury, and the proceedings suddenly conform to the romanticized paradigm of the "early days." With no judge present, Britt links the shirt to Scraggs and to the bloody shirt cuff found in Ned's cabin, and sends a man to rifle the villain's trunk to find a handful of gold nuggets mingled with ashes, which even the skeptical, fair-minded Brandon readily accepts as proof that these are the nuggets that Joe and Ned buried under their hearthstone. As Scraggs vainly pleads self-defense, the entire crowd rushes at him with lynching in mind; they agree to delay for one hour only because Joe recommends that they "let him live long enough to realize the doom that's waiting for him" (98). The townspeople fear and reject Josiah Scraggs because he threatens the myth of the West; they hang him because he is the serpent come to Eden, reminding them that their Siskiyou paradise is too good to be true, that the myth of the West is elevated far beyond the reach of actual experience.

To satisfy melodrama's demand for an ideal society, Campbell displaced the reality of California mining life with the more pleasant fiction. Most of California's gold has been found in hard-rock deposits, called lodes, but in the early years of the gold rush, the miners concentrated on placer deposits, usually riverbeds where the gold had settled after being eroded from the lodes. Placer miners used any of three methods to wash dirt or gravel to separate the gold from the rest, all of them based on the principle that gold, being unusually heavy, will sink to the bottom. The tool of romantic memory was a broad, shallow pan similar to a Chinese wok but with a flat bottom; the miner carefully swirled around a mixture of dirt and water, let the lighter sediment slosh over the side, and then sifted through the residue in search of gold. More efficient was the cradle, a wooden box mounted on rockers with a series of cleats or riffles nailed to the bottom and an open chute on the downhill end. The miner shoveled dirt and water into the top, then rocked the cradle to let the waste run out the lower end while the riffles caught the gold. A larger version was the Long Tom, a ten- to twenty-foot trough with riffles along the bottom that caught the gold as the miners shoveled pay dirt in the top and kept the dirt-and-water mixture running down to the end. A single man could pan for gold, but the cradles were more efficient with two men, and the Long Tom required three or four.

Yet placer mining was slow; a man, or even two men, could shovel only so much dirt and gravel in a day. Miners began to build ditches and flumes to carve the earth with water, and in 1853 in Nevada County, Edward E. Matteson revolutionized the process when he discovered he could increase the force of the water by running it through a hose and nozzle. Hydraulic mining companies used nozzles ranging from three to ten inches in diameter to spray high-pressure streams and wash dirt and gravel into a series of large sluice boxes, which caught the gold. According to Rodman Paul, this technique was well established after 1856–57 (*Mining Frontiers* 30); when Greeley visited the gold country in 1859, he noticed how such methods had muddied the water and silted up the beds in virtually all of the rivers and streams, and Blake, while she approved of the opportunity for the miners—"those great long-booted, red-shirted fellows, hairy and brawny, who stand so superbly in the midst of the roaring, rushing stream"—to work in the open air and sunshine, did offer a graphic description of how the immense force of water sprayed through a ten-inch nozzle could reduce a two-hundred-foot gravel bank to mere powder (178–79). In 1884 the hydraulic mines were closed in an attempt to restore the rivers and help protect nearby towns from flooding during the winter storms.

The more durable method was hard-rock mining, usually called quartz mining after the mineral whose veins most frequently held the gold. The miners dug long shafts down into the earth or straight into hillsides, following the veins. They loaded the ore into mine cars and took it to a stamp mill to pulverize the rocks, passed the dust over amalgamation plates to trap the gold in mercury, and then retorted the amalgam to remove the mercury. Even more than the hydraulic method, quartz mining required large crews of men, heavy machinery, and a considerable investment of capital. The quartz mines were owned and run by companies, so many of the miners became employees, trudging down into the tunnels every day, with helmets, picks, and lanterns, to crawl into narrow drifts and chip away at the rock. The quartz miner lived more like his counterpart in the coal fields and less like the idealized image of the well-bearded mountain man, crouched peacefully by a clear Sierra stream with his pan in his lap and his burro grazing on the bank. Samuel Bowles descended into a mine, and in 1866 reported the experience as unpleasant, dangerous, and even frightening. His party groped along a tunnel in the dim light and soon became disoriented in a maze of shafts, side tunnels, and ladders. They grew tired and discouraged, and so resolved to return to the surface, a project that proved more difficult than they anticipated, because

> the mine was oppressively hot and close; the mercury was up to one hundred degrees and more, and the sweat poured from us like water. . . . We only took in a sense of the thing after we had got started; each must carry his lighted candle, hold on, and creep ahead; a single misstep by any one, the fainting of our invalid, or of any of us, all weary and unstrung, would not only have plunged that one headlong down the long fatal flight, to become a very Mantilinean cold body at the bottom, but would have swept everybody below him on the ladder, like a row of bricks, to the same destination and destruction. (*Across* 319)

Blake, in 1883, regarded the quartz mine with horror.

> But the quartz mining . . . with its thunder of infernal machinery stamping and crushing the rock fed to it, with its fourteen hundred foot shaft leading men down to the bowels of the earth, to work, cramped for room, panting for air, one small candle only making a spot of light in the dreadful darkness, how different the toil for gold looked in this! . . . . Standing at the entrance to the dark chasm below . . . one could only think of the inscription which Dante placed over the entrance to his Inferno. (180)

The shafts reached deeper and deeper into the earth; in 1870, the Hayward Mine, in Amador County, reached a depth of 1,350 feet on the incline (Paul, *California Gold* 291).[28] The folksy prospector had become a rarity, replaced by the hard-rock miner who trudged down into the damp, stifling darkness to face cramped quarters, cave-ins and runaway ore cars.

The power of the myth of the West is evident insofar as it has been able to romanticize, to an impressive degree, so dangerous, dirty, and debilitating an occupation as mining, and displace the actuality with a highly pastoral image. The prospector bolsters the traditions of liberal humanism and rugged individualism that, according to popular belief and to Turner, form the bedrock of the American way of life and whose validity the pioneer—the man forced by circumstances to rely on his own strength, ingenuity, and luck—affirmed by constant and ongoing demonstration (30). The myth seeks to uphold this tradition, and so rejects the dehumanizing actuality of mining. Colton wrote of the "gold-diggers" returning at the end of the day: "Their wild halloos, as they come in, fill the cliffs with their echoes. All are merry, whatever may have been the fortunes of the day with them" (285–86). Buffum counts up the day's earnings and savors the entire experience.

> Our camp was merry that night. Seated on the surface of a huge rock, we cooked and ate our venison, drank our coffee, and revelled in the idea that we had stolen away from the peopled world, and were living in an obscure corner, unseen by its inhabitants, with no living being within many miles of us, and in a spot where gold was almost as plentiful as the pebble stones that covered it. (55–56)

Bayard Taylor marvels at the high percentage of "men of education and intelligence" in the goldfields of 1850: "A rough, dirty, sunburned fellow, with unshorn beard, quarrying away for life at the bottom of some rocky hole, might be a graduate of one of the first colleges in the country, and a man of genuine refinement and taste" (192). Taylor offers this observation ostensibly to pique his reader's attention with the idea that people are not always what they seem, but he covertly constructs the miners as men of whom eastern society could not but approve.[29] Blake construes the mining camp as a village almost in the manner of Washington Irving, or in anticipation of Norman Rockwell, enjoying "the most home-like small cottages we had seen out of New England nestled in their bright gardens, half hidden behind vines of gigantic roses, or climbing honeysuckle, and screened by clumps of red and white oleanders as large as small trees" (177). Her charming village resonates well with Taylor's conception of the miner as a new version of the classic whore-with-a-heart-of gold; both ambience and character types recall those of Harte, who idealized the labor and the life of mining.

Although Wing Lee refers to sleeping in a deserted mine shaft, which suggests the presence of quartz miners, when Joe reminisces about working his claim in the canyon, where "the dry leaves were a-dancin' in the wind, the birds singing in the branches, and the creek laughing among the boulders," he gives a pastoral impression more indicative of old-fashioned placer mining (73).[30] In other words, Campbell presents his miners not as unhappy employees laboring deep in the earth, but as free and independent men trying to realize the American promise. He reinforces this construction with the partnership between Joe and Ned.

No matter the specific method, placer mining was a small-time, personal operation that fostered interdependence and camaraderie among the miners. Shinn declared that the mining partnership was "almost as sacred as the marriage-bond."

> The legal contract of partnership, common in settled communities, became, under these circumstances, the brother-like tie and "*pard*"-nership, sacred by camp-custom, protected by camp-law; and its few infringements were treated as crimes against every miner. Two men who lived together, slept together, took turns cooking, and washing their clothes, worked side by side in dripping claims, and made equal division of returns, were rightly felt to have entered into relationships other than commercial. (111–12)

Josiah Royce, the Harvard philosopher who was born in the gold country in 1855, concurred, pointing out the moral effect of the cradle, which encouraged the men to cooperate rather than compete, and to band together rather than work alone. He called the miner's partnership "one of the closest of California relationships . . . widely and not unjustly celebrated in song and story," and interpreted the move from panning to the cradle as a form of social evolution, a rise from a primitive society to a form of social contract (227). In general, Shinn and Royce interpreted the miner's partnership as a somewhat idealized version of the relationship between nineteenth-century artisans working in a shop—coopers, tanners, smiths, and the like. The miners, however, lived far from the bustle of urban trade, working hard in the idyllic Sierra setting; Shinn and Royce cleansed the artisan model of commercial practice and even of the avarice that drove many to the goldfields in the first place. In *Two Men of Sandy Bar*, Sandy Morton describes his feelings toward his partner:

> There is one man, if he be living, knows me better than any man who lives. He has done me wrong—a great wrong, Concho—but I will forgive him. I will do more—I will ask his forgiveness. He will be a witness no man dare gainsay—my partner—God help him and forgive him as I do! (Loney 139)

Joe Saunders promotes this idealistic vision, referring to "My partner—better than a brother; for brothers they quarrel, but Ned and I have worked together in the same claim, eat out of the same pan, slept under the same blanket" (59). Campbell selects the nurturing influences of mining, and overlooks the greed and frustration.

THE "CHINEE"

Like most fiction writers who contributed to the myth of California, Campbell also whitewashed the Chinese question. In *My Partner*, as in most melodramas of the period, the intrigue was leavened with secondary comic characters and their interactions.[31] Sam is a trapeze artist trying to court Grace, who is principally interested in pretty dresses and flattery. Posie Pentland is a tight-lipped spinster looking for a man, and her prospects for inheritance attract the intention of Major Britt—orator, politician, stump lawyer, hard drinker—a character reminiscent of Harte's Colonel Starbottle (sans stammer) and offering just as much local color with his electioneering and broad rhetoric.[32] Yet the comic character most peculiar to the California experience is Wing Lee, the much-abused Chinese who saves Joe by producing the all-important torn shirt.

Chinese laborers were an integral part of California society even before the Southern Pacific hired throngs of them to build the western portion of the trans-continental railroad, and the journalistic commentary on them was, sometimes, openly calumnious. One of the first white Americans to write about the Chinese was Frank Marryat, who visited California during 1850–52, and in 1855 published a description of the stereotypical Chinese as thrifty to the point of avarice but addicted to gambling, so eager to get to work each morning that he takes no time to wash himself, hard-working and intelligent, and, of course, inscrutable. Most of all, however, he is deceptively evil.

> Many of the Chinese at the mines have abolished tails, and when their hair has grown in its natural manner, it is astonishing how villainous an appearance they present. Their hair grows low down on the forehead, and is invariably straight.
>
> An ordinary Chinaman in his loose dress, with his head shaved and hair drawn back, is rather an intellectual looking being, at the first glance, but take the same man, and allow his hair to grow, and divest him of a picturesque costume, and in the place of an apparent mild benevolence, you are struck at once with the small cunning-looking eyes and low forehead, which in the other garb escaped notice.   (297–98)

Greeley reported that each Chinese miner was taxed four dollars per month and even then restricted to diggings that white miners had abandoned. He described the typical "John" as "thoroughly sensual, and intent on the fullest gratification of his carnal appetites . . . an inveterate gambler, an opium smoker, a habitual rum drinker, and a devotee of every sensual vice" (246). Bowles described their oppression in some detail.

[W]e see them the victims of all sort of prejudice and injustice. Ever since they began to come here, even now, it is a disputed question with the public, whether they should not be forbidden our shores. They do not ask or wish for citizenship; they show no ambition to become voters; but they are even denied protection in persons and property by the law. Their testimony is inadmissible against the white man. . . . To abuse and cheat a Chinaman; to rob him; to kick and cuff him; even to kill him, have been things not only done with impunity by mean and wicked men, but even with vain glory. . . . [T]hey have been wantonly assaulted and shot down or stabbed by bad men, as sportsmen would surprise and shoot their game in the woods. There was no risk in such barbarity; if "John" survived to tell the tale, the law would not hear him or believe him. Nobody was so low, so miserable, that he did not despise the Chinaman, and could not outrage him. (*Our New West* 403–404)

The writer who, probably more than any other, shaped the popular conception of the Chinese was Harte. In 1870, he published a poem called "Plain Language from Truthful James," also known as "The Heathen Chinee" after a repeated phrase in the verse.[33] The poem describes a man named Ah Sin, whose smile is pensive, childlike, and bland as he sits in on a game of euchre and quietly out-cheats the dealer, who remarks that "we are ruined by Chinese cheap labor" and proceeds to assault Ah Sin and find both wax on his fingernails (used for marking the cards) and no fewer than two dozen jacks hidden in his long sleeves.

> Which is why I remark,
>   And my language is plain,
> That for ways that are dark
>   And for tricks that are vain,
> The heathen Chinee is peculiar,—
>   Which the same I am free to maintain.

Although Margaret Duckett maintains that Harte intended the poem as an ironic demonstration of the hypocrisy of white racism against the Chinese, many readers took the poem at face value.[34] The actual Chinese was eclipsed by the fictional stereotype of the "Chinee," which appeared on page and stage through the later nineteenth century. Harte himself wrote another poem on the subject, entitled "The Latest Chinese Outrage." A band of four hundred "Chinee" invade the camp of eight white men so that Ah Sin may complain that none of the miners has paid him for doing his laundry.

> You owe flowty dolee—me washee you camp,
> You catchee my washee—me catchee no stamp;
> One dollar hap dozen, me no catchee yet,
> Now that flowty dollee—no hab?—how can get?
> Me catchee you piggee—me sellee for cash,
> It catchee me licee—you catchee no 'hash;'
> Me belly good Sheliff—me lebbee when can,
> Me allee same halp pin as Melican man!

One Joe Johnson asks his friends, "Shall we stand here as idle, and let Asia pour / Her barbaric hordes on this civilized shore? / Has the White Man no country?" Shouting, "this 'yer's a White Man," he runs up the hillside after the "Chinee," who scatter before him as the other whites follow at a distance. They find no "heathen," but finally locate Johnson himself, his eyebrows shaved, his face painted "a coppery hue," leering down at them from a bamboo cage and stupefied by the opium pipe his adversaries have thrust between his lips.

In plays, the sinister qualities of the "Chinee" were trivialized to facilitate comic effect. Eastern theatre-goers probably saw their first "Chinee" in Harte's *Two Men of Sandy Bar*.[35] A minor character named Hop Sing explains, in broad pidgin, that an American named Alexander Molton has not paid his laundry bill: "Me washee shirt, Alexandlee Molton; he no pay washee. Me washee flowty dozen hep—four bittie dozen—twenty dollar hep. Alexandlee Molton no payee. He say, 'Go to hellee!' " (Loney 129) In *The Danites of the Sierras*, Washee Washee is too fond of brandy, reciting this soliloquy before a band of miners enters to arrest him for stealing their shirts. "Blandee! Blandee! Me likee blandee. [*Drinks again.*] Blandee makee Chinaman feel alee same likee flighten clock. [*Going to door.*] Melican man no comee. No catchee Chinaman. [*Drinks.*] Melican man he no comee. Chinaman he no go" (388).

Yet the most prominent stage "Chinee" was the title role in *Ah Sin* (1877), the disastrous collaboration between Harte and Mark Twain, conceived partly as an opportunity to trade on the popularity of Charles Thomas Parsloe's performance of Hop Sing. When Ah Sin first enters the action, a miner named Broderick serves as his straight man in a routine that would have fit easily into the vaudeville shows that were just becoming popular, and the "Chinee" employs the pidgin that, largely due to Harte's popularity, by that time had become customary and quite consistent: "Walkee bottom side hillee—stage bloke down—plenty smashee upee. Plunkee plenty helpee, plenty makee all rightee—plunkee vell good man" (10).[36] In an argument over a claim and a card game, Broderick kills (so he thinks, and so is the audience led to believe) Plunkett, another miner. Ah Sin finds Broderick's bloody jacket, archly offers " washee washee," but covertly withholds the incriminating garment when he sells the miner a bundle of clothing. Broderick then forces Ah Sin to doctor a jacket belonging to another man, York, to be used as evidence against him, and in the confusion, the miners' meeting suspects both York and Ah Sin. White juries would not accept Chinese testimony in California in those days, but Ah Sin reveals the truth by handing over Broderick's jacket, bloodstains and all, a denouement that Campbell borrowed for *My Partner*.

Wing Lee, therefore, is a stock comic character—the ubiquitous Parsloe played this role, too—that serves a larger purpose than providing a few laughs and facilitating a key twist in the plot. Like his counterpart "Chinees," he makes light of the genuine hatred that many white Californians harbored toward Chinese, and of the prejudice that actual Chinese faced. As with the nature of mining and of mining-camp justice, Campbell has selected and shaped his material to present the most pleasant image of California that he could conceive. He is not attempting a realistic portrayal of life in California in 1879 or even in 1849; he is trying to satisfy his eastern audience's preconceptions regarding an experience they have located in a rosy mythic context.[37]

PARADISE LOST

In creating a version of the pastoral, Campbell sought to control his audience's vision of the material. The pastoral summons a virtually unassailable set of associations that have to do with the oldest legends of Western civilization, cultural recollections that include the most hallowed icons of Christian myth and go back even farther, to the Biblical dawn of human experience in the original Eden. Leo Marx commented on the use of the pastoral ideal to inform the American experience, but his observation is all the more apt when applied to California:

> The ruling motive of the good shepherd, leading figure of the classic, Virgilian mode, was to withdraw from the great world and begin a new life in a fresh, green landscape. And now here was a virgin continent! . . . Soon the dream of a retreat to an oasis of harmony and joy was removed from its traditional literary context. It was embodied in various utopian schemes for making America the site of a new beginning for Western society. (3)

The recurring pæan to the California landscape is akin to an involuntary outcry of pained joy at having discovered the earthly paradise of legendary promise and collective memory. The acclamation of California's beauty is also a clamorous affirmation of the very definition of beauty, a conception overwhelmed by the pastoral æsthetic. Campbell, like others before and since, wrote not the truth of the experience, but rather the myth to which the experience had to appear to conform. By appropriating and prolonging the pastoral experience of 1849—itself a construction—Campbell preempted his audience's response, saying, in essence, that only certain reactions were possible, and excluding all others. Whatever is false or improbable must be overlooked, for the fable, as a whole, is unexceptionable. R. W. B. Lewis described the American Adam as

> an individual emancipated from history, happily bereft of ancestry, untouched and undefiled by the usual inheritances of family and race; an individual standing alone, self-reliant and self-propelling, ready to confront whatever awaited him with the aid of his own unique and inherent resources. . . . Adam was the first, the archetypal, man. His moral position was prior to experience, and in his very newness he was fundamentally innocent. The world and history lay all before him. (5)

Joe Saunders is Adam, the herdsman of Galilee, the Virgilian shepherd, and the wide-eyed benefactor of the breathtaking bounty of the new Eden.

To elevate experience in this way is to put the myth far beyond the reach of the actual experience, so to most Americans—and even recent immigrants—the West, and especially California, has been a source of disappointment. Wyatt refers to California as a "beautiful, vanished garden" (xvi), but the actual garden, no matter how idyllic, was never capable of satisfying the demands of mythic imagination. In his discussion of *Two Years before the Mast*, Wyatt proposes that Dana discerned the wonder of the landscape and its value to his self-actualization only after he left it, and so enacted "the first American version of what will become a familiar story, the discovery of California as paradise only once it is lost" (8). California is the last chance, and plays like *My Partner* express the reaction of the so-called mainstream American culture to the end of the westering tide, to our final attempt to incarnate our collective imagination in the illusory new Eden on the Pacific Coast. All of western culture's hopes were gambled on this last "new" world; Harold P. Simonson warns that the traveler who fails to find the Promised Land here has nowhere else to go and faces despair as space closes in upon him (104).

Melodrama of the West is doomed to fail from the outset, for melodrama must end in an affirmation of values that have little to do with untrammeled freedom, individualism, and romantic mission, and everything to do with the domesticity that Mary and Joe will undoubtedly establish once they marry and raise a family. Melodrama enforces a stability that runs directly counter to the restlessness and transience that Howard Mumford Jones finds so characteristic of the postbellum West (93). Indeed, the paradox of the westward movement, seen so clearly in the structure of melodrama, is that the "happy ending"—whether in a play, a story, or an actual episode in the life of a family or a town—required that the immigrants rob the West of the wildness that supposedly drew them out in the first place. That is, to move into the West is to destroy it and transform it into the East. Roderick Nash has argued that late nineteenth-century society valorized the pioneer in an attempt to bolster the faith in individual effort and ability, and that during the 1890s people began to realize that the wilderness was not "the villain of the national drama," diametrically opposed to the heroic pioneer, but rather the condition that made the pioneer and the frontier possible: "Pioneering, in short, came to be regarded as important not only for spearheading the advance of civilization but also for banging Americans into contact with the primitive" (145).[38] Melodrama is a means of affirming a belief in a reductive perception of reality, and to reduce a dream is to kill it.

The "West" was a myth in every sense; it did not truly exist outside of an immensely rich and hallowed cultural narrative. Turner believed in the myth, looking back, like many of us, to an era of "free" land. In pedestrian terms, the land was never free and was not settled freely, for although the Homestead Act of 1862 did make it possible for any man who was both the head of a family and a loyal citizen to claim a quarter-section of public land and buy it for $200, only 125,000 square miles were settled accordingly (Billington 83).[39] Nearly seven times as much land was sold through speculators, jobbers, railroad grants, and land grants for state schools, and many people moved west not out of irrepressible, spontaneous personal yearning but in response to the self-serving propaganda campaigns of speculators, railroad companies, territories, and states that wanted to sell land and establish towns (H. M. Jones 97). In broader terms, the land was not "free" because it was already inhabited by other human cultures as well as wildlife; the clarion of Manifest Destiny sounded only the call it wanted potential immigrants to hear, and part of their disappointment and failure stemmed from a misconception based on their ignorance of the truth. Most important, the land was not free because each immigrant paid a personal price to reach it, and, like Ephraim Cabot in *Desire under the Elms*, when the immigrant arrived he found not liberation but only himself. Richard Wattenberg has pointed out that both Turner and Campbell subscribe to a Romantic vision that refers not back into the fabled past, but "forward to a new and frilly transformed Romantic vision of the American future" (14–15). They *must* look forward, for what they seek never existed.

Yet the myth is immensely powerful; one indication is that it has almost completely displaced the ideology that gave it birth. The westward movement was, in mundane terms, an ongoing expression of ambition and imperialism. To posit the West as the inevitable destination of the American people was to legitimate greed and transform conquest into a welcoming embrace. The beauty and romance of the myth blind us to the motivations that inspired it; the sign usurps the idea.

The concept of Manifest Destiny carried with it a heavy responsibility. If God had given Americans—specifically white, Protestant, republican, and individualistic men—the right to expand their nation from coast to coast, and to bring "civilization" to the "wilderness," then He had also charged them with a mission to regenerate themselves as well as the "savages" they encountered, and to live up to the superiority that He seemed to affirm.[40] Manifest Destiny was a form of Romantic emplotment, casting the American Everyman as the hero in a cosmic drama of endless strivings toward a pinnacle of ultimate self-realization and cultural vindication. This grand play could not but eat its young, for even if California, that last bastion of western fantasy, validated every single dream that centuries of discourse had fastened to it, there still would be no place else to go, and succeeding generations would be doomed to disappointment. Joe defeats Ned's weakness and Scraggs's villainy, but in spite of his enthusiastic peroration, he finds not wonder but a quite ordinary existence. Any stage lover follows an arc, soaring through the exhilarating uncertainty of courtship and coming to rest in the stability of marriage, where the play mercifully ends, sparing the audience the commonplace routine that will follow. Joe's arc is all the higher because he came to the West as an argonaut, seeking the ultimate prize, and now has, although scarcely aware of it, sacrificed all for domesticity. Like Adam, the westering traveler must fail and fall, but not in God's eyes—in his own.[41]

6

Shenandoah (1889) and the Civil War

THE MOST FUNDAMENTAL assumption America now makes regarding the Civil War—one so ingrained in conventional cultural wisdom that we are hardly able to recognize it—is that the South is, and always was, an organic part of the United States. However else we may construct the war—as expression of tragic division, as proof of national resilience, as cultural crucible from which we emerged irrevocably bonded—it is therefore an interregnum, a historical aberration after which the nation returned to its "normal" state of political organization. Within such a paradigm, it is easy to conclude that the South actually desired Union, seceded reluctantly, and embraced the outcome with secret relief, all of which runs counter to the contemporaneous Southerners' perception that they were founding a new nation in the name of preserving their liberty and way of life. Secession took on strictly sectional connotations in 1861; the South insisted that it was an act of freedom in the finest tradition of 1776, while the North damned it as open treason. The first attitude defines the war as a revolution against tyranny, while the second rejects it as a rebellion; the first confers heroism on the secessionists, but the second allots them only shame and guilt which they may purge only through bloodshed, remorse, and magnanimous northern forgiveness. Because the South lost the war, the northern point of view has become, for the most part, the "American" point of view, and the northern-dominated culture has finished the war and Reconstruction by simply refusing to accept that the South did not want to rejoin the rest of the nation. Thus our collective recollection provides a classic example of the operation of hegemony, but—typical of the American experience—outside of the context of hierarchical class structure.

The Civil War provided the great American drama of the nineteenth century, but the professional stage did not embrace the topic with consistent enthusiasm until the late 1880s, when a series of plays began appearing: William Gillette's *Held by the Enemy* (1886) and *Secret Service* (1895), Bronson Howard's *Shenandoah* (1889), Augustus Thomas's *Surrender* (1892), David Belasco's *The Heart of Maryland* (1895), Clyde Fitch's *Barbara Frietchie* (1899) and James A. Herne's *The Reverend Griffith Davenport* (1899).[1] While the temperance dramas and *Uncle Tom's Cabin* had dealt with unresolved issues of present concern, the Civil War

"Phil Sheridan's Ride to the Front." From the cover of *Harper's Weekly*, November 5, 1864. (Courtesy of the Huntington Library, San Marino, California.)

plays looked back toward a conflict that was, militarily and politically speaking, finished. These plays appeared a full generation after the last surrender and well after the conclusion of Reconstruction, so they contemplated the war in retrospect, sometimes nostalgically, and sought to produce myth out of the raw materials of collective memory, to mediate in order to legitimate the past to the present. Yet their (re)construction of the war was not a virgin effort; their historiography was built on earlier texts, most of which, like the plays themselves, were northern in origin and presented a northern point of view either openly or disguised as an "American" perspective.

THE MYTH OF THE WAR

Even before Appomattox, there was no shortage of chronicles and histories; the publishing of the war had begun with comprehensive coverage in periodicals of various propensities and had continued with commensurately diverse book-length treatments. For example, the popular and prolific Joel Tyler Headley emphasized the purely military aspects of the conflict in *The Great Rebellion* (1863–66), Horace Greeley preferred more overt political comment and interpretation of causes in *The American Conflict* (1867), and *Harper's Pictorial History of the Great Rebellion* (1866–68) offered not only a thorough account of events but also engravings of maps, battle scenes, and prominent individuals. Although these and the many other histories made implicit claim to plain but thorough documentation, their exhaustive investigation of every aspect of the war served to legitimate the conflict and its conclusion.

Perhaps more compelling—and more relevant to the eventual development of Civil War drama—was the ongoing visual record. Periodicals like *Harper's Weekly* and *Frank Leslie's Illustrated Newspaper* published sketches and engravings based on the work of artists and photographers in the field, images that readers may have accepted as faithful representations, not realizing that, as Timothy Sweet has demonstrated, the engravers for *Harper's* modified the source photographs to avoid conveying a sense of discord (134–36). Originals were sometimes available, however, and Mathew Brady's exhibit, which opened in New York City in October of 1862, depicted the dead of Antietam so chillingly that the reviewer for the *Times* compared the show with leaving corpses in dooryards or on the sidewalks of Broadway (Sweet 116).[2] In 1866, Alexander Gardner, a Scot who had worked with Brady, published his *Sketch Book*, an album of photographs with long captions that guided the viewer's reading of the images. Gardner's photographs showed the battlefields after the fighting was over, torn landscapes peopled with corpses, and his narratives fostered the mystique, bravery, and danger of military action, in one paragraph comparing an assaulting column to a breaking wave, and in another marveling at the heroism and iron nerve of the army's scouts and spies. Plate 36, "A Harvest of Death, Gettysburg, July, 1863," shows a a southern soldier lying on his back, his arms stretched to the sides, his head flung back, and his mouth open in a wide oval toward the camera. The caption expresses both regret over the war and hope that it will be the last such conflict.

> Slowly, over the misty fields of Gettysburg—as all reluctant to expose their ghastly horrors to the light—came the sunless morn, after the retreat by Lee's broken army. Through the shadowy vapors, it was, indeed, a "harvest of death" that was presented; hundreds and thousands of torn Union and rebel soldiers . . . strewed the now quiet fighting ground. . . . [T]he distorted dead recall the ancient legends of men torn in pieces by the savage wantonness of fiends. Swept down without preparation, the shattered bodies fall in all conceivable positions. . . . Around is scattered the litter of the battle-field, accoutrements, ammunition, rags, cups and canteens, crackers, haversacks, &c., and letters that may tell the name of the owner, although the majority will surely be buried unknown by strangers, and in a strange land. Killed in the frantic efforts to break the steady lines of an army of patriots, whose heroism only excelled theirs in motive, they paid with life the price of their treason, and when the wicked strife was finished, found nameless graves, far from home and kindred.
>
> Such a picture conveys a useful moral: It shows the blank horror and reality of war, in opposition to its pageantry. Here are the dreadful details! Let them aid in preventing such another calamity falling upon the nation.

This is not exactly an attack on war itself; Gardner claims horrified dismay, but he achieves a subtly romantic tone with his "misty fields" and "ancient legends," and his choice of a Confederate corpse as the central figure helps distance the northern reader, encouraging a morbid fascination with the carnage and rendering the closing comment merely conventional. Plate 37, "Field where General Reynolds Fell, Gettysburg, July, 1863," shows five Union dead, all lying on the ground with their heads flung back, and the caption makes them seem beautiful and peaceful.

> Some of the dead presented an aspect which showed that they had suffered severely just previous to dissolution, but these were few in number compared with those who wore a calm and resigned expression, as though they had passed away in the act of prayer. Others had a smile on their faces, and looked as if they were in the act of speaking. . . . The faces of all were pale, as though cut in marble, and as the wind swept across the battle-field it waved the hair, and gave the bodies such an appearance of life that a spectator could hardly help thinking they were about to rise to continue the fight.

The caption reassures the northern reader who would like to think that the troops passed easily and with dignity from their patriotic mission into a sort of American Valhalla. Sweet has asserted that photographers like Gardner employed antebellum conventions of funerary portraiture and view scenes in order to transform "traces of violence" into "signs legitimating the Union" (85). Sweet sees in their method a pastoralism and an organicist æsthetic of unity—both analogous to Walt Whitman's approach to his war poems—that implied the indivisibility of the Union, which therefore approved of the war as a means to maintain the nation as a single whole (78, 137).

Fiction and parafiction appeared as soon as the war was over. In the North alone, nearly two million servicemen returned home to shape popular belief with their anecdotes and fireside recollections. Some such stories dwelt on lice, dysentery, and slaughter, while others conferred on memory the soft light of legend; with varying degrees of revision and mediation, all kinds found their way into print. *The Camp, the Battle Field and the Hospital* (1866) is a collection of tales that make military spies—honorable gentlemen all—look clever and daring by emphasizing disguises and last-minute rescues. In contrast, *Miss Ravenel's Conversion from Secession to Loyalty* (1867), a novel by John William De Forest, a former Union officer, anticipates Stephen Crane's more famous *Red Badge of Courage* (1895) in its realistic depiction of the confusion of battle from one officer's point of view.[3] The elated officer is not even fully aware that a bullet has hit his left arm. Dazed, he collapses under a tree and dozes before finding his way to the field hospital, which was "simply an immense collection of wounded men in every imaginable condition of mutilation, every one stained more or less with his own blood, every one of a ghastly yellowish pallor, all lying in the open air on the bare ground or on their own blankets with no shelter except the friendly foliage of the oaks and beeches." Beneath the operating tables are "great pools of clotted blood, amidst which lay amputated fingers, hands, arms, feet, and legs, only a little more ghastly in color than the faces of those who waited their turn on the table" (269).

Clearly, Northerners in the late 1860s had ample access to various perspectives on the war: as a composition of military strategies, as a political action, as a gallery of carefully depicted icons of heroism, as the source of ennobling narrative, and as a period of senseless horror. Yet the consistent thrust of most of the northern discourse was to legitimate the northern position to the exclusion of the southern enemy.

By the 1880s, the northern mood had shifted toward reconciliation with the South. President Johnson pardoned the rebels on Christmas Day, 1868, and in 1872, the General Amnesty Act restored to most former rebels the right to hold public office. Horace Greeley supported reconciliation in his presidential campaign of 1872, and the resolution to the contested election of 1876—the Democrats agreed to condone Hayes's election if he promised to remove federal troops from Louisiana and South Carolina—led to the collapse of the remaining carpetbag governments and the restoration of home rule to southern white Democrats. Union and Confederate veterans began holding joint reunions during the 1880s, and in 1888—the same year that the first version of *Shenandoah* opened in Boston—celebrated the twenty-fifth anniversary of the Battle of Gettysburg (Pressly 156).

As for literature, Joyce Appleby has discovered that calls for reconciliation had appeared in northern novels as early as 1865 (120).[4] During the 1870s, northern readers found a new way to reclaim the South by rediscovering and eagerly encouraging its romantic literary conception. *Scribner's* began publishing its "Great South" series in 1873, *Harper's Monthly Magazine* printed articles on the "New South" in 1874, and the *Constitution* published the first of Joel Chandler Harris's "Uncle Remus" stories on January 18, 1877. George Washington Cable's *Old Creole Days* appeared in 1879 and his *The Grandissimes* in 1880, and throughout the 1880s and 1890s, Harris contributed stories to such northern periodicals as *Century*, *Harper's*, *Scribner's*, *Atlantic*, *McClure's*, and *Youth's Companion* (Buck 229–30, 233, 235). Clearly, northern readers perceived the South not as a treasonous enemy, but as a fascinating and nostalgic fictional setting, a more compassionate, if no more accurate, construction.

Northern war literature lost some of its earlier diversity, gravitating toward heroism and grand military strategy. In *The Blue and the Grey* (1883), Theodore Gerrish and John S. Hutchinson offered stories and anecdotes that made heroes out of generals and private soldiers alike. After the battle of the Wilderness, a burial party find a young soldier—"only a smooth, thin faced lad, but nevertheless a brave soldier"—who is still alive and holding a bouquet of violets that he had gathered; when he dies, they lay the flowers on his grave (182–83). Another boy, during the battle of Chancellorsville, calmly asks a passing officer to cut the last shred of flesh that attaches his arm to his body (186). At Gettysburg, a rebel soldier hears one of the federal wounded crying feebly for water from the battlefield, and leaps over the breastworks to give him a drink from his own canteen. Both sides cease firing to cheer his kindness and bravery, and resume the battle as soon as he has returned to his post (329–30). During the siege of Petersburg, a Confederate general takes a leave of absence so he can return to Richmond for his wedding. Only an hour after the ceremony, Lee sends for him, and on the next day, the man is beheaded by a shell during the assault on Hatcher's Run (224–25).[5] Even William Dean Howells's ironic hand could not introduce a battlefield recollection without a romantic whiff of gunpowder. In *The Rise of Silas Lapham* (1885), we learn that the title character participated in a virtually suicidal charge against a rebel position.

> "About one in five of us got out safe," said Lapham, breaking his cigar-ash off on the edge of a plate. James Bellingham reached him a bottle of Apollinaris. He drank a glass, and then went on smoking. . . . Bromfield Corey remarked thoughtfully, "What astonishes the craven civilian in all these things is the abundance—the superabundance—of heroism. The cowards were the exception; the men that were ready to die, the rule." (1046–47)

The overt fictions complemented U.S. Grant's best-selling *Personal Memoirs* (1885) and the authoritative recollections, mostly by former generals on both sides, that *Century Magazine* published during the mid-1880s.[6] These works necessarily presented the war as seen by field commanders—Grant explains battles in terms of this general advancing, and that one falling back, as though there were no actual people under the generals' command—and tended to create the impression that the war proceeded as a result of the grappling of wills of "great" men such as Grant, Lee, and Jackson, and was more a matter of military strategy rather than personal battlefield suffering or the tortuous working-out of deeply seated internecine strife. *Century* published an account of the surrender at Appomattox as remembered by General Horace Porter, a member of Grant's staff; the piece encourages an Olympian interpretation of the meeting between Grant and Lee, and promotes the aura of chivalry and wistful intersectional conflict that pervaded much of the developing myth of the war. The *Century* articles, because they represented both North and South, legitimated the war as a glorious American achievement regardless of one's personal loyalties. Thomas J. Pressly has pointed out that the *Century* editors avoided using the incendiary word "rebellion" in their title and dodged the question of the causes of the war, all in an effort to present "something of a literary reunion of the Blue and Gray" and to acknowledge the bravery of both sides (158).

Grant, whose readers probably regarded his opinions with considerable respect, if not reverence—the original edition of *Shenandoah* includes quotations from the *Memoirs* for inclusion in program notes—enriched the myth of the war with his comments on its causes and effects. He stated plainly that he believed slavery to be the cause, not because its moral deviation outraged righteous Northerners, but because the system required "unusual guarantees for its security" and therefore involved the federal government in its protection, forcing everyone's complicity by means of the Fugitive Slave Act. He went on to legitimate the carnage by proposing that "we are better off now than we would have been without it," that "the war has made us a nation of great power and intelligence," and that he foresaw "great harmony between the Federal and the Confederate" (585, 589, 590). Grant's vision of one nation may not have represented the sentiments of many Southerners, but it validated the war as a restoration rather than a conquest.

This ongoing and intertwining discourse produced the myth of the Civil War, a set of beliefs that would help the American people—at least those in the North—accept and justify the slaughter they had endured. The war was, of course, regrettable because of the loss of life, destruction of property, and enormous redirection of effort. In fact, due to the use of photography, the civilian population enjoyed unprecedented access to gory battlefield horrors, and so was all the more informed regarding the personal price that so many paid. Yet the war was also desirable as a means to assert the preeminence and inevitability of the Union and to validate the American experiment. In fact, the war provided a way for a new generation to recapture the adventure and the mission of the Revolutionary experience, which was the predominant and overpowering mythic experience in a tradition still young and undergoing rapid formulation. Both Northerners and Southerners could claim to fight for liberty and the rights of man, and so stand as tall as their forefathers.

The war provided a means for soldiers to reclaim the manhood of their ancestors, to add their investment of blood to that which bought the nation's freedom. The more deplorable the specific experience of the war, the more noble the sacrifice made in the name of America.

THE VETERANS' MYTH ON STAGE

Although the professional theatre was slow to seize the chance, amateur companies restaged the conflict time and time again, starting in the late 1860s, in a steady series of scripts that attested to the participants' enthusiasm. Many of the plays were written specifically for the Grand Army of the Republic, a veterans' organization for those who fought on the Union side.[7] In addition to its other activities, the organization produced plays in what we might regard as a sort of special-interest community theatre or, less kindly, fraternal lodge pageantry. Some authors were, apparently, veterans and G.A.R. members, while others seem to have been professional or semiprofessional hacks writing for a specific amateur market.[8] Their point of view was fully supportive of the Union, so they validated their memories of themselves in their northern characters, and constructed the Southerners so as to explain the rebellion and justify the North's war of suppression. Whether or not leading professionals like Gillette and Howard ever read or saw these amateur contributions, they built their work on the fundamental conventions of Civil War melodrama as their predecessors established them.[9]

In several plays ranging from *The Drummer Boy* (1868) to *Lights and Shadows of the Great Rebellion* (1884), there is an almost formulaic method of initiating the action. In *The Spy of Atlanta* (1875), for example, the southern St. Clairs are visiting the northern Daltons when they hear news of the firing on Fort Sumter. Charlie Dalton exclaims that "the cowardly traitors at the South will soon be whipped into subjection, like unruly curs," but when his father expresses his hope that the St. Clairs will fight for the "maintenance of this government," Edward St. Clair disabuses him.

> I can speak for both my father and myself—we both were born and nurtured in the South—our homes are there, all our interests are centered around the dear old homes of our childhood, and we should be more than traitors, now that we are called upon to protect our sacred rights, should we be found wanting. (Ames and Bartley 7)

The young men call each other "coward" and "traitor" until Edwin Dalton demands that the St. Clairs leave his family's home. There is a complication, however— Edward has been courting Carrie Dalton, but because she will not go south with him and he insists on fighting for the Confederacy, they must part. In the ensuing scenes, both Edwin and Charlie Dalton enlist in the local company, and little Willie persuades his mother to let him join up as a drummer boy.[10] Farmer Dalton wipes a tear from his eye as he gives his consent.

> This is almost too much—to part from Willie, our youngest, our baby—but the dear old flag must be protected, although it takes our heart's dearest treasures. May God bless you my boy, guard and keep you from all harm, is the prayer of your father. (13)

The townspeople sing the national anthem, Carrie presents a flag to the colonel of the regiment, and the men march off to war. From that point on, the various plays pursue divergent stories, but nearly all of them include scenes of camp life and battle, demonstrations of northern heroism and southern villainy, gallantry on both sides, parodic nonsense from Irish and German ("Dutch") comic soldiers, a virtually obligatory foolish but loyal "darky," all finishing with the defeat of the South and the triumphant homecoming of the northern troops.[11]

The general pattern represents the efforts of the authors—some of whom were veterans—to find a shape in their recollections and develop a myth of their shared experience. In this veterans' myth, the war began with the attack on Fort Sumter—a point of origin that casts the South as the aggressor and obscures the deeper causes—and Lincoln's call for 75,000 volunteers, which led to the scenes of recruitment, mustering, and departure, and to drastic changes in these men's lives. The generic warplay itself was a combination of comedy and heroism, casting the Southerners as traitorous rebels and the federal troops as loyal citizen soldiers whose only aspirations were to lick the cowardly enemy and return home to their waiting families. The plays therefore valorized the Union soldier as a self-sacrificing hero who was all the more admirable because he was, at bottom, a common man who wore the uniform and marched to glory on a merely temporary basis.

The plays display what may seem to be a ludicrous naïveté and clumsiness in dramaturgy, but these apparently crude attempts were in fact endeavors to create completely unequivocal allegory. Realism trades on its ambiguity, but those designing the veterans' myth sought absolute clarity in their (re)construction of events and participants, and in the meaning they hoped to impart. A realistic technique would have confused the message, so the playmakers, like the temperance dramatists before them, employed exegetical representation to deliver the most explicit possible message. In *The Spy of Atlanta*, even after the Daltons and the St. Clairs so blatantly announce their sectional positions, the characters convey their attitudes less through the implications of their actions and more through repeated declarations. General McPherson needs to send "a courageous and resolute man" into the enemy lines, General Sherman wonders whether he knows a man who could perform such a "perilous duty," and McPherson asks Colonel Harrison to find him a "a trusty and courageous man—one in whom I can place the utmost confidence, to send upon a perilous mission" (Ames and Bartley 17). This concentrated reiteration prepares the entrance of Edwin Dalton, who, when McPherson tells him that success will bring promotion, establishes his selflessness and defines the stakes of his action so clearly that there is little room for doubt in the audience's minds.

> Perhaps, like many others, I desire to advance in position, but believe me, General, it is from no such thoughts as these that I accept this extremely hazardous undertaking, for the chances are that if I am not killed, I shall be made a prisoner, but if I can be of any service to my country, I will cheerfully make the attempt. (18)

Edwin seems slightly dismayed at the idea of becoming a spy—spying was not generally considered as honorable as fighting the enemy face to face—but assures the general that he will do "even that" for his country. Edwin is caught almost immediately by Edward St. Clair, who has been wailing impatiently for a chance to get him "in my power," and who recognizes him when a picket brings him into camp. Colonel St. Clair is surprised when Edward pulls off Edwin's false whiskers, wig, and blanket to reveal the Union uniform beneath.[12]

> ST. CLAIR: Is it possible, Edwin Dalton, that you have been foolhardy enough to enter these lines as a spy, knowing as you must, the penalty if captured.
> EDWIN: Colonel St. Clair, I knew full well my fate if taken prisoner, and small as would be my chance for mercy if captured by others, it is still less when in the hands of yourself and son.
> ST. CLAIR: . . . What was your object in entering our lines?
> EDWIN: That sir, the direst tortures you can inflict, will never cause me to answer.
> ST. CLAIR: Then sir, you shall be taken before a Military Court Martial, where you will be tried as a spy, and if found guilty, hung like a dog. (19–20)

The audiences of 1875 may have regarded such an interchange as quite plausible. Gerrish and Hutchinson recorded the last speech of a federal spy who faced hanging in Richmond in 1864; the rhetoric may be the precipitate of romantic convention, but the authors present it as genuine:

> When I consented to assume the dangerous task which I undertook, I knew well its penalty in the event of capture. I do not deny the charge of being a spy, and I am proud of the service I have rendered my country. I expect nothing else from your hands but death, and I meet that fate with the consciousness of having faithfully performed my duty to the best of my ability; while I thank God that I have been successful in doing more harm to the Confederacy then [*sic*] any other man thus far. I am satisfied with my lot. Go ahead with your hanging. (541)

Edwin escapes, of course, but when Sherman offers to promote him to major and assign him to his staff, he thanks the general for his kindness but asks to return to the ranks for the coming battle. The incidents are few and simple—Edwin volunteers, he is captured, he escapes—so the effect and interest of the sequence lie in the characters' constant declaration of intent. The declarations interpret the action and define such relevant values as courage, altruism, patriotism, and villainy;

they guide the audience's reading of the play. Insofar as Edwin is the Union soldier that the playmakers wanted to remember and present as typical, his valor becomes an allegory of Union bravery and virtue.

Underlying this use of exegetical representation is the fact that these plays were based on a war that was all too familiar to those involved. Whether the play depicted a specific battle or offered a generic panorama of the war, the participants knew that the play would end with (or at least anticipate) the Union triumph, and they expected that the admirable heroism of the Union soldiers would contrast favorably with the treachery of the rebels; there was no need to spend space and time in subtle characterization and the artful unfolding of events. For them, the interest in the play lay not in whether it would affirm valor, reveal rebel perfidy, and legitimate the Union cause, but in *how* it would do so. The use of declaration to achieve explication simultaneous with action, however inept it may seem, served to reassure and confirm the audience as to the nature and significance of events and participants, and to ensure a homogeneous, shared experience.

THE RATIONALE OF WAR

In their quest to validate the Union position, the playwrights had to present a satisfactory reconstruction of the reasons for fighting the war in the first place. In this context, a phrase that recurs over and over again is "the old flag"—an evocation of something worn by service and familiar by long usage, but still valiantly durable. The coinage represents an attempt to synthesize a long-standing tradition of patriotism for a nation that was still, in many respects, somewhat raw and new; neither the Constitution (effective 1789) nor the Stars and Stripes (adopted 1777) had yet endured for a century when the Civil War was fought. Nevertheless, to attribute long tenure to an institution or a belief is to confer a certain legitimacy, so in *Lights and Shadows of the Great Rebellion*, Guy Vincent refers to "the old flag that my forefathers fought and bled and died for" (Dawson and Whittemore 28). He and others like him dedicate themselves to "the old flag," for to raise it is to affirm America, and to align with that untouchable symbol is to take on its moral invulnerability.[13]

Several of the plays reenact a ceremony that was surely played out in many a northern town as the local company or regiment marched off to join the army—the presentation of a flag, sewn by the ladies of the town, to the departing soldiers. One young woman confers the flag as a sacred trust.

> We cannot follow you—we cannot share with you the hardships of the march, or the dangers of the conflict—but our prayers go with you for your safe return; and, with a deep sense of your heroism, we hopefully look to the future when through your bravery and self-sacrifice, this flag shall have been carried unsullied to victory, and brought back to your homes covered with glory—the harbinger of the blessings of a fruitful peace. (Renauld 13)

An officer accepts the flag and assures the townspeople that he and his men will punish the hateful, ambitious Southerners for their repeated insults and destroy their "foul rebellion."

> [W]e go, with sword in hand, to teach them lessons of loyalty to the proud banner they have insulted . . . the flag around which has banded, for nearly a century, the mightiest, the freest people on earth; but with that same flag to guide and cheer us on, we will battle and conquer—adding one more wreath to the crown of glory which is the heritage of the true American soldier! (14)

He legitimates the military action by associating it with past wars whose justice is, he assumes, no longer at issue. In *Gettysburg* (1879), a farmer presents the flag and exhorts the regiment by citing the revered name of Washington.

> Soldiers, this question is to you—not words, but swords must answer it—shall that old flag still live to bless the gave of him [*points to Washington*] who gave it birth, or shall it not? . . . Take it, and with it take its glorious past, and swear to all its foes abroad that glorious past shall still with it live on. Take it and swear to all its foes at home that those bright stars shall still shine on in union one—that this good land our fathers gave to us shall still for us and for the children of the world endure; "that this, the Government of the people, by the people, and for the people, shall not perish from the earth." (McKee 31)

His anachronistic quotation of Lincoln clarifies the ahistorical conflation of image, ideal, and event that informs this dramaturgy of the flag.

Reverence toward the flag functions like faith in God, and just as one can affront religious devotion either by denying God or by loving the devil, one can insult the flag either by assailing it or by setting up another in its rightful place. In response to an invitation to witness the firing on Fort Sumter, a loyal Northerner refuses on patriotic grounds.

> I have no desire for any such sight, to see the old flag fired upon, the old stars and stripes that have waved defiantly for years. No, never, nor no one but *a traitor* to his country could witness such a sight and not feel sick at heart. . . . Let them but dare fire on the old flag, and that fire will send its echo among the loyal hearts of the North, and arouse such a patriotic feeling that they will come down here in swarms. (*The Volunteer* 6)

Hearing of the southern defiance, a farmer rises grandly to condemn the rebels.

> And has it come to this?—that men, born and nurtured under freedom's flag, have become so base as to turn and rend it? trample it under their feet? stain its purity with fraternal blood? If so, they will deeply rue the day their impious hands were raised to do the accursed deed. (Barton 7–8)

When some Confederate soldiers prepare to hang a Union man beneath their rattle-snake flag, he says, "Let that flag, that sign and synonym of evil's self, now take my dying curse." He tears it and steps on it, declaring, "Thus do I right myself unto my country's love and curse Secession's serpent seed!" and one angry rebel shoots him, crying "Die, you mad dog!" (McKee 86, 87). Insults to the flag provide a focal point for northern indignation.

The play that most clearly foregrounds the flag as the object of the war and the pervasive symbol of the people's endeavors is entitled, appropriately, *The Old Flag* (1871). In the very first line of the play, Charles Sanford tells a friend, "It is the duty of every law-abiding citizen to lend his aid in sustaining our country and upholding the old flag which has so long floated over it" (Walker and Lewis 3). Charles's position represents exceptional commitment, for he is a native of North Carolina, and his father not only goes out of his way to trample on the Union flag, but rejects the son who has accepted a captaincy in a federal company. In a departure ceremony, Charles reverently accepts a flag, and he later receives his death wound while waving the banner and rallying his men to battle. As he lies dying, he will not loose his hold on the flag until he sees Alice, his hometown sweetheart who has remained loyal the South. She apologizes for rejecting him; he forgives her but asks for something more.

> But the Old Flag, Alice,—is there not an atonement needed there? I have stood by the Old Flag, Alice, and have sacrificed my life in its defense; with my dying grasp I have clung to it, resolving to relinquish it to none but you. I love the Old Flag, oh, how I love it; and it is indeed fitting that a thing so sacred to me should be my dying gift to you. Here, take it and cherish it for my sake, and when you look upon its tattered folds, stained with my life blood, and recall those happy days of the past, when your love for me and the Old Flag was one, you may feel that you have some share in the sacrifice. I thank God that we are reconciled at last. We may yet meet in Heaven, where there is but one flag, the bright banner of the cross. (40–41)

At his insistence, she swears allegiance to the flag, and when the war is over and the survivors are reconciled, she comes downstage to address the audience.

> And I see before me to-night many whose sympathetic tears tell me of loved ones lost in the holy cause of liberty and justice. Will you not unite with me in the noble mission of striving to keep ever green the memories of our blessed martyrs whose blood cements the union of which we are all so proud? . . . Mothers, teach your children, next to their duty to the Almighty Ruler of the Universe they owe it to their fallen sires, to ever revere and never falter in maintaining the glory and honor of THE OLD FLAG! (44)

So contextualized, the old flag is truly sanctified by virtue of the blood that martyrs shed to protect it, by its use as a gift of love and loyalty, by its association with the nostalgic past, by its equation with heaven (which, surely, also has a flag), and most of all by its connection with the ultimate American ideal of liberty.

The symbol eclipses the land, the government, and the ideals that it supposedly represents, and becomes an intrinsic reason for fighting the war. It is as though the flag has assumed a personality and become a cherished friend, now assailed and in need of rescue. One recruit tells a friend that "you know, and I know, and the people know, that this war is a war for the flag—a flag war, not a party war" (McKee 16). A farmer announces to the departing troops that they will "have assisted in causing the old banner to again wave from every mountain top, and over every town and hamlet in our once happy land, and hear the shouts of triumph ascend from a grateful people, proclaiming that once more we have one flag, and one country" (Dawson and Whittemore 16). He does not, of course, address the issue that the federal troops are marching off to force the South to return to the Union, and that most of the "grateful people" will probably be Northerners. In Act Two of *Gettysburg*, Percy Cook and Belle Kane debate the foundation of the war.

> PERCY: You say 'tis slavery's the cause. Cousin, you wrong us—or you dream!
> BELLE: It is the cause.
> PERCY: Slavery! Then 'tis slavery to the flag—that flag our fathers made—made sacred to us in one faithful blood. That is the cause—that flag. And would to heaven the South had one as fair, as pure, as just.
> BELLE: That flag thy cause! No, no—no, no, Percy. That Union flag but hides, conceals from you the real one, freedom to the slave! To that the North have sworn—for that will war us to the bitter end!
> PERCY: No, no. The North have sworn by deed that those "who would be free themselves must strike the blow." It dares not, cannot war for slaves. To war for slaves, who will not war themselves, would wrong, dishonor—yes, the best of flags, and d—n the best of men! . . . But . . . should once that North forget those Union stars, and chant its prayers for victory to these heathen gods—these slaves—then I for one forget the North and war the South no more. But that will never be. No; that flag—its rights began the war; that flag—its rights must end it. (McKee 9)

Percy insists that he aid his compatriots fight to preserve that sacred, just, and pure banner to which they are willing vassals, and on his way to arguing that position, he completely rejects the slavery issue, scorning the slaves themselves as unworthy of freedom.

This submersion of slavery is typical of the Yankee position as the plays depict it; almost no northern character mentions slavery as a reason for fighting.[14] Only Southerners cite slavery as a causative issue, but they spend virtually no effort on justifying the institution; perhaps the northern playwrights perceived their old adversaries as being so arrogant and intransigent on the subject that they would have scorned debate. Instead, the Confederates concentrate on the most radical of their opponents, and the word "abolitionist" becomes an insult beyond its specific meaning; the angrier rebels equate it with all who oppose their cotton kingdom. The Northerners are not only hirelings or mudsills, they are the "cowardly abolitionists," "insolent abolitionists," or "cursed abolitionists" who insult and disenfranchise the South. Southern rhetoric about the hated "abolition hosts" evokes an image of whole armies composed of manic caricatures of Garrison, come alive to overrun peaceful plantations. In *The Confederate Spy* (1887), Philip Bradley tells the Union commander that

> Abraham Lincoln, regardless of all moral, legal, and constitutional restraints, has sent his abolition hosts among us, who are murdering and imprisoning our citizens, confiscating and destroying our property, and committing other acts of violence and outrage, too shocking and revolting to humanity to be enumerated. (Stedman 23)

When Bradley finds a Union soldier embracing his sister, he snarls, "You miserable abolitionist. I'd like to tear your heart asunder" (27).

By the time these plays appeared, abolition was a fait accompli, so to turn "abolitionist" into such a furious insult was to make those who used it—Southerners all—appear ridiculous, while at the same time affirming an apparent historical inevitability. Yet when the comic darky enters the action, the essential abuse of slavery—white hegemony at the expense of black self-actualization—is covertly affirmed.[15] In *Lights and Shadows of the Great Rebellion*, Zeb first appears when a farmer named Ike pulls him into a recruiting scene.

> IKE: Here Captain, here's another recruit, 'list him we'll need him.
> ZEB: By jims, massa! I don't know nuffin 'bout dat business.
> IKE: Look here, Blackey, you must 'list, and go with us sojers, and help free the darkie.
> ZEB: Am dat what dis war am fur, massa?
> IKE: Yes, the politicians say the darkey is the bone of contention.
> ZEB: Now look heah, massa, did you eber see two dogs fightin' ober a bone?
> IKE: Yes, but what has that got to do with this war?
> ZEB: Well, massa, did you eber see de bone git up and fight too? (Dawson and Whittemore 9)[16]

Zeb is a cliché out of the minstrel tradition, given to puffing his own importance, eating whenever possible, drinking whiskey (which makes him feel "golly golluptious"), and malingering at every opportunity—he even entertains the audience with a song and dance. Like all the comic darkies, he is completely loyal to his white "massa," but while the playwrights may have intended his devotion as an indication of his fundamental humanity and worth, they persisted in defining that worth in relation to white needs; in other words, Zeb is a foolish fellow that we tolerate because he subordinates himself to us. The comic darky is a virtual duplicate of the plantation nigger that the southern aristocracy cherished and, during the antebellum era, promoted as evidence that slavery was, in practice, essentially benevolent. He is no more free than a dog who moves from one master to another; both expect him to chase the stick on demand. By including the comic darky, the playmakers further dissociate their work from any critique of slavery or any claim that slavery inspired the Union commitment to the war.

The southern characters invert the rhetoric to accuse the North of enslaving them. One of the more inflammatory secessionists refers to "our divine institution of slavery," associates Lincoln's election with the North's "persistent attempts to force upon us a government of ultra abolitionists and nigger worshippers," and scorns the ineffectual attempts of the "abolition spy . . . who is trying to arouse the niggers" (*Union Sergeant* 29). A Confederate major tells a northern friend, "You have at last brought on the issue by the election of a sectional President, and if we submit to his diction we well [*sic*] be but the slaves of a political despotism. All we ask is that you of the North will let us alone" (Muscroft 7). In *Harry Allen* (1872), Peyton Randolph complains of northern oppression.[17]

> I must say we have been basely imposed upon by those Ultra-Abolitionists. . . . [Y]ou have at last succeeded in electing for President one of the very worst leading negro worshipers of the whole abolition crew; and if we submit, we will be but little better than slaves to that tyrannical despot. All we ask is to be let alone. (Barton 7)

As Union troops are about to attack his position, an officer tells his men, "Remember now 'tis slavery you fight against, my men—slavery, the worst of slaveries, Yankee slavery and don't forget it" (McKee 87). A southern major dreams of "the complete emancipation of the South from abolition rule, and the establishment of a grand, new Southern empire" (Whalen 12). By protesting the North's alleged conspiracy to enslave the South, these Southerners condemn slavery, but only as applied to them; they insist on their rights as free men.

Both North and South fight for the hallowed ideals of liberty, freedom, and independence. When the governor of Massachusetts presents a flag to a departing regiment, he reminds them that "as our fathers fought, so strike you the blow for liberty" (*Union Sergeant* 17). One Union soldier believes that "duty says to go to the front, take up the musket [my] father dropped, and do as he would have done: fight till the stars and stripes shall again float over a free nation," and at the close of the play, he hopes that after the war, "under our beautiful banner of the free, protected by the Goddess of Liberty, the Gray and the Blue shall clasp hands over the bloody chasm" (Stedman, *The Confederate Spy* 11, 51). Southern characters apply more desperate rhetoric to "the holy cause of Southern liberty"; one insists that abolitionism and Lincoln's election have "*exasperated us beyond all endurance! Now* our motto is—*Independence* or *Annihilation*" (*Union Sergeant* 29). In *Gettysburg*, a southern newspaper insists on secession in the name of liberty.

> We say it once again we do not want a Union with the Yankees north. No! A Union with a nation of hyenas far were better—far better than with them. Union? No! Freedom is what we want and what we mean to have, and have we will, or have the freest fight for it this country ever had. It's freedom, Southern independence now, or war—a war unto the knife—the knife unto the hilt. (McKee 3)

In *From Sumter to Appomattox* (1889), Captain Julian Farnsworth of the Union debates the question with Major George Roberts of the Confederacy.

> FARNSWORTH: I fear that I shall be unable to make Major Roberts view the subject of secession as seen through Northern eyes.
> ROBERTS: I can view it in no other light, sir, than that of the attempt of a brave and chivalrous people to throw off the yoke of oppression which a tyrannical government has so long imposed upon them.
> FARNSWORTH: And to view it as it is regarded at the North, Major Roberts, you would see in it a gigantic conspiracy to destroy the best government that the world has ever seen; and to perpetuate the most atrocious system that God has ever permitted to exist. You see that our respective positions are too remote to permit us to discuss this question from any common standpoint. (Whalen 13–14)

Both sides claim to fight for their rights. One Southerner accuses his Yankee host of unpardonable insult because he and his family have been "driven from your door like dogs, simply because we have dared to maintain the rights of a people that have never known a master" (Muscroft 9). A southern cadet at West Point insists that "if to secure our rights we are obliged to inaugurate a war, we will not shrink from the responsibility," and Edward St. Clair feels "called upon to protect our sacred rights" (Kilpatrick and Moore 7, Ames and Bartley 7). Guy Vincent argues more than once that the Southerners fight for the just cause of preserving their rights, depicting the Northerners as invaders and promising that "we can defend our rights, even as our forefathers did against the minions of Great Britain" (Dawson and Whittemore 6). Yet even Northerners declare that they fight for their country's rights, while George Waterman, in *The Confederate Spy*, elevates the issue when he states simply that "I am fighting on the side of God and right" (Stedman 12).

Most Northerners enlist to suppress what they routinely refer to as the southern "rebellion," fought by those who were, by definition, traitors because they sought to tear apart the Union and because they cheerfully subjected the old flag to seditious artillery fire. When a federal officer refers to the trouble between the North and the South, a young woman corrects him, saying that the trouble is "between rebels and the Government," and when one Farmer Allen first hears of the firing on Fort Sumter, he exclaims, "The infamous rascals; every one of them ought to be shot down like dogs! . . . The traitors! Why, the Government will hang the last one of them. . . . [I]f these traitorous villains dare to attempt an open resistance, 'By the Eternal' we will hang them higher than Haman" (Andrews 12, Barton 7). He cites the memory of his great-grandfather, Ethan Allen, in promising that even if his own son supported secession, he would deny him the comfort of his fireside. Another farmer maintains that if one of his sons supported the secessionist treason, "I would smite him down, and pray Heaven he might never rise again," and yet another farmer voices a popular sentiment when he says that the rebels "ought to be hung as traitors, the last dog of them" (Muscroft 8, Dawson and Whittemore 3). Yet southern characters also find traitors in their midst—a sister who loves a Yankee, a wife who sides with her northern husband, or even Northerners who find themselves in the South when the shooting begins. The Northerners call the Southerners "cowardly traitors," while most Southerners assume that the Northerners are cowards by nature.

A major southern preoccupation was the defense of their homes, their land, and their "sacred soil." A general sends his troops out to preserve not only their rights but their homes, firesides, wives, and children, and a southern father scorns his son, a Union sympathizer, for having joined those who would invade the "sacred soil" and despoil the homes of his native land. Other Southerners are equally sentimental about the land itself; in *The Confederate Spy*, Maud Bradley muses that when she remembers "that the dear old home of my childhood is in the midst of the scene of carnage, it nearly drives me wild," and her brother tells a Union general, simply, "I am a Virginian by birth . . . this land where you now stand and where a part of your troops are camped, belongs to me. Reckless and unprincipled, you and your followers have invaded our soil" (Stedman 7, 23). Perhaps the most poignant expression of southern love of the land comes from Belle Kane in *Gettysburg*, whose love of homeland blinds her to all other considerations.

> I only know I love the South; my duty follows. . . . [M]y love's beyond control—beyond my own. The South, my home; 'tis with me always—comes in every thought, and lives in every breath; it speaks unto me now—recalls the past; its brightest fondest hopes; its joys and smiles, and all that is in memory worshipped dear; it comes to me in dreams, and sings again the songs it taught my early days; beats on my woman's heart, and wakes my sleeping soul to all that's highest, holiest, noblest, best there is in life, and bids it go. . . . I must be true to that or false to God! (McKee 9)

Like those who urged the flag, freedom, their rights, or the cowardice of the other side, Belle elevates her justification to an unassailable level.

WAR AS ROMANCE

To mythologize the war, the playmakers transformed it into a romance, interpreting the conflict as a troubled intersectional love affair. Within this paradigm, the question of the South's "true" attitude toward Union becomes commensurate with the question of a reluctant maiden's sincerity when she pushes her lover away. So treated, the lovers' trials become not only representative of those faced by actual individuals during the 1860s, but of the North and South in general. The reading of the war therefore begins with the question of whether North or South becomes male or female, and the interaction is relocated into the context of gender relations and courtship rituals.

In nearly every case where the man is a Southerner, he is also the villain of the piece, urging his unwelcome attentions on a distraught woman who almost always marries a Northerner by the end of the play. There are two models for this southern villain: the rejected suitor, who displaces his fury and resentment onto the woman's family, and the rapist, whom the woman never encouraged, but who takes advantage of the chaos of war to try to abduct her and force her to marry him against her will. In both cases, the villain usually commits a variety of war crimes along the way, and so reinforces his evil status. Edward St. Clair tries to have Edwin Dalton executed without proper authority, he forces Dalton's wife to see him starving in Andersonville, and he shoots little Willie for calling him a "cowardly traitor." In *Loyal Mountaineers* (1873), Alice Marks and her father live in Tennessee but remain loyal to the Union, and they suffer under the depredations of Fred Steel, the leader of a guerrilla band that goes from house to house in the dead of night to find and murder anyone suspected of hindering the Confederate cause. He continues his war crimes as commandant of Libby Prison, but returns to the Tennessee mountains to trick Alice into a tryst and to attempt to force her to marry him. She replies,

> and have I been led from home by your fiendish plottings? Lost, lost! just as I was about to see my vision of freedom realized, you cross my path to ruin all. Why do you torment me more? Are you not human, or have you lost all but the form of man? Leave me; the very sight of you is loathsome. Your foul breath is filled with rum and treason. Go, sir, I say, before I stain my hands with blood. (Culver 34)

In *The Dutch Recruit* (1879), another craven Confederate is about to force a woman to marry him when Union troops arrive to rescue her; he tries to stab her to death, but they shoot him down before he can do it.[18]

The presence of such a character invites the use of the conventional strategies and rhetoric of melodrama. One Southerner tells a woman's father, "Your daughter shall be my wife, though I wade through oceans of blood to obtain her," and later swears, "by all the powers of heaven and earth, she shall be mine!" (Vegiard 10) He imprisons the hero and promises to starve him to death unless he will join the Confederate army and resign his interest in the heroine, giving him the ultimatum, "tell Maude that you owe all to me, and rank and riches shall be yours. Refuse me and your tortures shall be tenfold" (38). When his captive escapes, he sends bloodhounds in pursuit. In *Surrounded by Fire* (1874), because Tom Clifton rebels not only against the Union, but also against his loyalist parents, he and the South appear as recreant youths who scorn wiser authorities. He loves Fanny Verne, his parents' ward, but turns against the whole family so thoroughly that he assigns one of his men to spy on their home and even orders his sergeant to restrain Fanny when she protests the treatment of a Union officer the family has been protecting. The hero of *From Sumter to Appomattox* hears that his cruel rival plans to force the heroine to marry him, and announces, "He shall be foiled in his devilish plot. I will save the woman I love from such a fate, or die in the attempt!" (Whalen 33).

To cast the South as a vengeful, rejected suitor is to demean the southern cause. The woman disdains her beau because he has announced his resolve to fight against her family (i.e., the North), which is so irreproachable a reason that when he expresses his resentment, he oversteps the bounds of genteel behavior. Even more devastating is to cast the South as a rapist, an aggressor who would abduct and violate the North. Beyond the intensity and violence of this image, it represented a drastic revision of the actuality of the war, for since the vast majority of the fighting took place in Confederate territory, it was the North who entered the South, rather than the other way around. This appropriation of rape is therefore ahistorical but expresses the playmakers' enduring anger and resentment at those who rent the Union, vilified the flag, and interrupted the grand experiment of the American republic; they could hardly find a more insulting way to characterize their old enemies. Such a casting pattern further lays the blame on the South, for if the North is a woman, passive and kind, none can attribute to her the responsibility for the breach. It is all the fault of the South.

When the man is a Northerner, he remains steadfastly loyal to his country, and the woman adjusts, often in response to some demonstration of strength and commitment from her suitor. In *Allatoona* (1875), Helen Dunbar rejects Harry Estes because he "would be a husband who would vow before heaven to be a woman's protector, and then, at the bidding of a lot of fanatical abolitionists, wantonly slay her people" (Kilpatrick and Moore 9). Yet when the war brings them together again and his life is in danger, she is distraught at the idea that he might be killed; she actually loved him all along. In *The Confederate Spy*, Maud Bradley's concerns are more personal than sectional—her lover is a Yankee, while her father and brother fight for the Confederacy—and although she rejects George Waterman at first, she changes her mind when he chivalrously helps her brother. In *From Sumter to Appomattox*, Clare Thorne has released her lover, Captain Julian Farnsworth, because he feels duty-bound to fight for the Union, so she leaves herself vulnerable to the dastardly attentions of Major George Roberts, who proves himself to be not only a radical secessionist but a rapist as well.

> ROBERTS: For three years you have avoided me, treating me with every mark of aversion. You have scorned my passion, and evaded my presence. I have borne your insults in silence, awaiting the hour of my triumph. That hour has at last arrived. Clare Thorne, you shall become my wife within the next half hour; and no power on earth can save you.
> CLARE: Become your wife, Major Roberts? Sooner than join myself to such a heartless villain as you I would die ten thousand deaths!
> ROBERTS: Indulge in all the high tragedy you please, my lady; you cannot escape me this time. I have laid my plans too well. There is not a soul within the sound of your voice, cry out as loudly as you will. (Whalen 37)

Roberts engages the services of a minister, who turns out to be Farnsworth in disguise and who reveals himself, calls Roberts a "cowardly poltroon," and rescues Clare, who finally relents and marries the Yankee officer. In *Hal Hazard* (1883), Nellie, the southern heroine, is a Union sympathizer from the start, and so requires neither correction nor reformation; when her Union suitor wonders whether she will accept the attentions of a federal officer, she sets him straight.

> Oh, we long for the halcyon days of peace under the beneficent government of our ancestors. There's many weary hearts all over the South, who sigh and pray for a restitution of the old Union in the glory and strength of its palmy days. . . . Hate you for fighting for the Old Union, Tom? There's not a soldier in Sherman's army that I do not honor and revere. Thank god that there are so many heroes in blue, who are ready with strong arms and stout hearts, to bear aloft the starry flag on their bayonets to victory. (11–12)

This scenario translates into a domestic scene where the South is a woman and the Confederacy her wayward brother; she looks to her more upright husband, the North, to restore the order of the family.[19]

Casting the North as a man affirms a classic patriarchal view of American society. The South, as a woman, is capricious and weak, while the North is sensible and strong; only through the intervention of the North can the South return to its senses. The war becomes a marital quarrel in which the husband must reprimand and then soothe a hysterical wife. By challenging the husband's authority, the wife violates her marriage vows and leaves herself open to censure and even rejection; she must think herself fortunate if the husband condones her return to "his" home.

The parallels multiply in light of the playmakers' treatment of the romantic couple as still in the courtship stage. The lovers are prisoners, each capturing the other, and when the war begins, they become prisoners of war, held hostage by their affection, and their unrequited love becomes a metaphor for the frustrated desire for Union that impels the North. In this northern vision, the sections are lovers whose compulsion toward each other makes the clash inevitable as long as one persists in pursuing contrary behavior. To present the war as a romance is to define the issues as emotional rather than political, which enabled the playmakers to rationalize the apparent chaos of the conflict. Their audiences would not expect a love affair to proceed logically—except that rapists and rejected suitors receive their just deserts, while honest men marry the heroines—and so perceived the arbitrary and unmotivated shifts in the plot as consonant with the model of narrative.

The tendency of the plays to interpret events on a personal level led to a conception of wartime action as a matter of individual heroism and even cloak-and-dagger intrigue, most often expressed in the character of the Union spy.[20] Although most of the spies are stalwart young recruits who bravely volunteer for one (usually disastrous) mission behind enemy lines, perhaps the most fully developed example is the title role in *Hal Hazard*. The hero's real name is George

Clarendon; he is a Georgian who has remained loyal to the Union, evaded Confederate impressment, and adopted the alter ego of Hal Hazard, an old hillbilly who assures us, "I hain't nary a drop o' secesh blood in me. I allers did hev a kind feelin' fer the flag, an' I say hurray fer the ole flag, an' hurray fer Ole Abe, through thick an' thin" (Andrews 5). As Hal, he is partly deaf and endearingly comic, so he moves unchallenged among the southern troops, who are far too dull and stupid to see through his disguise, and even gives them directions as to how to locate George (that is, himself), whom they are hunting. He saves two Union officers from an ambush, but without betraying his sympathies to the Confederates, and he repeatedly rescues his lady love from the clutches of the evil Captain Bilger. His devices are transparently simple; one of his operatives records information in a code where a = b, b = c, and so on.

Although this clumsy cloak-and-dagger routine resembles a little boy's fantasy, it serves to confirm the belief that the war turned not on large troop movements or battles where impersonal artillery felled thousands in the space of an afternoon, but rather on the cleverness and ingenuity of exceptional individuals. If Hal manages to fool the entire Confederate army, his triumph validates the power of a single man's initiative over the strength of the forces that both sides massed. To further reinforce this principle, the plays relegate general officers to their staff tents, far away from the "real" adventure and glory of battle, where they, stiff and lofty, give broad orders for vast plans that would go awry except that one imaginative volunteer saves the day.

To reinforce the concept of the war as not public but private strife, conflict between characters remains personal. The young southern aristocrat who declares for the Confederacy ultimately fights not for his principles but to avenge the "insult" of being turned out of the northern home where he once was welcome; he yearns for an opportunity not to rid the South of the invading federal armies, but to make life miserable for his former friends. The northern volunteer fights not only for his country but also to protect the woman he loves. There is no carnage involving thousands, but a series of marches, sorties, and expeditions in which only a few die, some deservedly and others in the name of heroic sacrifice.[21] This reduction obviates the need to explore the deeper issues of the war as such, as a civil conflict, and as a means of resolving complicated social, economic, and political disputes. If the war, as staged, is actually a matter of personal rivalry between two men, none of these factors applies. The war becomes a duel that has grown out of proportion, with each side seeking to erase the stain of insult from an otherwise honorable escutcheon.

This reductive treatment of the war stems from two sources. First, the plays tended to take the point of view of the common soldier, to whom grand strategy was largely obscure, even if it were accessible. As is probably the case with most soldiers, these men staged the war as a matter of what happened to the people in their particular company or regiment; a limited perspective which, in the context of the entire conflict, was virtually random. Second, the stagecraft and dramaturgy of these plays imposed severe limitations on their vision. There were attempts to depict the actual processes and consequences of battle—*The Drummer Boy* includes a potentially devastating scene of the wounded and dying on the field of Shiloh at night, and other plays offered scenes involving actual firing—but more often, the playwrights depicted battles through scenes at headquarters (driven by messengers, despatches, and hastily written orders) and confrontations, usually nonviolent standoffs, between small groups of soldiers far away from the principal fray.

On one hand, therefore, the plays construed the fighting as a gallant adventure, with minimal death and destruction. Yet characters die on these amateur stages—the little drummer boy, the Confederate colonel who repents his rebellion in his last breath, and the dedicated Yankee whose blood soaks through the flag that enfolds him—and even though they expire decorously and live long enough to make one last brave speech, theirs are the deaths that the playmakers remembered. These men took the stage as amateurs, but many of them had donned a uniform as amateurs as well, and learned terrible lessons that led them to take both the war and its dramatic reconstruction on an intensely personal level. The word "sacrifice" appears again and again in these plays—sacrifice for the flag, for the "temple" of the southern cause, for one's country. Like most soldiers, those who survived the war to re-create it in the theatre knew the tangible meaning of sacrifice, that a man might be maimed or wounded, that unrelievable suffering might obliterate any resemblance to the brave trooper that marched proudly out of his home town. In the preface to *Our Heroes* (1873), John B. Renaud delineated the rhetoric of sacrifice as he understood it, praising

> the almost endless acts of heroism performed by the Union soldiers, in their efforts to check and conquer a rebellion as desperate in its struggle as it was wicked in its aims. The author must pause before the number of their sacrifices and deeds of bravery, as well as before the fiendish modes of persecution invented by the Confederates, which furnish the subject of the darkest page of their history. . . . Patriotism, which so filled our volunteers' hearts; bravery, which so characterized their warfare; self-sacrifice, which was their constant virtue; and suffering, which was their inevitable lot, as well as the heroism and self-abnegation of our women, which so often gladdened the hearts of the soldiers, and cheered them on to further deeds of valor—should find a place in a play founded on the events of the late war. . . . (6)

The plays idealized the war precisely because they sprang from this rhetorical agenda, one that sought to validate the suffering of the war and raise its participants above the level of statistics in disasters like Marye's Heights and Cold Harbor. We now accept, as appropriate images of war, bodies piled on top of each other in common graves; such is the iconography that reinforces our post-Hiroshima, post-Vietnam guilt and ideology. The playmaking veterans had ready and ample access to the horrors of their war and could have conveyed what many of us would now regard as a highly realistic vision of the struggle; that is, as irredeemably bloody, destructive, and dehumanizing. Yet they chose to valorize the sacrifice, glorify the combatants, and idealize the conflict. Their representation was a matter not of misinformation or inability to perceive the material in terms more commensurate with our own, but one of considered choice carried out amidst a welter of theatrical and social conventions regarding heroism, the military, and the emotion of sectional dispute. The theatrical vision of the war worked synergistically with the melodramatic method typical of the period; both tended toward reduction and simplification. The result was a certain use of stage convention combined with a specific historiography of the war, one that almost without exception, conveyed a point of view presented either as northern or as generically American, a strategy that appropriated the South and denied the history of sectionalism.

SHENANDOAH

The professional plays of the mid-1880s confirmed the swing of popular northern sentiment away from sectionalism and toward reconciliation, extending the sorrow of sacrifice like an olive branch in order to embrace the South in one country.[22] In no play is this treatment clearer than in *Shenandoah*, which Bronson Howard drives toward reconciliation from the very beginning, leaving little cause for surprise when, once the war is over, the action retreats from the battlefield to a domestic setting, and no less than four pairs of lovers make preparations for marriage.[23] The playwright moves one step beyond the amateurs' pattern, not using love as a metaphor for the conflict, but shifting the issues almost completely into the private sphere, where love obscures politics and war altogether. As one man says, "Every woman's heart, the world over, belongs not to any country or any flag, but to her husband—and her lover. Pray for the man you love, sister—it would be treason not to" (600). Both men and women, ultimately, place love above duty.[24]

The play includes not one but two intersectional romances, arranged in a symmetrical pattern: Robert Ellingham of the 10th Virginia is in love with Madeline West, whose brother, Kerchival West of Sheridan's cavalry, is in love with Robert's sister, Gertrude.[25] These men are not the volunteers of the veterans' myth; they are West Point graduates, professionals who virtually divorce themselves from the politics that control them, and loyal officers whose sentiments regarding patriotism are identical except that they now salute different flags. They care less about sectional issues than about the manner in which the two of them will manage the difference of allegiance that circumstances have thrust upon them; Kerchival assures his friend that "one of us will be wrong in this great fight, but we shall both be honest in it" (576). In the introductory scenes for the men and for the women, who are also fast friends, Howard maintains a perfect balance between the northern and southern positions; each lover insists that his or her cause is just, but does not argue the point to the extent of jeopardizing friendship. This early dialogue includes none of the inflammatory rhetoric of the amateur formula; Robert refers to "the determined frenzy of my fellow Southerners" rather than his own dedication to the cause, and he assures his friend that the war is inevitable, thus begging the question of what he will or will not do to prevent it. General John Haverhill, who became the Ellinghams' guardian when their father died, continues the carefully nonsectional rhetoric when he expresses his relief that his old friend never had to choose between two flags; the remark gives each side equal merit. Because these are professional soldiers who serve whichever government commands their loyalty, there is none of the sentiment connected with mothers watching their sons enlist and townspeople sending off the local regiment with a newly sewn flag. Yet first and foremost, the principal characters are lovers, and the war impedes each romance equally.

Howard follows the amateur precedent by interpreting the war as a courtship gone awry. Kerchival's men capture Gertrude and suspect her of carrying secret information to the rebel lines, but every man, from General Buckthorn to Sergeant Barket, the Irish comic, is afraid to violate her delicacy and deny his gentility by actually searching her. The incident reduces the entire war to a matter of sexual etiquette, which turns itself back on the political history, as in the amateur plays, and defines the South as a tempestuous woman whom the the masculine North must somehow dominate without desecration. Furthermore, the play implies that if love is a valid metaphor for war, then the reverse is also true. Gertrude and Kerchival regard courtship as a game which they play as a mock battle, each trying to win a conversational advantage over the other; he tells her he loves her, but when she has stretched the moment out just long enough, the first rebel gun fires on Fort Sumter and she declares that they are enemies. After Gertrude's capture, Buckthorn makes her Kerchival's literal prisoner and even gives him a letter his men have found among her papers, one from a friend that alludes to her secret declaration of love for Kerchival, which is, of course, the last thing she wants him to know about. Her attitude is merely a strategic pose; when she sees him wounded, she drops to her knees and declares her love.[26]

Howard needs a villain to spur the action on, but his studied nonsectionalism prevents him from choosing either a Southerner or a Northerner, so he contrives a character who is neither: Thornton, a copperhead, a Northerner who has become a southern gentleman, but one whose loyalty is completely artificial and whom no one trusts. He has turned his unwelcome attentions on Haverhill's wife, Constance, who seems as distraught as if she had genuinely encouraged him, but in Howard's genteel fiction, the slightest impropriety can be cause for scandal. Robert tells Kerchival that Thornton has been "pressing, not to say insolent, in his attentions to Mrs. Haverhill" and reports that there was once a scandal when Thornton "entered a lady's room unexpectedly at night" and then killed the husband in a duel (577). Robert believes that while walking on the lawn he looked up and recognized Thornton's shadow on the curtains of Constance's room, and later tells

Thornton that he does not want him to escort Gertrude to visit a neighbor. Within the narrow bounds of honor in this play, such a remark is nearly a direct insult, so Thornton suggests, with perfect courtesy but scarcely veiled threat, that he and Robert might "chat over the subject later in the day" (578). In a soliloquy, Constance manages to convey both her anxiety and Thornton's depravity.

> If my husband should learn what happened in my room to-night, he would kill that man. What encouragement could I have given him? Innocence is never on its guard—but, the last I remember before I fell unconscious, he was crouching before me like a whipped cur! (580)

Thornton suggests delicately that he had mistakenly believed that Constance declined his attentions because she was preoccupied with Kerchival rather than with her husband; Kerchival calls him a scoundrel, and the two men go off to fight a duel as the deadline at Fort Sumter draws nearer. Kerchival hits his adversary but the wound is not fatal, leaving only a scar on Thornton's face and considerable resentment.

All of this late-Victorian chivalry carried a certain intrinsic interest to Howard's audience, but the characters' concerns also reinforce the play's underlying message: that form matters far more than content; the issues that engaged the attention of Howard's amateur predecessor—freedom, states' rights, rebellion, and the flag—simply do not apply here. War is a question not of national politics but of personal deportment, and although we witness the death on stage of Haverhill's estranged son Frank, we also see Robert Ellingham brought in ostensibly as a prisoner but more like a hockey player sent to the penalty box, unharmed but out of action for a time, free within his parole until his commander can arrange an exchange. Furthermore, the strict code of behavior between men and women enforces a commensurately strict conception of gender roles and imposes a rigid sexual politics that confers certain kinds of power on men and other prerogatives on women, but which definitely conforms to the traditional conception of the man as the gallant protector of the vulnerable woman.

Thornton's role as agent provocateur continues as Kerchival's men capture him, now a Confederate captain, in the Shenandoah Valley and find on him a miniature of Constance. Haverhill had given it to her to pass on to Frank, who is later reported dead but in fact assumes a false name, obtains a Union commission, and is subsequently assigned to Kerchival's regiment, where he volunteers for a hazardous reconnaissance mission and makes a favorable impression on the general, who finds the resemblance to his lost son disquieting. Thornton escapes, not back to his own lines, but to the hills, where he ambushes Kerchival, whose men carry him back to headquarters with a serious knife wound. An officer finds Constance's miniature in Kerchival's pocket and turns it over to Haverhill, who had suspected a liaison and concludes unhappily that his wife gave it to Kerchival. After the war, Haverhill finally confronts Constance with the miniature, but because Frank is dead and Kerchival is believed lost, there is no one to corroborate her story, and she disdains to protest her innocence. Thornton's evil seems to endure, but Frank's widow presents the letter he dictated while dying of his wounds; it reveals that Thornton took the miniature from him while he was a prisoner in Richmond.

As with the use of chivalry, this intricate manipulation of misprision adds more than a strong dose of theatricality to engage Howard's audience; it also indicates that the war was an extended misunderstanding and that evil itself is illusory. In fact, once Thornton has stabbed Kerchival, the renegade is no longer necessary and so disappears, but because convention demanded that Howard kill off the villain, during the final act, one of the officers mentions, almost casually, that he killed Thornton while heading north after his escape from a southern prison.

Aside from the firing on Fort Sumter, the key historical episode included in *Shenandoah* is Philip H. Sheridan's ride to rally his defeated troops at Cedar Creek, and it is from this incident that Howard most explicitly makes myth.[27] During the autumn of 1864, believing that Jubal Early had fled the Shenandoah Valley, Sheridan had led his men through the countryside to burn crops and destroy property in an effort to demoralize the residents. Early, however, was waiting for a chance to attack, and when the federal forces camped along Cedar Creek, he began moving his troops into position. On October 13, two Confederate divisions accidentally engaged the fringes of George Crook's 8th Corps, but even though he now knew that the enemy was nearby, Sheridan left for Washington on October 15 to confer with his superiors. While en route, he was given an intercepted Confederate despatch that purported to promise James Longstreet's support for Early's plan to rout the federals; he believed the signal to be a ruse, but nevertheless sent word to Horatio G. Wright, his second-in-command, to be prepared for trouble. On the evening of October 18, John B. Gordon's men moved as quietly as possible to take up a position on the Union flank, and as dawn approached, they attacked while Joseph Kershaw's division swept in from another direction. The federal camp was completely surprised; some soldiers ran without stopping for clothing or weapons.

Sheridan had spent the night in Winchester, about fifteen miles from his headquarters. His aides awoke him at 6:00 A.M. to report the distant sound of artillery, but he did not realize what had happened until he rode south and met his own army, panicky and demoralized, moving toward him. He posted a brigade to stem the flow of men, and then, on a black gelding named Rienzi, he rode on down the line, waving his hat and rallying his troops. The momentum of the battle reversed completely, and by the time it was over, Early's army had retreated all the way to New Market. Sheridan was a hero.[28]

The myth of Sheridan's ride began in the popular press. On the cover of its November 5 issue, *Harper's Weekly* featured an engraving of Sheridan riding his charger toward a point beyond the viewer's right shoulder while soldiers in the background wave enthusiastically. The accompanying article said that the victory reflected "peculiar credit on the brave commander to whose timely arrival upon the field the final success of the day must be attributed." The general rode in "so that the devil himself could not keep up with him," and when one of his staff described the situation as "awful," he told him, "it's nothing of the sort. It's all right, or we'll fix it right!" Sheridan waved his hat to the cheering troops, and then galloped down the line to reform the line and turn the rebels back.

In one of the earliest war histories, published in 1865, Samuel M. Schmucker suggested that "the army of the Shenandoah was for the first time defeated; not routed, but badly beaten" when Sheridan came riding up the pike from Winchester "at full speed, his noble horse completely flecked with foam, swinging his cap, and shouting to the stragglers, 'Face the other way, boys. We are going back to our camps. We are going to lick them out of their boots.' The effect was magical." The men cheered and followed him back to the battle, where he assured them that, "if I had been here, this never should have happened" (804). Under his influence, the federal troops "forgot their hunger, their thirst, and their weariness" and charged with "Sheridan himself dashing along the front, cheering them with his confident smile, and his emphatic assurances of success" (805). Schmucker compared the turnaround with those at Marengo and Shiloh.

In *The Great Rebellion* (1866), Joel Tyler Headley offered an account of Cedar Creek that closely resembles Schmucker's. He related that Sheridan heard "the thunder of the guns" as he rode back toward his command, and "the lion in his nature was roused" as he exhorted his men "to lick them out of their boots." Even the wounded cheered as he rode his foam-covered horse to the front of his army and ordered the retreat to halt. He assured them that, "if I had been here, this never should have happened," and "the excited soldiers felt a new strength infused into them by the confident bearing and language of their heroic Commander" (499–500). Because Sheridan's remarks were repeated, with little variation, in account after account, they helped to confer legendary status on the story and on its hero. Headley also drew the comparison with Marengo and Shiloh, but argued that those battles turned because of the arrival of fresh troops, while Sheridan won Cedar Creek simply because he appeared, alone, on the field and encouraged his men "by the power of his single presence as he dashed along the shattered lines, and the magic of his voice" (503).

Another early version of Sheridan's ride was Herman Melville's poem, "Philip" (1866), which rendered the horse more glamorous than the rider:[29]

House the horse in ermine—
  For the foam-flake blew
White through the red October;
  He thundered into view;
They cheered him in the looming,
  Horseman and horse they knew.

They faced about, each man;
Faint hearts were strong again,
He swung his hat in the van;
The electric hoof-spark flew.

With "Philip, king of riders," the horse led the countercharge. In "Sheridan's Ride" (1867), poet T. Buchanan Read also glorified the horse as the "black charger" who "saved the day" by bringing Sheridan down the road from Winchester.[30]

By the 1880s, the myth of Sheridan's ride had lost some of its luster. In one entry in the *Century Magazine* series, Wesley Merritt, who, as a brigadier general, had commanded one of Sheridan's three cavalry divisions, presented a relatively cool report of the episode, describing the tactics that led to the turnaround in the battle. As late as 1888, Rossiter Johnson repeated the "lick them out of their boots" speech, but when Sheridan himself published his *Memoirs* in the same year, he did not mention the famous exhortation at all. He described riding up to the crest of a hill to discover his "panic-stricken army" in confused retreat, and related his decision to restore his men's morale. While the historians of the 1860s have him shouting encouragement to his troops, Sheridan recalled his own behavior as more reserved than his men's.

> [W]hen they saw me they abandoned their coffee, threw up their hats, shouldered their muskets, and as I passed along turned to follow with enthusiasm and cheers. To acknowledge this exhibition of feeling I took off my hat. . . . I said nothing except to remark, as I rode among those on the road: "If I had been with you this morning this disaster would not have happened. We must face the other way; we will go back and recover our camp." (80–81)

For *Shenandoah*, Howard restored the romantic conception of the earlier histories. Haverhill's signal corps officer intercepts a Confederate message that Longstreet is coming to join Early with his corps of eighteen thousand men, and that Sheridan has gone to Washington; although the actual Early did not know of Sheridan's journey, Howard implies that the rebels feel more secure attacking while the redoubtable Union commander is absent, a twist that further elevates Sheridan.

The theatrical climax of the play is the Battle of Cedar Creek, a full day's action compressed into a few minutes. Madeline and Gertrude hear the sound of distant artillery, and Kerchival, wounded, staggers out of the house in time to see his sergeant run in with the news that their left flank has collapsed and that his regiment, with the rest of the army, is in full retreat. In spite of his wound and the fact that Haverhill has arrested him due to his suspicions regarding Constance, Kerchival calls for his horse, clenches his fists above his head, and runs out as soldiers begin to straggle across the stage. Gertrude, her southern sympathies forgotten, pleads with them to follow Kerchival and fight for the flag, but the troops continue their exodus, just as described in the histories, some without weapons, many wounded, and in complete disorder. Then they hear cheering in the distance;

Sheridan is coming, and as the men shout his name, the general gallops across the stage on his black horse. The men reverse direction, shouting and throwing up their hats, and the artillerists load their fieldpiece even as they manhandle it up the slope, back toward the enemy.

This is the stuff of which too many movies have been made, but it is also Howard's most vivid contribution to the myth of the war. The belief in the potency of the individual, that historiography so dear to the amateur playwrights, found its ultimate validation in Sheridan's ride, which Howard transformed into a compelling theatrical moment. Moreover, by showing Sheridan only in the midst of his ride rather than including him in the dialogue of the play, Howard avoids making him too familiar, and he appropriates for the play the general's potential for deification. Sheridan rides out of the past and into a war where all are winners; we see not the defeated Confederate army, but only the dispirited Union troops rediscovering their sense of commitment.

Howard's judgment was sound and the play was popular; the playwright earned $100,000 in royalties for the first three years of productions by companies under the management of Daniel Frohman, Al Hayman, and R. W. Hooley (Strang 2:213). In his review for the *New-York Times*, Edward A. Dithmar praised the verisimilitude of the production—the crowds, the battle noises, the torch signals, and Sheridan's ride—but assured his readers that "the battle for the Nation is kept in the background, and the battle of a few human hearts is the subject of the play." Dithmar was cognizant of Howard's effort to construct the war in a certain way.

> The author has spared no effort to emphasize the sentimental idea of the brotherhood of the contesting parties in our terrible war, and the recognition by individuals on either side of the natural ties which bound them to their foes. . . . Mr. Howard has made a popular play, which, happily, is good enough to deserve popularity, but he touches very lightly on the causes of the rebellion and the feelings that prevailed during that dreadful period, in spite of his background of carnage, his signal lights and bugle calls, and the fleeting vision of glorious Phil Sheridan on horseback.

In the *New York Dramatic Mirror*, Andrew C. Wheeler noted that the play

> very skilfully avoids a sectional bias. Heroism instead of partisanship is its theme, and there is an even-handed recognition of the bravery of Northern and Southern men that will make the play just as acceptable in South Carolina as it will be in Boston. (255)

RECONSTRUCTION ON STAGE

The Civil War provided a perfect opportunity for playwrights to employ melodrama as a theatrical expression of a polarized world view, to stage the division of America into good and evil, with the ultimate triumph of virtue an assured conclusion. Although some of the amateurs followed this pattern, Howard and his professional colleagues relocated evil to preserve the romance of intersectional strife and to express the values of melodrama's collective author, the middle class, who sought to preserve social stability. Within this perspective, the war itself is the archvillain, the disruptor that brings misfortune to powerless and inculpable individuals, thus creating the classic melodramatic situation wherein the victim bears no responsibility for the present calamity. The melodramatic historiography seeks a resolution that will disempower this great, threatening evil and restore order, and the melodramatic imperative worked neatly with the North's need to assume that the South was an inevitable part of the nation and that the South even desired to return. The lovers in *Shenandoah* begin and end the play with marriage in view, a prospect that assures the continuance of middle-class life as though four years of bloody fighting simply had not happened.[31]

The corpus of Civil War melodrama represents a concerted attempt to erase, submerge, or deny the Confederate position as unacceptably threatening to the Union; the plays force the South, as such, to the margin of American culture. By seceding, the South challenged the organicism of the Union and forced a reconsideration of "American" by, in essence, competing for that title, or for presence itself. To concede the South as a distinct polity was to admit that the Union was neither absolute nor inherent, that it existed only in terms of its difference from other entities and systems.[32] The war jeopardized "America" by threatening to dislocate fundamental values and insisting on a discourse that threw the terminology into limitless freeplay. The melodramas denied that discourse, trying to stabilize meaning and stop the play of *différance*. In other words, they did not investigate or debate the meaning of "American"; they took it for granted. The plays denied "North" and "South" as alternatives, substituting the terms "Union" and "rebel." As the equivalent of "Union," "North" is synonymous with truth and fidelity, and as "rebel," "South" is defined not as an element with inherent qualities, but as that which endangers the North; the South is therefore alien and transient. Yet by defining the South as "American," the North appropriated it and denied the distinctions that the South held to be essential. This myth of the war encourages the belief that the South(woman) feels no regret at rejoining the Union, and so reinforces the hegemony of the North(man) by denying that the quarrel had any real foundation. By casting out the South while simultaneously denying that it existed, the plays served the middle-class conservatism that demanded a return to the comfortable (but only putative) stasis that the northern bourgeois theatre audience embraced as the manifestation of the myth of America.

On stage, the Civil War was a foreordained struggle over who would inscribe the conflict in history and imagination, over who would control the semiotic repertoire—the images of flag and valiant soldier, the evocations of land and liberty—without which "America" could not exist. Signs, texts, and theatrical media worked harmoniously to create myth, a narrative configured through heroes and villains, composed of sentimental loyalties and selfless gestures, all aimed toward preserving old ways and institutions. But while this myth valorized individual commitment and sacrifice, it served a political expediency; it conveyed an ideology that ensured the hegemony of the northern position in spite of the apparent return of the southern states as equal partners in the Union. This operation of ideology and hegemony closely resembles the paradigm we derive from Karl Marx and Antonio Gramsci, yet the terms of the conflict have less to do with a typical hierarchical class system, instead cutting across complex fields related to region, race, and customs related to use of land and means of production, a situation exemplary of the intricacy of American culture and its resistance to simplistic analysis.

7

Staging the Myth of America

IN THE FIRST chapter, I proposed that any set of texts is analogous to an archipelago, a structure of elements that are simultaneously separate and connected. Having explored each island, I will now descend to the substructure which, I maintain, connects them; consequently, I will flout the most postmodern positions by alleging and elucidating the continuities between the plays.[1] I do not mean to suggest that one text necessarily leads logically into another or that any grouping of texts (according to time, geography, subject) necessarily reveals commonalities other than the operative one. Nor am I implying that these five plays demonstrate parallel relationships to their historical sources, or that they convey similar messages. Instead, I argue that all texts spring from the aggregate of human experience, which I posit as a sort of cultural reservoir, a wellspring that is constantly changing, a process rather than an entity, composed of currents, eddies, and variations in depth, temperature, density, and opacity which give each of its constituents the potential for uniqueness. In other words, I hold that we can understand (and articulate) discontinuity itself only in relation to the concept of continuity, and that chaos and order are themselves conventions that we accept in order to describe the relativities of experience. Another word for the continuity I seek is myth, and while the five plays I have examined address a variety of concerns and situations, insofar as they overlap, they stage a myth of America. It is not *the* myth of America, for there are many such myths, just as there are many diverse American melodramas, but it does represent a set of constructions of America that commanded large and enthusiastic audiences.

THE DISCOURSE AND CONVENTIONS OF AMERICA

The myth sets up a structure of values, and at the summit it places the very idea of America: a transcendental signified that establishes and preempts the moral high ground and becomes the standard against which all experience is measured. The myth employs—and, in a sense, is composed of—an American discourse, a rich complex of signs that have developed in response to the intersection of experience with idea, but it then presents that discourse as commensurate with the experience. Although experience theoretically produces discourse, the myth refers to the discourse to ascertain whether or not the present experience is desirable and valid. To be an American, whether on- or offstage, is not simply a matter of birth or citizenship, but of establishing a position in the discourse and a relationship to the idea.

The process of any discourse is largely an interplay of conventions. By "convention," I mean an idea on whose nature and significance certain people have agreed, either by deliberation or by custom, and according to which they act. Such an idea is therefore neither inevitable nor inherent in experience, even though its conventionalization makes it seem so. To accept an idea as a convention is to present it as an absolute, or as an externally imposed given, and so remove it from scrutiny. To challenge or even to examine a convention is to disable its function as such; it endures only as long as those who use it question neither its validity nor the process through which they developed it. A baseball player does not contest the rule of three strikes and four balls, or whether he should stand here or there; he asks only whether the pitch passed through the strike zone as he stood in the batter's box. A convention is a guideline that provides structure, however arbitrary it may seem from outside of the system, as a basis for both experience and its perception.

Convention makes communication possible. If, as de Saussure asserted, the relationship between the signifier (*signifiant*) and the signified (*signifié*) is arbitrary, then we are able to communicate, to contribute to discourse, only because we use and understand certain sign systems in intelligibly similar ways. Communication is both mimetic and referential as each participant repeats and re-uses signs. Like all mimesis, such communication offers not a precise re-creation of experience but, like Alice's mirror, a delicate transformation and dislocation of it; verisimilitude is merely relative.

Convention suffuses both the idea and the myth of America. The American tradition presents various principles—including freedom, autonomy, and certain unalienable rights—as conventions from which social organization and the American way of life are derived. Within the myth that the plays present, to be an American is to accept and acknowledge these ideas as conventions that, together, form the idea of America. As an idea, and as a structure of interrelated conventions through which text, image, and action refer, America itself becomes a convention.

Yet convention determines not only the medium and process of communication but also its content. Convention establishes our semiotic repertoire, and because we can know ideas only through their signification, the arbitrariness of the sign system extends to the ideas themselves. In other words, a sign can usurp the idea it was meant to convey; it can become autonomous and appear to be an idea itself, then requiring signification, or it might break free of its origin and take on new associations. It becomes less a means of communication and more, because it enjoys such ready acceptance, an obstruction to understanding. The observer fails to see the sign and accepts it as an unmediated fact. As a convention, "America" can fall into eclipse behind such retrograde signification. In the Civil War plays, for example, certain patriots posit the flag as a sign of America, but the flag develops so intense a presence that it becomes the ideal (and even the materiality) for which the men fight and die.

In the theatre, the participants agree on codes and customs, on the use of language, gesture, and image, on the rhythm and nature of the event, even on the etiquette and expectations governing their behavior or, more precisely, their construction of their participation.[2] More specifically, nineteenth-century American society developed conventions, especially concerning figuration, to which the stage then referred with its own set of conventions, so the theatrical representation of America becomes a discourse on convention more than on actuality. Michael Quinn has described "conventional figures, which may refer not to a specific individual but to a socially discriminated type, to a concept of personality in the social rhetoric of identity" (72). Heroes, heroines, and villains are quick and easy; once the performance sends the appropriate set of signals—an upstanding man reciting a popular sentiment, a pretty young woman expressing her helplessness and anxiety, or a sophisticated man shamelessly manipulating his text to gull the onstage listener— the audience is inclined to make quick (and probably accurate) conclusions regarding the disposition of each character and his or her ethical role in the story. The conventions are interactive; that is, the speech convention of "threat" helps reinforce the character convention of "villain," and "villain" makes "threat" predictable and virtually inevitable. In other words, text, character, costume, character objective, and character tactics are all parts of consistent patterns. If the object of representation is not empirical but rather a signified concept or a sign itself, mimesis becomes a means of representing signs instead of phenomena. That is, layers of convention can defer mimesis from experience as the performance refers not to an actuality but to a belief, or a belief about a belief, or to a sign that the audience accepts as indicative of a belief. The actor may refer not to life but to an image of life. Edwin Forrest played not a certain man, but a generalized American hero disguised as a stage Indian; the actors playing Cribbs and Scraggs played generalized embodiments of certain broadly drawn fears. The codes and customs of performance can therefore serve the culture's perception of the distance between appearance and actuality, and the mode of performance can slide between artificiality, ideality, and mimetic realism. What we call "style" is the result of the interactive use of semiosis and convention, all in service of a social vision. Since the object of mimesis was the image of life, not life itself, the theatre embraced a presentational style that transformed tangible phenomena—actors, costumes, scenery, and playhouse—into the ideal. The layers of convention grew ever deeper.

The trial that concludes *My Partner* renders a verdict not only on who murdered Ned Singleton, but on which man better serves as an American convention. Joe Saunders represents all men who would fulfill the promise of America, and Josiah

Scraggs represents all those who would confound him; such characters are generalities conceived to enact emblematic roles in relation to a conception of America. A play becomes a grand trial of signs and conventions, all measured against the standards and ideals that the myth presents.

AMERICA, THE SENTIMENTAL

The myth of America presents the American ethic as coterminous with the sentimental moral order. The myth takes on the sentimental vision as a project, a program to be pursued and legitimated. Because the myth so closely identifies America with the sentimental vision, it can support both American and sentimental values (insofar as it acknowledges any distinction) simultaneously. Virtue is the characteristic mode of the American experience, so that "American" and "virtuous" are synonymous. To be respectable or virtuous is to be an exemplary American; to protect and preserve the family is to defend America; to experience sympathy with one's fellow men and to act on it is to act on behalf of America. The sentimental project is all the more congenial to the American myth because sympathy supports democracy; that is, while sympathy encourages a community of feeling, democracy assumes a community of interests and abilities that supports a participatory, egalitarian form of self-government by mutual consent among partners. *My Partner* and especially *Shenandoah* end with affirmations of fellowship, confirmations that the characters understand each other and cherish similar concerns. Sentimentalism offers a guide for the construction of experience, one that the myth coopts in service of America, that makes its own demands on the American discourse, and that operates on the plays from beneath, providing the rationale and imperatives that shape character, story, narrative, and value.

Yet to make the sentimental vision succeed, the myth obscures certain aspects of the actual American experience. The same sympathy that supposedly guides the sentimental man also disables him as a pioneer or a capitalist; one preoccupied with his sense of fellowship can hardly succeed in the rigorous taming of a continent or in the aggressive competition of the marketplace. The actualities of the pioneer and capitalist experiences were that success was a matter of degree and that circumstances and competition entirely defeated some of the participants. The myth sidesteps the question by assuming that everyone can win and that the interests of one individual do not exclude the interests of any others. The sinister qualities and even the dangers of capitalism appear in *The Drunkard*, *Uncle Tom's Cabin*, and *My Partner*, but only as unfortunate quirks of the various situations rather than inherent and fundamental components of economic interaction. In Althusserian terms, the myth presents an "imaginary relationship" to the "real conditions of existence."

The myth achieves an even more challenging reconciliation when it resolves the question of primacy among the individual, the family, and the community. The

myth presents the ideal American society as a structure built on all three components, and it firmly denies that the interests of any one could undermine those of
the others. Joe Saunders pursues the freedom of the individual, but he finally marries
and, we assume, starts a family. Individuality is therefore a male condition that is
also temporary, and the dream is not to enjoy eternal autonomy, but rather to carve
out a homestead on which to settle and propagate. The myth resolves the conflict
between family and community by defining the community as family; to be an
American is to be part of the greater American family. The Civil War plays tend
to present Southerners as misguided people who misconstrued the intersection between their concerns and those of the community, and who either fell as a consequence or realized their error and returned to the fold. The collective author
never admits that interests might conflict; with the American system, the needs
of one family are synonymous with the needs of all others, and there is neither
friction, competition, nor ambiguity of duty.

THE AMERICAN SPACE

The myth configures the American subject as a virtual cliché: a white, Protestant, propertied, republican family man. He is The American; he is Walter, Edward
Middleton, George Shelby, Joe Saunders, or Kerchival West. The American maintains his autonomy but still conforms to the sentimental ideal and sustains a passionate loyalty to his community. He is a successful man, for the myth does not
admit that an individual could work and live according to the American ideal and
still fail, just as it does not admit that one who succeeds could in any way undermine
the idea of America. From outside of the melodramatic boundaries, the temporary
failure of an Edward Middleton or a Joe Saunders, like the temporary success of
a Fitzarnold or a Legree, is clearly only apparent. Edward or Joe may wonder
whether he will able to extricate himself from his predicament, but while the spectators may "enjoy" vicarious anxiety, they realize that the natural operation of the
myth will restore these deserving men to their rightful places and so validate
America.

Yet like any social construction, the myth of The American is a function of
the exclusion, erasure, and absence of those who do not fit the model—those who
are not male, not white, not propertied, and even, in the case of the Southern
rebels, those who would deny the ideology of America. These are the outsiders,
those whom the myth defines as interlopers in the American space, and whose
voice in the performance of America, and whose contribution and access to its
semiotic repertoire, are structured according to how they serve the white subject
and collective author. The myth defines The American in terms of his difference
from those who are not The American; the outsiders provide the contrast whereby
his essence may be clearly confirmed, and the signs of otherness rebound off of
one another in an endless freeplay of race, gender, power, and even geography.

The myth may take The American's whiteness for granted, implicitly accepting it as "normal," but it openly takes advantage of the potential to (re)present those of other races in relation to the subject model. Their nonwhite speech, appearance, and customs make them fascinating and even exotic, but also irretrievably alien and inherently inferior; that is, difference is equivalent to disadvantage.[3] The "Chinee" is a risible object of scorn, whom neither Campbell nor his white characters ever regard as anything but a foreigner, one visiting California on a temporary basis, whose eccentricities amuse as long as his ultimate departure is assured. The black man is likewise a foreigner, not truly an American because he was brought here against his will and because his "natural" home, where he would be happiest, is Africa; he may choose between transfiguration or transportation. Aiken, like Stowe, presents George Harris as a man neither black nor white who finally "chooses" to emigrate. The Indian is far more troublesome, for even rationalization cannot construe him as foreign, and the greater American myth needs him as a native emblem. Metamora is The American in all respects but ethnicity, which the play links with his so-called savagery to justify his destruction. The spirit of Metamora, however, and the ideals he reinforces, survive in Walter and Oceana, whose posterity becomes the new American nation. The American admires Metamora, George, and Uncle Tom, but does not accept them.

The myth assigns women an ambiguous status; The American must have a family, but the myth inscribes and represents gender according to the sentimental paradigm, which may concede respect and piety for the woman while reserving power for the man. The American is not only the subject of the myth, he is also the agent of its action. Women, like nonwhite men, are present as inspirations to action or objects of action. Although some women in *Shenandoah* and *Uncle Tom's Cabin* take the initiative and influence the course of events, they do so in the midst of crisis so that the situation may return to a quiescent state and they may return to their domestic roles. The myth defines the dream in male terms that set women aside and deny them access.

The myth's exclusionary configuration undermines its validity, for it claims to encompass America, yet it rejects some of its constituents. To dismiss the paradox and assure The American's predominance, the myth argues that only free, white men are present in America, so only free, white men can conceivably have power. If The American is the only true citizen, then no one can accuse him of dominating anyone, and he avoids violating sentimental, American principles of behavior. To exclude those who would contend with The American is to ensure that he wields power only against aliens, and hostility is always directed outwards from a cohesive center. In other words, the myth simply erases all those who might compete or who might claim their rights under America's own terms: this is the ultimate hegemony, the politics of the invisible. Yet within this myth of America, there is only one kind of American, therefore only one American ideology, and therefore—ostensibly—no operation of hegemony at all. The myth therefore presents two simultaneous and contradictory assertions: first, that The American is the only inhabitant of the American space, which implies that his ascendancy disempowers no one; and second, that The American's power is defined in relation to those outsiders whose presence the myth concedes, but whom the myth presents as alien and therefore not truly American.

The myth tends to conflate classes in order to insist upon a uniform ideology. The plays include laborers, bourgeoisie, and members of high society (the stratification of whites is most clear in *Shenandoah*), but the characters all subscribe to approximately the same sentimental, American values. In each play, the young lovers seek to marry and raise a family within the safety of American society, and even the comic servant types wish them well. They are able to claim autonomy as their due, but without taking advantage of anyone else: they will be independent but not autocratic. To so construct them is to deny the importance or even the existence of class stratification, a strategy that reinforces the American belief in social mobility so limitless as to mock hierarchy. Men like George Harris and Joe Saunders rise by means of bootstrap initiative, while men like Edward Middleton return to their "normal" state as though by the power of gravitation. Yet to scorn class distinctions and to erase them from discourse is to confound the concept of ideology. That is, if there is no class system in America, then there are no differences upon which to base a perception of relative ideologies.

American writings may, however, use "class" in a unique way; in fact, "American" may constitute a class by itself. Sacvan Bercovitch has pointed out that

> American literature . . . is . . . often obsessed with the idea of America, and . . . that idea, as it was made the exclusive property of the United States, is . . . transparently ideological. What could be a clearer demonstration of ideas in the service of power than the system of beliefs that the early colonists imposed on the so-called New World? What clearer demonstration of the shaping power of ideology than the procession of declarations through which the republic was consecrated as New Israel, Nature's Nation in the Land of Futurity? ("Afterword" 419)[4]

Such a paradigm reveals a paradoxical relationship to the idea of class. If we argue that "American" is a class in the sense that the aristocracy, bourgeoisie, or proletariat are classes, then we define the American class in relation to all non-Americans, thus fostering the ideology that Bercovitch presents, but we also confirm that within America there is only one class, which is the same as there being no classes, which is what we have wanted to believe all along. The paradigm is even more comfortable in that it assures our uniqueness and, in this stubbornly liberal culture, seems to affirm the teleological belief that American history demonstrates our ongoing evolution into the ultimate nation.

There remains the question of where to locate evil in the American space. Since neither The American nor the idea of America can be responsible for social or individual disorder, the myth posits "evil" as a way of defining and, particularly, excluding any forces of negation or failure. The exclusion is crucial, for if America is, by definition, the culture of virtue, founded on virtue and characterized by its virtuousness, then it cannot house evil. Evil is not only that which threatens America, evil is that which is not America. There cannot even be a truly American signification of evil; or, more precisely, the signification of evil is the semiotic negation of America. The myth defines and describes characters like Lord Fitzarnold, Lawyer Cribbs, Simon Legree, and Josiah Scraggs largely in terms of how they do *not* conform to the American configuration.[5] Thornton is the subtlest of all, fitting the description of The American except that he denies American values by acting treacherously, violating the conception of gentlemanly honor that the other men uphold so faithfully, and maintaining loyalty to neither North nor South.

The very mode of melodramatic performance includes the spectators in The American's success by playing to their values and allowing them to share in the onstage victory over evil. In addition to direct address and exegetical representation, many of the plays use, to borrow a term, the tirade—here, a protracted, desperate, and vituperative speech. The virtuous characters use the tirade to define and magnify what they perceive as the moral distance between themselves and those who assail them, as when the distraught drunkard excoriates the rum seller, or the northern heroine reviles the southern villain who would rape her. The more vehement the language and the more the performance pushes the emotional level to its highest possible pitch, the more the moment polarizes its elements, and because the invective is aimed at the avatar of evil, the speaker enlists the audience on his or her side and therefore reassures them that they, too are virtuous. The tirade defines the speaker as subject and the villain as object, and so suggests that they occupy disparate spaces, which encourages the audience's complacent and delusory belief that evil is not part of their society or culture, but somehow alien. The tirade therefore aids melodrama in preserving the status quo.

The American melodrama, therefore, does not merely push evil to the margins; it excludes and externalizes it altogether. The American fights all battles to cleanse America, whether of foreigners or of avatars of evil; there is no internal conflict. The myth defines evil as Un-American, located entirely outside of the American space; to defeat evil is to expunge it from the American space and return it to the Beyond where it belongs. Such a construction completely avoids the question of whether evil or sin derives from society, situation, or character, for evil is a force from outside. Evil is anything that jeopardizes, contradicts, or seeks to displace America, so evil is neither fixed nor evolutionary; it is a spontaneous manifestation of the fear that America is not inviolate.

AMERICAN HISTORY AS MELODRAMA

The myth does not offer a critique of culture; it rather affirms the status quo. The idea of America may change over time and from play to play, but no single text admits that the idea is changing or has changed; it rather refers to the idea as fixed and perfect. Men, or groups of men, may move within the space that the idea creates—they may improve their lot, as Joe and Ned seek to do by digging for gold—but the idea itself needs no improvement.

The entire motion of the myth is return; return to what was or return to what is imagined, but always return to what should be. The plays seem to be diachronic, but are in fact synchronic. That is, they purport to present change and evolution, but because that change is actually a matter of return and restoration, that history is static, so there can be no diachronicity. Melodrama is actually atemporal. If history is a narrative of movement, melodrama as history must continually repeat itself. A play may offer a depiction of progress, but it is illusory, because there is no true evolution or transformation, but rather return. *Metamora* looks back one-and-a-half centuries to champion those values that led to the establishment of a republic, an event its retrospection presents as inevitable. *The Drunkard* presents domestic life as blissfully and timelessly static, with drink as an evil energy that provokes temporary deviation in the individual without interrupting the fabric or the values of society. *Uncle Tom's Cabin* reduces societal dysfunction to a personal level and enacts an impossible fantasy of social change whose terms and interactions deny the validity of the problem and leave society essentially intact. *My Partner* offers an idyll that posits America as a matter of constant creation, but that really affirms eighteenth-century values without establishing anything new or progressive. *Shenandoah* interprets the Civil War as a rite of passage leading to the "inevitable" restoration of the Union, and in so doing erases the differences, not only between North and South, but between antebellum and postbellum experience. In each case, the text conveys a sense of motion in human affairs, a constant progression to the sentimental apotheosis that the future offers, but the action moves to a condition already tried, established, and accepted. If the present is unsatisfactory or disturbing, it is because some outside force has interrupted the equanimity of society.

Through the plays, the myth presents a conservative, even static vision of American history. Indeed, theatre's resemblance to myth leads to a puzzling con- clusion: on a theoretical level, at least, theatre, as a form of discourse and a mode of representation, tends to present a conservative position.[6] Because it is essentially social—that is, because it offers a means of communication less between individuals and more between groups—theatre, like myth, tends to adopt sign systems and conventions that permit collective address. Theatre works like myth in that both are allegorical and both invite the "reader" to identify with the represented actions, characters, and experience. Although the latter qualities contribute to the potential of theatre to legitimate virtually any vision, conservative or not, the use of widely accessible—and therefore traditional and conservative—semiotic repertoires bends content and message toward legitimating the status quo.

Theatre also affirms a conservative position by assuring a certain inevitability to its representation and thus making any exhortation to change seem pointless.

The very process of performance—of enactment or reenactment—locates inter-actions in the past, however immediate, and therefore establishes them as finished and no longer contingent. Theatre therefore has great potential for asserting—even seeming to create—faits accomplis. The audience enters the theatre, sees the pre-sentation of a problem, and even if the onstage action does not resolve the situation, even if the production attempts to galvanize the audience and provoke action, the event itself ends—the curtain falls, the houselights come up, and the audience departs. There is closure. The material conditions of theatrical production reinforce this tendency; typically, people in a theatre audience—those with the leisure and the opportunity to attend—are more likely to be aligned with the dominant class than not, and whatever social need or political outrage the play might address does not touch them directly, so their altruistic interest is vulnerable to sublimation through the process of the event.[7]

Mimesis also contributes to the conservative tone of theatre. Any form of communication uses "found" materials and so creates a collage of fragments drawn from the established vocabulary, but theatre does so most vividly, adopting the signifiers and therefore the signifieds of nontheatrical discourse and experience. Mimesis is imitation, even though imperfect, even when satirical or hostile, and to imitate is to replicate. If we reproduce the found world, we affirm it. Even if we replicate in order to expose and attack, we affirm the object's importance, bring it to life, and so validate it.

This theoretical conservatism suggests that all theatrical events gravitate toward some language or message that can speak to all people in all places, thus denying their differences and ultimately producing work of stupefying neutrality, yet the actual truth is that theatre artists have, on countless occasions, challenged the status quo, expressed myriad points of view, and even outraged their audiences. I am arguing that the essential process and method of theatre affirm established realities as fixed and even determined. To create theatre is to give form, to incarnate or reify, and therefore to reduce.

Four of the five plays take up strategically late positions in relation to their material; that is, those four address issues that have already become moot. The war is over, the West is won, or sobriety has become the norm. Only *Uncle Tom's Cabin* treats a subject of present concern, but it manages to deflate the issues in order to obviate action. Melodrama becomes an exercise in fomenting crisis and outrage over questions that are no longer compelling or even contingent, an ap-proach much in the tradition of a nation borne out of a revolution conducted by men who wished not to change society, but to restore it to the former condition that they preferred. Melodrama stages the vision of these conservative revolution-aries.

This equivocal representation of progress and change raises the question of whether there is change at all, and if so, whether it is evident in the individual, in society, or in values themselves. One set of axioms from the conventional study of melodrama-as-genre is that character is tantamount to caricature, that no one learns, no one changes, and behavior is a function of qualities simplistic and fixed enough to permit easy manipulation by the playwright. The difficulty with ascribing to an individual a change in self-awareness is that to do so is to imply either the possibility of more than one acceptable moral stance, or a moral equivocation on the part of the individual, an inner struggle that would deflect attention away from the spectator. As with society, if the individual changes, it is because the play depicts him in an aberrant and undesirable condition, and because he returns to his proper state so that the action may close. The drunkard, for example, returns to sobriety, or Mary Brandon atones for her sin and recruits her lost honor. Both conversion and revelation are means to return to the sentimental self. Even the grand romance of the Westward movement, presented so eloquently in *My Partner* and the texts surrounding it, is a matter of returning to a racial birthright, of rediscovering the lost garden through a process of pastoralization. To admit ambiguity is to invite debate, but the myth presents American values as immovable and unchallenged. American society may progress—or seem to progress—toward its teleological destiny, but that evolution is guided by unequivocal principles which the play firmly presents as eternal and organic.

Each play is a structure both presented and accepted as a spectacular phenomenon and a startling revelation of the truth about the American experience, but one conceived so judiciously as to offend no one, offering only false surprise. In the "sensation" scene in *Under the Gaslight*, Laura hacks at the door while Snorkey lies trussed on the tracks, helplessly awaiting the rushing train that will certainly obliterate him. Yet the danger is only ostensible, for the structure will not permit such a disaster—Laura *must* save him, or the moral bedrock dissolves. In each of these plays, the ideal society of melodrama is America itself, and America is somehow threatened but emerges unscathed from a conflict whose outcome is a foregone conclusion. The idea of America is equivalent to the moral order, and it is that which the action of each play restores. The myth—the melodrama as myth—offers its audience the sensation of America in jeopardy, but carefully designs its equations so that they always work out to zero and the progressive stasis of America endures. The plays function as historical texts, and their compositions of vision, form, and style present certain constructions of events, yet they are not merely melodramas presenting a certain version of history; they present history *as* melodrama, as a process of sentimental affirmation resulting from American heroes protecting their values against the assaults of villains from the outside. The fantasy of danger provides the faithful with an opportunity to renew their commitment in what amounts to a patriotic ritual.

Yet these plays may anticipate the deeper American fear, which became explicit in twentieth-century discourse—that we had failed from the start. The American is an overreacher, charting a journey which he defines in self-defeating terms: it is composed of virgin moments, but it always returns to a fixed point; and it is a romantic mission of grand scale, but it is defined in homely, sentimental paradigms. The journey is so demanding that The American, when he pauses to consider, wonders whether he missed his chance, whether he let the historical moment slip by at the very start and must now attempt to return to the crucial eddy in the cultural flow. The American bases his world view on the melodramatic conception of binary oppositions, but the actuality of his experience would form a diagram more like a multipolar mandala, with the trajectories of freeplay rebounding between overlapping pairs of points that are nearly but not quite opposite. The melodramas that compose this myth are morality plays, pitting virtue against evil under some ineffable divine hand, but they are also divine comedies, attempting to encompass the entire American experience by reducing it into stageable terms.

Notes

PREFACE

1. Johnson and McArthur have also written important studies. Bruce A. McConachie's *Melodramatic Formations* arrived in my mailbox just one week before I sent this manuscript to my publisher. McConachie offers a penetrating analysis of plays, their productions, and the operative social, political, and economic circumstances, which builds on his previous work to help lead the study of nineteenth-century American theatre out of the forest of information and toward sophisticated critical assessment of the operation and meaning of phenomena.

1. CONSTRUCTING AMERICAN IDEOLOGY

1. Throughout this book, I shall conform to popular and colloquial usage, however hegemonic, imperialistic, imprecise, and discourteous to other nations in the Western Hemisphere, in using "America" and "American" to refer to the United States of America, its people(s), and its culture(s).

2. Most nineteenth-century newspaper reviewers addressed issues of originality and verisimilitude—their prevailing æsthetic, the yardstick by which they measured the plays—so the reader must dig beneath the surface to find the attitudes and assumptions that produce and shape those concerns. See Roach on the treatment of æsthetics as separate from social concerns.

3. Even improvised theatre generates something that one could record as a playscript, and while we might argue the distinction that in such a case the production preceded the script rather than vice versa, it is rare for a playscript to finish a production process in the same condition in which it began; in both instances, production is necessary to complete the writing of the work.

4. I am using the word "ecology" quite carefully, implying that the text is an organism existing interactively within an environment.

5. There is also the question of whether performance is an act more of poetics or of hermeneutics. I am here using "poetics" to refer to the interactive functioning of poetic elements and structure, and "hermeneutics" to refer to the meaning that they convey.

6. See Williams on ideology as false consciousness (55, 69–70).

7. See McConachie on using the concept of hegemony to interpret theatre history. Lawner interprets hegemony as an equilibrium between *direzione* based on consent and *dominazione* based on coercion, or between civil society and political society (42). See Gramsci's *Prison Notebooks* for Hoare and Smith's discussion of the semantic and conceptual ambiguities between *egemonia, dirigere/direzione*, and *dominare/dominazione* (55 n. 5); we who read Gramsci in English would do well to mark the relationship of *egemonia* as "hegemony" to *direzione* as both "direction" and "leadership."

8. See Eagleton on the link between text and ideology (*Marxism* 6, 17).

9. See Eagleton on ideology as "a set of significations" that presents itself to a text (*Criticism* 64).

10. For definitions of myth, see Slotkin 269, and Slotkin and Folsom 5.

11. See Doty 6–8 for comments on myth denigrated as fiction.

12. "The social or natural affections, which our author considers as essential to the health, wholeness, or integrity of the particular creature, are such as contribute to the welfare and prosperity of that whole or species, to which he is by Nature joined. All the affections of this kind our author comprehends in that single name of natural" (Shaftesbury 2:293).

13. "To have the natural affections (such as are founded in love, complacency, good-will, and in a sympathy with the kind or species) is to have the chief means and power of self-enjoyment" (Shaftesbury 1:293).

14. "To deserve the name of good or virtuous, a creature must have all his inclinations and affections, his dispositions of mind and temper, suitable, and agreeing with the good of his kind, or of that system in which he is included, and of which he constitutes a part. To stand thus well affected, and to have one's affections right and entire, not only in respect of oneself but of society and the public, this is rectitude, integrity, or virtue. And to be wanting in any of these, or to have their contraries, is depravity, corruption, and vice" (Shaftesbury 1:280).

15. Shaftesbury was a student of Locke's.

16. I realize that "middle class"—a phrase that appeared early in the nineteenth century, close to the beginning of the period I am studying—is not a precise term, but I will use it for the sake of convenience to indicate those who are born into neither wealth and privilege nor poverty, and whose social and economic circumstances—relatively autonomous and comfortable without being carefree or lavish—are for the most part the result of their initiative and labor within the capitalist society over whose operations no individual enjoys significant control. See Bledstein for a different description, but one equally encompassing, and for a brief analytical history of the nature and position of the middle class in England and America (1–45).

17. Saum has established that while the public construction of the providential philosophy may have presented it as optimistic and oriented toward progress, the private writings of common people dwelt on providence as a means of rationalizing past sorrows rather than assuring future successes, and as a way of resigning oneself to an unknowable future (3–6). My preoccupation, however, is with the very public forum of the theatre, where providence did appear as a cause for hope.

18. There are obvious exceptions, such as Dion Boucicault, Augustin Daly, Bronson Howard, and Bartley Campbell, and their locations in time indicate that the relative insignificance to which I am alluding was more common earlier in the century when John Augustus Stone, W. H. Smith, and George L. Aiken were writing plays.

19. This anxiety offers an intriguing secular parallel to the old Protestant dilemma regarding salvation through predestination as opposed to good works.

20. As the play closes, the character who might be most inclined to view life as contingent is Pearl, the young woman who never doubted she was a Courtland until the very last moment, when she learns that she, not Laura, is the changeling.

21. Recent studies have clarified the complexity of nineteenth-century society; for examples, see Denning on class distinctions (45, 58), Lears on gender relations (221), and Halttunen on the contradictions that the evolving society enforced on gender roles.

22. One of the earliest and most daunting statements of the American sense of mission was in John Winthrop's 1630 sermon to the newly arrived Puritan settlers; he told them that "we shall be as a City upon a Hill," a model before "the eyes of all people."

2. *METAMORA* (1829) AND THE "INDIAN" QUESTION

1. The binarism has also created a legacy of semantic frustration. It should by now be axiomatic that there is no neutral term that refers generically to the many original peoples of the territory now known as the United States of America. Although "native" seems to connote,

pejoratively, "primitive" and evokes echoes of drums and the rattling of bone-bead necklaces, I will use it (and occasionally the phrase, "native American") when I wish to refer, in as objective a voice as possible, to those in question as actual people, reserving the word "Indian" to signal a white, Euro-American construct, perception, or perspective. I will use "Euro-American" to emphasize the European roots of those aspects of nineteenth-century American culture that I am examining. Finally, in opposition to "red," "native" or "Indian," I will sometimes use "white," and while I concede that it is just as generalizing a term as the others, its resonance is completely different. English-speaking whites chose "white" to describe themselves, but while they borrowed native place names freely, they resisted learning native names for the natives themselves, instead imposing terms of European origin and perspective. Furthermore, "white" has usually carried self-complimentary connotations deriving from centuries of colonial and imperial interracial politics. All of these terms, of course, exist historically in relation to each other: although the use of "white" to describe a fair complexion antedates William the Conqueror, only in 1604 does the *OED* find the first usage to denote difference from darker races; the first recorded application of "Indian" to native Americans dates from 1618.

2. The following summary of the events of the war is drawn from Leach 15, 23–43, 231–35, 241–46; and Jennings 289–96.

3. Like "Indian," the sachem's name presents a semantic problem. Although most whites today know him as King Philip, I will call him Metacomet when I refer to the actual man; when discussing another's writings about him, I will use whatever name that author conferred.

4. The war survives in white memory and imagination. After nine generations, my family still takes interest in the fact that on March 26, 1676, while the citizens of Marlborough were attending Sunday services, the natives attacked the village. As Moses Newton, my ancestor, attempted to carry an old woman to the safety of a garrison house, a warrior fired on him; the shot shattered his elbow and disabled him for life. As in the official histories of the war, this family tradition presents the colonist as a heroic victim of unprovoked aggression.

5. Drake's construction of Metacomet vacillated over time. In *The Book of the Indians of North America* (1833), the historian praised Philip and blamed the English for the war, but in his 1865 edition of Hubbard's *History*, he argued that Philip was "quite destitute" of any admirable qualities.

6. The very first noble savage in American literature may have been the hero of *Ponteach* (1766), but playwright Robert Rogers presents him as a nobleman in the European manner, with scarcely any recognizable reference to even an idealized native experience.

7. Ironically, Seeber reports that the historical John (or James) Logan's father was a white Frenchman; if so, the fact creates an amusing ambiguity in the case for noble-savage-as-classical-orator.

8. On December 19, 1829, the *New-York Mirror, and Ladies Literary Gazette* reprinted the piece under the heading "An Indian Memoir" (21–22), in honor of the opening of *Metamora* at the Park Theatre on December 15, thus encouraging its readers to associate Irving's point of view with Forrest's performance.

9. Bryant joined the editorial staff of the *Post* in 1826, probably in July, and became editor-in-chief in July of 1829. From 1823 to 1832, he wrote five "Indian" poems ("The Indian Girl's Lament" [1823], "An Indian Story" [1824], "An Indian at the Burial-place of his Fathers" [1824], "The Disinterred Warrior" [1832?], and "The Prairies" [1832]), three of which mourned the lost noble red man. Leggett also worked for the *Post*, serving as assistant editor from 1829 to 1836.

10. Stone's was not the first dramatic treatment of Metacomet; it followed Robert Montgomery Bird's *King Philip; or, The Sagamore* (1829) and James Kennicott's *Metacomet* (1829), both now lost. The anonymous *Philip; or, the Aborigines* (1822) is actually about the Pequot War of 1637; see Cox 121–25, M. J. Anderson, "The Image of the American Indian" 327–28

and 387–89, and Mulvey 87. For those seeking a comprehensive study of Indian plays, there are several that deal with them as a thematic genre; see B. J. Anderson, M. J. Anderson (both the article and the dissertation), Cox, Jones, Mulvey, Sears, and Wilmeth.

11. Grimsted says that Leggett probably wrote this speech (71).

12. See Ranny for a useful contemporaneous account of the riot.

13. One of Fitzarnold's servants, a man named Wolfe, later reveals that Walter is the very son that Sir Arthur lost to kidnappers years ago and then rescued, not realizing his true identity, from a New England shipwreck.

14. All page numbers refer to Moody's edition/compilation of the actor's "side" in the Forrest Home, the copy at the University of Utah which lacks Act Four, and the copy in the British Museum which lacks Act Five.

15. Metamora demonstrates a rhetorical resemblance to the Indian Chief in Noah's *She Would Be a Soldier*, a role that Forrest played in 1826 at the Bowery, where Stone was a member of the company.

16. Sears proposes three options for Indians in plays: cohabitation and acculturation, migration/escape (postponement), and defiance/death (87). Oceana suggests the first, but Walter scorns it on behalf of Metamora, who refuses the second, and so only the final alternative remains.

17. Alger's summary of the play includes several speeches that paraphrase those in the script Moody has edited, and at least two that appear nowhere else. Moody's textual scholarship is undoubtedly sound; the most likely explanation is that the play's evolution over four decades led to the interpolation of speeches that Forrest reported to Alger but which were never included in the extant manuscripts.

18. Sometime in the 1840s, possibly in 1845 or 1846, Forrest changed at least three of the characters' names to the ones we know now. Guy of Godalman became Mordaunt, Horatio became Walter, and Wiskunshe became Annawandah, although Alger refers to that character as "Aganemo" (245). To confuse matters further, the playbills in Toedteberg demonstrate variant spellings for several of the characters, the most diverse being as follows: Goodalmin, Godalming, Godalmin; Wiskoneki, Wiskinicke, Weskonkie; and Kaueshine, Haneshine, Kauishine, Koneshine, Kaweshine.

19. For the Henry parallel, see Sears 51.

20. Like many American plays of that period, *Metamora* is in part a stylistic mimicry of Shakespeare, whose works had provided a significant and recurring portion of American repertory since colonial days. Forrest himself aspired to compete with the best Shakespearean actors of the English-speaking stage; some of his favorite roles were Hamlet, Coriolanus, Macbeth, Gloucester, and Lear. He and his audience expected the new "tragedies" (as they called them) to strive for "Shakespearean" bombast, magnitude, and splendor. We may laugh at lines like "Lightning consume thee, meddling fool!" and "thy bridal hour has come; thy tauntings do but fan the flame that rages here," but to an audience reared on Sir Walter Scott yet committed in everyday life to an energetically egalitarian program, they were exciting examples of Stone's ability to use the conventions of high-flown stage speech to elevate the action. Consider Front-de-Bœuf's defiance from chapter 30 of *Ivanhoe* (1820): "And by mine honour, when we kindle the blazing beacon, for joy of our defence, it shall consume thee, body and bones; and I shall live to hear thou art gone from earthly fires to those of that hell which never sent forth an incarnate fiend so utterly diabolical!" Chapter 7 provides another bit of choice rhetoric: "Up, infidel dog, when I command you, or I will have thy swarthy hide stript off, and tanned for horse-furniture." *Metamora* is, inevitably, derivative, not of Shakespeare, but of the popularized Romantic interpretation of Shakespeare that may seem misguided to us but that suited Forrest's audiences quite well.

21. Metamora is also excluded from the "typical" Indian drama; in this play, the whites

commit no specific catalytic atrocity, there is no Great White Father who heals the discord, and Nahmeokee does not follow Pocahontas's example by falling in love with a white man and saving him from her tribesmen's cruel attentions (see Flynn 421). Of course, Forrest could hardly have wanted a Washington or a Pocahontas on stage to compete with him for the audience's acclaim, and so would not have approved a story that would have required such a casting structure.

22. M. J. Anderson has observed that nineteenth-century dramatists were careful to choose Indians from colonial times, thus avoiding direct confrontation with the Indian question of their own era ("The Image of the American Indian" 444).

23. In my summary of the events leading up to and away from the debate over removal, I am borrowing information and interpretations found in Berkhofer, *Salvation* 100–102; Berkhofer, *White Man's Indian* 135–36, 154–55, 159–60; Drinnon 115; Rogin 8, 181, 206, 212–13; and Satz 10–11, 100–101.

24. Of the two New York newspapers I will cite most often, the *Post* was the more polished and respectable, and the *Herald* the more popular and sensationalistic. The *Post* under Bryant supported Jackson as a matter of policy, while the *Herald* maintained no loyalty to any party or faction, but acted as a gadfly to public officials of any stamp.

25. Alger was not necessarily an infatuated stooge. I suspect that he pitched the biography in order to elicit the most favorable possible response from the public that Forrest himself may have (perhaps optimistically) described, including lush praise and hero-worship to reinforce attitudes that he or Forrest believed their potential readers had already cultivated.

26. Actually, one other actor may have played the role at least once. The Huntington Library holds a playbill that announces that on October 21, 1861 at the St. Louis Theatre, a Mr. Neafie appeared in *Metamora*, "an entirely new Indian tragedy," with a cast of characters including Lord Fitzarnold, Walter, Errington, Mordaunt, Sir Arthur Vaughan, Wolf, Church, Tramp, Kaweshine, Otah, Nahmeokee and, played by Miss L. Maddern, Oceana. Judging from the cast list, this was probably not "entirely new" at all, but Stone's play.

27. This run of the play was a financial success before the review even appeared, grossing $858.75 on December 26 and $1,408.75 on December 27 (Toedteberg). On March 27, 1845, in its review of the March 26 performance at the Princess Theatre, the *Times* of London conformed to the pattern set by American newspapers, bashing *Metamora* even harder than the *Herald* but arguing that Forrest's performance transcended and carried the play: "Such utter rubbish flaunting before the public in all the dignity of five acts and blank verse, was probably never seen in London. . . . Had it not been for the truthfulness and force of his acting, such a drama could not have been endured." The article also mentioned Irving's "Philip of Pokanoket."

28. The *Herald* critic then went on to claim that Forrest demonstrated little control over himself and his role, and that he employed, for the climactic scenes, "the very same voice, the very same manner, the very same action" as he had used for Macbeth's final encounter with MacDuff.

29. Some did acclaim Forrest in his own terms. In his 1888 biography of the actor, Harrison praised Forrest's "truthfulness to nature" in creating "a perfect portraiture of the highest type of the native Indians of the Western Continent" (37). He stated that Forrest's characterization was based on personal observations that led him to mimic even the Indian manner of breathing. The Push-ma-ta-ha story also served to confirm Forrest's reputed interest in physical culture; he was remarkable for his generation in that he pursued a regular program of exercise to develop and maintain the bulging muscles that were part of his theatrical attraction.

30. On July 25, 1834, Forrest's friends and admirers had gathered to celebrate the actor's career before he left on his first trip to Europe.

31. There is one divergent illustration in Toedteberg's collection, an 1842 engraving by

Rawdon Wright after a painting by Frederick S. Agate that shows neither pouch nor fringed leggings, many feathers, and the pelt of an animal, complete with head, thrown over Metamora's shoulder (1: 142). All of the images present Forrest as clean-shaven; while out-of-costume portraits from his younger years show him wearing, at most, a tuft of whiskers on his chin, virtually all of his mature portraits display a full mustache, which raises perplexing questions regarding his makeup for Metamora. The difficulty with all of these images is that they may represent not Forrest's actual appearance but what he or the artist wished to present.

32. See Wilmeth on the tendency to represent not actuality but legend or speculative destiny (45).

33. See McConachie on the probable tendency of Forrest's audiences to expect the exotic in romantic tragedy (3–4).

34. For the sake of scholarly precision, I should mention that I have been able to corroborate neither this incident nor its date. Hoole records performances of *Metamora* in Charleston on March 2 and 5, 1831, which makes the Augusta visit possible (183). Moody, however, does not mention a southern tour in early 1831 and does not place Forrest in Augusta until January or February of 1847 (*Edwin Forrest* 104, 239). The tale may be either inaccurately dated or even apocryphal.

35. The writers in question (as well as all the writers of the period whom I have mentioned in this chapter) were not only white but male, and they defined not only native but also woman as "other," a strategy that clarifies the hegemonic similarity between sexism and racism.

36. See McConachie on the similarity of the play's cultural values to those promoted by the Democratic Party from the mid-1820s to the 1850s (4, 8).

3. *THE DRUNKARD* (1844) AND THE TEMPERANCE MOVEMENT

1. During this chapter, unless I specify otherwise, when I refer to "temperance drama" I mean "*American* temperance drama." The distinction between American and English is, however, a bit blurry in both theatre and the temperance movement. English actors, managers, and playscripts remained prominent in American theatre during the antebellum period, and American temperance reformers addressed most of the same issues, and used many of the same tactics, as their counterparts in England; speakers even traveled back and forth across the Atlantic to deliver guest lectures.

2. I am following prevailing custom by accepting *The Drunkard* as an American play in spite of its author's nationality. Smith was born with the surname of Sedley in North Wales in 1806, took to the stage at the age of fourteen, and in 1827 migrated to the United States to spend the rest of his career here (see Moody, *Dramas* 277–78; Meserve, *Heralds* 152; and Smith, *Victorian Melodramas* 98). It is possible that Smith merely "doctored" a play by John Pierpont (1785–1866), a temperance poet who was pastor of a Boston church in 1844, so the authorship may be more American than Smith himself.

3. This response may have indicated a factional quarrel. The troupe was Washingtonian in origin and ideology, and may therefore have annoyed the more conservative ATU writers.

4. Rorabaugh estimates that the adult, per capita consumption of spirits rose from 5.1 gallons per year in 1790 to 8.7 in 1810, then hesitated a bit before reaching a peak of 9.5 gallons in 1830. Although consumption of cider fell over the same period of time, the ingestion of absolute alcohol reached an all-time peak of 7.1 gallons in 1810 and again in 1830. The reformers produced their own statistics; in 1831, the American Temperance Society adduced a cloud of speculative figures to "prove" that each adult male drank an average of 20 gallons of spirits per year, while the "confirmed drunkard" downed nearly 70 gallons per year (*Permanent Temperance Documents, Fourth Report* 77–78).

5. My discussion is gender-specific because most antebellum temperance discourse—es-

pecially the stories that engage my attention later in this chapter—located the problem in men, virtually ignoring the drinking problems of women; see Rorabaugh 12. Justin Edwards encouraged women to join temperance societies on the grounds that they were inherently moral and would provide a salutary influence, and the Martha Washingtonian societies recruited women with that idea in mind (Tyrrell 67–68, 179–82). For a thorough discussion of their efforts, with allusions to the problem of women who drank, see Alexander.

6. The Methodist Church recommended teetotalism in 1832, as did the Presbyterians in 1835 (Rorabaugh 207–208).

7. Until some temperance advocates started disseminating a chemist's analysis during the 1820s, many wine drinkers believed their beverage to be free of alcohol (Rorabaugh 101). The attack on wine also created a problem for those who revered it as an essential part of Holy Communion or Mass. Justin Edwards proposed that the Biblical wine had not been fermented (that is, it was mere grape juice) and Gerrit Smith argued that Christ could not have realized the ill effects of alcohol (Tyrrell 145–46).

8. The founders named the society to honor the memory of George Washington and to associate themselves with the cause of freedom; the former general and president had never been involved with any form of the temperance movement.

9. Tyrrell reports that the Washingtonians "often grossly exaggerated the poverty and degradation of the drunkard . . . in order to maximize the dramatic effect of conversion" (164).

10. Two gallons per capita seems to be the level to which the American drinking public gravitates. Consumption remained approximately stable for the rest of the nineteenth century, never rising above 2.1 gallons, although after the Civil War, the general preference shifted away from spirits and toward beer. Consumption rose from 1900 to 1915, dropped during Prohibition, and by 1945 reached two gallons again. Rorabaugh's figures for 1945 through 1960 show total annual ingestion of alcohol at 1.9 to 2 gallons per adult—only slightly higher than in 1845, and similar to the overall pre-Prohibition level. His tables then show an upward trend, and he estimates that in 1975, the most recent year in his study, the average adult drank 2.7 gallons of alcohol per year, composed of 2.4 gallons of spirits, 2.2 gallons of wine, and 28.8 gallons of beer (232–33). This translates into an approximate weekly consumption of six one-ounce shots of hard liquor, one six-ounce glass of wine, and one six-pack of twelve-ounce containers of beer.

11. Some of the scenarios enjoyed a certain durability; Justin Edwards used the idea of a mother supplying a hanging rope as the basis for one of his stories in *The Temperance Manual* (1846).

12. While working in New England stock companies before signing the pledge at a Washingtonian meeting, Gough played the leading role in a travesty of Lyman Beecher entitled *Departed Spirits; or, A Temperance Hoax* (Kobler 66–67). Beecher had, in 1826, preached a series of six temperance sermons that the American Tract Society then published for wide circulation in pamphlet form.

13. Arthur's temperance fiction made him famous, but it was only a portion of his output. His antebellum works alone form a long list of domestic and sentimental novels, novelettes, and stories with titles like *Family Pride: or, The Palace and the Poor House* (1844), *The Angel of the Household* (1854), and *Hiram Elwood, the Banker: or, "Like Father, Like Son." A story illustrating the doctrine, that moral qualities are transmitted by parents to their offspring* (1844).

14. See Tyrrell 72–73 and Dannenbaum 21–22.

15. For discussions of the ethic of self-improvement as an economically based ideology, see Tyrrell 6–7 and 125–26.

16. See chapter 3, part 2 of the *Manifesto*. It was published in 1848, right in the thick of the antebellum temperance movement, but while we may argue a confluence of ideas between

Marx and the reformers, it is unlikely that his work influenced their thinking, for it was not translated into English until 1883 as *Manifesto of the Communists* (New York: Schaerr and Frantz).

17. Tyrrell has pointed out that the entrepreneurial temperance advocates tended to acclaim the individual's ability to improve himself while blaming society at large for intemperance (128–29).

18. Because Gough was an orator, not a writer, I am quoting him as reported by John Marsh, a Congregationalist minister and editor of the *Journal of the American Temperance Union*; "Gough" may be in part Marsh's construction.

19. Respectability features explicitly in Arthur's *Ten Nights, Confessions of a Reformed Inebriate*, Edwards's *Temperance Manual*, Estes, Kitchel, Kittredge, Marsh's *Half Century*, W. H. Smith, C. W. Taylor, and *Who Slew All These?*

20. According to the national census, in 1850, 63.7 percent of the labor force worked on farms and 5.45 percent (420,000) were clerks and merchants; in 1860, 58.9 percent worked on farms and 7.43 percent (780,000) were clerks and merchants. Although the convergence is apparent, it may seem puzzling that the playwrights were concerned with a relative minority. Theatre, however, has always belonged to the cities, and we may assume that clerks and merchants formed a significant proportion of the urban population.

21. The other extant scripts are:

1848?—Harry Seymour's *Aunt Dinah's Pledge*
1848?—Harry Seymour's *The Temperance Doctor*
1850—G. D. Pitt's *The Drunkard's Doom*
1856—C. W. Taylor's *The Drunkard's Warning*
1858—John H. Allen's *The Fruits of the Wine-Cup*

Other plays produced but not extant include the following:

1830—*The Drunkard* in Nashville (Moody, *Dramas* 280)
1838—*The Drunkard* in St. Louis (Moody, *Dramas* 280)
June 1838—*The Drunkard's Warning* at the National Theatre, New York (Meserve, *Heralds* 152)
November 11, 1842—*The Drunkard's Progress* at the Arch Street Theatre (Quinn 442)
1843—*Moral Exhibition of the Reformed Drunkard* (Krout 256)
1844—*One Cup More, Or the Doom of the Drunkard* at the National Theatre, Boston (Ayer 62)
April 22, 1844—T. D. English's *Doom of the Drinker* at the National Theatre, Philadelphia (Quinn 442)
1845—*Another Glass; or, The Horrors of Intemperance* at the Chatham Theatre (Meserve, *Heralds* 152)
1848—I. Courtney's *Life; or, Scenes of Early Vice* at the Bowery Theatre (Meserve, *Heralds* 152)
1850—*Retribution; or, The Drunkard's Wife* at Barnum's Museum, Philadelphia (Quinn 478)
no date listed—*One Glass More* (Moody, *Dramas* 280)

None of the references explicitly indicates American authorship. The two early plays entitled *The Drunkard* were not the same as Smith's, and *The Drunkard's Warning* of 1838 was probably not the same as Taylor's 1856 play of the same title. I do not consider F. S. Hill's *Six Degrees of Crime* (first presented January 15, 1834) to be a true temperance drama because it exploits several different vices for sensational effect without attempting to argue the temperance position. Temperance drama flourished after the Civil War; there were at least forty-two temperance plays and collections of short pieces published from 1868 to 1898, and nearly half of those appeared from 1873 to 1879.

22. This date appears in Krout 254 and Meserve, *Heralds* 152, but Moody lists the premiere as February 25 (*Dramas* 277), Birdoff as February 26 (29), an Smith as March 16 (*Victorian Melodramas* 98). The latter may have been a misreading of Harry Watkins's journal entry for March 16, 1849 (Skinner and Skinner 70).

23 Moody reports that during the summer of 1850, Barnum's production eclipsed rival stagings of the same play at the Chatham, the National, and the Bowery, and ran for a record-breaking one hundred consecutive performances from July 8 to October 7 (*Dramas* 277–79). Smith lists the opening of that production as June 17 (*Victorian Melodramas* 98).

24. Jack Gelber and the Living Theatre offered one solution to this challenge in their 1959 production of *The Connection*.

25. I have chosen this phrase carefully. The *OED* notes the first appearance of "exegetical" in 1838, making it more than usually appropriate for a phenomenon of the era in question. "Exegesis" connotes explanation or exposition, especially of a text, and the interpretation is more direct and less sophisticated than in the case of formal hermeneutics. The association with scriptural readings is not, to my mind, misleading, for the temperance plays did serve an exhortatory purpose somewhat similar to that of the circuit minister's sermon.

26. Neither Smith nor Cribbs offers specifics regarding the act of atrocity; we are left to imagine the worst.

27. There are two subplots, one involving the honest Yankee, William, and his poor sister, Agnes Dowton, "a maniac" who regains her senses in the last scene, and the other concerning Cribbs's attempts to exploit Miss Spindle, a foolish spinster who imagines that Edward has made improper advances to her. Except that Agnes, once sane, enables the denouement by remembering where the crucial will is hidden, neither of the secondary stories is essential to the primary one; both, however, provide some welcome comic relief.

28. The stage direction "exults" appears in many plays of the period when one character is supposed to express joyful satisfaction over the actions of another. I wonder whether the word was an informal code for a stylized action or posture, grown familiar by custom, that the audience would easily recognize as conveying the appropriate attitude, and that the actor would accept as a fairly specific instruction.

29. The New York venue probably reflects Barnum's relocation to the city more familiar to his audience, and it indicates that the scripts we now have available were based on versions published not in 1844, but in 1850 or later.

30. Following is Rorabaugh's description of the affliction: "Delirium tremens . . . affects a heavy drinker after a binge, an illness, or a withdrawal from accustomed portions of alcohol. The disorder begins with a period of irritation and anxiety, frequently accompanied by muscle spasms called 'the shakes.' There ensues a period of paranoid hallucination, during which the subject commonly reports being chased by people or animals, usually either tiny or huge. During this highly excited phase restraints may be needed to prevent the subject from injuring himself. Finally, the victim falls into a deep sleep and enters an acute alcoholic depression. Either death or complete recovery follows" (169–70). Rorabaugh goes on to propose that the hallucinations seem to reflect both fear and a sense of guilt regarding failure in a competitive economy (172–73).

31. Mary might have played the role of "good angel" had Smith not rendered her so ineffectual. The morality struggle was even more explicit in *The Drunkard's Warning*; the drunkard has a friend who tries in vain to save him and who warns that "virtue and vice are contending for mastery over your soul" (7).

32. He also demonstrates the principle that the samaritan who helps the drunkard increases

his own respectability; Tyrrell has noted that the Washingtonians found satisfaction in proving that one did not have to be wealthy to perform the philanthropist's role (176).

33. In *The Drunkard's Warning*, Edward Mordaunt, after his drinking leads to gambling debts, forgery, and a term in prison, not only repents (and fortuitously saves his wife, who is about to expire from heartbreak) but suddenly acquires a stilted polish to his speech and scorns his former cronies as long as they refuse to sign the pledge.

34. In 1844, the Boston publisher E. P. Williams brought out a novelette called *The Drunkard*, listing no author but ascribing it to "the author of the moral drama of the same name." Because the playscript lists Smith as the adaptor, not the author, and because the novelette does not follow the play as closely as one would expect if the author were trying to capitalize on the popularity of the stage presentation, we might suppose that the novelette was the original that Smith used as his basis. However, the preface to the Samuel French edition of the play seems to indicate that certain parts of the story that do appear in the novelette were Smith's work: "The proprietor of the Museum . . . engaged a gentleman of known and appreciated literary acquirements. . . . Unfortunately his production, though eminently worthy of the gentleman and scholar, was from want of theatrical experience, merely a story in dialogue, entirely deficient in stage tact and dramatic effect. Under these circumstances, the manuscript was placed into the hands of Mr. W. H. Smith. . . . That gentleman revised what was written, altering what he considered ineffective, and introduced the entire underplot, together with the last scene of the second act, and the entire of the third, fourth and fifth parts. No claim is laid to originality of invention in the character of Cribbs, Agnes, or any other part in the piece" (vi).

The novelette sets up Edward Middleton, Cribbs, and the Wilsons much the same as in the play, but William is Edward's servant, not his foster-brother, and the self-righteous Miss Spindle is less comic and more an object of authorial disapproval, especially as she appears as an unwelcome and unbidden guest at the home of the three gossiping Drinkwater girls. We see much more of Edward's visits to the barroom at the Red Lion Hotel, where he demonstrates his susceptibility to peach brandy. After Edward flees to Boston (not New York; see note 29), William falls afoul of Cribbs, who tries to have him convicted of assault with intent to rob. The lawyer then gets Mary evicted from her tenement apartment. Rencelaw does not appear at all; a friendly farmer saves Edward by taking him in, weaning him off of the liquor habit with small doses of good brandy, and taking him to a temperance meeting, where he signs the pledge. Edward returns to his home village in search of Mary and meets mad Agnes, who gives him the old parchment she has dug up. It is the true will of Edward's uncle, who left his entire estate to Edward's father; Cribbs had forged a will to make himself the heir. Edward takes the coach back toward Boston but finds Mary and Julia by the side of the road, hungry and distraught, and the family are reunited with their newly discovered fortune. Cribbs has married Miss Spindle, but he goes to state prison while she must take in sewing and suffer the sneers of her neighbors, who treat her just as she treated Mary in earlier days.

35. The dry states and territories included all of New England plus New York, Delaware, Indiana, Michigan, Iowa, Minnesota, and Nebraska.

4. *UNCLE TOM'S CABIN* (1852) AND THE POLITICS OF RACE

1. As the composition of the Troy company demonstrated, theatre in antebellum America was frequently a family affair. Aiken (George Harris, George Shelby) and his brother Frank (Marks) were the nephews of Mrs. Emily C. Wyatt Fox (Ophelia), who was the mother of George Washington Lafayette Fox (Phineas Fletcher when the company moved to New York), Charles Kemble Fox (Gumption Cute; also Phineas Fletcher in Troy), and Caroline Emily Fox, aka Mrs. Howard (Topsy, Chloe), who was the wife of George Cunnabell Howard (St. Clare) and the mother of Cordelia Howard (Little Eva). Birdoff (48) reports that the Howards were

related, through Joseph Jefferson the First, to Mrs. Germon (Eliza Harris, Cassy), who was married to Greenbury C. Germon (Uncle Tom). Coincidentally, the two adult Howards, Mr. Germon, and all three Foxes appeared in the original production of *The Drunkard* (Birdoff 31–32).

2. This works out to nearly 7.6 performances per week. Birdoff reports that Purdy had booked the show in expectation of his usual lower-class audience but that the spectators represented more the elite of society, one-third of them being church members, their pastors, and Henry Ward Beecher himself (74–75). The script itself changed in mid-run; at Purdy's request, Charles Western Taylor revised it and added several characters, including Senator and Mrs. Bird, and the new version opened on January 9, 1854.

3. The many Tom plays were written without Stowe's consent. When Asa Hutchinson wrote her in 1852 to ask for her permission, Stowe declined on the grounds that the theatre was morally dangerous and that to hope for reform was impractical:

> If the barrier which now keeps young people of Christian families from theatrical entertainments is once broken down by the introduction of respectable and moral plays they will then be open to all the temptations of those who are not such, as there will be, as the world now is, five bad plays to one good. (qtd. in Kaye 26)

4. To refer to the popularity of "the play" is to conflate many scripts, including some that may have had little relation to Aiken's work or even to Stowe's novel. Minstrel troupes took over the story as early as 1853 (Toll 93–97, Birdoff 121), and some burlesques did not even refer to slavery or include black characters (Birdoff 121). Even Aiken's play evolved over time; contemporary reports indicate that Taylor's 1854 revision changed the script significantly, and when the Howard company played Baltimore in 1855, John E. Owens asked that they tone down the characters of Legree and George Harris, and make Marie more sympathetic, all doubtless to appease a border-state audience (Birdoff 101–102, 111–13). Furthermore, we might suspect an intermingling of the various versions in light of the appearance of Mrs. Howard as Topsy in an 1876 production of Conway's script (McConachie 25). If we seek to quantify the popularity of "the play"—as Toll seems to do when he claims that "escapist farces and burlesques . . . dominated stage productions" and that "the watered-down, pro-Southern versions of the play proved more in touch with the general public's tastes as the decade continued" (92)— we run up against the questions of which scripts to count and whether we should tally productions, performances, or total attendance to assess the relative effect of each version. Moreover, there are potential fallacies in referring to "northern" or "southern" audiences without investigating their characteristics in terms of socioeconomic status, ethnicity, gender, and educational level. In other words, I cannot conclude that, because "Tom" companies endured into the 1930s, Aiken's version sustained, over time, the same level and especially the same kind of popularity it apparently enjoyed in the 1850s.

5. Apparently some of the first group overcame their objections to the theatre and brought an unusual sensibility to the conventions of midcentury performance attendance; the review in the *New York Atlas* reports the presence of Methodists, Baptists, Presbyterians, and Congregationalists, who were more inclined to weep at Eliza's predicament than cheer the actress's presentation of her triumphant escape (174). McConachie speculates that the audiences for both Conway's and Aiken's plays may have included middle-income Protestants who would have favored antislavery views (24).

6. On March 9, 1851, Stowe wrote to Gamaliel Bailey, the editor of the *National Era*, offering as a serial the story she was planning. The first installment appeared on June 5, and the last on April 1, 1852, twelve days after the novel was published on March 20, and nearly three months after the first play was produced. Following is a partial record of early stage versions:

- By Professor Hewett, at the Baltimore Museum, January 5, 1852, entitled *Uncle Tom's Cabin as It Is; or, The Southern Uncle Tom*; a proslavery version that depicted Tom himself beating a character named Horace Courtney (Hirsch 359–60, Drummond and Moody 316).
- By Charles Western Taylor, at Purdy's National Theatre, August 23, 1852, to September 4; also in Dunkirk, New York on November 5, 1852. This version omits Topsy, Eva, and the St. Clares to focus on the persecution of Cassy and of George and Eliza Harris, whom Taylor renamed Edward and Morna Wilmot, possibly in honor of the congressman who sponsored the Wilmot Proviso. Tom survives to return to the plantation in Kentucky.
- By Mrs. Anna Marble, produced by J. B. Rice's company in Chicago, probably in summer or fall of 1852 (Arnett 898).
- By Aiken.
- By Clifton Tayleure, a "sketch," at the Detroit Theatre, October 2, 1852.
- By H. C. Conway, at William Warren's Boston Museum, November 15, 1852, and at P. T. Barnum's American Museum, November 7, 1853. This version included the characters Aunty Vermont (a revision of Ophelia) and Penetrate Partyside; Barnum touted the happy ending and assured potential patrons that the play did not try to elevate blacks above whites (Birdoff 88–89). In 1990, McConachie discovered a nearly complete promptbook of the Conway play in the Hoblitzelle Library at the University of Texas at Austin; see his article, "Out of the Kitchen and into the Marketplace."
- In Charleston, presented by Kunkel's Nightingale Burlesque Opera Troupe, *Uncle Tom's Cabin, or Freedom at the North and Service at the South (or Life among the Lowly)*, October 24–26, 1853. Hoole lists Aiken as the author but Dormon quotes the *Charleston Daily Courier* of October 24, 1853, as describing the play as "illustrating the real history of a fugitive, who, weary of living *free to starve* among abolition bigots, returns voluntarily to slavery" (Dormon 135, 201, 279–80; Hirsch 371–74; Roppolo 220–23).
- By Henry H. Stevens, at the Bowery Theatre, January 16 through March 11, 1854, featuring Thomas D. ("Jim Crow") Rice, the minstrel performer, as Uncle Tom.

Drummond and Moody also mention a lantern-slide production at the Franklin Museum and a burlesque by Christy's Minstrels, both running concurrent with Aiken's version at the National and Conway's at the American Museum (318, 321).

7. Unless I indicate otherwise, all quotations attributed to Stowe are from *Uncle Tom's Cabin*.

8. See Ammons, Gillian Brown, and Tompkins for feminist critiques of the pernicious effects of capitalism on the characters in the novel, and McConachie for an analysis of how Aiken and Conway, in their plays, actually reinforce the capitalist status quo.

9. Stowe's fiction ran closely parallel with more overt polemics; this passage conveys much the same message as Grimké, who wrote in 1836 that there was no ethical difference between the dealer and the client, and that "indeed, if slaves were not wanted by the respectable, the wealthy, and the religious in a community, there would be no slaves in that community, and of course no *slave-dealers*" (15).

10. Such questions were hardly abstract to Stowe's contemporaries. In 1834, Prudence Crandall had earned public rebuke for enrolling a black day student in her school in Canterbury, Connecticut. She then opened her boarding school exclusively for black girls, and after the town meeting denounced her, the state legislature passed an ex post facto law against her establishment. Crandall was found guilty at her second trial, but even though the case was thrown out

on appeal, the people of Canterbury had so harassed her and vandalized both her school and her home that she moved to Illinois (Richards 38–40).

11. The special commissioners who heard such cases were paid twice as much if they determined that the defendant was a fugitive than if they found he was not (Pease lxxvi).

12. Gara reports that during the decade the Fugitive Slave Law was in effect and enforced, only about 200 runaways were returned to the South. Some northern states passed personal liberty laws to impede the enforcement of the Fugitive Slave Law and to express their own interpretation of the principle of state sovereignty (235–36).

13. For anti-Tom novels, see Eastman, Hale, Page, Rush, Smith and Victor; for analysis, see Hirsch.

14. The critic for *The Liberator* spent most of his column implying that Stowe, like too many white Americans, took for granted that slaves, simply because they were black, should adopt a saintly level of nonresistance while waiting patiently for others to deliver them from their oppression. The review closed with regret over Stowe' s support of colonization. According to Filler, the abolitionists as a whole suppressed their objections because the novel succeeded in engaging so many people's emotions in the service of the antislavery crusade; outrage facilitated politicization (210). Gossett contends that the abolitionists said little about Stowe's novel and suggests that they did not generally find it congenial to their agenda and methods (175–76). Hirsch has analyzed the favorable reviews and concluded that as a group, they emphasized the reform-novel tradition, the Christian sentiments, the high moral purpose, the literary value, but most of all, the "truthful" depiction of slavery (215–21).

15. See Ames for excerpts from reviews in two newspapers in Troy; the journalists decided that the play would further the cause of the black slave, but more than that, found the production highly moving and dwelt on the wonders of Cordelia Howard as Eva. See Oakes for an analysis of newspaper response to Uncle Tom plays in selected cities in Wisconsin, Iowa, and Minnesota from 1853 to 1857. He concluded that except in Milwaukee "the play and book alone were not capable of instigating direct political action" (136–38, 140).

16. As was the case with the novel, some southerners condemned the play without seeing it. *The Liberator* gleefully quoted a short piece from the Charleston *Whig*, which denounced the "insulting play" that had recently been produced in that city and expressed the wish that Charlestonians had tarred and feathered the players rather than attending their performance ("Clerical Indignation"). *The Liberator* incredulously pointed out the play in question was a "burletta" (a musical farce); it was probably the Kunkel production. Garrison's letter to Helen E. Garrison, dated September 5, 1853, appears in Ruchames 248.

17. Some of these groups were the American Tract Society (1814), the American Home Missionary Society (1815), the American Education Society (1815), and the American Bible Society (1816).

18. Frederickson states flatly that Garrison did not lead the antislavery movement, that Garrison's influence was substantially limited to New England, and that his refusal to consider political action alienated him from the currents that led to the founding of the Republican Party. However, Frederickson does acclaim Garrison as the central figure in the crusade and one whom the South erroneously perceived as a genuine threat (*Arrogance* 73, 75).

19. Davis has observed that while most American men of the time were farmers, virtually no farmers joined abolitionist societies, a fact that further indicates the marginal position of the radicals (*Age of Revolution* 240). In response to concern over the presence of *The Liberator*, in October of 1831, Boston's Mayor Harrison Gray Otis made some inquiries and concluded that neither Garrison nor his journal was important enough to warrant official interference (Richards 21, Staudenraus 194).

20. We may find some indication of the northern conservative attitude toward slavery in

the review of Stowe's novel that the *North American Review*—which Blue describes as a Whig journal—published in 1853. The author held that black slavery was "rightfully imposed; for the white race are the natural rulers," and maintained that slavery did not violate the slave's rights because "his right, like that of all men, is to be governed for his own benefit." He reassured his southern readers that slavery was essential to the well-being of the negro, who was incapable of governing himself, and to the safety of the whites, living as they did among a "degraded" race (478–84).

21. In 1840 and 1844, the Liberty Party nominated James G. Birney for president; he garnered .29 percent and 2.3 percent of the popular vote. The Free Soil Party did better with former president Martin Van Buren in 1848, attracting 10.13 percent, but dropped back to 4.94 percent with John Parker Hale in 1852. During these four elections, frankly antislavery presidential candidates found their strongest support in Massachusetts, Vermont, Michigan, New Hampshire, and Wisconsin, but never drew more than 30 percent of the popular vote in any one state.

22. I am, of course, using "amalgamation" in the antebellum sense, to refer to the sexual and reproductive "mixing" of races.

23. The American Colonization Society (ACS) was founded in 1817, and four years later established the colony of Liberia on the west coast of Africa, sending the first settlers over in 1822. Although colonizationist ministers, especially Congregationalists and Presbyterians, presented Liberia as a missionary enterprise that would help Christian America to redeem dark Africa (Frederickson, *Black Image* 7), the American Society of Free Persons of Colour, in 1830, publicly condemned colonization (Staudenraus 188–93). Colonization suffered most under the pen of Garrison himself, who helped form the New England Antislavery Society partly to discredit and subvert colonization, which he saw as the tool of proslavery interests. In *Thoughts on African Colonization* (1832), he offered copious quotations from ACS literature to support his belief that the society represented a proslavery plot and a conspiracy between racist Northerners and southern slaveholders. Garrison and other abolitionists succeeded in so staining the colonization movement that any antislavery reformer who supported it invited the charge of equivocation if not downright collaboration with the slaveholders. Colonization dwindled during the 1830s and 1840s, and finally, because the United States refused to claim sovereignty over the colony, the ACS board directed the colonists to proclaim their independence, and in 1848, the Republic of Liberia elected its first president.

24. Actually, most Southerners seem to have boycotted the novel as too offensive to read, learning of it only by reputation.

25. The title page indicates that Stowe intended the play "expressly" for Mrs. Mary E. Webb, who gave readings of it in the United States and London in 1856. *Frank Leslie's Illustrated Newspaper* reported her appearance at the Stafford House, home of the Duchess of Sutherland: "The 'Uncle Tom' sympathy is still in full blast in London. . . . Without exactly acting the different parts, [Mrs. Webb] discriminated them with a great deal of nicety" ("Foreign Musical and Dramatic Items").

26. In their adaptations, Stowe and Aiken drew material from the same seventeen chapters: 5, 7, 8, 15, 16, 18, 20, 22, 25, 26, 28, 32–35, 40, and 41. In addition, Aiken made use of chapters 1 (Haley and Shelby), 3 (George and Eliza), 11 (George traveling in disguise), 17 (George and Phineas defending their party against the bounty hunters), 24 (Eva discussing the slaves and her impending death with St. Clare), 27 (following Eva's death), and 30 (the auction in New Orleans); while Stowe used chapters 4 (in Tom's cabin), 6 (Sam and Andy), 10 (Tom's departure with Haley), and 36, 38, and 39 (emphasizing Emmeline and Cassy). Neither drew from chapters 2, 9, 12–14, 19, 21, 23, 29, 31, 27, and 42–45, a body of material that includes Senator and Mrs. Bird, two of the Quaker scenes, the first auction, the journeys on the Mis-

sissippi and Red rivers, Alfred and Henrique, the long discussion between Ophelia and St. Clare, and the denouement.

Following are the source chapters for each act in *The Christian Slave*, with their correspondences with Aiken's play in parentheses:

Act 1—chapters 4–8, 10 (Act One)
Act 2—chapters 15, 16, 18, 20, 22, 25, 26, 28 (Acts Two through Four)
Act 3—chapters 32–36, 38–41 (Act Five, scene 3; Act Six)

27. Cassy's marked prominence in Act Three probably reflects Stowe's intention to create a theatre piece for Mrs. Webb.

28. I have transcribed the Spanish verse and its English translation exactly as they appear in the original, without attempting to make corrections.

29. In this scene, based on chapter 33, Stowe actually writes out Cassy's French insult to Legree in response to his asking how she likes picking cotton: "Beaucoup mieux que de vivre avec une bête telle comme vous"—"Much better than living with a beast like you" (52). In the novel, we know only that Cassy says something to Legree, whose face "becomes perfectly demoniacal in its expression."

30. Tompkins describes the novel as "the *summa theologica* of nineteenth-century America's religion of domesticity" (125).

31. Lynn has pointed out that the authors of antebellum southern romances presented the plantation society as a black-and-white extended family, an image that created an unintentional irony in light of the slave system's tendency to destroy families; Stowe turned this romantic rhetoric against its creators (viii).

32. Hirsch reports that even the hostile critics liked Eva (239); George F. Holmes, of the *Southern Literary Messenger*, approved of her, although he cited a precedent to prove that she was not an original creation.

33. According to Frederickson, the dominant eighteenth-century view of race was that all of mankind were descended from common ancestors and that difference was the result of environment; Samuel Stanhope Smith argued this position in *Essay on the Causes of the Variety of Complexion and Figure in the Human Species* (1787). Southerners probably first heard of polygenesis—the theory of various, separate, and unequal human races—in 1837 (*Black Image* 72, 74).

34. Moody has identified the sentimental Negro as a version of the noble savage (70–71), and Davis has suggested the eighteenth-century primitivists used the noble savage as a literary convention that applied to virtually any non-European (*Age of Revolution* 47).

35. Ironically, Stowe's views on the racial comparison were approximately consistent with those that Hale expressed in her anti-Tom novel, *Liberia* (1853): "The Saxon has not the indolent and docile nature of the African, but with strong passions and insatiate desires, he has mighty energies to incite them to activity, and a resolute will that hangs on to its prey with unyielding pertinacity" (94).

36. See Zanger for an analysis of the antebellum "tragic octoroon."

37. In a passage unique to *The Christian Slave*, an elaboration of an incident in chapter 20 of the novel, Stowe presents Topsy as a diverting little clown.

> OPHELIA. Let me see if you can say your catechism; and if you can you may go and play. Did all mankind fall in Adam's first transgression?
>
> TOPSY. [*Repeating very rapidly.*] Covenant being made with Adam not only for hisself but for his posterity, all mankind 'scending from him by ordinar transgression, sinned wid him, and fell in him, in that fust generation.

OPHELIA. Stop! stop!! stop!!! Topsy. Why, how are you saying it?

ST. CLARE. Why, what 's the odds? I don't see but that it makes as good sense one way as the other.

OPHELIA. St. Clare! now — how can I teach this child if you will talk so? And now you're laughing!

ST. CLARE. I'm done. Proceed. Topsy! you careless hussy, mind yourself! Be sure you get everything in right end first. Now for it!

OPHELIA. Into what state did the fall bring all mankind?

TOPSY. Fall brought all mankind into a state of sin and misery. Please ma'am—?

OPHELIA. What, Topsy?

TOPSY. Dat ar state Kintuck? De Lor' knows dey has sin and misery 'nough dar!

OPHELIA. Hush, hush, Topsy!

ST. CLARE. No personal reflections, Topsy!

TOPSY. Please missis, can't I go play? Dat ar 'bout the generations was so curus! Never kin get it right nohow!

ST. CLARE. O, yes, coz, let her go. I want you to go up stairs and look at a new carpet I've been buying for Eva's room. There, Tops, there 's some candy for you. Next time get the words straight. (41–42)

When one of the boys warns her that she will go to "torment" because she is so wicked, she assures him that she is sure to go to heaven because Ophelia will not have anyone else to wait on her.

38. Aiken used material from twenty-four of Stowe's forty-five chapters, passing over chapters 2, 4, 6, 9, 10, 12–14, 19, 21, 23, 29, 31, 36–39, and 42–45. Act Four, scene 1; Act Five, scenes 2 and 4; and Act Six, scenes 2, 4, and 6 are original, while Act One, scene 5 and Act Four, scene 3 are extrapolations from action implied in the novel. The relationship of scenes to chapters is as follows:

1.1	3	2.1	15	3.1	18, 25, 22
1.2	1	2.2	16, 20	3.2	22, 25
1.3	5	2.3	11	3.3	26
1.4	7, 8	2.4	20, 24	3.4	26
1.5	extrapolation	2.5	17		
1.6	8	2.6	17		
4.1	original	5.1	30	6.1	34
4.2	27, 28	5.2	original	6.2	original
4.3	extrapolation	5.3	32, 33	6.3	35
4.4	28	5.4	original	6.4	original
				6.5	40, 41
				6.6	original

39. Aiken may have included this section to develop the role of Legree, but his concerns may have been less dramaturgical than reflective of company politics. We can only speculate about his situation as a hack playwright, writing on commission and trying to please the various members of a tightly knit, provincial theatre company. His casting structure is notable for how evenly it spread the responsibilities among the principal players in Troy; with doubling (in addition to the members of the extended Howard family, Mr. Lemoyne played both Wilson and Perry, and Mr. Davis played both Haley and Legree), the script gave substantial assignments to seven men and three women, but no one performer appeared on stage for more than one-third

of the play. In other words, everyone got a chance to shine for the audience, but no one dominated the show.

40. Senelick writes, "The first scene between the mulattoes George Harris, represented with a brick-red face, and Eliza, depicted as a pretty white girl, made no more impression than the usual tender farewell of any lover and mistress" (65).

41. See Slotkin on the use of captivity mythology in slave narratives (441–43).

42. See 307 (chapter 22) in the novel.

43. The review overlooked the abolitionist question entirely; explicitly stated that sympathy with the play, its characters, or its apparent message did not imply interference with southern affairs; but sought to present a brave face by insisting on the North's right to "discuss . . . any question."

44. As feminist and black activist, both Ammons and Baldwin write from outside of the white male power structure; perhaps it is not so surprising that the views from any part of the margins are somewhat similar. Tom's emasculation is a paradigm for the dominant group's treatment of the subordinates.

45. According to Gossett, the tradition of playing Tom as meek, subdued, and elderly began only when J. Lingard replaced G. C. Germon as Tom in August of 1853, during the run at the National (277–80).

46. E. P. Christy wrote "Old Folks at Home," and the review in the *New York Atlas* branded the inclusion of a minstrel song "an insult to the intelligence of the city, and to those who are the legitimate friends of the objects set forth by the author of Uncle Tom's Cabin."

47. Robson has pointed out that both Tom and George Harris were remarkable stage Negroes for their time; their predecessors had "been characterized as either stupidly servile or as savages" (71). Gossett believes that in spite of the demeaning stereotypes, Aiken's play encouraged its audience "to think about blacks in a new and better way than they had in the past" (283).

48. For a discussion of antislavery as extension of the philanthropic tradition, see Davis, *Western Culture* 333–64.

5. *MY PARTNER* (1879) AND THE WEST

1. Wilt reports that *My Partner* ran through October 18 before going on a tour that included a run at Hooley's Theatre in Chicago from February 9 through February 22, 1880. The play also appeared at the Olympic Theatre in London from April 10 through May 8, 1884, and in translation as *Mein Kumpan* at the Residenztheater in Berlin on September 15, 1883 (Wilt xlvii–xlviii).

2. Joseph A. Nunes wrote *Fast Folks*, and Joaquin Miller also wrote *Forty-Nine* (1882). Earlier plays on the subject, but with no record of professional production, were Warren Baer's *The Duke of Sacramento* (1856), Alonzo Delano's *Live Woman in the Mines* (1857), and Charles E. B. Howe's *Joaquin Murieta de Castillo* (1858). For a discussion of produced plays whose scripts are no longer extant, see Gaer 15, 23, 54–57 and 84–97; Gagey 84–85; and MacMinn 236–37.

3. Narcissa and Marcus Whitman brought their mission to Oregon in 1836, and the first wagon train reached California in 1841. I acknowledge that in constructing the westward movement in terms of trappers, loggers, farmers, and miners, I am making an omission that may seem strange to those unfamiliar with the chronology. When Americans today consider the concept of the West, we tend to fix on the myth of the Old West and its emblem, the cowboy, that lonely, independent vanguard of American individualism, dressed in ten-gallon Stetson, vest, chaps, and finely tooled boots, riding the Chisholm Trail through the limitless range, cutting Joseph Glidden's barbed wire to confound the homesteaders, fighting with the sheepherders for

pasturage, ready to lynch a cattle rustler at the point of a Colt .45, cherishing each "little dogie," loving his horse as a brother, and gazing off into the sunset, with a saddle-leather face and a discreet chaw thrust into his lip. The actual cowboy flourished shortly after the Civil War and diminished in the 1890s, a stretch of years that included not only a bloody series of so-called "Indian Wars"—another source of twentieth-century popular romanticism—but also the careers of such heroes and "bad men" as the James gang, Wild Bill Hickock, John Wesley Hardin, Billy the Kid, and the Earp Brothers, who shot it out with the Clantons and the McLaurys at Tombstone's O.K. Corral on October 26, 1881, an event that, in retrospect, marks the apotheosis of the Wild West. Yet the legend of the cowboy developed too late to influence the cluster of theatrical Westerns that appeared in the 1870s. The long cattle drive first appeared in fiction with Arthur Morecamp's *The Live Boys* in 1878, Buffalo Bill opened his Wild West show in 1883, Prentiss Ingraham introduced the fictional cowboy hero in *Buck Taylor, King of the Cowboys* as part of Beadle's Half-Dime Library in 1887, and Owen Wister began publishing his Lin McLean stories in *Harper's* in 1892, then firmly establishing the legend with *The Virginian* in 1902. During the 1870s and 1880s, therefore—the period of *My Partner*—the cowboy was only beginning to enter the popular imagination.

4. James Marshall discovered a gold nugget at Sutter's Mill on January 24, 1848, and the Treaty of Guadalupe Hidalgo took effect on February 2.

5. Garcí Ordóñez de Montalvo wrote *Las sergas de Esplandián* ca. 1510; he invented the island of California, populated by tall, bronzed Amazons, replete with gold and griffins, and ruled by Queen Califía.

6. See Merk on Manifest Destiny of the middle to late 1840s, the period of the Mexican War and the gold rush (24–39).

7. As I write this passage, the Columbian Quincentenary is the subject of growing controversy. There is no doubt that the Europeans and their descendants appropriated this hemisphere with scant regard for the prerogatives of those who were already living there. (No one knows what the native Americans would have done had they been the first to cross the water.) Perhaps we may better understand, if not condone, the European treatment of the Americas if we acknowledge the immense force of ancient myth as a spur to a certain course of action.

8. In his popular account, Frémont described a journey of over fourteen months (May 29, 1843 to August 1, 1844) during which, including layovers, he and his party traveled an average of fifteen miles per day, so his report, although often tersely factual, renders an impression of constant movement and therefore of adventure. Wyatt writes that Frémont's "was the most widely read official document to come out of the West, and it was read as epic. Joaquin Miller was propelled westward after hearing his father read the *Report* on his Ohio farm" (18).

9. Despite his enthusiasm, Dana conceded the tedium and misery of much of his voyage, and was quite ready to leave California when the time came.

10. Genus *Platanus*, more commonly known as the sycamore.

11. His last recorded latitude was 35° 17′ 12″, so this pass could have been either Walker or Tehachapi Pass. The long quotation is taken from his entry of April 14, 1844.

12. The syntax of this last phrase is confusing; she probably means that the sunlight passed through the clear, pure air to bathe the fir trees with luster.

13. The smog and dust of contemporary California life have made experiences like King's virtually unavailable. I have driven over Pacheco Pass many times since the 1960s, and rarely have I been able to see the Sierra at all, much less discern its beauty.

14. One dissenting voice in the California chorus was that of Hinton Rowan Helper, who called California "overrated," argued that the benefits of gold do not justify the deleterious effects its acquisition has on those who seek it, and debunked the land as being mostly desert. He also cited "the unexampled debauchery and lewdness of the community" and generally tried

to dissuade people from migrating (281). Twain, although he admired much that he found in California, detested San Francisco's climate and could not understand why anyone would prefer the California landscape to the lush green summer of New England: "The idea of a man falling into raptures over grave and sombre California, when that man has seen New England's meadow-expanses and her maples, oaks and cathedral-windowed elms decked in summer attire, or the opaline splendors of autumn descending upon her forests, comes very near being funny" (365).

15. Leland Stanford drove the Golden Spike on May 10, 1869.

16. Wattenberg writes, "Rather than dominating their environment [Harte's characters] are victimized by it" (10).

17. All page numbers refer to the edition by Wilt, who includes two endings to Act Two; one taken from his copy-text, a manuscript owned by Campbell's son, Robert, and the other taken from a manuscript once owned by Louis Aldrich, who created the role of Joe Saunders. Although the variants are not relevant to my discussion, I have noticed that in his analysis of the authenticity and chronology of the two versions, Wilt does not mention the facts that (1) the "second" ending includes a stage direction for a curtain drop just after Joe is arrested, and (2) the remainder of that text is virtually identical to that of the "first" ending. This "second" ending is therefore a composite, and the inclusion of two curtain drops seems to indicate a typist's, printer's, or editor's error of some kind. Furthermore, Wilt does not acknowledge that unless Joe is arrested, Act Three fails to make much sense. I believe that in spite of Robert Campbell's assertion to the contrary, Wilt's study of the newspaper reviews indicates clearly that the *first* portion of the "second" ending was the one used in the early productions. The "first" ending—which focuses attention on Wing Lee—may have been used only in productions where Parsloe, who played that role, had more clout.

18. Campbell set the play in Siskiyou County, a mountainous, still relatively isolated area on the Oregon border. This was a somewhat unusual setting for a gold-country play, since the Klamath mining region was far from and less productive than the better-known lodes of the Sierra Nevada.

19. Miller employed a similar story structure in *The Danites in the Sierras*.

20. Meserve asserts that the "western" plays of the 1870s and 1880s equate East with female and West with male (62). According to Paul's analysis of the early census records, the population of California in 1850 was over 90 percent male, and he believes that the imbalance in the mining camps was even greater (*Mining Frontiers* 17).

21. There are anecdotes of miners, in the early days of the gold rush, who, hearing that a child was going to arrive in a mining camp, would wait there patiently in hopes of a glimpse; the sentimentality is, apparently, not entirely Harte's fabrication.

22. In *The Girl of the Golden West* (1905), David Belasco offered an apparently western woman, living on her own and running the Polka Saloon with the help of her "little wepping," but he finished the play by sending her back east to marry Dick Johnson and shed her unwomanly ways.

23. Perhaps Campbell's essentially male vision perceives all nonheroes (that is, both women and villains) as alien and marks them with a certain general manner and quality.

24. In our more pliable time, audiences are likely to accept Mary's considerable remorse as satisfactory payment of her moral debt, not realizing that the social conventions of Campbell's age and stage would have condemned her transgression as unforgivable.

25. The *New-York Times* reviewer commented, "We advise Mr. Campbell, by the way, to cut out that portion of *Saunders's* speech (act 4) in which he seeks to exonerate *Mary*; for, while it is rank sentimentalism to overlook her fault, we can sympathize with his course all the same. As it is, the play seems to be written to prove that a woman's shame is excusable as long as a woman is young and innocent."

26. Had Joe Saunders appeared in a typical dime novel—another potent means of constructing the West—of the middle 1870s, he would have been more polished to ensure his conformity with eastern values and manners and to demonstrate the opportunity for social advancement; see D. Jones 47. The western heroes of dime novels of the 1860s were rougher, but also more likely to be woodsmen and hunters, in the tradition of Leatherstocking, Boone, and Crockett, than dogged miners.

27. Paul points out that if a camp had no jail and no officer to hold prisoners in custody, a jury could act on a guilty verdict only by whipping, branding, banishing, or executing the condemned man (*Mining Frontiers* 24).

28. The depth of a mining shaft may be measured on the incline, which would be its actual length as one walks down its slope, or in vertical feet, which would be its elevation relative to its starting point. Grass Valley, which became an important quartz-mining center in the 1850s, now rests on a network of over 350 miles of tunnels, some reaching to 11,000 feet on the incline and a vertical depth of over a mile, which puts them well below sea level.

29. As early as 1886, Royce, a native of Grass Valley, was sensitive to the way Easterners had constructed California's gold country: "Bayard Taylor . . . is an observer sufficiently optimistic to suit the most enthusiastic. . . . [H]e saw whatever illustrated life, hope, vigor, courage, prosperity. It was not his business to see sorrow or misery" (239).

30. Paul reports that the Klamath River miners adopted the more efficient techniques later than did their counterparts in the Sierras, using the rocker as late as 1856 (*California Gold* 97).

31. There is also at least one scene that Campbell undoubtedly intended as highly dramatic but that today's audiences might find unbearably funny. After Scraggs has killed Ned and left with the gold, Joe reenters to ask for a reconciliation and talks for a full minute to Ned's corpse, slumped over the table, before he realizes that something is wrong.

32. The *New-York Times* reviewer mentioned the Starbottle/Britt similarity and praised Britt as "Mr. Campbell's most valuable contribution to our stage."

33. "Plain Language from Truthful James" first appeared in the *Overland Monthly* in September 1870.

34. Duckett reports that Harte responded to misinterpretations of "The Heathen Chinee" by writing "Wan Lee, the Pagan" (1874), which included Hop Sing, "an intelligent, sophisticated, and admired gentleman" (113). Yet his use of the "Chinee" in *Two Men of Sandy Bar* and *Ah Sin* seems to indicate that he had few compunctions either way. Mrs. Frank Leslie, who wrote a breathless, sensational account of her 1877 visit to an opium den and a brothel in San Francisco's Chinatown, embraced Harte's "Heathen Chinee" with neither irony nor skepticism, and Mary Blake assured her readers, in 1883, that "hatred of the Chinese is the one point on which all Californians, good, bad or indifferent, agree" (159).

35. The first stage "Chinee" may have been a nameless "Chinaman" in Delano's *A Live Woman in the Mines* (1857). Later theatrical examples included Win-Kye in George M. Baker's *Nevada* (1882), Hop Se in Milton Nobles's *From Sire to Son* (1887), Hop Sing in L. L. Ware's *Gyp, the Heiress* (1892), One Lung in Charles Townsend's *The Golden Gulch* (1893), and Sam Wong in Augustus Thomas's *Arizona* (1899).

36. Duckett reports that in his opening night speech, and apparently without irony, Twain described Parsloe's caricature of Ah Sin as a virtually perfect portrayal of the "Chinaman" (153).

37. The *New-York Times* review of *My Partner* indicates that the play was set in 1859, but because the available editions of the play locate the action in 1879, I am assuming that either the reviewer or the typesetter made a mistake.

38. White, on the other hand, argues that the postbellum East prized industrial progress and so condescended to the western wilderness; "man had become nature's architect instead of

her worshiper" (46). White points out that in the late 1870s and early 1880s, a man with $300 could buy a transcontinental train ticket and travel in a comfortable Pullman car (47).

39. A section is a square mile, or 640 acres, and the statutory price was $1.25 per acre. 125,000 square miles is equivalent to half a million quarter-sections—certainly a major factor in the westward movement and a significant opportunity for migrating small farmers, but perhaps not as dominant a phenomenon as some suppose.

40. See Merk on Anglo-Saxon "superiority" and sense of mission (261–65). Wattenberg has suggested that Manifest Destiny "certainly had a melodramatic dimension—that is, the taming of the continent even against great odds could be rationalized as a victory of virtue over evil" (7).

41. Wyatt observes that Royce structured *California* around the myth of the Fall (30).

6. *SHENANDOAH* (1889) AND THE CIVIL WAR

1. Probably the first professional play to use the Civil War—and then only as background for the ongoing lives of the characters—was Augustin Daly's *A Legend of "Norwood"* (1867). Other early productions, whose scripts are now lost, included *Returned Volunteers* (1870), *Ulysses* (1871), and *Colour Guard* (1873). Dion Boucicault's *Belle Lamar* was produced in 1874 and is still extant. Of *The Reverend Griffith Davenport*, only a portion of Act IV and a synopsis are extant.

2. Another interesting source of Civil War iconography is the body of *carte de visite* photographs, which had more to do with portraiture and military aspirations than actual battle conditions.

3. The novel was originally intended for serialization in *Harper's Monthly* but its realism discouraged the editor.

4. Appleby also points out that while the war and related issues preoccupied southern writers, only 5 to 6 percent of northern novels, of nearly one thousand published from 1865 to 1880, dealt with the war (127–28).

5. This anecdote probably represents a (willful?) conflation of two incidents. Mary Chesnut reports a rumor that one of Lee's aides, Major Walter Taylor was married in April 1865, called back to the front almost immediately, and killed (Woodward 794). General John Pegram was married in Richmond and killed two or three weeks later at Hatcher's Run.

6. Grant was impoverished and dying, and so wrote the book to provide for his family after his death. Serialized in *Century* and then distributed through door-to-door sales under Mark Twain's supervision, it sold 300,000 copies in two years. The *Century* articles were serialized from November 1884 through April 1888, and then collected into four volumes edited by Johnson and Buel.

7. The G.A.R. was founded during the winter of 1865–66. Membership rose to 30,000 by 1878, and to 409,000 in 1890 (Buck 246).

8. Among the G.A.R. titles were *The Drummer Boy* (1868), *The Color Guard* (1870), *Foiled* (1871), *True to the Flag* (1871), *The Volunteer* (1871), *The Union Sergeant* (1872), *Loyal Mountaineers* (1873), *Surrounded by Fire* (1874), *The Virginia Veteran* (1874), *Our Regiment* (1884), *The Confederate Spy* (1887), and *The Midnight Charge* (1892).

9. Like most interpretations of the war, the amateur plays represented the northern perspective. Exceptions include *The Confederate Vivandiere* (1862), performed in Montgomery as a benefit for the 1st Alabama Cavalry; *The Tyrant of New Orleans* (1873), a forthright attack on Major General B. F. Butler, who "insulted" the ladies of New Orleans while serving as a military governor there; and *A Southern Rose* (1893), performed in Akron, Ohio, but depicting the Southerners more sympathetically than the Northerners.

10. The heroic little drummer boy, who longs to serve and sometimes bravely falls in

battle, was not as common a character type as one might expect, but he does appear in *The Drummer Boy* (1868) and *Lights and Shadows of the Great Rebellion* (1884).

11. Producers assured potential audiences of the thoroughness with which they would depict the war. A playbill dated Tuesday evening, February 6, 1872, announces, "The Comrades of Encampment Farragut Post, No. 27, Department of Vermont, respectfully announce to the citizens of East Wallingford and vicinity, that they will present the most thrilling Historical War Drama, The Union Sergeant; or, The Battle of Gettysburg! . . . It presents in the most vivid and life-like manner the stirring scenes of Camp, Bivouac, Picket Line and Battlefield; the terrible tortures of the Rebel Prison-pens, and the heroic life and death of our gallant martyrs of the Union."

12. An earlier version of such an episode appears in *The Drummer Boy*, when Frank Rutledge recognizes Martin Howard as a spy, and Major Rutledge reluctantly presides over the young Northerner's trial and sentencing.

13. The Civil War experience probably made a substantial contribution to America's growing reverence for its flag. In spite of the implicit assumptions so self-righteously cherished by politicians hoping to reinforce their standing with certain of their constituents, Americans have not always recited the Pledge of Allegiance (first published in 1892), nor have we always restricted the flag's use to patriotic ceremony. Our current obsession with ritual and hatred of desecration have developed by stages over two centuries and have no absolute status.

14. One of the very few Union characters to adduce slavery as a motivation is General Thomas in *General Grant* (1868): "I stood by the South to the last: her arrogance and madness have forced me to arms against her; and never will I lay them down until slavery, the cause of this rebellion, is swept away and forever! The South has invited the contest: she shall *fall* before it" (9).

15. Comic darkies appeared in *The Old Flag* (1871), *True to the Flag* (1871), *The Volunteer* (1871), *The Union Sergeant* (1872), *Harry Allen* (1872), *Our Heroes* (1873), *The Spy of Atlanta* (1875), *Lights and Shadows of the Great Rebellion* (1884), *The Confederate Spy* (1887), *From Sumter to Appomattox* (1889), *In the Enemy's Camp* (1889), and *The Spy of Gettysburg* (1891). In *The Drummer Boy* (1868) and *Loyal Mountaineers* (1873), the servant is more loyal than comic, a treatment the professional playwrights adopted for Uncle Dan in *Belle Lamar*, Uncle Rufus in *Held by the Enemy*, and Jonas in *Secret Service*.

16. The bone story may have been based on one of those that appear in *True to the Flag* (1871) and *The Dutch Recruit* (1879). It is also possible, if not likely, that all three scenes drew from oral traditions.

17. Peyton Randolph was the name of the Virginian who presided over the Continental Congress for a total of two months during 1774–75.

18. These southern villains were usually incorrigible, but in a rare departure from the standard patterns, Guy Vincent (in *Lights and Shadows of the Great Rebellion*) realizes that the southern position has no merit, so he serves through the war as a double agent acting on the North's behalf, and finally marries Carrie Johnson, his northern sweetheart.

19. In most of the professional Civil War plays—*Held by the Enemy, Secret Service, The Heart of Maryland, Barbara Frietchie*—the southern heroine simply cares more about her northern suitor than about questions of sectional loyalty.

20. Southerners were rarely cast as spies, and then they recanted their sectional commitment in order to appear sympathetic: Belle Kane, in *Gettysburg*, sacrifices her espionage career to help her northern cousin, who is trapped behind Confederate lines; and the title character in *The Confederate Spy* gives up the southern cause after his sister's northern lover helps both of them and teaches him "the value of *true friendship*."

21. According to official records, nearly 365,000 Union combatants died (less than 40 percent of those in battle, and many of the remainder of illness) and over 280,000 survived

their wounds, for a total casualty rate of of almost 30 percent. Confederate casualty figures are unavailable.

22. Buck observes that the plays followed the example set by the novels and stories of the period in emphasizing mutual valor, divided loyalties, and "the glorious climax of reunion" (241).

23. The Boston Museum produced an early version of *Shenandoah* on November 19, 1888; Howard then revised the piece for Charles Frohman, who produced the opening at the Star Theatre in New York on September 9, 1889, to an audience including General Sherman himself. Frohman moved the show to Proctor's Twenty-third Street Theatre, where it closed on April 19, 1890, after 250 performances (Moody 572). In "History in a Play," Howard recalled Grant's remark concerning "great harmony between the Federal and Confederate," and went on to say of himself, "With these words in his mind, he could write only in kindness and gentleness of our Southern fellow-citizens. He was so greatly influenced by them that he even retraced his steps and blotted out every line in the preceding acts that might have hurt a Southerner's feelings" (287). That article makes specific reference to the following sources, which Howard apparently consulted while writing the play: Grant, Pond, Stevens, Crowninshield's "Cedar Creek," and Nicolay's *Campaigns of the Civil War*.

24. See Ryan for a discussion of Howard's earlier plays on the Civil War: *Feds and Confeds; or, Taking the Oath* (1869) and *Drum Taps* (1873). Both texts are lost.

25. James S. Rogers offered a similar double romance in *Our Regiment* (1884), but Ryan has established that Howard first used the idea in *Drum Taps*.

26. One secondary love affair involves Captain Heartsease and Buckthorn's daughter, Jenny, who has been raised in army camps and even, like her lover, flirts in military terms; he hopes that "if you ever decide to assume command of any other man, I—I trust you will give me your orders" (586) and after he has escaped from the rebels, assures her that he has become her prisoner instead.

27. In "History in a Play," Howard wrote that he was less interested in Sheridan's arrival than in "the change from a broken and dispirited retreat of the Union army to an enthusiastic advance," and he referred to Sheridan as being "merely a part of the machinery of the piece" (282).

28. I have based this summary on Lewis 139–58, which is itself not primary research, but rather a recent compendium of others' efforts.

29. As "Sheridan at Cedar Creek," the poem was collected in *Battle-Pieces and Aspects of War* (New York: Harper's, 1866).

30. In his review of *Shenandoah*, Dithmar referred to Sheridan's ride as "made immortal in verse by Thomas Buchanan Read."

31. None of the professional plays treats Lincoln's assassination; perhaps the playwrights considered it so incendiary an incident that they could not conceive of a satisfactory denouement that would leave their dramatic Union intact.

32. This was, of course, a more popular sentiment in 1776, but by 1861, the revolutionaries' grandsons had become the accepted power structure and had adopted appropriately conservative attitudes.

7. STAGING THE MYTH OF AMERICA

1. See Bank for an extension of Foucault into theatre historiography.

2. See McConachie for comments on conventions as clues to the changing relationship between audience and actor in the context of social class in the nineteenth century (55–56).

3. In a largely different context, Case has proposed that "ethnicity is a racist construction which signifies" the supremacy of whites in representation.

4. Elsewhere, Bercovitch has argued that "American" itself is an ideological term, the emblem of a system of beliefs and meanings ("America as Canon" 102–3).

5. Regarding Legree, Stowe presents him as the worst American, while Aiken deflates the implied indictment by killing him and by providing Cute as a harmless alternative.

6. I do not mean to disparage theatre by arguing that it tends toward a conservative construction of experience. I simply mean that theatrical representation tends to affirm, confirm, and sustain the status quo, rather than question, challenge, or shatter it. Whether this is desirable or not depends on one's relationship to the status quo.

7. This "alignment" may not be actual in terms of class interests; it may be more a matter of perception under the influence of Gramscian coercion through hegemonic means.

Bibliography

PREFACE

Grimsted, David. *Melodrama Unveiled: American Theatre and American Culture, 1800–1850*. Chicago: U of Chicago P, 1968.

Hewitt, Bernard. *Theatre U.S.A., 1668 to 1957*. New York: McGraw-Hill, 1959.

Hornblow, Arthur. *A History of the Theatre in America from Its Beginnings to the Present Time*. 2 vols. Philadelphia: J. B. Lippincott, 1919.

Hughes, Glenn. *A History of the American Theatre, 1700–1950*. New York: Samuel French, 1951.

Johnson, Claudia D. *American Actress: Perspective on the Nineteenth Century*. Chicago: Nelson-Hall, 1984.

McArthur, Benjamin. *Actors and American Culture, 1880–1920*. Philadelphia: Temple, 1984.

McConachie, Bruce A. *Melodramatic Formations: American Theatre & Society, 1820–1870*. Studies in Theatre History and Culture. Iowa City: U of Iowa P, 1992.

Meserve, Walter J. *An Emerging Entertainment: The Drama of the American People to 1828*. Bloomington: Indiana UP, 1977.

———. *Heralds of Promise: The Drama of the American People during the Age of Jackson, 1829–1849*. Contributions in American Studies 86. New York: Greenwood, 1986.

Moody, Richard. *America Takes the Stage: Romanticism in American Drama and Theatre, 1750–1900*. Bloomington: Indiana UP, 1955. Millwood, NY: Kraus, 1977.

———. *The Astor Place Riot*. Bloomington: Indiana UP, 1958.

———. *Edwin Forrest: First Star of the American Stage*. New York: Knopf, 1960.

Moses, Montrose J. *The American Dramatist*. Boston: Little, Brown, 1925.

Quinn, Arthur Hobson. *A History of the American Drama from the Beginning to the Civil War*. 2nd ed. New York: Appleton-Century-Crofts, 1943.

———. *A History of the American Drama from the Civil War to the Present Day*. Rev. ed. New York: Appleton-Century-Crofts, 1936.

Watts, Steven. "The Idiocy of American Studies: Poststructuralism, Language, and Politics in the Age of Self-Fulfillment." *American Quarterly* 43 (December 1991): 625–60.

Wilson, Garff B. *A History of American Acting*. Bloomington: Indiana UP, 1966.

———. *Ye Bare and Ye Cubb: Three Hundred Years of American Drama and Theatre*. Englewood Cliffs, NJ: Prentice-Hall, 1973.

1. CONSTRUCTING AMERICAN IDEOLOGY

Althusser, Louis. "Ideology and Ideological State Apparatuses." *"Lenin and Philosophy" and Other Essays*. Trans. Ben Brewster. New York: Monthly Review Press, 1971. 127–86.

Bennett, Susan. *Theatre Audiences: A Theory of Production and Reception*. London and New York: Routledge, 1990.

Bercovitch, Sacvan. "Afterword." Bercovitch and Jehlen. 418–42.

Bercovitch, Sacvan and Myra Jehlen. *Ideology and Classic American Literature*. Cambridge Studies in American Literature and Culture. Cambridge: Cambridge UP, 1986.

Bledstein, Burton J. *The Culture of Professionalism: The Middle Class and the Development of Higher Education in America*. New York: Norton, 1976.

Brooks, Peter. *The Melodramatic Imagination*. New Haven: Yale UP, 1976. New York: Columbia UP, 1984.

Denning, Michael. *Mechanic Accents: Dime Novels and Working-Class Culture in America*. London: Verso, 1987.

Derrida, Jacques. "Structure, Sign, and Play in the Discourse of the Human Sciences." *The Structuralist Controversy: The Languages of Criticism and the Sciences of Man*. Ed. Richard Macksey and Eugenio Donato. Baltimore: Johns Hopkins UP, 1970, 1972. 247–65. Delivered as a paper in October 1966.

Doty, William G. *Mythography: The Study of Myths and Rituals*. University, AL: U of Alabama P, 1986.

Eagleton, Terry. *Criticism and Ideology: A Study in Marxist Literary Theory*. London: NLB, 1976.

———. *Marxism and Literary Criticism*. Berkeley: U of California P, 1976.

Garcia, Gustave. *The Actors' Art: A Practical Treatise on Stage Declamation, Public Speaking and Deportment for the Use of Artists, Students and Amateurs*. London: T. Pettitt, 1882.

Gerould, Daniel C. "The Americanization of Melodrama." *American Melodrama*. New York: Performing Arts Journal Publications, 1983. 7–29.

Gramsci, Antonio. *Selections from the Prison Notebooks*. Ed. and trans. Quintin Hoare and Geoffrey Nowell Smith. New York: International, 1971.

Halttunen, Karen. *Confidence Men and Painted Women: A Study of Middle-Class Culture in America, 1830–1870*. New Haven: Yale UP, 1982.

Hirsch, E. D., Jr. *The Aims of Interpretation*. Chicago: U of Chicago P, 1976.

Jehlen, Myra. "Introduction: Beyond Transcendence." Bercovitch and Jehlen. 1–18.

Kristeva, Julia. *Revolution in Poetic Language*. Trans. Margaret Waller. New York: Columbia UP, 1984.

Lawner, Lynne. "Introduction." *Letters from Prison*. By Antonio Gramsci. New York: Harper & Row, 1973. 3–56.

Lears, T. J. Jackson. *No Place of Grace: Antimodernism and the Transformation of American Culture 1880–1920*. New York: Pantheon, 1981.

McConachie, Bruce A. "Using the Concept of Cultural Hegemony to Write Theatre History." *Interpreting the Theatrical Past: Essays in the Historiography of Performance*. Ed. Thomas Postlewait and Bruce A. McConachie. Iowa City: U of Iowa P, 1989. 37–58.

Roach, Joseph R. "Theatre History and the Ideology of the Aesthetic." *Theatre Journal* 41 (May 1989): 155–68.

Saum, Lewis O. *The Popular Mood of Pre–Civil War America*. Contributions in American Studies 46. Westport, CT: Greenwood, 1980.

Shaftesbury, Anthony Ashley Cooper, Third Earl of. *Characteristics of Men, Manners, Opinions, Times, Etc.* 1711. Ed. John M. Robertson. 2 vols. 1900. Gloucester, MA: Peter Smith, 1963.

Slotkin, Richard. *Regeneration through Violence: The Mythology of the American Frontier, 1600–1860*. Middletown, CT: Wesleyan UP, 1973.

Slotkin, Richard and James K. Folsom, eds. *"So Dreadfull a Judgment" : Puritan Responses to King Philip's War, 1676–1677*. Middletown: CT: Wesleyan UP, 1978.

Williams, Raymond. *Marxism and Literature*. Oxford: Oxford UP, 1977.

2. *METAMORA* (1829) AND THE "INDIAN" QUESTION

Works Other than Plays

Alger, William Rounseville. *Life of Edwin Forrest, The American Tragedian*. 2 vols. Philadelphia: J. B. Lippincott, 1877.

"American Drama." *American Quarterly Review* 1 (June 1827): 331–57. Calls for a national drama.

Anderson, Brenda Jean. "The North American Indian in Theatre and Drama from 1605 to 1970." Diss. U of Illinois, 1978.

Anderson, Marilyn J[eanne]. "The Image of the Indian in American Drama during the Jacksonian Era, 1829–1845." *Journal of American Culture* 1 (Winter 1978): 800–810.

———. "The Image of the American Indian in American Drama: From 1766 to 1845." Diss. U of Minnesota, 1974.

Berkhofer, Robert F., Jr. *Salvation and the Savage: An Analysis of Protestant Missions and American Indian Response, 1787–1862*. Lexington: U of Kentucky, 1965. New York: Atheneum, 1972.

———. *The White Man's Indian: Images of the American Indian from Columbus to the Present*. New York: Knopf, 1978.

Bird, Robert Montgomery. *Nick of the Woods; or, The Jibbenainosay*. 1837. Rev. ed. 1853. Ed. Curtis Dahl. The Masterworks of Literature Series. New Haven: College & University Press, 1967.

Bryant, William Cullen. *The Poetical Works of William Cullen Bryant*. Ed. Henry C. Sturges and Richard Henry Stoddard. 1903. New York: AMS, 1969.

[Cass, Lewis.] "Documents and Proceedings Relating to the Formation and Progress of a Board in the City of New York, for the Emigration, Preservation, and Improvement of the Aborigines of America. July 22, 1829." *North American Review* 30 (January 1830): 62–121.

Catlin, George. *Letters and Notes on the Manners, Customs, and Condition of the North American Indians*. 2 vols. 1841. Minneapolis: Ross & Haines, 1965.

Church, Thomas. *The History of Philip's War*. Boston: B. Green, 1716. Ed. Samuel G. Drake. 1827. 2nd ed. Exeter, NH: J. B. Williams, 1829.

Cooper, James Fenimore. *The Last of the Mohicans*. 1826. Rpt. in vol. 1 of *The Leatherstocking Tales*. Ed. Blake Nevius. New York: Library of America, 1985.

——. *Notions of the Americans, Picked Up by a Travelling Bachelor*. 1828. New York: Frederick Ungar, 1963.

——. *The Wept of Wish-Ton-Wish*. 2 vols. Philadelphia: Carey, Lea & Carey, 1829. New York: AMS, 1972.

Cox, Paul Ronald. "The Characterization of the American Indian in American Indian Plays 1800–1860 as a Reflection of the American Romantic Movement." Diss. New York U, 1970.

Drake, Samuel G. *The Book of the Indians of North America*. Boston: Josiah Drake, 1833.

"Dramatic Literature." *American Quarterly Review* 8 (September 1830): 134–61. On *Metamora*.

Drinnon, Richard. *Facing West: The Metaphysics of Indian-Hating and Empire-Building*. Minneapolis: U of Minnesota P, 1980.

Eastburn, James Wallis [and Robert C. Sands]. *Yamoyden, a Tale of the Wars of King Philip*. New York: James Eastburn, 1820.

Flint, Timothy. *Indian Wars of the West*. Cincinnati: E. H. Flint, 1833.

Flynn, Joyce. "Melting Plots: Patterns of Racial and Ethnic Amalgamation in American Drama before Eugene O'Neill." *American Quarterly* 38 (1986): 417–38.

Forrest, Edwin. *Oration Delivered at the Democratic Republican Celebration of the Sixty-Second Anniversary of the Independence of the United States, in the City of New-York, Fourth July, 1838*. New York: J. W. Bell, 1838.

Freneau, Philip. "The Prophecy of King Tammany." 1782. Rpt. in *The Poems of Philip Freneau*. Ed. Fred Lewis Pattee. 3 vols. 1902. New York: Russell & Russell, 1963. 2:187–89.

Grimsted, David. *Melodrama Unveiled: American Theatre and American Culture, 1800–1850*. Chicago: U of Chicago P, 1968.

Harrison, Gabriel. *Edwin Forrest: The Actor and the Man*. Brooklyn, 1889.

Heckewelder, John. *An Account of the History, Manners, and Customs of the Indian Nations, Who Once Inhabited Pennsylvania and the Neighboring States*. Philadelphia: Abraham Small, 1819. Vol. 12 of *Memoirs of the Historical Society of Philadelphia*. Philadelphia: Historical Society of Pennsylvania, 1876. New York: Arno, 1971.

Hoole, W[illiam]. Stanley. *The Ante-Bellum Charleston Theatre*. [Tuscaloosa]: U of Alabama P, 1946.

Hubbard, William. *The History of the Indian Wars in New England, Etc.* 1677. Ed. Samuel G. Drake. Roxbury, MA: W. Elliot Woodward, 1865. New York: Kraus, 1969.

Irving, John Treat, Jr. *Indian Sketches*. 2 vols. Philadelphia, 1835. Ed. John Francis McDermott. Norman: U of Oklahoma P, 1955.

Irving, Washington. "Traits of Indian Character" and "Philip of Pokanoket." 1814. Rpt. in *The Sketch Book of Geoffrey Crayon, Gent.* 1819. New York: Dodd, Mead, 1954. 285–97 and 298–316.

Jefferson, Thomas. *Notes on the State of Virginia*. London: John Stockdale, 1787. *Writings*. New York: Library of America, 1984.

Jennings, Francis. *The Invasion of America: Indians, Colonialism, and the Cant of Conquest*. Chapel Hill: U of North Carolina P, 1975.

Jones, Eugene H. *Native Americans as Shown on the Stage 1753–1916*. Metuchen: Scarecrow, 1985.

Kappler, Charles J., ed. *Indian Affairs*. 2 vols. Washington: Government Printing Office, 1904.

Leach, Douglas Edward. *Flintlock and Tomahawk: New England in King Philip's War.* New York: Macmillan, 1958. New York: Norton, 1966.

Levin, Harry. *The Myth of the Golden Age in the Renaissance.* Bloomington: Indiana UP, 1969.

Mather, Increase. *A Brief History of the Warr with the Indians in New-England.* 1676. As *The History of King Philip's War, by the Rev. Increase Mather, D.D.; also, A History of the Same War, by the Rev. Cotton Mather, D.D.* Ed. Samuel G. Drake. Boston and London, 1862.

McConachie, Bruce A. "The Theatre of Edwin Forrest and Jacksonian Hero Worship." *When They Weren't Doing Shakespeare: Essays on Nineteenth-Century British and American Theatre.* Ed. Judith L. Fisher and Stephen Watt. Athens: U of Georgia P, 1989. 3–18.

Meserve, Walter J. *Heralds of Promise: The Drama of the American People during the Age of Jackson, 1829–1849.* Contributions in American Studies 86. New York: Greenwood, 1986.

Miller, Perry. *The New England Mind: The Seventeenth Century.* New York: Macmillan, 1939.

Moody, Richard. *The Astor Place Riot.* Bloomington: Indiana UP, 1958.

———. *Edwin Forrest: First Star of the American Stage.* New York: Knopf, 1960.

———. "Lost and Now Found: The Fourth Act of *Metamora.*" *American Literature* 34 (November 1962): 353–64.

"Mr. Forrest's Oration." *United States Magazine and Democratic Review* 3 (September 1838): 51–57.

Mulvey, Kathleen A. "The Growth, Development, and Decline of the Popularity of American Indian Plays before the Civil War." Diss. New York U, 1978.

Murdoch, James E. *The Stage; or, Recollections of Actors and Acting.* Philadelphia: J. M. Stoddart, 1880.

New-York Evening Post December 11, 1829: 2. On Indian removal.

New-York Evening Post May 28, 1830: 2. On Indian removal.

New-York Evening Post December 14, 1831: 2. On Indian removal.

[New York] *Evening Post* July 17, 1834: 2. On Forrest.

[New York] *Evening Post* July 29, 1834: 2. On Forrest.

[New York] *Evening Post* December 6, 1837: 2. On Indian removal.

[New York] *Morning Herald* October 11, 1837: 1. On Indian removal.

"New-York Stage, The: The New Tragedy of Metamora—A Bird's Eye View of Mr. Forrest's Performance." *Irish Shield and Monthly Hilenan* 10 (December 1829): 467–69.

[New York] *Weekly Herald* November 4, 1837: 386. On the natives.

Pearce, Roy Harvey. *The Savages of America: A Study of the Indian and the Idea of Civilization.* 1953. Rev. ed. Baltimore: Johns Hopkins UP, 1965. (Rpt. 1967 as *Savagism and Civilization.*)

[Ranny, R. H.] *Account of the Terrific and Fatal Riot at the New York Astor Place Opera House, on the Night of May 10th, 1849; with the Quarrels of Forrest and Macready, Including All the Causes which Led to that Awful Tragedy! Wherein an Infuriated Mob Was Quelled by the Public Authorities and Military, with Its Mournful Termination in the Sudden Death or Mutilation of More than Fifty Citizens, with Full and Authentic Particulars.* New-York: H. M. Ranney, 1849.

Rees, James. *The Life of Edwin Forrest.* Philadelphia: T. B. Peterson, 1874.

Rev. of *Metamora*. [New York] *Evening Post* October 11, 1837: 2.

Rev. of *Metamora*. [New York] *Morning Herald* December 28, 1837:1.

Rev. of *Metamora*. *New-York Mirror, and Ladies' Literary Gazette* December 19, 1829: 190–91.

Rev. of *Metamora*. *The* [London] *Times* March 27, 1845: 4.

Richardson, James D. *A Compilation of the Messages and Papers of the Presidents, 1789–1897*. Vol. 2. Washington: Government Printing Office, 1896.

Rogin, Michael P. *Fathers and Children: Andrew Jackson and the Subjugation of the American Indian*. New York: Knopf, 1975.

[Saltonstall, Nathaniel.] *The Present State of New-England with Respect to the Indian War*. London: Dorman Newman, 1675. *A New and Further Narrative of the State of New-England; Being a Continued Account of the Bloody Indian War*. London: Dorman Newman, 1676. Rpt. in *The Old Indian Chronicle*. Ed. Samuel G. Drake. Boston: Antiquarian Institute, 1836.

Satz, Ronald N. *American Indian Policy in the Jacksonian Era*. Lincoln: U of Nebraska, 1975.

Sears, Priscilla. *A Pillar of Fire to Follow: American Indian Dramas, 1808–1859*. Bowling Green: Bowling Green U Popular P, 1982.

Seeber, Edward D. "Critical Views on Logan's Speech." *Journal of American Folklore* 60 (1947): 130–46.

Simpson, Alan and Mary Simpson. "Introduction." *Diary of King Philip's War 1675–76*. By Colonel Benjamin Church. Chester, CT: Pequot, 1975. 1–63.

Slotkin, Richard and James K. Folsom, eds. *"So Dreadfull a Judgment": Puritan Responses to King Philip's War, 1676–1677*. Middletown, CT: Wesleyan UP, 1978.

Toedteberg, Augustus. *Forrestiana: Portraits, Playbills and Obituaries Relating to Edwin Forrest. Collected and Arranged for Augustin Daly*. 2 vols. New York: n.p., n.d. Scrapbooks collected in the Huntington Library.

Trumbull, Henry. *History of the Discovery of America, of the Landing of Our Forefathers, at Plymouth, and of Their Most Remarkable Engagements with the Indians, in New-England, from Their First Landing in 1620, until the Final Subjugation of the Natives in 1679*. Norwich: privately printed, 1812.

———. *History of the Indian Wars*. Boston: Phillips and Sampson, 1846.

Tyson, Job R. *Discourse on the Surviving Remnant of the Indian Race in the United States*. Philadelphia: A. Waldie, 1836.

Webster, Noah. *An American Dictionary of the English Language*. New York: S. Converse, 1828. Anaheim, CA: Foundation for American Christian Education, 1967.

Whittier, John Greenleaf. "Metacom." 1829. Rpt. in *The Complete Poetical Works of Whittier*. Cambridge Edition. Boston: Houghton Mifflin, 1894. 488–90.

Williams, Stephen K., ed. *Cases Argued and Decided in the Supreme Court of the United States*. Rochester, New York: Lawyers Co-operative, 1882, 1883.

Wilmeth, Don B. "Noble or Ruthless Savage?: The American Indian on Stage and in the Drama." *Journal of American Drama and Theatre* 1 (Spring 1989): 39–78.

Plays

Doddridge, Joseph. *Logan*. Buffaloe Creek, VA: privately printed, 1823.

Noah, M[ordecai] M. *She Would Be a Soldier, or The Plains of Chippewa*. New York: Longworth's, 1819. Park, New York, June 21, 1819.

Philip, or the Aborigines. New York: 1822.

Rogers, Robert. *Ponteach; or, The Savages of America.* London: privately printed, 1766. Rpt. in *Representative Plays by American Dramatists, 1765–1819.* Ed. Montrose J. Moses. New York: E. P. Dutton, 1918. New York: Benjamin Blom, 1964.

Stone, John Augustus. *Metamora; or, The Last of the Wampanoags. Dramas from the American Theatre 1762–1909.* Ed. Richard Moody. Cleveland: World, 1966. 205–227. Park, New York, December 15, 1829.

3. *THE DRUNKARD* (1844) AND THE TEMPERANCE MOVEMENT

Works Other than Plays

Alexander, Ruth M. " 'We Are Engaged as a Band of Sisters': Class and Domesticity in the Washingtonian Temperance Movement, 1840–1850." *Journal of American History* 75 (December 1988): 763–85.

Arthur, T[imothy] S[hay]. *The Club Room, and Other Temperance Tales.* Philadelphia: E. Ferrett, 1845.

———. *Illustrated Temperance Tales.* Philadelphia: J. W. Bradley, 1850.

———. *Six Nights with the Washingtonians.* Philadelphia: L. A. Godey & Morton M'Michael, 1842. (Rpt. as *Temperance Tales; or, Six Nights with the Washingtonians.* 2 vols. Philadelphia: W. A. Leary, 1848, 1850.)

———. *Ten Nights in a Bar-Room, and What I Saw There.* Boston: L. P. Crown, 1854. Ed. Donald A. Koch. Cambridge, MA: Belknap-Harvard UP, 1964.

Ayer, Mary Farwell. *Early Days on Boston Common.* Boston: privately printed, 1910.

Barnum, P. T. *Struggles and Triumphs: or, Forty Years' Recollections.* Hartford: J. B. Burr, 1869. New York: Arno, 1970.

Beecher, Lyman. *Six Sermons on the Nature, Occasions, Signs, Evils, and Remedy of Intemperance.* New York: American Tract Society, 1827.

Birdoff, Harry. *The World's Greatest Hit.* New York: S. F. Vanni, 1947.

Booth, Michael R. "The Drunkard's Progress: Nineteenth-Century Temperance Drama." *The Dalhousie Review* 44 (1964): 205–212.

Caruthers, William A. *The Drunkard; from the Cradle to the Grave.* Savannah: W. T. Williams, 1840.

Confessions of a Reformed Inebriate. NY: American Temperance Union, 1844.

Cruikshank, George. *The Bottle.* London: David Bogue, 1847.

———. *The Drunkard's Children.* London: David Bogue, 1848.

Dannenbaum, Jed. *Drink and Disorder: Temperance Reform in Cincinnati from the Washingtonian Revival to the WCTU.* Urbana: U of Illinois P, 1984.

Dodd, Jill Siegel. "The Working Classes and the Temperance Movement in Ante-Bellum Boston." *Labor History* 19 (Fall 1978): 510–31.

Dorchester, Daniel. *The Liquor Problem in All Ages.* New York: Phillips & Hunt, 1884. New York: Arno, 1981.

Drunkard, The: or, The Fallen Saved. By the Author of the Moral Drama of the Same Name, Which Has Been Performed Nearly One Hundred Times at the Boston Museum, to Overflowing Houses. Boston: E. P. Williams, 1844.

Eagleton, Terry. *Marxism and Literary Criticism.* Berkeley: U of California P, 1976.

Edwards, Justin. *On the Traffic in Ardent Spirit. The Temperance Volume.* Tract 125.

———. *The Temperance Manual*. New York: American Tract Society, [1846].

———. *The Well-Conducted Farm. The Temperance Volume*. Tract 176.

Estes, Benjamin H. *Essay on the Necessity of Correcting the Errors Which Have Crept into the Washingtonian Temperance Movement and of Bringing to Its Aid the Church of God*. New York: privately printed, 1846.

Gusfield, Joseph R. *Symbolic Crusade: Status Politics and the American Temperance Movement*. Urbana: U of Illinois P, 1963.

Harrison, Brian. *Drink and the Victorians: The Temperance Question in England 1815–1872*. Pittsburgh: U of Pittsburgh P, 1971.

Hitchcock, Edward. *An Essay on Temperance, Addressed Particularly to Students, and the Young Men of America*. 2nd ed. Amherst: J. S. & C. Adams, 1830.

Kitchel, H. D. *An Appeal to the People for the Suppression of the Liquor Traffic*. New York: Oliver and Brother, 1848.

Kittredge, Jonathan. *Address on the Effects of Ardent Spirits. The Temperance Volume*. Tract 221.

Kobler, John. *Ardent Spirits: The Rise and Fall of Prohibition*. New York: G. P. Putnam's Sons, 1973.

Krout, John A. *The Origins of Prohibition*. New York: Alfred A. Knopf, 1925. New York: Russell and Russell, 1967.

Marsh, John. *A Half Century Tribute to the Cause of Temperance*. New York: American Temperance Union, 1851.

———. *Temperance Recollections*. New York: Charles Scribner, 1866.

Meserve, Walter J. *Heralds of Promise: The Drama of the American People during the Age of Jackson, 1829–1849*. Contributions in American Studies 86. New York: Greenwood, 1986.

Moody, Richard, ed. *Dramas from the American Theatre 1762–1909*. Cleveland: World, 1966.

Mouffe, Chantal. "Hegemony and New Political Subjects: Toward a New Concept of Democracy." *Marxism and the Interpretation of Culture*. Ed. Cary Nelson and Lawrence Grossberg. Urbana: U of Illinois P, 1988. 89–101.

Permanent Temperance Documents of the American Temperance Society. Vol. 1. Boston: Seth Bliss, 1835.

Quinn, Arthur Hobson. *A History of the American Drama from the Beginning to the Civil War*. 2nd ed. New York: Appleton-Century-Crofts, 1943.

Rorabaugh, W. J. *The Alcoholic Republic: An American Tradition*. New York: Oxford UP, 1979.

Rush, Benjamin. *The Effects of Ardent Spirits upon the Human Body and Mind. The Temperance Volume*. Tract 25.

Skinner, Maud and Otis Skinner. *One Man in His Time: The Adventures of H. Watkins, Strolling Player, 1845–1863, from His Journal*. Philadelphia: U of Pennsylvania P, 1938.

Smith, James L. *Victorian Melodramas*. London: Dent, 1976.

Temperance Manual of the American Temperance Society for the Young Men of the United States. Boston: Seth Bliss, 1836.

Temperance Volume, The; Embracing the Seventeen Tracts of the American Tract Society. New York: American Tract Society, [1834?].

"Theatrical Exhibitions." *Journal of the American Temperance Union* (August 1843): 125.

Tyrrell, Ian R. *Sobering Up: From Temperance to Prohibition in Antebellum America, 1800–1860.* Contributions in American History 82. Westport, CT: Greenwood, 1979.

Who Slew All These? The Temperance Volume. Tract 247.

Plays

Allen, John H[enry]. *The Fruits of the Wine-Cup.* The Acting Drama 56. New York: Happy Hours, n.d. Old Bowery, New York, 1858.

Hill, F[rederic] S[tanhope]. *The Six Degrees of Crime: or Wine, Women, Gambling, Theft, Murder and the Scaffold.* Spencer's Boston Theatre 15. Boston: Wm. V. Spencer, 1856. Tremont Theatre, Boston, January 15, 1834.

Jerrold, Douglas. *Fifteen Years of a Drunkard's Life.* French's Standard Drama 347. New York and London: Samuel French, n.d. Royal Coburg, London, 1828.

Pitt, G[eorge] D[ibdin]. *The Drunkard's Doom; or, The Last Nail.* French's Standard Drama 345. New York: Samuel French, n.d. Barnum's Museum, New York, 1850.

Pratt, William W. *Ten Nights in a Bar-Room.* Boston: W. H. Baker, [1889?]. New York: French, 1898. Rpt. in *Hiss the Villain: Six English and American Melodramas.* Ed. Michael Booth. 1964. New York: Benjamin Blom, 1967. National Theatre, New York, August 23, 1858.

Seymour, Harry. *Aunt Dinah's Pledge.* New York: Dick, [1853?].

———. *The Temperance Doctor.* French's Standard Drama 356. New York: Samuel French, n.d.

[Smith, W. H.] *The Drunkard; or, The Fallen Saved. A Moral Domestic Drama in Five Acts. Adapted by W. H. Smith.* French's Standard Drama 86. New York: Samuel French, n.d. Rpt. in *Dramas from the American Theatre 1762–1909.* Ed. Richard Moody. Cleveland: World, 1966. 281–307. Boston Museum, Boston, February 12, 1844.

Taylor, C[harles] W[estern]. *The Drunkard's Warning.* Ames' Series of Standard and Minor Drama 185. Clyde, OH: A. D. Ames, n.d. Barnum's Museum, New York, 1856.

Taylor, T[homas] P[rochis]. *The Bottle.* The Minor Drama 20. New York: John Douglas, 1847. London, 1847.

4. *UNCLE TOM'S CABIN* (1852) AND THE POLITICS OF RACE

Works Other than Plays

American Anti-Slavery Society. *Address to the People of Color, in the City of New York.* New York: S. W. Benedict, 1834. Rpt. in Pease. 191–96.

Ames, Edgar W. "First Presentation of *Uncle Tom's Cabin*." *Americana* 6 (November 1911): 1045–52.

Ammons, Elizabeth. "Heroines in *Uncle Tom's Cabin*." *American Literature* 49 (May 1977): 161–79.

Arnett, Frank S. "Fifty Years of Uncle Tom." *Munsey's Magazine* 27 (September 1902): 897–902.

Baldwin, James. "Everybody's Protest Novel." *Partisan Review* 16 (June 1949): 578–85.

Beecher, Catherine E. *An Essay on Slavery and Abolitionism, with Reference to the Duty of American Females.* Philadelphia: Henry Perkins, 1837.

Birdoff, Harry. *The World's Greatest Hit.* New York: S. F. Vanni, 1947.

Birney, James G[illespie]. *Examination of the Decision of the Supreme Court of the United States, in the Case of Strader, Gorman and Armstrong vs. Christopher Graham, Delivered at its December Term, 1850: Concluding with an Address to the Free Colored People, Advising Them to Remove to Liberia.* Cincinnati: Truman and Spofford, 1852. Rpt. in Pease. 44–48.

Blue, Frederick J. *The Free Soilers: Third Party Politics 1848–54.* Urbana: U of Illinois P, 1973.

Bowditch, William Ingersoll. *Slavery and the Constitution.* Boston: Robert F. Wallcut, 1849.

Brown, Gillian. *Domestic Individualism: Imagining Self in Nineteenth-Century America.* The New Historicism: Studies in Cultural Poetics 14. Berkeley: U of California P, 1990.

Buffum, Arnold. *Lecture Showing the Necessity for a Liberty Party, and Setting Forth its Principles, Measures, and Object.* Cincinnati: Caleb Clark, 1844. Rpt. in Pease. 418–27.

Chapman, Maria Weston. *"How Can I Help to Abolish Slavery?" or, Counsels to the Newly Converted.* Anti-Slavery Tract 14. New York: American Anti-Slavery Society, [1855].

"Clerical Indignation." *The Liberator* 23 (December 16, 1853): 195. On Kunkel's production in Charleston.

Cooper, James Fenimore. *Notions of the Americans, Picked Up by a Travelling Batchelor.* 1828. New York: Frederick Ungar, 1963.

Davis, David Brion. *The Problem of Slavery in the Age of Revolution, 1770–1823.* Ithaca: Cornell UP, 1975.

———. *The Problem of Slavery in Western Culture.* Ithaca: Cornell UP, 1966.

Delany, Martin Robison. *The Condition, Elevation, Emigration, and Destiny of the Colored People of the United States.* Philadelphia, 1852. New York: Arno, 1968.

Dillon, Merton L. *The Abolitionists: The Growth of a Dissenting Minority.* DeKalb: Northern Illinois UP, 1974.

Dormon, James H., Jr. *Theater in the Ante Bellum South, 1815–1861.* Chapel Hill: U of North Carolina P, 1967.

Drummond, A. M. and Richard Moody. "The Hit of the Century: *Uncle Tom's Cabin*— 1852–1952." *Educational Theatre Journal* 4 (December 1952): 315–22.

Eastman, Mary H. *Aunt Phillis' Cabin; or, Southern Life as It Is.* Philadelphia: Lippincott, Grambo, 1852. New York: Negro Universities P, 1968.

Emerson, Ralph Waldo. "Address on Emancipation in the British West Indies." 1844. Rpt. in *Miscellanies*. Vol. 11 of *Emerson's Complete Works*. Boston: Houghton, Mifflin, 1878, 1887. 131–75.

———. "The Fugitive Slave Law." 1854. Rpt. in *Miscellanies*. Vol. 11 of *Emerson's Complete Works*. Boston: Houghton, Mifflin, 1878, 1887. 205–30.

"Extracts from the Annual Report." *The Abolitionist* 1 (February 1833): 20–23. Concerning the annual meeting of the New-England Anti-Slavery Society.

Filler, Louis. *The Crusade Against Slavery, 1830–1860.* New York: Harper & Row, 1960.

Fitzhugh, George. *Sociology for the South, or the Failure of Free Society.* Richmond, VA: A. Morris, 1854.

Foner, Eric. *Free Soil, Free Labor, Free Men: The Ideology of the Republican Party before the Civil War.* New York: Oxford, 1970.

"Foreign Musical and Dramatic Items." *Frank Leslie's Illustrated Newspaper* 2 (August 23, 1856): 167. On Mrs. Webb's reading of *The Christian Slave*.

Foster, Stephen S[ymonds]. *The Brotherhood of Thieves, or A True Picture of the American Church and Clergy*. New-London: William Bolles, 1843.

Frederickson, George M. *The Arrogance of Race: Historical Perspectives on Slavery, Racism, and Social Inequality*. Middletown, CT: Wesleyan UP, 1988.

———. *The Black Image in the White Mind: The Debate on Afro-American Character and Destiny, 1817–1914*. New York: Harper & Row, 1971.

Gara, Larry. "The Fugitive Slave Law: A Double Paradox." *Civil War History* 10 (September 1964): 229–40.

Garnet, Henry Highland. *The Past and Present Condition, and the Destiny, of the Colored Race*. 1848. Miami: Mnemosyne, 1969.

Garrison, William Lloyd. *Thoughts on African Colonization*. Boston: Garrison and Knapp, 1832. New York: Arno, 1968.

Goodell, William. *Slavery and Antislavery*. New York: W. Harned, 1852. New York: Negro Universities P, 1968.

Gossett, Thomas F. Uncle Tom's Cabin *and American Literature*. Dallas: Southern Methodist UP, 1985.

Grimké, Angelina Emily. *Appeal to the Christian Women of the South*. 1836. New York: Arno, 1969.

Grimsted, David A. "Uncle Tom from Page to Stage: Limitations of Nineteenth-Century Drama." *Quarterly Journal of Speech* 56 (October 1970): 235–44.

Hale, S[arah] J[osepha]. *Liberia; or, Mr. Payton's Experiments*. New York: Harper, 1853. Upper Saddle River, NJ: Gregg, 1968.

———. *Northwood; A Tale of New England*. Boston: Bowles and Dearborn, 1827. Louisville: Lost Cause Press, 1967.

Harper, Robert Goodloe. Letter to American Colonization Society, dated August 20, 1817. *First Annual Report*. American Colonization Society: 1818. Rpt. in Pease. 18–32.

Hirsch, Stephen Alexander. "Uncle Tom's Companions: The Literary and Popular Reaction to *Uncle Tom's Cabin*." Diss. SUNY Albany, 1975.

[Holmes, George F.] Rev. of *Uncle Tom's Cabin*. *Southern Literary Messenger* 18 (October 1852): 630–38.

Hoole, W[illiam] Stanley. *The Ante-Bellum Charleston Theatre*. [Tuscaloosa]: U of Alabama P, 1946.

Kaye, Joseph. "Famous First Nights: 'Uncle Tom's Cabin.' " *Theatre Magazine* (August 1929): 26, 65.

Kinmont, Alexander. *Twelve Lectures on the Natural History of Man, and the Rise and Progress of Philosophy*. Cincinnati: U. P. James, 1839.

"Letter from New York." *New Orleans Daily Delta*. January 29, 1854: 7. Regarding the Aiken version.

Lumer, Robert. "Good Ol' Slavery and the Minstrel Show." *Zeitschrift für Anglistik und Amerikanistik* 33 (1985): 54–61.

Lynn, Kenneth S. "Introduction." *Uncle Tom's Cabin*. Cambridge: Belknap-Harvard UP, 1962. vii–xxiv.

McConachie, Bruce A. "Out of the Kitchen and into the Marketplace: Normalizing *Uncle Tom's Cabin* for the Antebellum Stage." *Journal of American Drama and Theatre* 3 (Winter 1991): 5–28.

Moody, Richard. *America Takes the Stage: Romanticism in American Drama and Theatre, 1750–1900*. Bloomington: Indiana UP, 1955. Millwood, NY: Kraus, 1977.

Oakes, Harold Rasmus. "An Interpretive Study of the Effects of Some Upper Mid-West Productions of *Uncle Tom's Cabin* as Reflected in Local Newspapers between 1852 and 1860." Diss. U of Minnesota, 1964.

Page, J. W. *Uncle Robin in His Cabin in Virginia, and Tom without One in Boston.* Richmond, VA: J. W. Randolph, 1853.

Pease, William H. and Jane H. Pease, eds. *The Antislavery Argument.* American Heritage Series. Indianapolis: Bobbs-Merrill, 1965.

Ratner, Lorman. *Powder Keg: Northern Opposition to the Antislavery Movement, 1831–1840.* New York: Basic Books, 1968.

Rawley, James A. *Race & Politics: "Bleeding Kansas" and the Coming of the Civil War.* Philadelphia: J. B. Lippincott, 1969.

Rev. of *Uncle Tom's Cabin. New York Atlas* October 16, 1853. Rpt. in *Theatre U.S.A. 1665 to 1957.* By Barnard Hewitt. New York: McGraw-Hill, 1959. 173–78. On the Aiken version.

Rev. of *Uncle Tom's Cabin. New York Herald* September 3, 1852: 4. On the Taylor version.

Rev. of *Uncle Tom's Cabin. The Liberator* 23 (September 23, 1853): 152. On the play as produced in Philadelphia.

Rev. of *Uncle Tom's Cabin. North American Review* 77 (October 1853): 466–93. On the novel and the *Key.*

Richards, Leonard L. *"Gentlemen of Property and Standing": Anti-Abolition Mobs in Jacksonian America.* New York: Oxford UP, 1970.

Robson, Mark. "Aiken's Dramatic Version of *Uncle Tom's Cabin*: A Success Story for the Negro Characters." *Publications of the Arkansas Philological Association* 10 (1984): 69–78.

Roppolo, Joseph P. "Uncle Tom in New Orleans." *New England Quarterly* 27 (June 1954): 213–26.

Ruchames, Louis, ed. *From Disunionism to the Brink of War, 1850–1860.* Vol. 4 of *The Letters of William Lloyd Garrison.* Ed. Ruchames and Walter M. Merrill. Cambridge, MA: Belknap-Harvard UP, 1975.

Rush, Caroline. *The North and South; or, Slavery and Its Contrasts.* Philadelphia: Crissy & Markley, 1852.

Saum, Lewis O. *The Popular Mood of Pre–Civil War America.* Contributions in American Studies 46. Westport, CT: Greenwood, 1980.

Saxton, Alexander. "Blackface Minstrelsy and Jacksonian Ideology." *American Quarterly* 27 (March 1975): 3–28.

Senelick, Laurence. *The Age and Stage of George L. Fox, 1825–1877.* Hanover: UP of New England, 1988.

Slotkin, Richard. *Regeneration through Violence: The Mythology of the American Frontier, 1600–1860.* Middletown, CT: Wesleyan UP, 1973.

Smith, William. *Life at the South.* Buffalo: Georg H. Darby, 1852.

Sorin, Gerald. *Abolitionism: A New Perspective.* New York: Praeger, 1972.

Staudenraus, P. J. *The African Colonization Movement, 1816–1865.* New York: Columbia UP, 1961.

Stowe, Harriet Beecher. *The Key to Uncle Tom's Cabin.* 1853. Boston: John P. Jewett, 1854. New York: Arno, 1968.

———. *Uncle Tom's Cabin or, Life among the Lowly.* Boston: J. P. Jewett, 1852. Rpt. in *Three Novels.* New York: Library of America, 1982.

Thoreau, Henry David. "Slavery in Massachusetts." 1854. Rpt. in *Reform Papers*. Ed. Wendell Glick. Princeton: Princeton UP, 1973. 91–109.

Toll, Robert C. *Blacking Up: The Minstrel Show in Nineteenth-Century America*. London: Oxford UP, 1974.

Tompkins, Jane. *Sensational Designs: The Cultural Work of American Fiction, 1790–1860*. New York: Oxford UP, 1985.

" 'Uncle Tom.' " *New Orleans Weekly Picayune* August 30, 1852. Regarding a production in Boston.

" 'Uncle Tom' on the Stage." *The Liberator* 23 (September 9, 1853): 142. On the Aiken version.

Victor, Metta Victoria. *Maum Guinea, and Her Plantation "Children;" or, Holiday-Week on a Louisiana Estate*. New York: Beadle, 1861. Freeport, NY: Books for Libraries, 1972.

Walters, Ronald G. *The Antislavery Appeal: American Abolitionism after 1830*. Baltimore: Johns Hopkins UP, 1976.

Ward, John William. "Afterword." *Uncle Tom's Cabin*. New York: New American Library-Signet, 1966. 478–94.

Wittke, Carl. *Tambo and Bones: A History of the American Minstrel Stage*. Durham: Duke UP, 1930. New York: Greenwood, 1968.

Zanger, Jules. "The 'Tragic Octoroon' in Pre–Civil War Fiction." *American Quarterly* 18 (Spring 1966): 63–70.

Plays

Aiken, George L. *Uncle Tom's Cabin: or, Life among the Lowly*. New York: Samuel French, [1858?]. New York: Samuel French, [1967?].

Stowe, Harriet Beecher. *The Christian Slave*. Boston: Phillips, Sampson, 1855.

5. *MY PARTNER* (1879) AND THE WEST

Works Other than Plays

Bank, Rosemarie. "Frontier Melodrama." *Theatre West: Image and Impact*. Ed. Dunbar H. Ogden with Douglas McDermott and Robert K. Sarlós. DQR Studies in Literature 7. Amsterdam: Rodopi, 1990. 151–60.

Billington, Ray Allen. *The Westward Movement in the United States*. Princeton: D. Van Nostrand, 1959.

Blake, Mary E. *On the Wing: Rambling Notes of a Trip to the Pacific*. Boston: Lee and Shepard, 1883.

Bowles, Samuel. *Across the Continent: A Summer's Journey to the Rocky Mountains, the Mormons, and the Pacific States*. Springfield, MA: Samuel Bowles, 1866.

———. *Our New West*. Hartford: Hartford Publishing, 1869.

Brace, Charles L. *The New West: or, California in 1867–68*. New York: G. P. Putnam, 1869.

Bryant, Edwin. *What I Saw in California*. New York: D. Appleton, 1848.

Buffum, E. Gould. *Six Months in the Gold Mines, from a Journal of Three Years' Residence in Upper and Lower California 1847-8-9*. Philadelphia: 1850. Ed. John W. Caughey. [Los Angeles]: Ward Ritchey, 1959.

Colton, Walter. *Three Years in California*. New York: A. S. Barnes, 1850. Ed. Marguerite Eyer Wilbur. Stanford: Stanford UP, 1949.

Dana, Richard Henry, Jr. *Two Years Before the Mast*. New York: 1840. 2 vols. Ed. John Haskell Kemble. Los Angeles: Ward Ritchie, 1964.

Duckett, Margaret. *Mark Twain and Bret Harte*. Norman: U of Oklahoma P, 1964.

Farnham, T. J. *Travels in California*. New York: 1844. Ed. Joseph A. Sullivan. Oakland, CA: Biobooks, 1947.

Frémont, John C. *Report of the Exploring Expedition to the Rocky Mountains in the Year 1842, and to Oregon and North California in the years 1843–'44*. Washington: 1845. Rpt. as *The Exploring Expedition to the Rocky Mountains*. Washington, DC: Smithsonian, 1988.

Gaer, Joseph, ed. *The Theatre of the Gold Rush Decade in San Francisco*. 1935. New York: Burt Franklin, 1970.

Gagey, Edmond M. *The San Francisco Stage: A History*. New York: Columbia UP, 1950. Westport, CT: Greenwood, 1970.

Greeley, Horace. *An Overland Journey from New York to San Francisco in the Summer of 1859*. New York: Saxton, Barker, 1860. Ed. Charles T. Duncan. New York: Knopf, 1969.

Harte, Bret. *Writings of Bret Harte*. Standard Library Edition. 20 vols. Boston: Houghton, Mifflin, 1896–1920.

Helper, Hinton Rowan. *The Land of Gold: Reality versus Fiction*. Baltimore: Henry Taylor, 1855.

Ingraham, Prentiss. *Buck Taylor, King of the Cowboys*. Beadle's half-dime library 497. New York: Beadle and Adams, 1887.

Jones, Daryl. *The Dime Novel Western*. Bowling Green, OH: Popular Press–Bowling Green State U, 1978.

Jones, Howard Mumford. *The Age of Energy: Varieties of American Experience 1865–1915*. New York: Viking, 1971.

King, Clarence. *Mountaineering in the Sierra Nevada*. Boston: James R. Osgood, 1872.

Leslie, Mrs. Frank [Miriam Folline Peacock Squier Leslie]. *A Pleasure Trip from Gotham to the Golden Gate*. New York: G. W. Carleton, 1877.

Lewis, R. W. B. *The American Adam: Innocence, Tragedy and Tradition in the Nineteenth Century*. Chicago: U of Chicago P, 1955.

MacMinn, George R. *The Theater of the Golden Era in California*. Caldwell, ID: Caxton, 1941.

Marryat, Frank. *Mountains and Molehills, or Recollections of a Burnt Journal*. New York: Harper and Brothers, 1855. Ed. Marguerite Eyer Wilbur. Stanford: Stanford UP, 1952.

Marx, Leo. *The Machine in the Garden: Technology and the Pastoral Ideal in America*. New York: Oxford, 1964.

Merk, Frederick. *Manifest Destiny and Mission in American History: A Reinterpretation*. New York: Knopf, 1963.

Meserve, Walter J. "The American West of the 1870s and 1880s as Viewed from the Stage." *Journal of American Drama and Theatre* 3 (Winter 1991): 48–63.

Morecamp, Arthur [Thomas Pilgrim]. *Live Boys*. Boston: Lee and Shepard; New York: C. T. Dillingham, 1879.

Morrow, Patrick D. "Bret Harte, Popular Fiction, and the Local Color Movement." *Western American Literature* 8 (Fall 1973): 123–31.

Nadal, E. S. "Bret Harte." *North American Review* 124 (January 1877): 81–90.

Nash, Roderick. *Wilderness and the American Mind*. New Haven: Yale UP, 1967.
Paul, Rodman Wilson. *California Gold: The Beginning of Mining in the Far West*. Lincoln: U of Nebraska P, 1947, 1967.
————. *Mining Frontiers of the Far West, 1848–1890*. Histories of the American Frontier. New York: Holt, Rinehart and Winston, 1963.
Rev. of *My Partner*. *New-York Times* September 17, 1879: 5
Richardson, Albert D. *Beyond the Mississippi*. Hartford: American, 1867. New York: Johnson, 1968.
Royce, Josiah. *California from the Conquest in 1846 to the Second Vigilance Committee in San Francisco: A Study of American Character*. 1886. Ed. Robert Glass Cleland. New York: Knopf, 1948.
Shinn, Charles Howard. *Mining Camps: A Study in American Frontier Government*. New York: Scribner's, 1884. Ed. Rodman Wilson Paul. New York: Harper & Row, 1965.
Shirley, Dame [Clappe, Louise Amelia Knapp Smith]. *The Shirley Letters. 1854–55*. Ed. Richard E. Oglesby. Santa Barbara: Peregrine Smith, 1970.
Simonson, Harold P. *Beyond the Frontier: Writers, Western Regionalism and a Sense of Place*. Fort Worth: Texas Christian UP, 1989.
Smith, Henry Nash. *Virgin Land: The American West as Symbol and Myth*. Cambridge, MA: Harvard UP, 1950, 1970.
Taylor, Bayard. *Eldorado; or, Adventures in the Path of Empire*. New York: Putnam, 1850. Ed. Robert Glass Cleland. New York: Knopf, 1949.
Turner, Frederick Jackson. *The Frontier in American History*. 1920. New York: Holt, Rinehart and Winston, 1962.
Twain, Mark. *Roughing It*. 1872. Rpt. in vol. 2 of *The Works of Mark Twain*. Ed. Franklin R. Rogers and Paul Baender. Berkeley: U of California P, 1972.
Wattenberg, Richard. "Americanizing Frontier Melodrama: From *Davy Crockett* (1872) to *My Partner* (1879)." *Journal of American Culture* 12 (Spring 1989): 7–16.
White, G. Edward. *The Eastern Establishment and the Western Experience: The West of Frederic Remington, Theodore Roosevelt, and Owen Wister*. New Haven: Yale UP, 1968.
Wilt, Napier, ed. The White Slave *and Other Plays*. Vol. 19 of *America's Lost Plays*. Princeton: Princeton UP, 1940. Bloomington: Indiana UP, 1965.
Wister, Owen. *The Virginian*. New York: Macmillan, 1902.
Wyatt, David. *The Fall into Eden: Landscape and Imagination in California*. Cambridge Studies in American Literature and Culture. Cambridge: Cambridge UP, 1986.

Plays

Baer, Warren. *The Duke of Sacramento*. 1856. San Francisco: Grabhorn, 1934.
Baker, George M[elville]. *Nevada; or, The Lost Mine*. Boston: Walter H. Baker, 1882.
Belasco, David. *The Girl of the Golden West*. New York: S. French, 1933. Rpt. in *American Melodrama*. Ed. Daniel C. Gerould. New York: Performing Arts Journal Publications, 1983. 183–247.
Campbell, Bartley. *My Partner*. The White Slave *and Other Plays*. Ed. Napier Wilt. Union Square Theatre, New York, September 16, 1879.
[Delano, Alonzo.] *A Live Woman in the Mines; or, Pike County Ahead! . . . By "Old Block."* Minor Drama 130. New York: Samuel French, [1857]. Rpt. in *California Gold-Rush Plays*. Ed. Glenn Loney. 65–101.
Harte, Bret. *Two Men of Sandy Bar*. Boston: James R. Osgood, 1876. Rpt. in *California*

Gold-Rush Plays. Ed. Glenn Loney. 103–75. Union Square Theatre, New York, August 28, 1876.

Howe, Charles E. B. *Joaquin Murieta de Castillo*. San Francisco: Commercial Book and Job Steam Printing, 1858. Rpt. in *California Gold-Rush Plays*. Ed. Glenn Loney. 21–63.

Loney, Glenn, ed. *California Gold-Rush Plays*. American Drama Library Series. New York: Performing Arts Journal Publications, 1983.

Miller, Joaquin. *The Danites in the Sierras*. San Francisco: 1882. Rpt. in *American Plays*. Ed. Allan Gates Halline. New York: American Book Company, 1935. August 22, 1877.

———. *Forty-Nine: An Idyl Drama of the Sierras*. 2nd ed. San Francisco: California, 1882.

Nobles, Milton. *From Sire to Son; or, The Hour and the Man*. Philadelphia: Ledger, 1887.

Nunes, Joseph A. *Fast Folks; or, The Early Days of California*. Philadelphia: Barnard & Jones, 1861. American Theatre, San Francisco, July 8, 1858.

Thomas, Augustus. *Arizona*. New York: R. H. Russell, 1899.

Townsend, Charles. *The Golden Gulch*. New York: Fitzgerald, 1893.

Twain, Mark and Bret Harte. *Ah Sin*. Ed. Frederick Anderson. San Francisco: Book Club, 1961. Daly's Fifth Avenue Theatre, New York, July 31, 1877.

Ware, L. L. [Lew Ward] *Gyp, the Heiress; or, The Dead Witness*. Ames' Series of Standard and Minor Drama 311. Clyde, OH: Ames, 1892.

6. *SHENANDOAH* (1889) AND THE CIVIL WAR

Works Other than Plays

Appleby, Joyce. "Reconciliation and the Northern Novelist, 1865–1880." *Civil War History* 10 (1964): 117–29.

Brockett, L[inus] P[ierpont]. *The Camp, the Battle Field and the Hospital; or, Lights and Shadows of the Great Rebellion*. Philadelphia: National, 1866.

Buck, Paul H. *The Road to Reunion, 1865–1900*. New York: Vintage, 1937.

De Forest, John William. *Miss Ravenel's Conversion from Secession to Loyalty*. 1867. Ed. Gordon S. Haight. New York: Holt, Rinehart and Winston, 1955.

[Dithmar, Edward A.] Rev. of *Shenandoah*. *New-York Times* September 10, 1889: 4.

Gardner, Alexander. *Gardner's Photographic Sketch Book of the War*. Washington, DC: Philp and Solomons, 1866. 2 vols. Rpt. as *Gardner's Photographic Sketch Book of the Civil War*. New York: Dover, 1959.

Gerrish, Theodore and John S. Hutchinson. *The Blue and the Grey*. Portland, ME: Hoyt, Fogg & Donham, 1883.

Grant, U.S. *Personal Memoirs of U.S. Grant*. New York: Charles L. Webster, 1885. Ed. E. B. Long. Cleveland: World, 1952.

Greeley, Horace. *The American Conflict*. Vol. 2. Hartford: O. D. Case, 1867.

Guernsey, Alfred H. and Henry M. Alden. *Harper's Pictorial History of the Great Rebellion*. New York: Harper, 1866–68. Chicago: Star, 1894.

Headley, J[oel] T[yler]. *The Great Rebellion; a History of the Civil War in the United States*. 2 vols. Hartford: American, 1866.

Howard, Bronson. "History in a Play." *Liber Scriptorum*. New York: Authors Club, 1893. 282–87.

Howells, William Dean. *The Rise of Silas Lapham*. 1885. Rpt. in *Novels 1875–1886*. New York: Library of America, 1982.

Johnson, Robert Underwood and Clarence Clough Buel, eds. *Battles and Leaders of the Civil War*. 4 vols. New York: Century, 1884–88. New York: Thomas Yoseloff, 1956.

Johnson, Rossiter. *A Short History of the War of Secession 1861–1865*. Boston: Ticknor, 1888.

Lewis, Thomas A. *The Shendandoah in Flames: The Valley Campaign of 1864*. The Civil War. New York: Time-Life Books, 1987.

[Melville, Herman.] "Philip." *Harper's New Monthly Magazine* 2 (April 1866): 640.

Merritt, Wesley. "Sheridan in the Shenandoah Valley." Johnson and Buel 4: 518–20.

Moody, Richard, ed. *Dramas from the American Theatre 1762–1909*. Cleveland: World, 1966.

"Phil Sheridan Riding to the Front." *Harper's Weekly* 8 (November 5, 1864): 706.

Pond, George E. *The Shenandoah Valley in 1864*. Campaigns of the Civil War 11. New York: Charles Scribner's Sons, 1883.

Porter, Horace. "The Surrender at Appomattox Court House." Johnson and Buel 4: 729–46.

Pressly, Thomas J. *Americans Interpret Their Civil War*. Princeton: Princeton UP, 1954. New York: Collier, 1962.

Read, T. Buchanan. "Sheridan's Ride." New York: Privately printed, 1867.

Ryan, Pat G. "The Horse Drama, with Supernumeraries: Bronson Howard's Semi-Historical *Shenandoah*." *Journal of American Drama and Theatre* 3 (Spring 1991): 42–69.

Schmucker, Samuel M. *The History of the Civil War in the United States*. Philadelphia: Jones, 1865.

Sheridan, P. H. *Personal Memoirs*. 2 vols. New York: Charles L. Webster, 1888.

Stevens, George T. *Three Years in the Sixth Corps*. 2nd [rev.] ed. New York: D. Van Nostrand, 1870.

Strang, Lewis C. *Plays and Players of the Last Quarter Century*. 2 vols. Boston: L. C. Page, 1902.

Sweet, Timothy. *Traces of War: Poetry, Photography, and the Crisis of Union*. Baltimore: Johns Hopkins UP, 1990.

Wheeler, Andrew C. ["Nym Crinkle"] Rev. of *Shenandoah*. *New York Dramatic Mirror* September 14, 1889. Rpt. in *Theatre U.S.A. 1665 to 1957*. By Barnard Hewitt. New York: McGraw-Hill, 1959. 254–56.

Woodward, C. Vann, ed. *Mary Chesnut's Civil War*. New Haven: Yale UP, 1981.

Plays

Ames, A. D. and C. G. Bartley. *The Spy of Atlanta*. Ames' Series of Standard and Minor Drama 79. Clyde, OH: A.D. Ames, 1879. Plymouth, OH, September 23, 1875.

Andrews, Fred G. *Hal Hazard; or, The Federal Spy*. Clyde, OH: A.D. Ames, 1883.

Barton, Joseph. *Harry Allen, The Union Spy*. Lansing, MI: W. S. George, 1872.

Belasco, David. *The Heart of Maryland*. 1895. Rpt. in The Heart of Maryland *& Other Plays*. Ed. Glenn Hughes and George Savage. Vol. 18 of *America's Lost Plays*. Ed. Barrett H. Clark. Princeton: Princeton UP, 1940. Bloomington: Indiana UP, 1965. Grand Opera House, Washington, October 9, 1895.

Boucicault, Dion. *Belle Lamar*. 1874. Rpt. in *Plays for the College Theatre*. Ed. G. H. Leverton. New York, 1932. Booth's Theatre, New York, August 10, 1874.

Brown, J. S. *A Southern Rose*. Clyde, OH: Ames, 1899. Akron, OH, February 19, 1893.

Brown, S. J. *In the Enemy's Camp; or, The Stolen Despatches*. Boston: Walter H. Baker, 1889.

[Clark, William Adolphus.] *General Grant; or, The Star of Union and Liberty*. By Anicetus. French's Standard Drama 351. New York: Samuel French, 1868.

Cornish, O. W. *Foiled; or, A Struggle for Life and Liberty*. Chicago: Dramatic, 1871. Birmingham, CT, January 25, 1871.

Culver, J. N. *Loyal Mountaineers: or, The Guerrilla's Doom*. Rev. ed. St. Albans, VT: E. A. Morton, 1873.

Daly, Augustin. *A Legend of "Norwood;" or, Village life in New England*. New York: printed for the author, 1867.

Dawson, J. H. and B. G. Whittemore. *Lights and Shadows of the Great Rebellion; or The Hospital Nurse of Tennessee*. Ames' Series of Standard and Minor Drama 194. Clyde, OH: A.D. Ames, 1885. North Auburn, NE, August 14, 1884.

Fitch, Clyde. *Barbara Frietchie, the Frederick Girl*. New York: Life, 1900. Broad Street Theatre, Philadelphia, October 10, 1899.

Gillette, William. *Held by the Enemy*. New York: Samuel French, 1898. Criterion Theatre, Brooklyn, February 22, 1886; revised for reopening at Charles Frohman's Madison Square Theatre, New York, August 16, 1886.

———. *Secret Service: A Romance of the Southern Confederacy*. New York: Samuel French, 1898. Broad Street Theatre, Philadelphia, May 13, 1895.

Herne, James A. *The Reverend Griffith Davenport. The Early Plays of James A. Herne*. Ed. Arthur Hobson Quinn. Vol. 7 of *America's Lost Plays*. Ed. Barrett H. Clark. Princeton: Princeton UP, 1940. Bloomington: Indiana UP, 1965.

[Hodgson, Joseph, Jr.] *The Confederate Vivandiere; or, the Battle of Leesburg*. Montgomery: John M. Floyd, 1862.

Howard, Bronson. *Shenandoah*. New York: Samuel French, 1897. Rpt. in *Dramas from the American Theatre 1762–1909*. Ed. Richard Moody. Cleveland: World, 1966. 575–609. Star Theatre, New York, September 9, 1889.

Kilpatrick, Maj.-Gen. [Hugh] Judson and J. Owen Moore. *Allatoona*. French's Standard Drama 376. New York: Samuel French, 1875. October 22, 1877.

Lang, T. E. *Surrounded by Fire*. Salem: Salem Post, 1874.

McKee, W. J. *Gettysburg*. Pittsburgh: Nevin, Gribbin, 1879.

Muscroft, S[amuel] J. *The Drummer Boy: or, The Battle Field of Shiloh*. Detroit: Daily Post, 1868. Pittsburgh: A. A. Anderson, 1871. Mansfield, OH: L. D. Myers, 1872.

Power, Thomas F. *The Virginia Veteran*. Boston: Lea and Shepard; New York: Lee, Shepard and Dillingham, 1874.

Renauld, John B. *Our Heroes*. New York: Robert M. De Witt, 1873.

Rogers, James S. *Our Regiment*. Boston: printed for the author, 1884.

Stedman, W. Elsworth. *The Confederate Spy*. French's Standard Drama 402. New York: Samuel French, 1887.

———. *The Midnight Charge*. New York: Samuel French, 1892.

Thomas, Augustus. *"Surrender!!"* Typescript in New York Public Library.

———. *The Spy of Gettysburg*. Boston: Walter H. Baker, 1891.

Tyrant of New Orleans, The. Atlanta, GA: Herald, 1873.

Union Sergeant, The; or, The Battle of Gettysburg. Springfield, MA: Geo. W. Sargent, 1873. East Wallingford, VT, February 6, 1872.

Vegiard, J. T. *The Dutch Recruit; or, The Blue and Gray*. Clyde, OH: Ames, [1879].

Volunteer, The. Norwich, CT: n.p., 1871.

Walker, G. H. and E. A. Lewis. *The Old Flag: or, the Spy of Newbern!* Brattleboro: F. D. Cobleigh, 1871.

Whalen, E. C. *Front Sumter to Appomattox.* Chicago: T. S. Denison, 1889.

Winston, Sergeant James. *True to the Flag, or The Tennessee Unionist.* Boston: Charles Boutelle, 1871.

7. STAGING THE MYTH OF AMERICA

Bank, Rosemarie. "The Theatre Historian in the Mirror: Transformation in the Space of Representation." *Journal of Dramatic Theory and Criticism* 3 (Spring 1989): 219–28.

Bercovitch, Sacvan. "Afterword." Sacvan Bercovitch and Myra Jehlen. *Ideology and Classic American Literature.* Cambridge Studies in American Literature and Culture. Cambridge: Cambridge UP, 1986.

———. "America as Canon and Context: Literary History in a Time of Dissensus." *American Literature* 58 (March 1986): 99–107.

Case, Sue-Ellen. "Seduced and Abandoned: Inclusionary/Exclusionary Practices between the White Lesbian Feminist and Chicana Texts." Association for Theatre in Higher Education Convention. Seattle, August 8, 1991.

McConachie, Bruce A. "Pacifying American Theatrical Audiences, 1820–1900." *For Fun and Profit: The Transformation of Leisure into Consumption.* Ed. Richard Butsch. Philadelphia: Temple UP, 1990. 47–70.

Quinn, Michael L. "The Comedy of Reference: The Semiotics of Commedia Figures in Eighteenth-Century Venice." *Theatre Journal* 43 (March 1991): 70–92.

Saussure, Ferdinand de. *Course in General Linguistics.* Trans. Roy Harris. La Salle, IL: Open Court, 1983, 1986.

Index

abolitionism and abolitionists, 91, 93, 95, 96–101, 102, 104

"abolitionist" as insult in Civil War plays, 168–69

Ah Sin (Harte and Twain), 127, 151

alcohol, consumption of in America, 62, 66, 204*n4*, 205*n10*

Alger, William Rounseville: on Forrest as American, 40–41; as Forrest's biographer, 203*n25*; on Indian, 23–24; on *Metamora*, 55–56

Althusser, Louis, on ideology, 8–9

America: as concept, 19–22, 184–86; as convention, 188, 189–90; ideology of, 54, 89, 185–86, 191–93; as transcendental signified, 187; myth of, 21–22, 89, 131, 187–98

"American" as self-construction, 33, 47, 185–86

American, The, as concept, 191–94

Arcadian myth, 25, 31, 33–34, 55, 130, 144, 152

Arthur, T. S., 72, 205*n13*; as temperance advocate, 70; *Ten Nights in a Bar-Room*, 85–86

Astor Place Riot, 39–41

Baldwin, James, on *Uncle Tom's Cabin* (Stowe), 93, 108, 115, 122

Barbara Frietchie (Fitch), 155

Bottle, The (Taylor), 76

Bryant, William Cullen, 38, 201*n9*

California: early plays concerning gold country of, 215*n2*; myth of, 129–38, 152–54; source of name, 216*n5*

Cass, Lewis. *See* Indian removal

Catlin, George, 54, 55

Cedar Creek, Battle of: in histories and chronicles, 181–83; in Melville's "Philip," 182–83; in *Shenandoah*, 183–84, 221*n27*

"Chinee," 149–52, 192, 218*n35*

Christian Slave, The (Stowe), 105–108; excerpt from, 213–14*n37*; in relation to novel, 212–13*n26*; intended for Mary E. Webb, 212*n25*, 213*n27*

Christianity: in *The Christian Slave*, 106–108; Eva as perfect disciple of, 110; as motive for colonization, 101–103; and race, 112, 113, 115; as source of antislavery position, 95; and Stowe's antislavery sentiments, 103–105; in *Uncle Tom's Cabin* (Aiken), 121, 122–23, 125; as validating influence on slave system, 92. *See also* evangelicalism, Indian removal, religion

Christians as rum-sellers, 70

Church, Benjamin, 28; as character in *Metamora*, 42, 45

Civil War plays, 154–55; conventions of, 162–63, 178; early examples, 219*n1*; patterns in amateur efforts, 162–65; rationale for war in, 165–72; romantic construction of war in, 172–78; sacrifice as theme in, 176–77; sponsored by G.A.R., 219*n8*; slavery as submerged issue in, 168–69; favorable to southern point of view, 219*n9*

Civil War: fiction about, 159–60, 219*n4*; histories of, 157, 160–61; myth of, 157–65; visual representations of, 157–59

class: in America, 19–20; complexity of, 86–87; conflation of in myth of America, 193; conflict within temperance movement, 62, 64–65, 66–67, 68; consciousness in *My Partner*, 143; Forrest's scorn for aristocracy, 40; and Harte's Mexican characters, 137; and hegemony, 8; interdependence of in slave system, 92; lower, in England, 91; middle, 12, 22, 200*n16*; middle-class status as temperance motive, 71; prejudice in southern society, 100; in reformism, according to Marx, 76; and sentimentalism, 13; slaves as, 92; struggle and ideology, 7, 8; in temperance movement, 76;

JEFFREY D. MASON has published articles and delivered papers on American melodrama and on the work of Arthur Miller, Eugene O'Neill, Sam Shepard, Adele Edling Shank, and Tom Stoppard. He teaches courses in theatre studies and performance at California State University, Bakersfield, where he holds an appointment as Professor of Theatre and Chair of the Fine Arts Department.

ACP 8563   5/4/94

PS
336
M44
M36
1993